BABYLON EAST

Babylon East

PERFORMING,
DANCEHALL,
ROOTS REGGAE
AND RASTAFARI
IN JAPAN

MARVIN D. STERLING

DUKE UNIVERSITY PRESS *Durham & London 2010*

Designed by Jennifer Hill
Typeset in Chaparral Pro by Keystone Typesetting, Inc.

*Library of Congress Cataloging-in-Publication Data
appear on the last printed page of this book.*

For my mother,
Winnifred Sterling,
and in memory of my father,
Kenneth Sterling

CONTENTS

This book explores Japanese engagement with Jamaican popular culture. I begin this exploration with "The Politics of Presence: Performing Blackness in Japan." In that chapter, I locate Jamaica and Japan on the map of a global imagination of blackness, an imagination which I argue turns significantly on racial demography and political history. The four following chapters root this broad theoretical discussion in ethnography, exploring the lives and performances of the practitioners of Japan's Jamaican subcultures. Although I discuss performance in each subculture in general terms, I also focus on particular modes of performance. I have done so not because I feel each performance mode is exclusive to a given subculture, but simply because I believe that it offers particularly interesting insights into the life of this subculture. Chapter 2, "Music and Orality: Authenticity in Japanese Sound System Culture," explores the creative use of Jamaican music and spoken language by Japanese sound systems members as well as DJs, tracing the transnational routes these performers take to accumulate this musical and verbal symbolic capital. In the chapter, I explore how, once back in Japan, they draw upon these resources in the process of creating an "authentic" Japanese dancehall culture, both for their Japanese audiences and more subtly for each other.

"Fashion and Dance: Performing Gender in Japan's Reggae Dance Scene" is the third chapter. It addresses the cross-cultural issues of gender and sexuality, morality, and class invoked by the dress and dance of Japan's reggae dancers. Disturbing the moral conventions of Christian, middle-class, British-identified Jamaican womanhood (Cooper 1997, 2004), the dance scene is the primary space for female participation in Jamaican dance-hall culture, one otherwise dominated by male declarations of lyrical agility, sexual bravado, and willingness to use violence. I use fashion and dance to explore the extent to which the gendered body politics evidenced in the Jamaican case also appear in Japan.

The next two chapters shift from dancehall to Rastafari. The fourth chapter, "Body and Spirit: Rastafarian Consciousness in Rural Japan," picks up on the previous chapter's concern with embodiment but focuses on its relation to Rastafarian notions of spirituality. The chapter explores how Japanese express their identification with the movement in bodily terms, including the wearing of dreadlocks, diet, and medicinal practice. I will consider how one group's participation at an annual festival in several of the the members' hometown becomes a vehicle through which they bridge the gap between their selves as dreads and as residents of their rural community, and between their global experiences and those of a mythologized local.

The fifth chapter is "Text and Image: Bad Jamaicans, Tough Japanese, and the Third World 'Search for Self.'" The first part of this chapter explores the interest of some Japanese dreads in a body of popular writings in which Japanese are imagined to be the true ancient Israelites. Jamaican Rastafarians make the same claim for themselves; the independent existence of this literature appears to these Japanese dreads to help legitimize their own claim to Rastafari. In the second part of the chapter, I examine nonfictional and fictional writings on Japanese travel to Jamaica. I link these works to the recent discourse of *jibun sagashi* (search for self)—a popular term in Japanese public discourse since the 1990s—particularly as this search has centered on narratives of Japanese travel overseas. I focus on a novel by Jah Hirō (1991), about a Japanese man who travels to Jamaica to discover himself through contact with the third world. I explore the author's textual "performance" of the protagonist's search for a stronger, ideologically actu-alized self, in part through an analysis of the novel's imaging of Jamaicans.

I use the sixth and final chapter, "Jamaican Perspectives on Jamaican

Culture in Japan," to resolve my discussion of how Jamaican subcultures afford insight into the performance of social identity in Japan. I begin to consolidate my discussion of race in a global context by exploring Jamaican perspectives on the popularity of Jamaican culture in Japan. I leave this discussion to the end of the book, at some risk of appearing to marginalize this perspective. But it is precisely because of the importance of a focused discussion of this Jamaican point of view that I have left it for the end. This discussion leads into what I consider the bigger picture of this research: what is in the social scientific literature a still-underexplored concern with the global politics of race and ethnicity beyond the West and the African diaspora, including as evidenced in Afro-Asian contact. With this concern in mind, I identify three key discourses of global race evident in this research.

Many people have been instrumental in the completion of this book. I first want to thank Eduardo Brondizio, Jeanne Sept, and Richard Wilk, in their capacity as chairs of the Department of Anthropology of Indiana University, Bloomington, for their support of my work. Thank you to Joelle Bahloul, Sara Friedman, Paula Girshick, Shane Green, Sarah Phillips, Anya Royce, Nazif Shahrani, Beverly Stoeltje, Dan Suslak, and Catherine Tucker, and all my other colleagues, graduate students, and staff in the Department of Anthropology, the Department of East Asian Languages and Cultures, and Indiana University's "Variations on Blackness Workshop," particularly the organizers, Matt Guterl and Vivian Halloran. My gratitude to E. Taylor Atkins, Carolyn Cooper, Donna Hope, Minako Ikeshiro, Minako Kurosawa, Jalani Niaah, Sonjah Stanley-Niaah, Shinichiro Suzuki, and Yasuko Takezawa for conversations about music, religion, and race in Jamaica and Japan. Thank you to Sachi Shitara of the Embassy of Japan in Jamaica for introducing me to some of the players on the Jamaican scene.

I am grateful to my friends Jeannine Bell, Stan Huey, and Lanita Jacobs-Huey for all their encouragement. Thank you to Mai Kaneko for introducing me to many of the key players in this research, and for accompanying me to several interviews in which she felt her mediation would be helpful. I would like to thank her family—Mieko-san, Motomu, and Tsuguru—and my friends Joe Essertier and Tsutomu Saito, as well as their families, for their kindness during my stays in Japan.

Thanks to Fujiko, Riki, Ruri, and everybody in Yoshino, and to all the artists whose generosity with their time and their experiences made this research possible. Many thanks to Junko Komatsu, who has been instrumental in this study both as a liaison between me and many of the artists who appear in this book, and in providing me access to several of the events I attended in the course of this research.

This book grew out of my dissertation at the University of California, Los Angeles, and I wish to thank my dissertation committee: the co-chairs Mariko Tamanoi and Marcyliena Morgan of the Department of Anthropology, and Kyeyoung Park, also of the Department of Anthropology, and Miriam Silverberg of the History Department. Thank you to John Russell of Gifu University, my field advisor in Japan, whose work I admire not only for its intellectual merit but also for its great social value. Thank you to two of my first advisors at UCLA, Peter B. Hammond and Douglas Hollan, also of the Department of Anthropology. Although all these individuals have contributed much to the realization of this book, I want to express my particular gratitude to Miriam, who passed away in 2008. It was Miriam who first introduced me to this research topic twelve years ago. The support of a scholar as respected as she was meant a great deal to me, probably more than she realized, and I regret that I did not tell her so while she was alive.

Many thanks to Ken Wissoker of Duke University Press for his kindness and patience, and to the reviewers whose comments have helped me greatly improve this manuscript.

My deepest thanks go to my family: Dorothy Thompson, Wendell Thompson, Beryl Johnston, Byron, Randy, Naoko, and O'Neil. Thank you to Wayne Sterling, for always lending an ear to my ideas, for being such a good big brother, and for continuing to show me the way. Thank you to my mother, Winnifred Sterling, whose wisdom, warmth, and love will always be a deep blessing to me. Thank you to my father, Kenneth Sterling: "Old Paw," this is your book. I should have given it to you sooner. But you knew I would get it done. Rest in peace.

On the upper floor of a rural *ryokan* (inn) overlooking a hillside in Nara prefecture, home to one of Japan's ancient capitals, seven men in their twenties, thirties, and forties dress for a *matsuri* (festival) for which this small town enjoys some national renown.

It is midmorning, early in July 2000. Standing about the dimly lit, tatami-matted room, the seven men are dressed only in *handako* (short laborers pants) and *tabi* (socks). Tiny pockmarks make similar patterns on each of their sinewy backs. As they move, massive dreadlocks like tree roots sway across their backs, chests, and thighs. Some of the men have bound their locks with *hachimaki* (ceremonial headbands), or contained them in tams.

As the one woman in the room moves busily about, the men work in pairs. One man in each pair stands with his arms raised to shoulder level, lengths of *sarashi* (a long spool of white cloth about the width of a forearm) wrapped tightly around his ribs. The second man grips the other end of the cloth. Pulling away from his partner with all his strength, he grunts as, with loud snaps, he tugs the sarashi taut. The first man revolves slowly to wrap the cloth around his upper body. When the men are wrapped, they begin strapping towels to their shoulders.

Finished, the men sit cross-legged on the floor, chatting quietly. The decorative centerpiece of the room is a painting, framed by lines of red, green, and gold—Rasta colors—of three Hindu deities. Lord Vishnu, seated, plays a sitar on the left; Ganesh, robed in gold, sits on the right; and Lakshmi, in the center, cradles two red lotus flowers. Two white elephants, trunks solemnly aloft, face each other in the background.

The men, reggae musicians, listen to a portable radio that plays a tape of their recent live performance of "Exodus," originally recorded by Bob Marley, the Jamaican reggae superstar.

> Exodus, movement of Jah people,
> Open your eyes and look within.
> Are you satisfied with the life you're living?
> We know where we're going; we know where we're from.
> We're leaving Babylon, we're going to our fatherland.
> Exodus, movement of Jah people.

Soon it is time to leave. The men—still bare-chested except for the sarashi wrapped tightly around them—gather their belongings, walk downstairs, and wait outside.

A minivan picks the dreads up and whisks them through the town, whose trees are gaily decorated by origami frogs. The men arrive at a restaurant. Loud and energetically happy, they eat omelets stuffed with fried rice and tiny bits of meat, and drink iced *ocha* (green tea).

The men soon leave the restaurant, without paying. Their expenses have been covered. Today is a special day.

Late on a Friday night a few months earlier, only days before the start of the new millennium, much of the city of Kawasaki has grown still. Most of its glass-fronted boutiques, restaurants, and cafes have closed, or are about to. A few clerks and businessmen move along the darkened sidewalks toward the nearest train station. Now and then a car passes, edging through the narrow streets toward the highway home.

But one upscale mall in this city between Tokyo and Yokohama grows more crowded by the minute. Here, dozens of people in their teens and early twenties mill about or sit on the ground outside a wide, attractive building. Above its closed doors, the words "Club Citta" glow brightly in silver letters. The young people chat with each other or into tiny *keitai denwa* (cellphones). Laughter and the sudden roar of motorbikes punctuate the chatter.

Mixing the styles of Kingston rudie, b-boy, and West Coast slacker, the men wear baseball, ski, and Muslim skull caps; huge down jackets; baggy pants; and limited edition sports shoes. Some have shaved heads; others wear their hair long; and still others have short, salon-managed dreadlocks. Many of the women wear hooded, thigh- or ankle-length pink-and-white down coats, and black, calf-high platform boots. Several women wear their hair in perms or braids. Others have frizzy hairdos bound with woolen bandanas.

The club doors open to the crowd, now numbering in the hundreds. As the loud young people file inside, they shed their jackets, revealing—in the case of the women most steeped in Japan's dancehall reggae culture— bodies clad in tight pants, skirts, or short shorts, and torso-baring tops. They cram their winter coats, purses, and book bags into 200-yen[1] coin lockers.

Before long, farther inside the club, the dance floor has become a pulsing fray of darkness, bodies, and bass. People push toward the elevated stage. Directly in front of them, spotlit in white from high above, about four young men work in a maze of amplifiers, turntables, and mixers, each machine linked to the others by wiring lying tangled on the floor. With electronic effects and his own shrieking voice, the MC punctuates the roar of the crowd, the organic bass, and the gruff voices of infamous Jamaican artists. Turrets of speakers flanking the stage thunder a heavy sound. One of the four young men—the group's selector—rifles through crates of records stacked toward the rear of the stage, carefully placing one record after the next on the turntable. The throng includes a few Jamaican men and women, many from the naval base in nearby Yokosuka. Attendance at this event otherwise appears to be exclusively Japanese.

Based on two years of research conducted in Japan between 1998 and 2000, as well as briefer periods of fieldwork in Japan, Jamaica, and New York between 2000 and 2010, this book explores contemporary Japanese engagement with Jamaican culture. Like in Jamaica, this engagement manifests itself as a continuum ranging from the sacred, as illustrated in the first vignette above, to the popular cultural, as illustrated in the second. Many Japanese drawn to Jamaican culture on both ends of this spectrum involve themselves with it only superficially. Some attend dancehall events as fans with only a general interest in a range of so-called black music, perhaps including hip-hop and rhythm and blues as well as reggae. Many Japanese who dreadlock their hair know or care little about Rastafari, the anticolonialist movement that views Ethiopian Emperor Haile Selassie as black people's messiah. (Much the same, of course, might be said for "fashion dreads" in other countries, including Jamaica itself.) Although I explore the entire spectrum of Japanese interest in Jamaican popular culture, I focus on the lives and performances of the artists who are most fully steeped, *as practitioners*, in reggae music. I consider the smaller number of Japanese—like the men in the first vignette—engaged not only with reggae, but also with Rastafari as a spiritual movement, who use the religion as a primary means by which to lead their spiritual lives.

In this book, I argue that reggae and Rastafari represent productive lenses through which to view a range of aspects of social identity—such as gender, class, ethnicity, and nationhood—in contemporary Japan. The motivations for Japanese engagement with Jamaican popular culture are at least as complex as the notion of identity itself. The presence of such subcultures in the country should partly be understood as belonging to a new spirit of internationalism in Japan today. This internationalism demonstrates a shift from the long-standing dialectic between Japanese particularity and Western universality, in which the Japanese are seen to construct a sense of modern nationhood primarily in relation to the West, to a broader Japanese engagement with the world at large. This broader engagement is informed by Japan's ongoing status as global power, on the one hand, and its economic decline in recent years, on the other hand.

I argue that both of these aspects of the contemporary Japanese situation mobilize diverse—and, thus, diversely consumable—imaginings of ethnic and racial difference, including that of blackness. Indeed, while the study has an ethnographic focus on the performance of social identity in such aspects as class, gender, ethnicity, and nationality, I focus on race. A significant aspect of the Japanese cultural encounter with the Jamaican evidences itself, albeit discreetly in many cases, in racial terms. Blackness in consumerist, information-age Japan is a commodity that is largely divorced from its human referents, to be enjoyed through, for example, the playful consumption of dancehall music. However, especially given Japan's long economic recession, which began in the early 1990s, blackness can also be something deeper, a way of rethinking one's life circumstances, such as through immersion in Rastafari. (This is not to say that it is only possible to identify with dancehall as something superficial and with Rastafari as something deep.)

"Race" in Japan, must be seen in terms of its particular ethnonational inflections. Nevertheless, it remains powerfully informed by its Western provenance. This provenance is of great importance for the way in which the Afrocentrisms evident in dancehall, reggae, and Rastafari are consumed in Japan. The significance of this provenance becomes especially pronounced as Japanese travel beyond Japan to such spaces as Jamaica, New York, and England. Thus a major concern of this study, both within and beyond the ethnographic center of Japan, is thinking about blackness beyond the African diaspora and, more broadly, race in a global context. I frame this interest largely within the emergent scholarship on the intersections between the African and the Asian experiences in the modern world, and I regard this study as one of if not the first multi-sited ethnographic monograph of the Afro-Asian. I inflect this Afro-Asian focus to further position the study as a rare ethnographic monograph on blackness in a global context, and on the transnational cultural exchanges between Japan and a non-Western country as well as between two non-Western countries in general. By positioning the study in these ways, I wish to destabilize the tendency to view ideas of race as sited within the West, and between the West and the postcolonial non-West. I want to open up the conversation to include how these ideas of race also flow within more rarely considered realms of the non-West (such as Asia) and across them (such as between the African and Asian diasporas).

Babylon East

The concept of Babylon is one point of entry for considering the implications of my framing in this way the presence of reggae and Rasta in Japan. "Babylon" is the Rastafarians' term for the immoral West as a space, a history, and a way of thinking. It cites the biblical city riven by vice and confusion. Imperial Britain particularly was Babylon, as is capitalist Euro-America and the destructive neoliberalism of such institutions as the International Monetary Fund and the World Bank. Jamaica, too, until recently a colonized country dominated by these pirates and their allies, was Babylon: in the famous Rasta idiom, "Jamaica is an island, but it is not I [my] land." Jamaica is hell, and Africa is true home. Paradoxically, Jamaica localizes the irredeemable evil that is Babylon, but it is also the site of a long-running hope for its eventual suppression.

By using this term in the title of this book,[2] I want to recognize a connection that many of my research subjects made between the Jamaican and Japanese situations. This connection has to do with the sense that Japan, like Jamaica, is part of the Babylonian world dominated by the West, including through the adoption of Western ways of thinking. When the reggae musician Sawa lyrically describes himself as a "raggamuffin inna Tokyo City / raggamuffin inna Babylon City," for instance, he invokes a sense of himself as a rebel, rejecting life in an exploitative, soul-crushing Japanese city that is as Babylonian as anywhere else. At the same time, Japan—like Jamaica, a land in which Rastas have much invested—is not a place of irredeemable evil. Japan remains powerfully home, the seat of a Japaneseness intimately experienced in familiar landscapes, among family and friends, in the familiarity of faces (even those of strangers), in food, in religion, and in the ease of one's own language.

But even as Jamaica and Japan have much in common viewed vis-à-vis Babylon, the two are differently positioned in the overall political and economic order of nations. When some Japanese practitioners of Rasta describe Japan as Babylon, they object to modern Japan's participation not only in a capitalism that has exploited many Japanese, but also one that exploits poor people around the world. They object to a Japanese colonialism that has done great harm to its Asian neighbors. "Babylon East," then, speaks to the domestic and international political terms of Japan's engagement with the Jamaican: Japan as the East dominated by the West, and as such partnered with Afro-Jamaica; Japan as partner in the colonial and capitalist domination of non-Western people, thus linked to Western power and distanced from Afro-Jamaica; and Japan as a domestic space experienced as independent of the international. "Babylon East," therefore, complicates African diasporic assumptions of Babylonian power as strictly Western, and deepens the recognition that the effects of its oppressiveness, as well as resistance to this oppressiveness, evidence themselves outside of the African diaspora. None of this, however, is meant to ignore the fact that the heavier ideological investments of the practitioners I focus on are balanced by easier mainstream consumptions of the difference of the Afro-Jamaican.

Before discussing these issues in fuller ethnographic depth, I will say something about the Jamaican cultural forms that will be the lens through which I explore this encounter between the Jamaican and the Japanese.

Reggae, Rasta, and Dancehall in Jamaica:
A Brief Introduction

Reggae is a genre of folk music emerging from the Afro-Jamaican under-class in the late 1960s. It belongs to a musical genealogy that can be traced back to mento music of the colonial period and to even earlier West African musical practices, but more immediately to ska and rocksteady. Best known for its up-tempo, trumpeted, syncopated beat, ska conveyed the exuberance of the Jamaica that gained its independence in 1962. The message of reggae's more immediate musical predecessor, rocksteady—slower and heavier than ska, its syncopated beat now played on guitar—dominated the Jamaican musical scene briefly in the mid- to late 1960s. Lyrically, rocksteady spoke to the experiences of tough, urban "rude boys" who were often recent migrants to Kingston from the countryside. Reggae—its beat even slower and heavier than rocksteady's—emerged in the late 1960s. It soon gave rise to a number of subgenres, most notably roots reggae. This music is deeply influenced by the message of Rastafari.

The term "dancehall" has been used in a number of ways. The first refers generically to Afro-Jamaican social gatherings going as far back as the days of slavery (Stolzoff 2000). The second refers more specifically to such gatherings in the period immediately after the Second World War, when records (especially African American rhythm and blues and, later, Jamaican music) were played at entertainment venues. A third use of the term "dancehall" refers to a new form of reggae music that began taking shape in the 1970s, even as roots reggae was at the peak of its popularity. In this third aspect, dancehall is a direct ancestor of several genres of popular electronic music today, including hip-hop. One aspect of this kinship is the development of the "toasting" style of speech-song pioneered by Count Machuki as he introduced the records he played at parties in the 1940s and 1950s. Another is the remixing of records, pioneered by King Tubby in the late 1960s. Tubby's sampling of prerecorded songs, and combining them in the studio with the toasting of DJ U-Roy in the early 1970s, set the musical stage for the development of dancehall as it is known today.

From the 1970s to the early 1980s, live dancehall, in this third aspect, involved toasting over live musical instrumentation and is associated with such artists as Sugar Minott and Yellowman. The fourth aspect of dancehall—also called "ragga" or "raggamuffin," especially in the United Kingdom—is the specifically digitized form of the third aspect and has dominated Jamaican popular music since the mid-1980s. (Some argue that the third kind of dancehall is a general category to which the fourth belongs.) When I use the term "dancehall," I refer to all these readings, but most immediately to the fourth—that is, dancehall as patois-based toasting to digitized beats, and the subcultures associated with it.

Regarding these associated subcultures, dancehall today consists of two, largely gendered scenes. The first is centered on the sound system. Sound systems can refer both to mobile audio equipment and to the small group of people, usually young men, who play records on this equipment at clubs and outdoor venues. In sound-system culture, the MC introduces musical selections and urges the crowd on throughout live events. DJs are vocal artists who perform over musical tracks. They might do so as recording artists whose records are played by sound systems at live events, or as live performers over digital musical tracks—"riddims"—laid down by the sound systems. (In dancehall and hip-hop culture, then, MCs and DJs play opposite roles.)

Donnettes make up the second scene. They are the extravagantly dressed—and often underdressed—women who attend dancehall events, either as individuals or "posses" in the audience, or as professional dancers on stage. Many Jamaican social commentators see dancehall, with its materialist, erotic aesthetic, as lacking the dignity and spiritual uplift of roots reggae, its predecessor. But as was the case with roots reggae at one time, dancehall's status as "vulgar" black ghetto music has not stopped it from becoming a commercial force within, nor hindered its expansion well beyond, the island.

Enter the Japanese

The annual World Clash and National Dancehall Queen competitions are the two events, respectively, with the highest profiles in these two scenes. Sound clashes are competitions between rival sound systems, and the winner is the system that judges determine have received the most cheers from the audience. In the World Clash of 1999, held in Brooklyn, New York, Mighty Crown, a Japanese sound system, was the only non-Jamaican competitor. Wielding to the surprise of many the agonistic, subculturally deep patois needed to "big up" their sound system and down their rivals, Mighty Crown stunned the international dancehall community by winning the event. Three years later, Junko Kudo, a dancer from Japan's burgeoning donnette scene, became the first non-Jamaican to compete in Jamaica's National Dancehall Queen competition. In this event, contestants are judged, among other things, for their skill in erotic dance to the beat of dancehall tunes, for the creativity of their (often minimal) costume, and, in the manner typical of beauty contests, for their performance during a brief interview. Victory guarantees the winner at least minor celebrity status on the island and in the Jamaican diaspora of North America and Great Britain.

In what might have been an even more surprising turn of events for the dancehall community than Mighty Crown's victory, Kudo won the event. As Jamaica's National Dancehall Queen for 2002, she became a Jamaican celebrity, one of the most popular dancehall queens since the legendary Carlene Smith—who, as a measure of her success, has had her own television talk show. Mighty Crown is also very well known in the sound-system scene on the island and remains a major force in international competition. In fact, the group again won the World Clash competition in 2007.

Jamaican Popular Culture in Japan

How did the Japanese interest in reggae music come about? How did the Japanese scenes that produced Mighty Crown and Kudo evolve? Japanese engagement with Jamaican culture may be traced through five phases, which I delineate below.

1. BIRTH: MID-1970S TO EARLY 1980S

The oldest Japanese reggae fans I consulted during this study reported first discovering reggae and Rasta culture through a number of sources. As was the case for many reggae fans in other countries outside Jamaica, the 1973 Jamaican film *The Harder They Come*, starring reggae singer Jimmy Cliff, was what introduced some of the fans I interviewed to the music. Others reported first hearing it not on Jamaican reggae albums per se, but on punk music albums imported from Britain.[3] With the opening in the late 1970s of a small number of shops specializing in reggae imported directly from Jamaica, Japan had a true pipeline to the island's music. A few tiny reggae bars, clubs, and live houses opened across the country. Tokyo's Club 69, established early in this first period, is credited with being the first such establishment; this regularly packed club, which played only roots reggae, was run by Jah K. S. K., one of several Japanese who were part of the hippie scene before becoming attracted to reggae and Rasta culture. Other early clubs were Hot Corocket, Chocolate City, and Pigeons (More 1994).

Bob Marley, reggae's main international messenger, performed in Japan in 1979, and it is Marley to whom most early Japanese reggae fans trace their first exposure to the music. Marley's only concert tour of the country brought reggae at the time most fully to the attention of mainstream Japanese audiences, and helped to distinguish it from calypso, an older genre of Caribbean music which some years before had been briefly popular.[4] Reggae did not immediately achieve *būmu* status ("boom": a full-fledged, mainstream popular cultural fad): Marley, around whom an underground youth interest had developed, and around whom such a būmu could have been centered, died of cancer in 1981 at age 36. However, even today, fans and practitioners who attended talk and write about the '79 tour with something close to reverence, as a "legendary," once-in-a-lifetime event (Tagawa 1985). Even after Marley's death, Japanese interest in reggae music has remained intensely centered on his iconic figure, as well as, particularly during this first stage, such artists as Sugar Minott, the Mighty Diamonds and Freddie McGregor.

2. LAYING THE FOUNDATIONS: EARLY 1980S TO MID-1980S

From the early to mid-1980s, something of the corporate foundation of Japan's reggae scene was being laid. Overheat Music began publishing *Riddim*, and Tachyon published *Sound System*, which would evolve into the industry mainstay *Reggae Magazine*. Through the magazines and sponsorship of reggae concerts and club events, the two companies would evolve into major managers of reggae's later popularity in Japan. While *Reggae Magazine* is no longer in business, as of this writing, *Riddim* still exists as a free paper with a national circulation of 75,000, has a presence on the Internet,[5] and has long been a main artery of information about the reggae scene in Japan.

Recognizing the potential market for reggae in Japan, representatives from small music companies like Overheat traveled to Jamaica in the early 1980s to form business relations with reggae musicians there, and thus served as conduits between the most famous Jamaican talent and the relatively small number of fans in Japan at that time. During the early to mid-1980s, Overheat signed several major Jamaican artists to album deals, and in 1985 promoted the Mighty Diamonds' live Tokyo performance. At an outdoor venue with a capacity of 3,000, the performance drew about 2,500 fans: a modest success. Although the scene was still small, this was an early sign of the viability of reggae music in Japan. Reggae Sunsplash, a world tour of Jamaican reggae artists, began including Japan as part of its circuit around this period, and, along with the concerts of a number of individual artists, was another major route through which reggae music continued entering the country.

During this second period, a number of local reggae artists who would become the main figures in the third period of Japanese reggae began establishing their careers. These include artists like Nahki; PJ and his band, Cool Runnings (credited with being the first all-Japanese reggae band); Chieko Beauty and Sister Sayoko; and ska bands like Mute Beat, the Ska Flames, and the internationally renowned Tokyo Ska Paradise Orchestra (which fuses ska, jazz, and rock, and which is largely responsible for creating the category "J-ska"). Not only would Rankin' Taxi, now the elder spokesman of Japan's reggae scene, go on to become one of the first big Japanese dancehall reggae DJs, but his Taxi Hi-Fi became the country's first popular sound system. A number of early Japanese DJs emerged from Taxi's crew of vocal artists. Banana Size, based in Yokohama, was also among the very earliest sounds; other early sound systems included the Tokyo-based Massive and V.I.P., and Osaka's Brainwash and Earthquake.

3. BOOM: MID-1980S TO MID-1990S

In 1985, Tachyon held its first Reggae JapanSplash concert. The concept behind this annual tour for the dozen years it was run by Tachyon was to bring not only established but also new, up-and-coming Jamaican musicians to Japan. This way Japan would have direct access to Jamaica's biggest stars even before they hit their stride back home. Reggae JapanSplash grew into a major concert event in Japan, drawing tens of thousands of fans every summer. At the height of roots reggae's popularity in 1994, the tour drew over 100,000 fans nationwide, making it the largest outdoor concert tour in Japan.

As evidenced by the success of this annual event, reggae, Rasta, and other things Jamaican during this third period truly boomed in Japan. Many books, articles, and television documentaries about the Caribbean island appeared in the Japanese media. In Tokyo alone, scores of tiny reggae bars and clubs opened. Specialty and mainstream record shops sold not only reggae CDs, but also movies, documentaries, and concert videotapes made in and about Jamaica. During the 1990s, more and more Japanese tourists, including many honeymooners, began traveling to Jamaica. According to Jamaica's Ministry of Justice, the number of Japanese visitors to the island rose every year between 1980 and 1995, from 29 to 11,534. Managerially linked to Reggae JapanSplash, *Reggae Magazine*, the industry mainstay until it went out of business in 1997, helped galvanize interest in reggae music with its record reviews, profiles of Jamaican musicians, information on upcoming club events, and advertisements for local reggae bars, craft shops, clothing stores, and record stores. Nearly all major Jamaican reggae stars performed in Japan, and their concerts, even with other reggae events taking place at the same time, sold out quickly. This third period saw a flowering of the Japanese reggae scene. For instance, Nahki—who has released nine albums and who had one single sell 400,000 copies—is a veteran of Japan's reggae scene. The Japanese release of the 1993 Disney feature film *Cool Runnings*, about Jamaica's bobsled team, became part of this Jamaican craze, and as a result of the movie, the real Jamaican bobsled team received an ovation at the Nagano Winter Olympics. Jamaica's soccer team, dubbed "the Reggae Boyz," were minor celebrities in Japan in 1998.

4. CONTRACTION OF ROOTS REGGAE: MID-1990S TO LATE 1990S

By the late 1990s, Jamaica was already close to fifteen years into the transition from the dominance of roots and early dancehall—that is, dancehall in its third aspect as discussed above—to the prevalence of the digital riddims of contemporary dancehall reggae. Japanese popular awareness of reggae music in the late 1990s, however, continued to be dominated by roots and early dancehall. Only in the fourth period did contemporary dancehall become predominant. Both the waning roots and the rising dancehall had significant fan bases at this point. As a result, although in Jamaica the distinction between roots and dancehall can be made more clearly according to fan age—these respective musical genres having each run fuller courses on the island—in Japan, where one mature musical import arrives soon after the last, interest in these genres is less distinctly differentiated along generational lines. This is not to say that Japanese fans and performers of roots and dancehall cannot be distinguished at all according to age: after all, as discussed above, many older Japanese became interested in reggae music as early as the mid-1970s, and most dancehall practitioners and fans have emerged much later, since the late 1990s. However, most roots fans were first popularly introduced to that music in the early to mid-1990s, and most dancehall fans were introduced to dancehall music not much later (often indirectly through the popularity of roots reggae), starting in the mid-1990s. (The youngest dancehall fans are teenagers currently being introduced to the music.) Whether one is a roots or dancehall fan in Japan thus depends less on age and more on personal choice, itself a reflection of factors such as area of residence. Although there are many exceptions, the majority of young, urban dancehall fans from such cities as Yokohama, Tokyo, and Osaka, though able to appreciate the kinship between roots and dancehall, have comparative difficulty connecting with the former; while in rural areas, where much of the postboom roots scene is now to be found, roots' naturalistic vibe has followers, old and young, who see dancehall as nothing but grating noise and chatter.

Although reggae in the Japanese popular consciousness near the end of the third period was defined by a mix of roots and early dancehall, with roots predominating, by the late 1990s, the roots reggae boom was clearly contracting. Many of the roots bars and clubs that had cropped up across the country were closing their doors for lack of business. The number of Japanese travelers to Jamaica, while still high, began a steady decline. The format for Reggae JapanSplash changed dramatically when Tachyon folded in 1997, ceding the name "Reggae JapanSplash" to the management of Inter FM, a national radio station. During this period, Reggae JapanSplash booked big-name Jamaican reggae (as well as non-Jamaican, nonreggae) stars, much to the chagrin of many purists who miss the days when young Jamaican unknowns had their first shot at stardom on a Japanese stage. Those fans miss the days when all of the biggest Jamaican reggae musicians flocked to Japan, rather than only a couple, and rather than only musicians like, during this period, Diana King, Big Country, and En Vogue, whose music reflected an American crossover appeal.

When Tachyon and *Reggae Magazine* went out of business, a major route through which Jamaican artists had reached the country, as well as a major conduit of information about the reggae scene in Japan, closed. Reggae now had to compete more directly with other cultural imports like tango; salsa; Indian dress, cinema, and cuisine; and, indeed, the *esunikku* (the ethnic), a hybrid stew of global ethnic culture. Roots reggae as a distinct trend in Japan during this period did not hold nearly the same level of interest it had a decade earlier. Little does in the ever-changing mixture that is popular culture in Japan. Yet roots reggae still has an appeal for Japanese—

measured not only in raw numbers of fans, or in the stories of those who have shed their dread wigs for trendier or more conservative wear, but also in the stories of those for whom an interest in reggae culture has deepened over time to become a way of life.

Artists who flourished during the third period found it necessary to come to terms with the new musical economy of the fourth. Nahki and Rankin' Taxi, two veteran artists mentioned above, and Sister Kaya serve as illustrations. The popularity of Nahki, one of Japan's first and most successful reggae musicians, came in part from a combination of his close links with Tachyon, the marketing of his "alien" mystique (discussed below), and the fact that, having lived in Jamaica and the United States for several years, he uses English and Jamaican Creole with ease. Nahki's verbal delivery reflects the deejaying popular in Jamaica in the late 1970s, and, accordingly, his style as a musician has revolved around live instrumental production. His career took shape during the early 1980s, when the DJing style of speech-song was well under way in Jamaica, but when the rough vocal quality and multiple DJs' use of single digital riddims, all common in contemporary dancehall, were not. Instead of riding this bandwagon, at the time of our interview in 2000, Nahki was experimenting with a "salsa ragga" sound, fusing the live sound of earlier dancehall reggae with salsa music. This move toward salsa ragga was apparently intended to use his reggae credibility to increase his popularity at the time of a salsa craze in Japan. More recently, Nahki has moved into the realm of contemporary dancehall, producing an album for three of the biggest stars on the scene today, the dancehall duo Megaryu, and Pang, a female singer. Nahki continues to perform, including a 2006 appearance with these artists at a sold-out event at Crash Mansion (whose capacity is about 1,500) on New York City's Lower East Side. The performance there appears to be in recognition of New York's status as a city where Japanese artists, including reggae musicians, develop their skills and prove their worth beyond the confines of Japan.

The veteran DJ and MC Rankin' Taxi has not had far to go in order to adapt to the new trends, because he has long performed in contemporary dancehall's musical idiom. Taxi still performs as a DJ; his sound system, Taxi Hi-Fi, appears at many major dancehall events across the country. He is now an elder statesman who educates up-and-coming Japanese talent on deejaying and the art of the sound system. Sister Kaya has used her success as a roots singer to create a niche for herself within Japanese dancehall in several capacities. She has promoted a number of dancehall events and produced albums and videos showcasing female talent, even while she most often performed at strictly roots events. I discuss below one of the DVDs her company produced, on Japan's reggae dancers—as female dancehall dancers are now known in Japan.

5. THE RISE OF DANCEHALL: LATE 1990S TO THE PRESENT

By the late 1990s, dancehall in Japan, as had happened many years earlier in Jamaica, had surpassed roots reggae as an urban subcultural force. More recently, however, it has also moved to some degree into the realm of mainstream culture. Dancehall reggae in Japan has not only achieved a boomlike glory equaling that of its roots predecessor in the 1990s: in many ways, remarkably, it has exceeded this popularity, as measured by record sales and concert attendance. When I asked fans and people in the industry about dancehall's popularity, the very consistent reply was that it had to do with Mighty Crown's victory in 1999, as well as Kudo's in 2002. Mighty Crown's Masta Simon, in describing the growth of the dancehall scene in Japan since 1999, said:

> It took time. It took two, three years [for the music to] spread to the people. Because nobody knew what World Clash was all about, [except for] industry people. The underground street kids, they knew what was going on. They were, like, "Yo, Mighty Crown beat 'jaro, 'jaro that we used to listen to way back." Because nobody really thought that a Japanese sound could beat Kilimanjaro. So it was . . . history . . . right there.[6]

This great ebullience surrounding Mighty Crown's and Kudo's victories has much to do with the sense that they helped legitimize Japanese reggae internationally, and therefore in Japan itself. The degree of enthusiasm for Japanese acts, I think, significantly distinguishes this most recent boom from the first boom, of roots reggae. This enthusiasm resonates recognizably with other Japanese excursions into the international. The upsurge of interest in reggae following these victories is not just about love for reggae music, but also about the possibilities of Japanese accomplishment on the international stage. It is very much part of the pride Japanese have felt about other Japanese successes overseas, including animation, comic books, dolls, and horror films (Kelts 2006; Tobin 2006; Belson and Bremmer 2004). Another expression of Japan's global cultural power (McGray 2002) has been the success of Japanese athletes like the baseball players Hideo Nomo, Ichiro Suzuki, and Hideki Matsui. Sometimes there are specifically racial dimensions to this pride. Many Japanese revel in Matsui's accomplishments, particularly as a power hitter able to compete with some of the most prolific (black, white, and Latino) home-run hitters in American baseball. Japanese television, films, literature, magazines, and comic books routinely work through similar anxieties and enthusiasms about Japanese performance in other sports requiring strength and speed, such as track and field, professional wrestling, mixed martial arts, and boxing. Slight Japanese youth are depicted in manga (comics) for boys, for instance, as overcoming the knotted, hulking, black and white athletes they compete against. Similar anxieties manifest themselves in a more nuanced way in Japanese engagement with such art forms as jazz (Atkins 2001) and tango (Savigliano 1995), to whose progenitors certain ethnoracial passions, which Japanese sometimes imagine themselves as lacking, are ascribed.

This pride, however, is only part of the story of Japanese dancehall's rise in recent years. Another is the way in which Japanese dancehall has become linked to Jamaican dancehall as mediated through the United States. Jamaican dancehall artists have been making incursions in the American market since Shabba Ranks in the early 1990s. The early 2000s have witnessed a similar process. Flavoring their dancehall sound with hip-hop and rhythm and blues, the Jamaican DJs Shaggy and Sean Paul have had significant crossover success. Shaggy had a no. 3 hit in the U.S. *Billboard* Hot 100 Charts in 1995 ("Boombastic") and two no. 1 hits after that ("It Wasn't Me" and "Angel" in 2001). Sean Paul has had three no. 1 hits ("Get Busy" and "Baby Boy" in 2003, and "Temperature" in 2006). Newcomer Sean Kingston's singles "Beautiful Girls" in 2007 and "Fire Burning" in 2009 reached no. 1 and no. 5, respectively, on these charts, and continues the tradition of reggae-hiphop fusion. Bounty Killer, Elephant Man, and Beenie Man, Jamaica's three most popular DJs for many years, have also enjoyed some success in the United States. Dancehall's crossover into American markets has guaranteed a heightened popular-cultural (as opposed to strictly subcultural) profile for dancehall in Japan, given the country's sensitivity to U.S. trends. In 2004, "Good to Go," an album by Elephant Man—whose extreme savvy in courting the Japanese market has led to a sold-out tour by the same name as the album—went gold (sold over 100,000 copies) in the country. "V.I.P. Presents Dancehall Lovers Best," an album compiling songs by such Jamaican dancehall artists as Beenie Man and Elephant Man, was the eighth most popular album on Oricon's (comparable to *Billboard* in the United States) "Western music" charts in late May 2007.

In addition to Mighty Crown's and Kudo's victories, an early major milestone in the rise of what is now called "J-reggae" in Japan—a sign of the growing sense that reggae music in Japan is distinct from Jamaican reggae—was the Osaka DJ Miki Dōzan's no. 1 hit, "Lifetime Respect," in 2001. Delivered with an adroit lyrical flow and in regional dialect, the love song, which sold around a million copies, was a favorite at wedding parties that year. In summer of that same year, several television stations across the country ran reports on Japanese dancehall culture as a hot new discovery. In June 2006, Megaryu's second album, "Garyu Senpu," hit no. 1 on the national charts. "Day by Day," a song from this album, was featured in a national Yokohama Tires television ad campaign. In addition to these artists, among the most well-known reggae DJs and singers are Moomin, Ryo the Skywalker, Fire Ball, Hibikilla, Pang, Chehon, Papa B, Pushim, Minmi, Munehiro, Shonan no Kaze, U-Dou and Platy, and Mighty Jam Rock. Many of these artists were part of the underground dancehall scene years before it boomed nationally.

Riddim remains a major published source on dancehall in Japan; the publisher of the free paper *Yokohama Reggae Times* has also begun a new, more expensively produced free paper called *Strive*. A new, major monthly magazine called *Rove: Reggae Life-style Magazine* has recently appeared on the scene, and other magazines have run special editions on dancehall music. A further manifestation of the increased mainstream presence of dancehall in Japan was that dancehall fashion as of summer 2004 was clearly a style boom: two fashion magazines published special editions on dancehall fashion in the same month that year. Noticeable since 1998, when I began my fieldwork, is a significant overlay of a key element of Japan's reggae subcultural imagery—the Rasta colors of red, green, and gold—with the black, green, and gold of the Jamaican flag still favored in the videos of Elephant Man and other Jamaican artists in heavy rotation for a while on MTV.

As a result of Mighty Crown's acclaim, Yokohama, the group's hometown, has today developed Japan's strongest dancehall following (dancehall is also popular in Osaka). In the summer of 2004, Yokohama Reggae *Sai* (festival), produced by Mighty Crown Entertainment, attracted around 20,000 fans. In 2006, that number reached over 30,000, making it arguably the largest one-day reggae concert in the world. Mighty Crown has done much to brand its name, as Yokohama Reggae Sai illustrates. A high point of this effort was announced at the 2006 event: the sound system received a shoe contract with Nike. The basketball shoe features the Nike logo at the sides with small impressions of the sound system's logo—the letters MC topped by a crown—imprinted all around. (In 2007, they were being sold on ebay.com for between $210 and $290 a pair.)

Another major reggae event is the One Love Jamaica Festival inaugurated in 2004, and held in Tokyo's Yoyogi Park. That year, 30,000 people attended the two-day event.[7] It featured a Bob Marley "sing alike" competition, the winner of which received tickets to travel to Jamaica. There were stalls all around promoting many aspects of Jamaican culture and industry; I remember getting on one extremely long line for the most expensive jerk chicken I have ever had. The event also included several reggae dance performances. I was struck by this because, when I began my fieldwork, the erotic dance and fashion of the donnette scene was entirely underground. The One Love Jamaica Festival, however, was a massive event held in broad daylight in the most public of venues.

Dancehall's popularity represents a kind of delayed snowball effect in the way that it gained initial force from the preceding boom in roots reggae. Some artists in this fifth phase perform both roots reggae and dancehall. However, the effect of dancehall's surge on the continuing roots movement remains to be seen. Reggae JapanSplash has returned after a brief hiatus, probably thanks to the renewed interest in Jamaican music generally that the surging interest in dancehall has generated. Outside the immediate subculture, many DJs and singers inflect their sound by recording and performing in a broad range of Jamaican musical styles. However, other indications are that if roots is to regain anything of its former popularity, it will have to do so independently of dancehall's success, given the rifts between the two subcultures (discussed below). Yet roots reggae continues to survive, even thrive, especially in the summertime. Urban reggae bands—also somewhat removed from the Rastafarian element—keep the tradition of live instrumental reggae alive as inflected in their own original styles. Ska, two evolutionary steps behind reggae (with rocksteady in between), also continues to have a presence in Japan, with older groups like Tokyo Ska Paradise Orchestra and Ska Flames, as well as newer ones like the Determinations. The naturalist vibe of roots reggae, appealing most to those living in the countryside, is represented by bands like Dub Sensemania, Zion High Players, the Bandories, and the Hemptones. Mighty Massa, Sweet Jamaica Muzik, Shandi I, Jah Works, and Direct Impact are sound systems identified not so much with the Jamaica-New York dancehall circuit but rather with the more ethereal, dub reggae sound (also discussed below) centered in Britain.

Japan as Difference, Difference in Japan

Japanese engagement with Jamaican popular culture deepens what is for many the mystery of Japan, a country doubly orientalized (Said 1979) as, on the one hand, a tradition-bound society (of demure geisha and disciplined samurai) and, on the other hand, the society which defines postmodern consumerist excess. Japan has indeed posed various challenges to the Western effort to know the non-West. To the Americans whose unwelcome arrival helped end the Tokugawa shogunate's two centuries of near-seclusion from the outside world, Japan in the mid-1800s appeared as the barbaric, historically arrested Orient of western—including Western anthropological—imagination. Yet Japan's rapid industrial modernization during the Meiji period (1868–1912) and its military victories in the Sino-Japanese and Russo-Japanese wars (1894–95 and 1904–5, respectively) complicated efforts to envision the nation as essentially different from the modern West. Japan also problematizes the Western tendency to imagine non-Western and indigenous peoples as necessarily marginalized by the forces of modernity (economic, military-industrial, aesthetic, and epistemological), as being forced to play a Western game at which they, newcomers to the modern scene, are ill equipped to succeed. Japan, a country which has never been colonized—despite ideological and other Western (pre)occupations—developed relatively earlier, and more fully than other non-Western nations, the apparatuses of modernity (national universities, academic societies, media industries, the military-industrial complex), inventing traditions (Hobsbawm and Ranger 1983) such as those invested in the figure of the emperor, through which a sense of Japanese citizenship could be inculcated (Gluck 1985).

Therefore, while anthropologists today are increasingly concerned with non-Western vulnerability in the new global economy, Japan, despite being a non-Western country, has been as much an agent of these realities as a subject of them. Consumption is a key way in which this situation has been explored (Clammer 1997): from tourist travel to the purchase of major American corporations, from English-language schools to parks with European nations as their themes (Hendry 2000). Yet I would suggest that particularly in the past fifteen years there has been a significant development in Japan's public discourse about its national identity understood in relation to its consumption of the outside world. Joseph Tobin (1992b) in describing this earlier discourse, centers his analysis of Japan's self-making consumption of the West. Many Japanese see this consumption, Tobin argues, as a means of asserting cosmopolitan identities in a homogeneous Japan. Peter Dale's (1986) analysis of *nihonjinron* (theories of the Japanese), a body of popular and scientific speculation on what makes the Japanese unique as a people, also demonstrates the Japanese tendency to frame the particularity of Japaneseness in relation to the universal West. However, I argue that the public discourse of Japaneseness in Japan today has come to more self-consciously invoke the world at large beyond the West. I also argue that while these discourses depart from the ironic Eurocentrisms of nihonjinron, they are of a kind with nihonjinron-like assumptions about the Japanese as a unique people.

It is true that Japan has long culturally engaged countries outside East Asia and the West, as is evidenced in the reputation of the Japanese as international travelers. The Japanese preoccupation with the West and the anxieties that underlie it remain profound. The new fascination with the non-Western world, then, can still in some measure be seen in terms of this anxiety surrounding Western power, and as such is not new at all. Yet this fascination is distinctive for the way it involves a collective spectatorship of individual self-actualization in these non-Western spaces. In the new accounts in the mass media and elsewhere of Japanese, especially youth, travel overseas, the travelers tend not to travel in large groups, but rather, expressly, alone.

Many important works have explored global cultural flow as an ethnographically rich local situation of a West variously posited as the global. These include James Watson's (1997) edited volume on the cultural terms of McDonald's localization across Asia. A more specifically Japanese, and more recent, example is Masamichi Inoue's (2007) exploration of the development of Okinawan resistance to the American military presence; this resistance is partly expressed through a human-rights discourse that has helped facilitate Okinawa's internationalist identifications. Japanese engagement with the non-West provides a valuable analytical complement to these works on continued Japanese negotiation of Western hegemony. Analyses of how non-Western countries—marginalized in varying degrees in the global political landscape—imagine each other in the present moment of globalization complicate the easy dichotomies of West and non-

West, North and South, oppressor and oppressed. Such analyses, while continuing to speak to the devastating consequences of Northern economic domination of the South, may also disclose some of the complex interactions among non-Western societies.

The presence of Jamaican subcultures in Japan represents one element of the latter country's domestications of the esunikku. For most Japanese, engagement with this global ethnicity, including Jamaican culture, is temporary: a honeymoon in Montego Bay, a Jamaican DJ's concert in Shinjuku's Liquid Room, a cup of Blue Mountain coffee sipped at an expensive Shibuya cafe, a Rasta tam—fake dreadlocks attached—removed in time for work the next day.[8] And yet, when Japanese consumption of Jamaican culture goes beyond the disposable, when it involves forsaking the *sararii-man* or office lady[9] path to become a DJ or donnette, this consumption can represent a significant remove from the mainstream. The decision to cultivate real dreadlocks, or a Rasta-inspired critique of Japanese social politics, can come from a profound sense of personal investment in Rastafari. This sense of investment can be especially charged since the Jamaican cultural forms in question bear ideological content to which Japanese, citizens of a relatively safe, prosperous Asian nation, would initially appear to have little claim.

Social Performance

In investigating the Japanese encounter with the ethnic difference of the Jamaican, I ethnographically center this book on the performance of social identity.[10] I define "social performance" as the public expression of social identification (gendered, ethnic, class-based, racial) through management of given symbolic resources. I represent performances as taking place in basically two settings: proximal and remote. In proximal settings, performer and audience are located within a physically designated space, in which the deployment of the symbolic resources that define the event usually occurs within a restricted time frame. In the context of this research, performances revolving, for instance, around onstage speech, music, fashion, and dance in Japanese dancehall fall most clearly into this category. In remote settings, the audience, although physically absent, is implied in the production of the work, consuming it after a delay. Japanese representations of Jamaicans through mass-mediated texts and images are examples of performances taking place in remote settings.

In line with a general concern these days in the social sciences, perhaps especially in anthropology, with understanding the terms under which cultural phenomena like reggae music and Rastafari are no longer bound to single sites (Basch, Schiller, and Blanc 1994; Bestor 2004; Clifford 1997; Malkki 1995; Ong 1999), another term I wish to define is "performative field." Depending on the context and analytical focus, this refers to a local, national, or transnational network of (sub)culturally circumscribed, politically complex spaces whose coherence as such is critically effected in performance. It is a network of spaces in which performance represents a definitive mode in which the commonalities—and often the complex differences —between participants are worked through. These politically complex alliances and differences—definable in such terms as race, class, ethnicity, and gender—help inform the terms under which any given node is constituted as belonging to this broader network of spaces. In this book, I explore the performative field not in conceptual abstraction, but rather do so by privileging the ethnographic analysis of specific performances to reveal the workings of social power that surround them. For instance, I discuss the Jamaican powder room as a space in which Japanese and Jamaican dancers converge out of a sense of connection within the performative field of a transnational, politically complex (in this case, seen in gendered and economic terms) dancehall culture. The stages of the dancehall queen competitions and sound clashes—in which Jamaicans and Japanese compete in such cities as Montego Bay, New York, London, and elsewhere—are other nodes within the broader performative field of transnational dancehall culture. While these nodes can be fixed in time and place, as these examples suggest, that is not always the case. This is so given that performance and the politics surrounding it emerge not only in proximal, but also in remote, terms. As an example of how these nodes are not fixed in time, in Japanese readership of Japanese-authored writings on travel to Jamaica, a sense of Japaneseness is literarily performed, but not simultaneously consumed. The bus taking the contestants to the International Dancehall Queen Competition, where donnettes informally perform for each other before arriving in Montego Bay, is an example of shifting place. I also use the notion of performative field to explore how Rastafari as encountered in Jamaica is resituated in rural Japan. This term, then, draws attention to the various terms under which Jamaicans and Japanese come together—sometimes easily, sometimes not—to perform at least nominally as subcultural peers in these transnational settings. Among the transnational politics of performance that I discuss as being relevant to this coming together are those pertaining to race and racism.

On Race and Racism

Most studies of the performative have centered on gender.[11] Some analyses, however, have also recognized race as a key aspect of social identity worked through in performative terms (Benston 2000; Butler 1993; Johnson 2003; Rahier 1999). In this book, I will consider a range of ways in which Japanese perform Jamaican culture, including in gendered, class-based, ethnic, local, national, and transnational terms. However, I will focus my analysis, especially in the international context, on race and particularly blackness, including as linked to the other terms above.[12]

It is with reservation that I place transnational discourses of black otherness so close to the center of this study. Such a focus potentially deepens the objectification of black people. It permits little room to consider what is interpersonally—beyond broad, hegemonic discourse—the absolute fluidity of selves and others: so-called others often can and do return the gaze of so-called selves (hooks 1992). (With this in mind, in the final chapter, I explore Jamaican takes on the Japanese interest in reggae and Rastafari.) However, despite the fact that analyzing blackness in countries where there are few black people complicates efforts to represent its lived humanity, it is crucial to explore the terms under which deconstructed blackness has circulated around the globe, including to East Asian countries like Japan. It is crucial not only in academic terms, but also to understand the racial political globe in which this lived humanity must assert itself.

A few older and some more recent works (such as Dikötter 1992, 1997a; and Wagatsuma 1967) have explored how the Western concept of race has come to be situated in East Asia. Some have investigated issues of race and racism as they have emerged in given modes of subcultural and mass-mediated performance (Atkins 2001; Condry 2006; Kelsky 1994, 2001; Robertson 1998; Russell 1991a, 1991b, 1991c, 1998). A number have been focused on the histories and rememberings of Japan's colonialism and militarism in Korea, China, and Japan itself in the period before and of the Second World War (Doak 2001; Eskildsen 2002; Tamanoi 2000; Weiner 1995). One goal of this study is to build on these works on race in East Asia by exploring how racial politics are performatively worked through not only domestically, regionally, and in relation to the West, but also in the wider third world. This includes my consideration of Jamaican blackness seen as a symbol of the fight against, but also domination by, Western power; as the pure (blackness as natural) but also the impure (blackness as impoverished and corrupt); as the cosmopolitan (blackness as belonging to the exciting global) but also the primitive (blackness as the third world regressed); and as the desired but also the devalued (precisely given its status as the desired which, possessed, becomes diminished). By considering the imagination of blackness in these complex terms, I hope to avoid the reductionism that an analysis of mass-mediated blackness can invoke.

In addition to essentialization, another concern that might be raised about placing race at the analytical center of this study is that by doing so, the Japanese appropriation of Jamaican culture will not be appreciated on Japanese terms. Here I reiterate my earlier point that I will consider race as only one point (albeit a significant one) around which Jamaican musical and religious subcultural identities are crafted in Japan. I further note that I regard as important the analysis of race beyond the West in local historical context. Still, "race" is not one of the many English loanwords commonly used in Japanese. It was certainly used very rarely by the individuals who participated in this study, in English or in Japanese (usually rendered as *jinshu*). How productive, then, can race be as the analytical center of a study of Jamaican musical and religious subcultures in Japan?

For now I will say that although the Western term "race" is not much explicitly invoked in Japan, racial discourse is clearly in evidence (Oguma 2002; Takezawa 2005). Japan's very birth as a nation was largely defined by the adoption of Western institutions and ideologies—including racial ones —that remain with Japan even today. Frank Dikötter notes:

> Far from being a negligible aspect of contemporary identities, racialized senses of belonging have often been the very foundation of national identity in East Asia in the 20th century . . . It is not a necessary precondition to use the word 'race' in order to construct racial categories of thought . . . Racial discourse in . . . Japan thrived and evolved over time because it reconfigured pre-existing notions of identity and simultaneously appealed to a variety of groups, from popular audiences to groups of scientists. (Dikötter 1997b, 2, 3, 8)

Early modern Japanese intellectuals applied Social Darwinist ideas to Japan's various others at home and overseas (Dikötter 1997b). Race manifests itself in such forms as Japan's popular-cultural and literary imaginings of itself in relation to whiteness (Creighton 1995; Kelsky 1994, 2001) and to blackness (Russell 1991a, 1991b, 1991c, 1998). It manifests itself in everything from the common representation of the Japanese characters in manga and *anime* (animation) as phenotypically white, to the very popular golliwog-like dolls called *Dakko-chan* and blackface performers appearing on Japanese television. It may very well be this omnipresence and perhaps even the naturalness—for too many and for too long—of black objectification and idealizations of whiteness that has made it possible to miss the presence of racial thinking in Japan.

Given the commonness of these images; given a series of remarks by high-level Japanese politicians from the 1980s through the early 1990s in which blacks were variously described as dirty, fiscally irresponsible, and unintelligent; given the works of female writers who have garnered popularity among Japanese readers in part through explicit descriptions of their liaisons with sexually stereotyped black men; given a certain lurid fascination in the Japanese media with the excesses of African American servicemen, Japan has been described by some Western observers as the most racist country on earth. Although it is hard to determine what such rankings are based on (or to see them, in some cases, as anything but self-serving and hypocritical), it is not hard to conclude that racism is a reality in Japan. It is not just comments and images like those described above, nor just the simultaneous fascination and wariness with which foreigners generally are often regarded, including as racial others. Foreigners in general are subject to housing discrimination and to restricted employment opportunities; they are rarely able to become Japanese citizens. (It is interesting that even as so many Japanese celebrate travel to and take up residence in countries all over the world, Japan's own immigration policy is so extremely restrictive.) But while foreigners might generally be seen as other, and might all be subject to a certain generalized discrimination, individual groups of foreigners often have certain racial stereotypes associated with them. For example, while both black and white men (regardless of nationality) might be considered impure, extreme in their sexual endowments and appetites, tending toward violence and so forth, the otherness of black foreigners is inflected far more regularly and far more singularly in these terms. White men are routinely imagined as kind, romantic, and sophisticated in ways that black men, reducible to their phalluses, are not.

If racism is imagining, representing, or treating individuals socially recognized as belonging to another race according to a narrow set of ideas associated with that race, in ways that—directly or not—sustain the structural (economic, political, and so forth) marginalization of these racialized individuals, then the above imaginings of black people are racist. These stereotypes are born of and help sustain a reductive view of black humanity, one which works to limit full black participation in social life, domestically and internationally. I want to focus here on racism's structural aspect. "Structural racism" might generally be seen as describing how racism is effected through government agencies, corporate employers, banks, real-estate agencies, schools and universities, the media, the family, and other institutions. Racism in this structural aspect is not necessarily avowed and can take place without conscious effort on the part of institutions' human constituents. The managers of the U.S.-based plant of a Japanese car company do not have to explicitly mandate not promoting black executives in order for black executives to not be promoted: the company's historical exclusion of people of color from its upper ranks, along with its making no provisions to deal with the interpersonal difficulties that might occur should black people be promoted, makes it that much more difficult to even imagine such promotions taking place.

Structural racism, then, does not necessarily have to do with conscious insensitivity on the part of the individual toward racialized others. But it is precisely this "not necessarily" aspect of structural racism that I want to foreground. Structural racism preserves itself in part through an institution's intense decentering of individual responsibility, in which the mandate to recognize racist wrong becomes lost within the workings of the institution. In contemporary capitalist societies like those of Europe, the United States, and Japan, many institutions belong to massively impersonal systems (ideological, infrastructural, material-cultural) of global production and consumption, a gross impersonality that makes it easy for the lone consumer to dismiss the damage wrought by this global production and consumption. Among these moral effects is the muting of the voices of producers, the occlusion of the dissent of the consumed. These producers often belong to a racialized underclass—one legacy of colonialism—whose cultural productions emerge out of unequal economic relationships with first-world agents (governments, corporations, lending institutions, consumers); silencing their voices is necessary for capitalist consumption to proceed smoothly—that is, without guilt, and so that much more profitably for these first-world agents.

In light of these considerations, is it (ethno)racist when Japanese youth as part of their engagement with Jamaican dancehall and reggae wear dread wigs or tan their skin? Seen in structural terms, I think it is. Japanese embodiments of blackness in Japan are usually undertaken with the discreet understanding that *black people have no say in the matter*. Racialized people's structurally facilitated inability to complexly represent themselves as full human beings is a fundamental aspect of racism generally. Japanese adoptions of ethnoracial blackness without need for sensitivity to black people's opinion about how they and their cultural productions are represented and consumed situates Japan within the first-world sociopolitical order in which such concerns have been made structurally irrelevant. It is reasonable to expect Japanese people to adopt reggae, this music they love, on terms that they can understand; how this is done is indeed an anthropologically important issue that I will explore in this book. Yet this adoption is realized through structural racisms which facilitate the first world's gazing at, and taking from, black people with little need for concern about black opinion. Few of these black people can speak directly to the terms under which the cultural expressions they create—often the only means at their immediate disposal to challenge the economic, sociopolitical, and other difficulties they face as a people—are reproduced elsewhere. As the progenitors of these cultural forms, and as the people with whom these forms are globally identified, they rightly feel they have an investment in the forms even beyond the sites of their original production.

Is there a realistic scenario in which Japanese today can avoid engaging in structural racism in their adoptions of Jamaican culture? For me, the short answer is no. This is as true for the Japanese as it is for anyone else who engages the cultural production of politically marginalized racial others with a structurally facilitated indifference to the opinions of these racial others (as seen in anything from tourism to some approaches to anthropology, past and present). This indifference reflects, and thereby reproduces, the marginality of these cultural producers. However, I want to foreground the agency of the individual in structural racism in order to consider the possibility that individual Japanese, though to some degree necessarily working within orders of structural racism, can still engage in reggae subcultural and Rasta religious practices that might undermine this racism. Although I have not seen it as my job particularly to judge whether one or another research participant is racist, I regard situated ethnographic analysis as critical in exploring the extent to which the personal motivations behind such engagement, and the practices through which it takes place, might be complicit with or challenge structural and other forms of racism. Japanese who wear dread wigs render as cheap and disposable an embodied symbol that devout Rastafarians crafted, in the not-so-olden days of Jamaican colonialism, as a critique of colonialized mentality—including the perceived Anglophilia symbolized by neatly cropped hair. For many Japanese people, dreadlocks are an easy joke, partly because they do not need to be anything more serious, a condition partly sustained by the forces of structural racism.[13]

On the other hand, choosing to cultivate long, waist-length dreadlocks can reflect a more sensitive engagement with Rastafari. To be sure, even cases such as these give evidence of structural racism as described above: they can be of a fetishizing, stylistically superficial kind with the dread wig. The choice to cultivate real dreadlocks remains a choice, one usually made within and one which thus supplements a broader symbolic economy in which the signs of blackness are readily appropriated as self-styling things to be consumed. Yet the choice to have dreadlocks, rather than being singularly about consequence-free play, is for a small number of serious Japanese practitioners of Rastafari an intimate, embodied expression of identification with the struggle of Afro-Jamaicans as fellow colored people, of dissent against political apathy in Japan. In seeking out Jamaican people as they often do, these Japanese most directly encounter the dissonance that many other Japanese do not, that between blackness as symbol and blackness as lived, an encounter which potentially upsets the insidious system of representational nonavowal through which structural racism proceeds. Thus individuals such as these represent an important front in the fight against racism in Japan. Rather than just stigmatizing as racist all Japanese bodily and other appropriations of the Jamaican, then, I want to first fully acknowledge the complexity, insidiousness, and seeming intractability of structural and other forms of racism in Japanese and other societies. This acknowledgment becomes a point of departure from which to consider how the practices of individual Japanese reggae fans and practitioners, however compromised, might come to challenge reductionist representations of Afro-Jamaican people.

In considering this potential, Japanese engagement with Jamaican culture needs to be understood not only vis-à-vis an overdetermining symbolic economy of Western racialism. It needs to be understood not only vis-à-vis a Japanese society appreciated on its own terms.[14] It also needs to be seen as it emerges in the spaces of subcultural practice, in the performative fields of a Japanese-Jamaican encounter informed by, but also potentially subversive of, familiar views of Japan as bound to the West or as uniquely self-contained. In this way, what comes into view is not only Japan as avid consumer of the West (in which I uncomfortably include African America)[15] but also of the world beyond; not only of Japan as marginalized non-West or slumping superpower but also, still, a powerful first-world nation; not only, therefore, a view of the Japanese practice of taking the best and leaving the rest as innocently entertaining (for Japanese consumers and non-Japanese consumers of Japan alike), but also as of issue for those taken from and disposed of; not only a trivial Japanese pursuit of Jamaican culture, but also a pursuit in which some of these practitioners are deeply invested; not only a foreclosed "Jamaican culture" easily consumed by and becoming part of a thus foreclosed "post-modern, consumerist Japan," but also a potential for new meanings realized in the intersocial spaces of Jamaican-Japanese contact. Among the ways in which these issues of intersocial contact emerge in my analysis of subcultural practice are the efforts of dancehall divas traveling to Jamaica to articulate a sense of sisterhood with Jamaican women (see chapter 3); the Japanese effort to deeply identify with Rastafari in part through travel to Jamaica (see chapter 4); and the literary effort to link the oppressions faced by the Japanese working class to those of the Jamaican underclass (see chapter 5).

Method and Positionality

As an anthropologist of Japan, my primary concern in this study is with using Jamaican-Japanese cultural exchanges to understand aspects of contemporary Japanese society. In doing so, I take a multi-sited approach to this research, partially placing this book within the emergent field of Afro-Asian scholarship. This Afro-Asian perspective requires taking into account how racial ideas and racially informed cultural production flow and settle outside the West (even where informed by Western colonial ideology and by Western-dominated neoliberal capitalist modes of production, circulation, and consumption). While each of these non-Western societies might judge itself and other non-Western societies in Western ideological terms, the West can become peripheral in non-Western peoples' lived encounters with each other. For example, I explore in chapter 3 the extent to which women's engagement with dancehall dance frees them from the gendered norms that are not only originarily Jamaican or Japanese but also, less consciously, of the modern West. In these ways, then, the Afro-Asian perspective of this research represents one among many other potential interventions into the hegemony of the West in investigations of Japan's ventures around the cultural globe.

But beyond the fact that I have chosen to center my analysis of Jamaican-Japanese cultural exchange on Japan (again, given my primary identification as an anthropologist of Japan), and although these exchanges are being initiated mostly by Japanese (given the popularity of Jamaican culture in the country), I do not assume any de facto primacy of Japan any more than I do a primacy of the West in understanding these exchanges. Given what can be the charged interethnic, and sometimes specifically racial, politics that such exchanges can invoke, I argue that it misses too much of what Japanese dancehall, roots reggae, and Rastafari are to privilege these phenomena as Japanese things onto themselves. Beginning the analysis with the assumption of an already completed Japanese adoption of Jamaican popular culture forecloses consideration of the sometimes contentious terms—including ethnic, racial, and national ones—under which Japanese work toward adopting these subcultures. Even where motivated by cultural relativist sensitivity to Japan as a non-Western society, such an assumption ironically risks dismissing the opinions of Jamaicans, a third-world people, about Japanese engagement with their culture. This is something I wish to avoid, given the marginalization of Jamaica throughout so much of the global political arena, relative to a country like Japan—itself marginalized as merely imitative of other peoples, but nonetheless an economically and politically powerful force in the world today. This assumption also risks dismissing, as I discuss later, the ways in which Jamaican-Japanese exchanges have come to inform Jamaican culture in Japan. An issue that I wish to address in this book, then, most directly in the last chapter, is how Rastafari and reggae in Japan invoke discourses of race, culture, and power in which Japan is not only marginal as a non-Western country vis-à-vis the hegemonic West, but is also a powerful first-world country vis-à-vis poor countries like Jamaica. Many Japanese people's reading of Jamaican culture is informed by both these positions (Japan as non-Western and as first world); many Jamaicans' reading of Japanese consumption of reggae is informed by Western stereotypes of Asians and by Jamaica's status as a fledgling postcolonial society in a rapidly neoliberalizing world. Far from undermining appreciation of Jamaican culture in Japan, then, I see this multi-sited approach as a valuable tool with which to mine its richness.

Given this concern with both countries, in the decade of conducting this research, I have made several of trips to Jamaica, attending numerous dancehall events there as well as meeting and speaking with members of the Rastafarian community. The majority of the fieldwork for this research, however, was conducted in Japan beginning in 1998. While my research was centered in the Tokyo metropolitan area, I traveled extensively across the country—to Osaka, Nara, Kyoto, Nagano, and Okinawa—wherever I could find people, places, and events related to dancehall, roots reggae, and Rastafari. These included such venues as clubs, concerts, Jamaican themed-restaurants and bars, record shops, craft shops, and similar spaces. As I became friends with many of my research participants, research sites came to include homes, workplaces, recording studios, and other less public spaces. It was at this point that I began audiotaping research participants, since earlier use of this equipment, I feared, would be intrusive. These interviews tended to be open-ended and conversational in tone. For major performers and other industry figures (such as magazine publishers and promoters) to whom my access was relatively restricted, I tended to conduct briefer, tape-recorded, semistructured interviews (in which I asked a scripted set of questions while going with the flow of the conversation). These interviews tended to last anywhere from half an hour to a couple of hours. Other major methodological approaches included content analysis of popular media representations of Jamaican culture in Japan, and archival research on related Japanese-language material—both popular and academic—unavailable in the United States.

In the early days of my research, I often introduced myself as a Jamaican graduate student at the University of California, Los Angeles, conducting research on Jamaican popular culture in Japan. Since I was a Jamaican frequently in settings with many people interested in Jamaican culture, and in a country where there are few Jamaicans, many research participants became interested in me personally. Many chose to speak with me not in Japanese or in English but rather in Jamaican patois. Early in the research, this tendency no doubt had to do with the fact that I was still struggling with conversational Japanese, despite two years of graduate study. Throughout my stay, however, I grew able to communicate more comfortably in Japanese; still, people who I met for the first time at this point in my research tended to speak to me in patois.

Many of my research participants have traveled to Jamaica, New York, and London, where they spent much time learning Jamaican musical and religious culture, including patois. I believe their speaking to me as a Jamaican in patois represented a way for them, consciously or otherwise, to perform their subcultural identifications as reggae artists, reggae dancers, or Rastafarians. Despite the high premium on learning English in mainstream Japan, I know of many Japanese immersed in Jamaican culture whose interest in patois did not at all extend to standard English, despite the genealogical links between the two. I read this respect for patois as no different from my own for Japanese, and I suspected that many Japanese who were willing to speak with me in their language did so despite thinking how weird it was to be speaking Japanese with a foreigner (perhaps especially a Jamaican). Therefore, despite my initial discomfort in speaking in patois with Japanese people—I had lived in the United States for many years at that point and felt there was a kind of presumptuousness in some people's speaking with me in patois—I became increasingly willing to do so, especially with those participants who became my close friends.

Ethnonationality (my being Jamaican) and language were not the only factors influencing my interactions with research participants. Gender was another. For instance, although I was able to meet and talk at length with several reggae dancers, the fact that I am a man may have restricted my access—or afforded me a different kind of access—in ways I may never fully know. I think particularly about the backstage areas of reggae dance competitions, or the powder rooms I discuss later. I did not attempt to gain direct access to these areas, but I have been able to compensate for this to some degree through reporting—interpersonal and mass-mediated—about what goes on in these spaces. However, the same fact of my being a man may also have provided me greater—or different—access to and rapport with the Japanese men who dominate the sound system and Rasta scenes.

With regard to race independently of ethnonationality, the visible fact that I am black (leaving aside the socially constructed nature of race) could have made it easier for some respondents to speak to me about race (I could relate to what they were saying), but more difficult for others (they worried that they might say something that would offend me). Those aspects of my discussion of race that are based on these interactions have been written with careful consideration of this fact. (This is not to say that I see my data as more potentially compromised than that of, say, white researchers, racialized as they also are in Japanese eyes.)

Another issue that I wish to address here, relating to the positionality of my research participants, is marijuana use. Marijuana consumption is an important part of Rastafarian religious practice in Jamaica. It is found among many Jamaican roots reggae and some dancehall reggae artists. As in Jamaica, marijuana possession and use is illegal in Japan. Many of my research participants were quite candid with me about their use of marijuana, and I have presented some of their stories in this book. However, I have chosen to exclude some of the ethnographic details of this consumption, details that I think would have enriched appreciation of the performative and other terms under which Jamaican culture is adopted in Japan. In ritual terms, this includes, for instance, the lighting of the chalice by the person to the left of the individual holding it; the invocation of the words "Jah Rastafari"—always by this person seated to the left, as well as, often, by the others at the table—as the chalice bearer smokes the marijuana; the consistent passing of the chalice to the left; or one Japanese dread's gestural conjunction of sacraments by scraping the ashes or unused portion of the herb with a knife, wiping it into his hand, and stroking it into his dreads. These collective and individual practices, conducted much as they are in Jamaica, performatively reference the authority of the Jamaican as one way of authenticating Rasta in Japan, and in so doing making it less immediately subject to that Jamaican authority. In this way, what comes into view is a gap whereby ganja and (full-on, organic—as opposed to fashionable salon) dreads are clearly treated as sacraments through Jamaican Rasta rituals, but their meanings become less singularly Afro-Jamaican. This retooling of Jamaican cultural symbols according to Japanese prerogatives will be of general concern for me in the chapters that follow. Despite withholding the broader ethnographic context of marijuana consumption in the interest of protecting my research participants, I believe that what details I do provide later in the book accomplish enough in the way of explaining the significance of this consumption.

A final issue pertaining to positionality is that of the text itself. I realize that the readership of this book—primarily academic but also more casual—is likely to be diverse. This is because of the geographic (Jamaica, Japan) and topical range (race, gender, class, ethnicity, nation, religion, music, subculture, and so forth) necessary for a study of Jamaican popular culture in Japan. I realize that it will be impossible to satisfy all audiences. My bottom-line approach in trying to address all of these audiences is to introduce complexity ultimately as relevant to an appreciation of the often complex—but also, I confess, often entertaining—issues at hand. I am no fan of complexity for its own sake. But I obviously want to avoid common views of Japanese as bizarre, wacky, and superficial consumers of foreign culture; of Jamaicans as easy-going natives whose only exertions are to make music, run, and dance; and of both groups as all the more amusing for actually having an interest in each other. I hope that in trying to represent this encounter in a thoughtful manner, both as appreciated within my discipline and by my research participants, readers will feel I have reached some acceptable middle ground.

1

The Politics of Presence
PERFORMING BLACKNESS IN JAPAN

How have Jamaicans and Japanese, their islands oceans apart, come into the kinds of contact that have made Jamaican culture so popular in Japan? What are the cultural, historical, and ideological vectors along which this distance is traversed? How, specifically, are the ideas about blackness that inhere in Jamaican culture worked through in Japan? In this chapter, I provide a context for my argument that the various terms in which the idea of blackness has circulated around the world have a significant impact on the consumption and reproduction of Jamaican culture in Japan. In doing so I focus on the case of Afro-Jamaican popular culture, I argue that blackness as encoded in these popular-cultural movements represents a flexible, often performatively realized metaphor through which black as well as nonblack peoples in a range of global sites voice their various sociopolitical concerns. I argue that much of the variability in how blackness is constructed around the world turns importantly on racial demography—specifically the relative presence of black people—in a given site. I focus this discussion on performativities of blackness in Japan, given their relevance to my explorations of Jamaican popular culture in the country.

Perspectives on Global Blackness

Especially over the last two decades, globalization has come to exert a powerful influence on processes of cultural production and consumption. This influence is one of accelerated flows of people and commodities, of capital and information within an increasingly interlinked global economy (Appadurai 1996; Clifford 1997). Ideas also transcend national boundaries. One of these is that of blackness.

The presence of the modern racial idea of blackness on the international stage, however, is not particular to the current era of globalization. One aspect of the historical construction of global blackness—the worldwide movement of black peoples, as well as of the dynamic complex of cultural and ideological expression associated with black peoples—is the notion of diaspora (Gilroy 1993; Roach 1996). Black people were originally categorized as such according to a Western scientific regime employed in part to morally justify their abduction from Africa and enslavement throughout the New World. Rastafarians, roots reggae musicians, and many dancehall musicians (Luciano, Capleton, Sizzla, and Anthony B) invoke the diaspora as the ancestral memory of this uprooting and the desire for repatriation to the continent. The religious and musical movements that have valorized Africa and called for pan-African unity have developed great followings throughout much of the continent (Savishinsky 1994). They also effect a sense of political and cultural community among black people in places where the diaspora intersects with the metropolitan West, including such sites of Jamaican immigration as New York (Manuel and Marshall 2006) and London (Cashmore 1983).

In addition to the diaspora, a second—related, and more recently ascendant—dimension of the scholarship on blackness around the world concerns the politicization of black identity in Latin America (Green 2007; Harris 1993; Lewis 1995; Wade 1995; Whitten and Torres 1998). Of concern is how peoples of African descent in this region have come to claim this heritage not only against domestic valorization of whiteness and/or racial mixedness, but also across national boundaries. Many Afro-Latin peoples have seen in roots reggae and Rastafari internationally recognizable modes through which to performatively realize their racial political identities— both long-standing and emergent, deeply felt and opportunistic—as black citizens. The renowned Brazilian band and cultural group AfroReggae uses the popularity of reggae and other African diasporic music as a way of addressing issues of social justice—urban poverty, police brutality, and drug violence—that have long faced Afro-Brazilian peoples (Yudice 2001). Maroons in Suriname, French Guiana, and Colombia have used reggae music as a way of communicating their sense of kinship with black people not only in Jamaica and their own countries but also in other parts of the African diaspora (Bilby 1999, 2000).

A third recent perspective on global blackness is one which to date remains almost entirely disconnected from the scholarship mentioned above on blackness internationally: work on race in modern East Asia. In this literature, the assumption that race as a Western notion does not apply to Asia gives way to analysis of clear manifestations of racial thinking in the region, including Japan's racializations of its Asian colonial subjects (Robertson 1998; Tamanoi 2000). This broad body of literature also includes works dealing with blackness, such as those on the Afro-Asian (Gallicchio 2000; Jones 2001; Jones and Singh 2003; Mullen 2004; Prashad 2001; Raphael-Hernandez and Steen 2006). These are usually critical-theoretical analyses, as well as cultural and political histories of African and Asian peoples' encounters within international spaces structured by Western power. Another vein within this work on race in East Asia that is relevant to blackness explores the contemporary encounter between blacks and Asians in East Asia (Russell 1991a, 1991b, 1991c, 1998; Sautman 1994), and to this extent as understood from an East Asian perspective.

Mapping Global Blackness

Given this sense of Asia's disconnection from discussions about blackness in the modern world, it might be useful to identify some criteria with which to map, if only at this point in a broad way, discursive construction of blackness globally. One possible approach is to group countries according to their historical relations to black transatlantic slavery. In doing so, one also groups these countries according to the relative numbers of black people resident in each country. By extension, this allows a discussion of the terms under which the humanity of black people is realized in interpersonal terms or is more fully the province of the mass media, with all the complexities both possibilities imply.

Applying this historicized politics of presence to explore global blackness —with examples from the Afro-Jamaican case—three broad regions present themselves. The first is the so-called peripheral (Wallerstein 1974) societies of Africa, South America, and the Caribbean. Here there are significant numbers of black people, who nevertheless have had to struggle with the direct as well as the indirect legacies of colonial rule to develop stable political and economic infrastructures. While largely or even predominantly composed of black people, these societies are often dominated by a minority of white, light-complexioned, or otherwise Western-identified peoples. This elite is often committed to the notion of nationhood not so much out of a sense of democracy but rather because, on the most practical level, it provides a structure through which to preserve and augment their power. In these countries, nationhood can be celebrated through Afrocentric cultural institutions that often offer the black citizen only symbolic investment in the nation, as these institutions are primarily managed by and reflect the interests of the neocolonial elite. Even in predominantly black countries, the conditions of European privilege and black marginalization, and of agentive Western selfhood and objectified black otherness, linger.[1] Some Rastafarians question a national independence based on the motto, "Out of Many, One People," since about 92 percent of Jamaica's population is of African descent, and since, for these Rastas, such a motto unduly privileges Jamaica's upper socioeconomic classes, a relatively large percent of whose members are of lighter complexion.

A second set of countries in which discourses of blackness may be seen as critically informed by racial demography are the so-called core countries, in which formerly colonized black people live as minorities among former colonizers. These include the countries of Western Europe and North America. In the case of the United States, the majority of the black population has been living in the country for several generations; in the case of Western Europe, most of this population arrived after the Second World War from the former colonial "periphery."[2] For its part, Europe has had to come to terms with the arrival of black peoples from Africa and the Caribbean (as well as peoples from Asia) with the independence movements of the 1950s and 1960s. One dimension of how blackness is constructed in Afrocentric Rastafari overseas has been its status among the children of Jamaicans immigrating to Britain immediately after the Second World War as a means of expressing resentment of British racist and xenophobic exclusion (Cashmore 1983; Gilroy 1991).

While nonwhite peoples imagine themselves and are imagined by other non-white peoples in many uniform ways (including through their shared adoption of the West's political, educational, cultural, and other institutions), I would suggest that the global imagination of African diasporic peoples has been particularized by the vast drama of black slavery. I am not arguing here for or against the uniqueness of black suffering under slavery. Comparisons like those of blacks and Jews are interesting to me in the context of this discussion only in considering why each group has come to assume the prominent place they have in the global imagination. (In the case of African diasporic peoples, it is largely through Western corporate, mass-mediated, globally circulated tellings of the epic of slavery and its consumable legacies in the contemporary world, including the way it is told through such musical genres as reggae and hip-hop. In the case of Jews, it was through the horror of the Holocaust as a technologically modern phenomenon; through their status in international Christianity as protagonists of the Old Testament and, among anti-Semites, villains in the New Testament; and through stereotypes of their management of an international capitalism that is one definitive aspect of the modern experience.) Rather, I am acknowledging what I see as a powerful perception throughout much of the world of black people as being uniquely victimized. The staggering number of Africans abducted and sold across the Atlantic (11 million between 1500 and 1880); the millions who died in transit and on arrival in the Americas; the attempts to deny transplanted African people their heritage; the fact that the legacies of all these linger even now; and, crucially, black resistance (political, religious, and aesthetic) against all of these assaults— all have made a powerful impression around the world.

Given its multiple international rootings, blackness is flexibly, opportunistically constructed through a range of often contrasting terms. These include ideas of blackness and black people as apathetic slaves and as resistant maroons, as the vulgarity of the donnette and the nobility of Rastafarians, as rude-boy belligerence and dread spirituality, as impoverished vice and impoverished purity. Even as black and other peoples have moved to assert blackness in progressive terms, U.S. corporations today still circulate around the world images that clearly reference Western caricatures of blacks from the nineteenth and early twentieth centuries. Several print ads and television commercials produced for Latin American audiences as recently as the late 1990s illustrate this point. For instance, in 1997, Goodyear ran a television commercial in Peru likening the thickness of its tires to that of a black man's lips; in 1996, a Domino's Pizza ad in Guatemalan newspapers featured a family of blacks ("negros")—rendered in the familiar black-skinned white-lipped iconography—whose "cannibalistic" appetites could be satiated by offering them this company's product. There was a recent controversy over the 2005 issue of stamps in Mexico celebrating a popular comic-book character, a boy called Memín Pinguín. This character's bulbous, whitened lips and hapless demeanor recall similar caricatures of blacks originally produced in the United States. Many in Mexico dismissed American criticism of the stamps. They regarded Memín Pinguín affectionately, as a nostalgic reminder of the 1940s, the era when this character was created. The Mexican historian Enrique Krauze asserts that among Mexicans, the "wise-cracking," come-uppance-delivering character is "felt to represent not any sense of racial discrimination but rather the egalitarian possibility that all groups can live together in peace" (Krauze 2005). These interpretations do speak to the need to place any analysis of global blackness in national and local context, and the complex investments in such representations there. But however popular Memín Pinguín may be, whatever present-day resonance he may have among what Krauze refers to as Mexico's "poorer people," the character also illustrates the remarkable pervasiveness and range of so-called darky iconography around the world. Images like these reflect the common ways in which their global recreations and appeal depend on erasures of provenance, on the sustained voicelessness of "the poorer people" who are both readily represented and underrepresented.

Representations of Blackness in Asia

Africans and Asians both at home (in Africa and Asia) and throughout their respective diasporas have forged cultural, ideological, and other alliances with each other. These alliances, famously emblematized by the encounter between W. E. B. Du Bois and Chairman Mao in 1959, are often a result of their mutual recognition of their marginalization by the hegemonic West (Prashad 2001). However, the alliances can contain tension—for example, when Asian-Americans move to become full, respected producers, not just consumers, of hip-hop (Wang 2006); when African Americans and Korean Americans live together in Los Angeles (Park 1996); and throughout the Caribbean between people descended from East Indians and those descended from Africans (Lopez-Ropero 2006). Just as understanding a people too narrowly in terms of their resistance can flatten appreciation of the fullness of their sociocultural life, assumptions about a given, reified solidarity between two resisting peoples can obscure the more complex political relations between them.

Part of the difficulty in these relationships can be understood by looking at the way blackness in Asia, a main region of the third of the three sets of countries (the other two being former colonies and metropolitan centers), is defined not so much in interpersonal terms as according to the range of the globally mass-mediated representations described above. This third region is defined by its having few people of African descent within its borders, given a lack of such an indigenous population and given its location outside the primary circuits of the Atlantic and Arab slave trades. Many Japanese imagine Afro-Jamaicans to be like the Western, mass-mediated stereotypes of them as happy-go-lucky and dangerous, as fond only of sex and dancing. On the other end of the Afro-Asian equation, many Jamaicans bear the Orientalist view of Japanese as exotic women and martial artists. Blackness, like Orientalism (Said 1979), is a discourse of the non-Western other that has circulated and taken root beyond the West. Part of the challenge of Afro-Asian scholarship, therefore, might be to investigate how Asians and blacks negotiate their relationships with each other vis-à-vis these globally circulated, locally situated discourses.

Here, however, I want to focus on the case of mass-mediated blackness in the Asian imaginary. In some metropoles and former colonies, there may be some politically and economically empowered black people who are able to interrogate stereotypical representations of black people, but throughout Asia there are very few such people. Discourses of blackness in the first two regions are partly based in the need to situate flesh-and-blood black people safely within given political, economic, and ideological orders often dominated by whites or white-identifying people. In Asia, however, a region with few black people, blackness today is often more purely shadow, stripped of its human substance. Blackness there is simulation (Baudrillard 1994) in the purest sense, copies whose integrity disturbingly comes to surpass that of their original human referents. Among the characters of a South Korean children's show aired in Los Angeles in 1998 was an "African" mascot wearing a grass skirt, with thick white lips, and a bone through its hair. Chinese karate films in the 1970s featured black hoodlums whose jive talk presaged whooping by otherwise gentle leading men. The logo of Darkie Toothpaste, manufactured by Hazel and Hawley Chemical Company in Hong Kong (Colgate-Palmolive bought half the shares of the company in the mid-1980s) and marketed all across Asia for decades, featured the image of a blackfaced minstrel (McGill 1989). Advertisements that feature black people as Sambos, mammies, and savages are still easily found throughout Japan, despite efforts to remove these images following inter-national criticism. These widely disseminated images of blackness are not unrelated to how real black people are viewed throughout much of Asia. While the abandoned children of American GIs and Asian women are often ostracized in Japan, Korea, Vietnam, and other Asian societies, this ostra-cization can be more profound when the father is black (Gage 2006). African students have been the victims of racial attacks by Chinese students in China (Dikötter 1992; Sautman 1994).

At the same time, African diasporic culture, particularly music, has been popular in many of these countries. (Felt valorization and belittling of black-ness can both come from the perception of blackness's essential difference, in this third space profoundly severed from real black people.) For instance, Ferguson (2006) links the emergence of a roots reggae scene in Thailand in the 1970s to the entry of Western popular music in the preceding decade. Her analysis is ethnographically centered on such sites as reggae pubs in the country, where the staff is dressed in Rasta wear, including dreadlocks. She explores the music of Caraboa, a popular Thai musician who uses reggae music—including his cover of several Bob Marley songs on one album—to call attention to such political issues as the situation of the Shan, a minority people at war with the Burmese military. At first glance, therefore, what is for many the seemingly improbable figure of the Thai (or Japanese) dread may lead to assumptions that Rasta is pursued here only as consumerist play. However, the serious local political context in which this adoption can take place suggests otherwise. Rasta in Jamaica is a religion, a political movement, a way of life, and more, all rolled into one: to understand the movement's deepest significances in Jamaica, no one element is separable from the other. However, that separation necessarily takes place as the movement is transmitted especially to countries like Japan. In the final chapter, I consider whether the Japanese manifestation of the movement—given this separation—might be understood as Rastafari.

Historicizing Blackness in Japan

What is the social and historical context in which these globally circulated ideas, images, and ideologies of blackness have taken root in Japan? Given my contemporary focus on Jamaican popular culture, how have they mani-fested themselves specifically in performative terms? In the following sections, I address these issues as evidenced in premodern, early modern, and postwar Japan.

PREMODERN JAPAN

Black people first arrived in Japan in the mid-1500s as the slaves of Portuguese traders and visiting officials (Leupp 1995). Blacks manned Portugal's Asian empire as deep-sea sailors, men-at-arms, and bodyguards. Arnold Rubin reports: "As early as 1547, the Portuguese captain Jorge Alvarez wrote that the Japanese 'were very inquisitive and most desirous to find out all they could about Europe and its inhabitants, nor were they in the least bigoted or narrow minded.' The Japanese were intrigued by the black crewmembers: 'They would often come thirty or forty miles to see them, and entertain them honorably for three or four days at a time'" (Rubin 1974, 8).

Insider-outsider status is one potential framework for understanding how the Japanese may have viewed these Portuguese traders and black crewmembers. Elites in the Tokugawa period (1600–1868) saw their world largely in Confucian terms, divided between civilized Japanese selves and barbarian foreign others (Weiner 1995, 2004). In addition to this elite Confucian perspective, Weiner notes at the popular level there were folk mythological constructions of "the excluded or demonic other": "within pre-Restoration nativist discourses, these subordinate, outsider roles were ascribed mainly to foreigners (Europeans), the Ainu of Hokkaido, and the eta outcastes, whose exclusion was informed by occupational taboos and sanctioned by Tokugawa law" (1995, 437). As I discuss later, outcaste *eta* (otherwise known as burakumin) as well as Chinese-Japanese are among those Japanese minorities who have employed the flexible metaphor of blackness as encoded in reggae and Rasta as a way to articulate their identities as such.

Direct evidence of how these early preconceptions about the demonic outsider may have been mobilized in the interpersonal encounter with blacks is hard to come by. But given my concern with the performative political dimensions of black representation in Japan, a certain aspect of Japanese painters' (remote performative) renderings of foreigners is worth noting here. What the painters sought was not simply to reproduce the observed in a direct, one-to-one sense. Rather, the paintings capture the impression the foreigners made, mobilizing those codes at the artist's disposal to make sense of the phenotypic difference of the foreigner. The socially constructed fact of the difference of the European, in keeping with Weiner's speculations, was indeed encoded in part through features associated with demons (*oni*), such as long, red noses and a glaring aspect. Interestingly, blacks, rather than being painted as fundamentally different creatures from whites, have been represented using similar aesthetic conventions. Their difference from the Portuguese was communicated by differences in skin color and dress, not through such physical markers as the shape of lips and noses. To this extent, blacks and whites were similarly circumscribed as foreign others.

However, on the question of actual indigenous valuations of skin tone—as opposed to simple observation of differences in it—the anthropologist John Russell notes that "in Japan as in Europe the color black has traditionally carried negative symbolic connotations . . . Certainly neither Heian nor Nara Period aesthetics leave any doubt as to the value associated with white skin" (Russell 1991a, 5). Hiroshi Wagatsuma has also noted that "'white' skin has been considered an essential characteristic of feminine beauty in Japan since recorded time. An old Japanese proverb states that 'white skin makes up for seven defects'; a woman's light skin causes one to overlook the absence of other desired physical features" (Wagatsuma 1967). As a consequence of this privileging of white skin, Wagatsuma asserts, and given the profound cultural association of whiteness with purity in Japan, Japanese are aesthetically predisposed against dark-skinned peoples. However, while acknowledging the possible importance of indigenous valuations of "white" skin over dark for understanding how people of African descent are viewed in Japan, Russell distinguishes between blackness as an indigenous social construction—as reflected, for instance, in its association with outdoor labor—and blackness as a specifically racial idea arriving from the West.

MODERN JAPAN

Soon after U.S. naval forces arrived off the shore of Japan in 1853, with an aggressive demand that the long-secluded country open its doors to Western trade, came an intense effort to unify and therefore strengthen Japan as a nation. Ironically, modern nationhood in Japan subsequently developed in part as a colonial enterprise, both domestically and regionally. In defining the extreme boundaries of the Japanese nation, Ezochi—"Ainu land"—to the north was claimed as Hokkaidō, and the Ryūkyū islands to the south became Okinawa. Yet even as Japan demanded that these territories' inhabitants adopt mainland (i.e., national) ways, it also stigmatized them as primitives, doomed to live within their sociopolitical and intellectual limitations. These uncivilized others came to be seen as aspiring to a Japaneseness of which they were unworthy, and they gave mainland Japanese a means by which to measure their own march toward modernity. Meiji leaders represented the Emperor as the semidivine head of a consanguineous nation-state, the direct descendant of the common ancestor of all Japanese people. Many rituals assumed to be of ancient provenance, including a performatively realized imperial divinity, were introduced by Meiji bureaucrats during the modern era to foster this sense of nationhood (Gluck 1985).

It is during this Meiji period that Japan encountered the idea of race as a concept specifically of Western provenance.[3] How has racial blackness manifested itself throughout the course of early Japanese modernity? How might this be figured especially in performative terms? After concluding a treaty with the Japanese, Commodore Matthew Perry—who led the 1853 U.S. naval expedition—entertained Japanese officials with a minstrel show by white sailors in blackface (Yellin 1996). The Japanese would themselves have a tradition of blackfaced minstrelsy, an adoption very much in keeping with the ethos of the Meiji period. During this period, adoption of the arts, technologies, dress, manners, and political and educational institutions of the West became means of achieving equality with it. What was at stake in these adoptions was demonstrating that Japan was as civilized as any Western country and entitled to all the rights of that civilized status. (Among these rights was the basic security of a Japan, and later its empire, endangered by Western imperial ambitions. This demonstrates how discourse, including in its performative dimensions, is not necessarily expression with little bearing on the material conditions of national life, but is often deeply embedded in, and helps realize the relations of, material power.) Much as the state disciplined the bodies and minds of female high-school students as evidence of Japan's progress—or rather Westernization—in matters of gender (Czarnecki 2005), blackface in Japan might here be regarded as a negative performative means of asserting Japan's status as a civilized, therefore rightly powerful nation. Japanese and Euro-American blackface performances do not only serve the purposes of immediate entertainment, but also performatively index a black subordination that supports Japan's claim of equality with Europe and the United States (Russell 1998).

The popularity of jazz music is another way to consider the historical performativities of blackness in Japan. During the first half of the twentieth century, jazz became the art form through which musicians around the world—from India to China to Sweden to Russia—artistically expressed the headlong energy of the modern world materializing around them (Atkins 2003). It was the ultimate expression of the high-speed, urbane, popular-cultural modernity to which many of these societies aspired. Jazz was a prominent element of Japan's intensified exposure to Western popular culture. The historian E. Taylor Atkins, in his excellent book on jazz in Japan (2001), explores Japanese adoptions of the music as a universal art form that transcends the boundaries of race and nation. Arriving in the country soon after its birth in the early 1900s in the United States, jazz was both celebrated and reviled as Americana transposed onto a Japanese cultural landscape increasingly filled with movie theaters, cafes, and department stores (Silverberg 1991).

In Atkins's narrative, it appears that it is within the community of Japanese jazz musicians that jazz in Japan was most explicitly, most intensely worked through as African American music. Atkins discusses the assumptions many African Americans and Japanese had about each other as jazz musicians, including those of natural black giftedness and Japanese imitativeness. However, once these anxieties are worked through, jazz could come to be imagined beyond its immediate African American origins and more readily projected into the social mainstream. It could become exotic not just as African American, but also as American;[4] universally modernizing in contrast to the "primitive," ethnoracially particular African American; and distinctively Japanese as Japanese musicians reworked jazz in musicological and ideological terms to make it recognizably their own.

What I am speculating about is a subtext I hear in Atkins's narrative that seems familiar to my own. At risk of putting it too straightforwardly, Japanese musicians need to personally or collectively reckon with the blackness of black music in the subcultural backstage before presenting the music in, or as being appropriately of, the Japanese mainstream. Similarly, reggae is most particularly regarded and most intensely worked through as Afro-Jamaican music privately, in the personal and subcultural backstage. Much emotional labor is sometimes required by the Japanese who are most invested in dancehall, roots reggae, and Rastafari so they can find a certain place for themselves as Japanese in these profoundly Afrocentric subcultures. (The stories of Junko Kudo in chapter 3, and of Brother Taffy and Ras Tanki in chapter 4, illustrate this point.) Once this is accomplished, "J-Reggae" can be seen as a Japanese domestication of a music seen as universal —not so much in modern terms, as was the case with jazz, but rather in terms of a cultural globalization which today dominates contemporary Japanese discourses of the world beyond its shores. If rooting jazz comprehensibly in Japan required a gaze at progressive America and more broadly the West, in all the complexities and contradictions that the modern idea of progress has implied, rooting Jamaican culture comprehensibly in Japan required a gaze at the Jamaican as an exemplar of a more heterogeneous (including the third world) international (despite the particularities of the Jamaican case). The meanings of jazz as well as reggae and Rastafari in Japan turn in part on a historical mystification of blackness, a blackness which attracts practitioners but which must be managed in getting it to speak beyond the subaltern enigma of itself.

POSTWAR JAPAN

The growing Westernization of Japanese society that jazz represented enthralled some and outraged traditionalist others, the latter group gaining power as the nation moved toward war. After Japan's defeat in the Second World War, the United States occupied the country between 1945 and 1952 (maintaining administrative control over Okinawa until 1972). Part of the American influence during these years was in the realm of material culture. Japan became not only an outpost of American-style consumption, but also of American production, including of goods associated with America's racial others. The U.S. government, for instance, manufactured in Japan, for American consumption, dolls stereotyping black people's physical features (Goings 1994).

Japanese interpersonal contact with black people in Japan was then, and remains largely, restricted to African American military personnel. White GIs warned Japanese to stay clear of blacks, describing them as "little more than savage, carefree children in adult guise" (Thornton 1983, 32). The sexual relations between black men—often American GIs—and Japanese women have long been part of the contemporary Japanese imagination of blackness. Russell notes that "with the Vietnam War, the rise of the counterculture and the influx of black popular music and culture, disaffected Japanese youth came to see the African American as a counter to the values of the Japanese establishment, and the black Other was adopted as a symbol of defiance, forbidden fruit, and their own alienation from the Japanese mainstream" (Russell 1991a, 20–21). These uses of blackness as resistance to Euro-American power, domestic patriarchy, and sexual inhibition have more recently taken the form of sexually graphic fiction by such writers as Murakami Ryū (1976) and Yamada Eimi (1987), in nonfiction by authors like Takeda Mayumi (1999), and in late-night television reports on sexual relations between black males and Japanese females (Russell 1991a, 1998).

Early in the postwar period, Japan experienced a so-called introspection boom, during which Japanese social critics excoriated the Japanese character. These critics looked into the recent past in order to understand why Japanese modernity had gone so terribly wrong, in the hope of making the nation more democratic (Gordon 1993). Japan then went through a period of spectacular economic growth that led to the development of its mass media and its industrial, transportational, and other facilities. This postwar growth has been read in Japan under the discursive aegis of nihonjinron. Nihonjinron is characterized by a vast popular literature that asserts Japanese uniqueness and accomplishment in terms of climate, biology, and social psychology, especially in contrast with Europe and the United States. The goal of nihonjinron writers is not necessarily objective comparison of Japan with the West: "what must be understood is that these ideas are symbolic, not empirical" (Dale 1986, 43). Nihonjinron is a product of the national pride that occasioned Japan's phenomenal postwar development into the postindustrial, information-age society that it is today. By the 1970s, having found in economic success at least a partial answer to the depressed soul-searching of the immediate postwar period, Japan was again positioned to positively assert its sense of ethnonational identity in relation to the West.

Nihonjinron is not heard so much any more in Japanese public discourse. I would argue, however, that as a product of the ongoing historical moment from which it emerged—a period of great economic accomplishment, despite the recession; of new possibilities for collective and individual self-making through consumption—nihonjinron remains a definitive influence on the discursive construction of nation and ethnicity in postmodern Japan (Miyoshi and Harootunian 1989). The economic prosperity which nihonjinron emerged out of and reflected would facilitate a heightened consumption of the West and, later, third-world countries like Jamaica. It is interesting to compare the sometimes spectacular claims of some nihonjinron theorists in explaining the uniqueness of Japanese relative to Westerners with speculations by some Japanese practitioners of Rastafari that the Japanese are descended from one of the lost tribes of Israel (Goodman and Miyazawa 1995). In the former case, popular academia is mobilized to authenticate a collective imagination of the Japanese as a unique people, especially relative to the West. In the latter, as I discuss in chapter 4, some Japanese followers of Rastafari, as one means of authenticating their identifications with the movement, point to an enormous body of popular writing claiming that the Japanese are descended from the ancient Israelites (Jamaican Rastas make this claim for themselves). Suggestions such as these not only facilitate individual and collective Japanese identifications with Rasta relative to Jamaicans. Beyond the Rasta community, they also mobilize very nihonjinron-like beliefs about the Japanese generally as a unique people relative to Western people, vis-à-vis their claims to a Jewishness more authentic than that of Euro-American Jews.

If nihonjinron expresses a sense of Japanese uniqueness in relation to the West, the discourse of *kokusaika*, or "internationalization," that was most popular in the 1980s and 1990s was precisely an extension of nihonjinron claims of Japanese uniqueness now in relation to the world at large (still sometimes a covert, as well as an explicit, working through Japan's anxious relation with the West). In nihonjinron, anything that was imagined to exist in Japan, but not in the supposedly universal West, was easily assumed not to exist anywhere else in the world. Kokusaika extends this logic: anything that is imagined to exist in Japan, but not in the world at large (rather than just the West), affirms Japanese uniqueness. Kokusaika seen in these terms accords well with its provenance as a Japanese government buzzword through which Japan's greatness among other nations is to be asserted. As reflected in what is still a very restricted foreign presence in the country (Lie 2001; Linicome 1993), and in the general wariness about sustained interpersonal contact with the foreign (White 1988, 1993), kokusaika ironically reinforces Japan's status as a unique, ethnically uniform nation (Befu 1992). Indeed, as I discuss later, while Japan's participation in the dancehall scene can be read in terms of a freeing of local attachment to Japan, including in the form of life-changing travel to Jamaica, there is also a clear current of national, even racial pride that has occasioned the recent Japanese victories in international dancehall competitions. Similarly, a consistent theme emerges throughout my research in which experiences gained from travel to Jamaica are planted in the soil of the Japanese local as signs of Japanese accomplishment.

Performing Social Identity in Contemporary Japan

I focus in this book on the ways in which Afrocentric Rasta, reggae, and dancehall permit exploration of various aspects of social identity in Japan. The notion of a powerful Japanese group consciousness such as that assumed in nihonjinron has long been a major point of analysis of this Japanese social identity (Benedict 1946; Doi 1981; Lebra 1976; Smith 1983). Japanese and non-Japanese alike have imagined the Japanese as a group-oriented people who put their sense of collective belonging—national, local, professional, familial—above all other identities. In recent years, however, these claims have been qualified on psychological, anthropological, economic, gendered, and ethnic fronts. Mathews asserts that differential valuations of *ikigai*, or that which makes one's life worth living (1996, 718), among his interviewees demonstrates the need for more careful consideration of Japanese selfhood—seeing it not just as a generalizable social construct, but also as experienced in individually particular terms. Other scholars argue that the thesis of group-orientedness is primarily an effort to direct Japanese social energies principally toward profit, of which the ruling class of corporate heads, politicians, high-level civil administrators, and other power brokers enjoys a disproportionate share (Befu 1992; Dale 1986; Kawamura 1980; Sugimoto and Mouer 1980; van Wolferen 1990). Class difference in Japan intersects importantly with gender. Public discourse continues to confine Japanese women largely to the domestic sphere; female part-time workers, traditionally expected upon marriage to leave the workplace for the home, are often treated as second-class employees (Kondo 1990; Ogasawara 1998). The wives of Japan's male white-collar workers often express resentment that company demands on their husbands' time harm the men's relationships with their families (Allison 1994). Critics further argue against assumptions of a homogeneous Japanese group identity by noting the presence of the Ainu, Okinawans, burakumin, Chinese, Koreans, and other groups variously marginalized in mainstream social life. As I will demonstrate in the upcoming chapters, dancehall, roots reggae, and Rastafari are performative means by which to situationally dissociate oneself from or identify with a supposedly homogeneous Japaneseness constructed in these gendered, class-based, ethnic, and personal terms.

RACE, ETHNICITY, AND PERFORMATIVE THIRDNESS

The tendency to view as "superficial" Japanese engagement with foreign culture emerges from Japan's reputation as a society of voracious consumers (Sato 1991; Tobin 1992a). From jazz to salsa, from choro to hip-hop to Southeast Asian arts and culture—everything, it seems, is fair game. Partly because of this assumption of superficiality, the more complex dimensions of Japanese consumerism go unremarked. This includes Japanese love of the foreign, though not necessarily the foreigner, including domestic ethnic others who reproduce many Japanese cultural forms. A number of prominent Japanese entertainers and professional athletes, for instance, have been of Korean and Chinese descent but have been required to identify themselves as Japanese to establish and sustain their careers (Lie 2001). An interesting subtext in many sumo wrestling matches is a sort of ethnic transvestism, whereby a wrestler like Akebono, from Hawaii, becomes Japanese by taking a Japanese name and by mastering the set of practices, inside and outside the ring, associated with this perhaps most Japanese of sports.[5] (This is comparable to how the spectacle of *onnagata*— the female role played by male actors in kabuki—as well as *otokoyaku*—the male role played in the all-female Takarazuka Revue—valorizes Japanese womanhood and manhood. The years of training required to play another— or even, in the case of Takarazuka's *musume*, one's own—gender, with all its traditionalist proprieties, performatively valorizes the gender played.) Everyone knows he is not Japanese, but the spectacle of his ethnic difference performatively inhabiting Japaneseness naturalizes the authority of this Japaneseness. The gap, then, is a sign that celebrates the signified.

Seen straightforwardly, this is the way in which the gap—Akebono's difference in this culturally Japanese space—is a sign that works to valorize the signified of Japaneseness. Japaneseness as ethnonational and gender ideology is made powerful by its regulation and thus domination of this difference. Read less straightforwardly, however, the signified might be seen not only as the end of Japaneseness valorized. Seen in a different way, it might also be the end of the sign system that is conventionally regarded as the means through which this valorization takes place. That is, the gap is also a sign signifying itself. In this way, the gap foregrounds not so much Japaneseness, but the aesthetic code of *rikishi* (the sumo wrestler), onnagata, otokoyaku, and musume as values onto themselves. It is in this thirdness—not man or woman, not foreign or Japanese, but the performances/performativities thereof—that the potential for subversion (of ethnic Japaneseness, manhood, or womanhood) most powerfully discloses itself.

Another dimension of this gap, this thirdness as the sign system itself, emerges in a comparison of how it manifests itself in two different cases: among non-Japanese performing Japanese art forms (Akebono as rikishi), and among Japanese performing non-Japanese art forms (Japanese reggae artists). This comparison reveals the complexity with which thirdness finds its particular meanings. Akebono performs within the heavily regulated spaces of a Japanese cultural institution, one in which thirdness is more readily (though never necessarily) resolved in the master narrative of traditional Japaneseness. In contrast, the gap between Japanese and reggae artist, especially in the very earliest days of the reggae scene in Japan, resolves itself more explicitly in the nominally unregulated spaces of an emerging youth subculture. Japan's geographical distance from the authority of the Jamaican permits greater room for play. However, now that Japanese reggae has become more commercially successful, and thus more fully accountable to the prerogatives of the consuming ethnonation, Japanese reggae is in some ways becoming, to some degree always was, a conservative enterprise. This includes the way in which Japanese participation in Jamaican popular-cultural scenes has been co-opted to represent not so much the value of ethnic difference, but the nationalized signs of the Japanese powers of cultural assimilation and consumption. The uncomfortable gap between the authentic Afro-Jamaican and the Japanese imitation becomes a circle more comfortably inclusive of Japanese subcultural practice.

Thirdness here, then, represents a given manifestation of a range of possibilities which the Japanese may mobilize in staking a claim to Jamaican popular culture. Ethnoracially ambiguous approximation of Afro-Jamaican cultural practices can be as compelling for Japanese practitioners and consumers as pure, originary (Afro-Jamaican) blackness. Japanese reggae magazines and the dancehall editions of urban magazines routinely feature photo spreads of Afro-Asian models in Jamaica-identified fashion and accessories; in other cases, Japanese models are photographed with their skins darkened, in addition to having the other racial symbolic

The CD cover of a Japanese reggae collection. Artwork by Ryoono. © 2007 Ki/oon Records Inc.

accouterments (dreads and braids, rude-boy gear, diva fashion) associated with the subculture. Japanese fans I have spoken with have said there is just something about the veteran deejay Nahki that is unlike other Japanese dancehall artists. On at least one magazine cover, it is named specifically as an "alien" (in English) mystique. To my eye, in some photographs of him especially earlier in his career, Nahki's dark skin, his fade (a hair style that was popular among black men in the 1980s and 1990s), rounded forehead, and full lips are made to signify a hybridized iconicity that is somewhere between the African and the Asian. To name that someplace "black," or "trying to be black," or even "racial" misses the point: it is the ambiguity that tantalizes, that matters.

Racial thirdness raises the question of the status of blackness itself in contemporary Japanese society. Although not a primary site in which race, ethnicity, and nationality have been worked through in Japan, blackness remains an important one. It remains important in part given its relationship with whiteness, which *is* a primary site in which these issues have been worked through in the country.

The notion of a universal whiteness—whiteness as an intellectually, ideologically, and aesthetically hegemonic idea in the world today—can indeed powerfully invoke that of blackness. Given the vast tragedy of the colonial encounter, one mythology—whiteness as the way of the modern world—often engages the other—blackness as counterpoint to this way. The meanings underlying how blackness is used in Japan, then, are often to be found not on social surfaces, but beneath them. Blackness, rendered into an object for mainstream consumption, can of course achieve a popular, mass-media presence. But blackness is always imagined and feared as something that might become unmanageable, set loose in the modern world. It inhabits, in Morrison's (1992) metaphor, the space of shadows. Rastafari, and the roots reggae music subsequently associated with it, for instance, have today been made into acceptable international symbols of Jamaica and primary draws for the island's tourist industry. But not so long ago, these Afrocentric, anticolonialist, anticapitalist Rastafarians were institutionalized as mad people by the Jamaican colonial government and remain ostracized from much of Jamaican society even today. It is blackness mythologized in this way as menace that can make it such a felt means of expressing dissent from the West's ways of feeling and knowing, a West whose politically corrective forgetting, whose ability to easily imagine itself as an unambiguously civilizing presence, is viscerally disrupted on encountering Sambo, Mammy, and their global cousins in the most unexpected places.

The particular caricatures and stereotypes of blackness that appear in other parts of the world—for instance, in appearance, black face, white lips, grass skirt, and a bone binding the hair or run through the nose; and in behavior, simple-mindedness, cannibalism, and hypersexuality—fully evidence themselves in Japan. The anthropologist John Russell, in discussing the recurrence of the trope of the childish black in Japanese postwar fiction (Endo 1973; Itsuki 1966; Oe 1958), writes: "The popularity of child and animal tropes is not limited to literary narratives. The association of blacks with children as 'playmates' also finds expression in consumer goods, such as the 'Dakko-chan' *ningyō* . . . popular during the '60s and the recent line of Sambo products marketed here, products which often blur the boundary between human—or perhaps more accurately homunculoid—and animal. For example, black character dolls are sometimes placed next to stuffed apes and other stuffed animal toys in shops" (Russell 1991a, 8). Black characters in Japanese comic-book illustrations have often been "in the sambo mode; comical entities with bulging eyes, misshapen ears, and bulbous white lips, a depiction not noticeably different from American animated cartoons of [the 1930s]" (12).

Similar images make their appearance in Japan in relation to the popularity of reggae in the country. During a 2005 Rasta-themed "Go! Shiodome Jamboree," the premises of Nippon Television (the event's sponsor), in Shiodome, Tokyo, were bedecked in the Rasta colors of yellow, red, and green. Included in the event was a large illustration of three Rastas sprinting, one while eating a banana. In a second display, the logo of an organization associated with the event—the "&" sign with eyes at the top—was specially decorated for the jamboree. This included adding dreadlocks on the logo's head, striping it in Rasta colors, and placing a bunch of bananas in its hand. Another display featured oversized bananas, with an oversized boombox above them. The event's staff wore T-shirts with the same stripes as the logo had, and one person wore a tam with fake dreadlocks attached. Rasta at this event was reduced to reggae (the boombox), the tropical (bananas), a certain wildness (dreads running), and weirdness (the logo), rendered as cute and thus supposedly innocent. These images are not quite in the mode of the black-skinned, white-lipped characters commonly found in Japan until a storm of overseas protest in the early 1990s. Yet they clearly belong to this same symbolic economy of race that literally as well as figuratively belittles black people.

For Russell, liaisons with blackness can give the Japanese a metaphor through which to exorcise anxieties about their relationship with the West. He argues that blacks can be fellow victims of Western oppression, or disposable props in Japanese efforts toward parity with Euro-America. One example of the latter is the Japanese wearing of American-style blackface, for instance on television variety shows. Nina Cornyetz contends, however, that American "blackface" is qualitatively different from Japanese "black face," as the latter "masks the Japanese self with a realistic black visage." Russell has argued convincingly that the new popularity of black style in

Japan reproduces old stereotypes, yet I think that for some Japanese youth, reconfigurations of themselves in black images mark a processing of blackness qualitatively different from earlier representations and reveal a subject of racial and erotic desire" (Cornyetz 1996, 114).

Yet, to rephrase a point I made earlier, however one nuances the differences between American "blackface" and Japanese "black face," the two commonly turn on the dearth of black voice and gaze to interrogate these representations. The anthropologist Karen Kelsky has written about "yellow cabs," Japanese women so labeled in the Japanese media because Western men can supposedly hail them as easily as taxis, but who are ultimately to be seen as sexual agents in their own right. She argues that these women, by exercising their sexual initiative, "have unwittingly reversed the Orientalist trope of Madame Butterfly; now it is the Japanese woman who can travel to the West, buy the Western man, discard him, and then write about him" (Kelsky 1994, 476). But here, too, the black man finds that while his sexuality has been elevated from disdained to desirable (or desirable because disdained by the mainstream society), he remains essentially unable—despite his status as emissary of Western power, and as a man—to participate fully in this Western Orientalist discourse.[6] This in itself is unregrettable, but it points out that despite the so-called progress that Japanese women may have made, and despite the fact that particular black men might not object to being used in this way, black men generally remain marginalized within this global sexual economy.

Hip-hop has been one front line in this sexual, and material, fetishization of blackness in contemporary Japan (Condry 2006; Cornyetz 1996; Kelsky 1994; Wood 1997). Japanese women steeped in this culture often braid their hair to copy the image of the African American women they see in black fashion magazines and hip-hop videos, some tanning their skin in expensive parlors. Some frequent hip-hop clubs in areas like Tokyo's Roppongi to seek out black men as boyfriends, the ultimate accessories in their identifications with hip-hop. Japanese men and women can engage in hip-hop with various gender-political ends in mind: "Hip-hop style, which is marked in Japan with black skin, is interwoven with the phallus as a signifier . . . of masculine, heterosexual *body* power. Young men seek to incorporate this power by remodeling themselves in hip-hop style. For young women, hip-hop style includes the acquisition of male African-American lovers, bound to the same subtext of phallic empowerment, but transgressive of assumed (racial exclusive) Japanese male access to their sexual bodies and belittling of Japanese masculine identity" (Cornyetz 1996, 115).

Similar claims about blackness as a performative proxy through which to speak to issues of sexual and gendered political power in Japan may be made for dancehall in Japan. When the Jamaican dancehall deejay Elephant Man, during his tour in Japan in 2006, receives a mild cheer from his audience as he describes his admiration of the petite behinds of Japanese women, then receives a great cheer as he describes how he also admires the round behinds of black women, there a sense that the sexual energy of the dancehall is not generalized, but is importantly informed by racialized ideas about the bodies of Afro-Jamaican women compared with those of Japanese women. (Later I discuss how Japanese reggae dancers discuss their being stereotyped by Japanese men, including their boyfriends, for their participation in this erotic, Afro-Jamaican, female dance form.)

However, it is difficult to say that blackness as encoded in dancehall is significantly understood as a means of phallic empowerment, which in turn works to address issues of sexual and gendered power in Japan. Although in Japan's dancehall scene, male artists do make sexual references in their lyrics, the most extreme of such references do not tend to be anatomically very explicit. When such references take place, they tend to be humorous, even self-effacing. This is in contrast to the explicit (though, if the deejay is any good, also clever) way in which many Jamaican dancehall artists can glory in their own—as well as those of their conquests—sexual parts and performances, to say nothing of the former's perceptions of the latter's physical peculiarities and shortcomings.

Furthermore, a small, but I think significant, part of the menace and appeal of hip-hop in Japan in the terms Cornyetz describes is interpersonal: this perceived menace and appeal is made visceral by the small but actual (and made much of) presence of African-American servicemen in Japan. There is also an even smaller number of Jamaicans who travel to Japan, relationships with whom can be made to pose an interpersonal threat, as opposed to one existing only as public discourse, to gendered and racial values in Japan. While Japanese can and do travel to Jamaica to absorb reggae music, sometimes having sexual liaisons (as well as raising families) with Jamaicans, these liaisons are less radical because they take place outside Japan. In this way, they are less of a female Japanese complaint against male social power in Japan, or a male claim of masculine power and sexual worth to Japanese women. The use of blackness as a sexual political statement that men make to women and women make to men is even more diluted in the roots reggae music and Rastafarian scenes. While there is much room in Jamaican roots reggae for the erotic, where this erotic is expressed it is more often phrased in romantic terms. The monogamous maternalism that Rastafari conventionally expects of female followers also does not make it an ideal means of expressing sexual dissent. Here, then, is evidence of the flexibility of blackness as performatively realized through given, globally circulated subcultures: not only the phallic, but also the romantic, the humorous, the spiritual, and the traditional.

The anthropologist Ian Condry (2006) has also discussed the construction of race in Japan's hip-hop culture. He presents the idea of *genba* (actual sites)—hip-hop nightclubs, recording studios, and similar spaces—from which global hip-hop is realized in Japan. He argues that genba is a critical space which other agents of Japanese hip-hop cultural production—the media, record companies, fans, and artists—gravitate toward and draw energy from. This productive concept applies well to the reggae music scene in Japan. The insert for *Masters of Rab-a-Dub 1999*, a Japanese reggae CD of a live event at a club in Osaka, mobilizes the term *genba* to explain "rub-a-dub." In Jamaica as well as Japan, rub-a-dub refers to a show in which several DJs perform over tracks laid down by a sound system, in this case Red Spider. "Rab-a-Dub Time" is described in the insert as a live *hapuningu* (happening) in which reggae dance and music fanatics find their passions at their highest. The CD's reference to and status as a product of a live event at Sound Bar Yo on April 18, 1999, well illustrates Condry's point: how, in instances like this one, record companies draw on the heat of genba to facilitate new forms of dancehall cultural production and consumption—the CD.

Condry sees race as less immediately salient for an analysis of hip-hop culture in Japan, reworked as this concept is in Japanese context—and perhaps given his decision to not explore African-American–Japanese interpersonal engagement with hip-hop. Condry ethnographically centers his analysis of genba as the local siting of global hip-hop primarily in Japan, viewing it as a critical coordinate for hip-hop cultural production in the country. Condry and I therefore have a common interest in the performative constitution of our respective musical scenes, including the ways in which racial politics as configured in these largely Afrocentric musical scenes are retooled in Japan. However, one difference between our works is that while

Condry's concern with the relationship between power and location is largely that among the media, record corporations, fans, and artists in relation to genba, my concern about the relationship between power and location has been framed more in ethnoracial terms and as worked out across a transnational range of actual sites. This focus emerged from the ethnographic context I encountered in my research. For example, the national media and record companies played a comparatively small role in what was, when I began my research, a very underground scene. (I later discuss the increased corporatization and commoditization of dancehall culture in recent years.) Furthermore, the ethnoracial encounter between Afro-Jamaicans and Japanese, including in Jamaica—given the international success of Japanese dancehall artists—was more explicitly relevant.

The flexible metaphor of blackness is performatively inflected and mobilized in Japan, as it is elsewhere around the world, according to a broad range of influences. Among these are the racial demography and political history of the society in question; local constructions of social identity and difference; and the status of blackness as an oppositional figuration of supposedly universal Western power. Arriving primarily through the mass media in information-age Japan, where there are few foreigners, blackness —when viewed as ideology through the lens of Jamaican religion and musical subculture—is potentially a means of resisting but also playfully complying with Euro-American power; salve for the wounds of classist oppression masked in the myth of a homogeneous middle class; a resource in performative self-making through the ambiguities of cool thirdness; cuteness and the iconic grotesque; and a tool through which to express sexual agency and sexual worth. In the next few chapters, I provide ethnographic substance to these racial and other social terms under which Jamaican popular and religious culture is performatively reseeded in Japan. Picking up with the second vignette from the introduction, I begin with those surrounding the sound system culture.

2

Music and Orality

AUTHENTICITY IN JAPANESE SOUND SYSTEM CULTURE

The next tune trickles in, bassless and tinny. The MC, head bound with a black do-rag, repeats in a shriek the recorded DJ's cries. "Yo!" yells the DJ. "Heeeey! Waaay!" Suddenly the tinny sound surrenders to bass pounding from Club Citta's speakers. Now recognizing the tune and the gruff voice of Buju Banton, one of Jamaica's most popular DJs, the young men on stage and everyone in the audience shout and jump about, rhythmically thrusting their index fingers into the air.

I make my way through the crowd, right up to the stage. One of the young men onstage, noticing my recording equipment, approaches.

"A no sell you a go sell di tape?" he inquires, shouting above the noise. When I explain that I am not planning to sell tapes of the show, he rejoins his partners.

The patois used by the man I came to know as Sticko did not surprise me. In the course of my research, I had met many DJs, selectors, and MCs able to speak the Jamaican vernacular. Nor did the question Sticko asked. Several videocameras were on hand to record this event in late 1999, which was billed as a celebration of Japan's two biggest sound systems. Mighty Crown and Judgment Sound Station had over the last few months become increasingly popular, given their recent successes in international sound clashes (Mighty Crown won the World Clash in the United States, and Judgment won the Global Cup Sound Splash, in the United Kingdom, both in 1999). For Japanese youth seeking places for themselves in the black musical cultures they enjoy so much, the victories were enormous, as the large turnout at this event shows.

In this chapter, I argue that events such as these represent a means by which Japanese sound systems dramatically constitute Japan and, more locally, Yokohama as an authentic node within the transnational performative field (again, a network of socioculturally, economically, and politically defined spaces whose coherence as such is significantly constituted in performance) of international dancehall culture. Extensive knowledge of Jamaican musical culture as well as linguistic command of patois are critical components of the subculturally recognized symbolic capital (Bourdieu 1984) that Japanese sounds like Mighty Crown and Judgment must draw on in this effort. For Bourdieu, symbolic capital refers to forms of social value expressed by those in (or negotiating their way into) positions of power in ways that reflect, as well as work to reproduce, this social value. Depending on one's location within the performative field of the (Jamaican-Japanese) dancehall, this value is differentially constituted. In Jamaica, New York, and elsewhere, both Jamaican and Japanese dancehall artists' use of subcultural patois and deep knowledge of Jamaican music are forms of symbolic capital that work to sustain the integrity of the dancehall as a subcultural space and, perhaps more broadly, that of the Afro-Jamaican experience from which dancehall originates. At the same time, for Japanese in Japan, this use is the sign of a prestige deployed in the service of a pleasurable effort to socialize Japanese fans into Jamaican culture. In this way, it works to privilege Japaneseness in its aspect as the ability to "domesticate" the Jamaican (and the foreign in general; I deliberately use Tobin's [1992b] term to foreground the tensions, discussed later, that can arise especially when the foreign culture being domesticated is not that of the powerful West). In addition to this goal, Japanese sound systems performatively use patois, records, and other symbolic capital associated with dancehall culture to socialize the performers themselves into an intimate sense of subcultural belonging.

In making these arguments, I provide an overview of sound systems as one element of dancehall culture in Jamaica and Japan. I then discuss the performative constitution of an authentic Japanese sound system culture. In doing so, I will be concerned with the global routes that Japanese DJs and the members of sound systems take in becoming socialized into dancehall culture, including the acquisition of the subcultural symbolic capital of Jamaican music and language. I focus on one Japanese DJ and one sound system member to explore the evolution of their involvement in dancehall culture, which is representative in many ways of the experiences of other Japanese DJs and sound system engineers. My ethnographic focus is on the use of this capital at one sound system event, as an example of Japanese efforts to authenticate and sustain dancehall in Japan, and even to transcend the ethnoracial energies discreetly associated with Afro-Jamaican dancehall culture.

Sound System Culture in Jamaica

Since at least the mid-1980s, contemporary dancehall reggae has been Jamaica's most popular music. Sound systems, dancehall's sonic heart, began to emerge when, along with hundreds of thousands of other Jamaicans, the live-band musicians who had long been the staple of social gatherings across the island began migrating to Britain. Britain had been drawing people from its present and former colonies to provide low-waged labor for its reconstruction after the Second World War. To meet the resulting shortage of musicians in Jamaica, audio engineers still on the island began rigging record players to public-address systems, playing their record collections at various venues. The sound-system technology evolved beyond these basics to include amplifiers that could distinguish and emphasize treble, mid-range, and bass frequencies (the last critical to the dancehall sound of today). Another important element of today's dancehall sound is the emergence in the 1960s of a music industry in Jamaica that created ska, rocksteady, and reggae music records for play in local dancehalls (the early history of the sound systems had been dominated by jazz, soul, and rhythm and blues). Still another is the introduction in the late 1960s of two-track recording, in which the instrumentals are recorded separately from the vocals.

Related to this development, and arising at the same time, was King Tubby's creative use of "dub versions" (also simply known as "versions"), re-recordings of songs in which the vocals are removed and the instrumentals creatively reengineered. (Sometimes fragmented echoes of the vocals remain, becoming more fully part of—rather than something more readily heard as independent from—the sonic gestalt of the dub version).[1] King Tubby also brought the "toasting," speech-song style of DJs like U-Roy into the recording studio, a style that is an integral part of dancehall today. Given his endeavors, King Tubby is credited with the creation of dub music as well as, even more significantly, the invention of remixing. Remixing is the basis of subsequent forms of electronica. This includes hip-hop, which further bears Tubby's direct imprint—through a Jamaican immigrant to the United States, DJ Kool Herc, generally considered the founder of hip-hop—in its coupling of toasting with this creative reworking of previously recorded music (Chang 2005; Rose 1994).[2] In the mid-1980s, digital riddims increasingly came into use.

Shaped by these developments, the sound systems, which had faded from the scene in the late 1960s, made a return in the early 1980s. Dancehall during this revival has included rub-a-dub events, in which multiple live DJs toast over riddims supplied by the sound system. "Juggling," in which the sound consecutively plays "tunes" (songs) recorded by different DJs, but which share the same underlying riddims or similar lyrical themes, later appeared on the scene.

In addition to musical technique, vocal style, and increasing specialization of events, dancehall's evolution might also be considered in sociopolitical terms. In the context of the present discussion, dancehall constitutes a local (in the context of this discussion) performative field in which race, class, gender, political affinity, and other key forces in Jamaican society can be worked through. Carolyn Cooper (2004) mobilizes the metaphor of clashing to speak to the multiple lines of social tension running through and demarcated by Jamaican dancehall culture. These social tensions, which have played themselves out in the past and present of dancehall, were especially significant during the 1960s. Many members of the vastly predominant black lower class rejected celebrations of Jamaica's purported racial and ethnic unity, believing such celebrations failed to come to terms with the nation's real problems—many of them legacies of the colonial era. The island was riven by rioting as well as violence between Jamaica's two political parties, the Jamaica Labour Party (JLP) and the People's National Party (PNP). The political violence became especially intense in the months leading up to the 1980 elections, which saw the end of Michael Manley's left-leaning PNP and the rise of Edward Seaga's pro-American JLP. The anthropologist Norman Stolzoff (2000) suggests that this political change facilitated an increase of American-style consumerism in Jamaican society which helped displace the Rastas' spiritualist message of the 1970s. This consumerism, and a commentary on the violence between the two major political parties, powerfully informs the lyrics of much of contemporary dancehall music.

Sound System Culture in Japan

Although dancehall has been the most popular music in Jamaica since the 1980s, dancehall culture in Japan has until recently remained largely undiscovered by most mainstream Japanese audiences. But a smaller number of Japanese more in tune with the changes in reggae music have been pursuing dancehall for many years. The members of Mighty Crown had been attending dancehall events in Yokohama since the early 1990s. They had been drawing large crowds wherever they performed in Japan even before 1999, the year they first won the World Clash title. Since word of this victory reached Japan, dancehall in the country, including sound system culture, has been on a steady rise. The first edition of the dancehall free paper *Strive*, published in 2001, confirms the existence of at least 150 sound systems in Japan; its publisher told me she was confident that the number is significantly higher. (Masta Simon of Mighty Crown, which has a close affiliation with *Strive*, recently suggested that there are now about 300 sound systems, a credible number since the 150 figure was suggested before the dancehall boom.) Jamaica's population is only a fraction of Japan's (2.5 million compared to 127 million), but the very safe figure of 150 sound systems remains impressive, since in all of dancehall-saturated Jamaica there are only about 300 sounds.

Two sound system cultures are present in Japan: one, currently the more popular, is oriented around dancehall music, and the other around dub. (I will focus on the dancehall element of sound system culture in this chapter, briefly touching on the dub aspect later.) In addition to Mighty Crown, the most popular dancehall sound systems are Mighty Jam Rock, Jam Tek, Sunset, Infinity 16, Blast Star, Red Spider, and King Ryūkyū. Dub music has recently had little current presence in dancehall-dominated Jamaica but has been a stronger cultural force in Britain. Dub-based sound systems share the digital musical manipulation and MC orality of dancehall even as they tend to retain more of roots reggae's Rasta-influenced message of spiritual uplift. This message is evoked in the distinct sound of dub's ethereal remixing of previously recorded as well as original roots reggae tunes.

Among the major Japanese dub sound systems are Mighty Massa, Direct Impact, Shandi I, and Jah Works.

IMMERSION IN THE SOURCE: NEW YORK AND JAMAICA

Dancehall sound system members, DJs, and fans became interested in dancehall in a number of ways. Few older roots fans—say, those in their late twenties and older during the initial period of my research, between 1998 and 2000—have gone on to express interest in the emerging dancehall culture. However, many younger fans grew interested in dancehall after being introduced to roots reggae around the mid- to late 1990s. Other young Japanese became interested in dancehall culture when their high-school or college friends, eager to impress them with something they had never heard before, loaned them dancehall CDs or took them to local dance-hall events. Despite, or perhaps because of, the fact that most young Japanese flock to the familiar J-pop, a few search for novel underground music. Dancehall fits the bill.

Those who go on to become deeply involved in dancehall culture—including, of course, performers—often travel to dancehall's two main international centers, New York and Jamaica. (England represents an important third center, especially for dub sounds.) A clear pattern emerged throughout my research in which sound system members and DJs reported traveling to these two sites specifically to develop their skills. From Japan they go to New York to establish contact with Jamaican and Jamaican American DJs and sound systems at dancehall events held in such largely Jamaican communities as Crown Heights and Bedford-Stuyvesant. Many stay in New York for months or years, not only to become acclimatized to New York's dancehall scene but also to experience life in general in this city that figures greatly in the popular Japanese imagination of the West. Many earn a living at part-time jobs unrelated to dancehall culture.

From New York, these musicians then make something of a pilgrimage to Jamaica (many, of course, travel directly there from Japan). Depending on their resources, some might stay in Jamaica for only a few days, while others remain for several months, even a year or two. A key form of symbolic capital obtainable in Jamaica is knowledge and possession of many Jamaican dancehall records. Given the huge Japanese interest in roots reggae a few years ago, as well as the more recent interest in dancehall, there is little delay between the release of new tunes in Jamaica and in Japan. Jamaican vendors in New York also sell mix tapes or more recently

CDs of new dancehall tunes and events; Japanese artists who happen to be in the city return to Japan with this edge. Japanese entrepreneurs live in Jamaica and ship thousands of dancehall records to Japan each month, feeding the appetites of Japanese consumers who want to hear the most recent Jamaican dancehall tunes as soon as they are produced.

But for the most competitive sound systems, nothing short of immersion is enough. Their members regularly travel to Jamaica or New York to stay on top of the most popular songs at Jamaican dances as well as over the airwaves. In addition to awareness of what is going on in Jamaica musically, the ability to speak patois is a second key form of subcultural prestige. Less skilled Japanese MCs and DJs can speak only in Japanese, with a few terms drawn from Jamaican dancehall records and DVDs. The more skilled ones learn Jamaican Creole, particularly the vocabulary of dancehall culture. While in Jamaica, Japanese sound system members often make business contacts with major Jamaican DJs. A primary purpose for this contact is to obtain "dub plates." Dub plates are similar to dub music in that both are versions of songs. (Again, dub music as a genre emphasizes the record producer as artist, who creatively remixes the instrumentation of previously recorded, but sometimes original, songs.) Dub plates are recordings in which the vocal track is stripped from the riddim—the musical element of a tune— and a new vocal track with similar lyrics is overlaid. A Japanese sound system will pay a Jamaican DJ to make a dub plate of one of his popular songs. In the new lyrics, the DJ sings the customized praises of the paying sound system, and marvels at the foolhardiness of those rival systems that attempt to compete. In dancehall everywhere, dub plates, especially at sound clashes—competitions between sound systems—are the lingua franca or ammunition of the sound system's subcultural power. Although both the DJs and the sound systems try to keep payment figures secret, a DJ usually makes between a few hundred U.S. dollars to well over a thousand or a couple thousand for a dub plate, depending on his or her fame and relationship with the Japanese sound system. The members of some sound systems have reported to me that they paid reduced prices to DJs with whom they have had long-term relationships; other systems report receiving dub plates at no charge, in exceptional cases.

The Japanese musicians return home from Jamaica, sometimes by way of New York. They then put into play in Japanese dancehall clubs across the country the skills and capital they acquired in Jamaica, New York, London, and other expatriate Jamaican communities. Once this primary transnational socialization has been completed, the musicians travel occasionally to Jamaican communities to keep on top of subcultural developments there.

SINGERS AND DJS

While Japanese sounds have recently been enjoying some international success, to date there has been little effort to move Japanese DJing outside Japan. Nahki, perhaps the most popular DJ in Japan from the late 1980s to the mid-1990s, has been something of an exception to this rule. He speaks patois and English fluently, and to my knowledge, he is the only Japanese DJ to have performed in Jamaica's Reggae Sunsplash. I have already mentioned the 2006 performance he, Megaryu, and Pang gave in New York; the veteran DJ duo Ackee and Saltfish has performed internationally, including in Jamaica. Sister Kaya has performed at an annual reggae concert in San Diego. Besides these and a few others, there are few established Japanese DJs and singers on the international reggae scene.

Nevertheless, the surge in popularity of dancehall singing and deejaying in Japan has been one of the most noticeable trends in Japanese dancehall over the last few years. DJs like Miki Dōzan, Papa Bon, Papa U-Gee, Chozen Lee, Ng Head, Cone Head, Yoyo-C, Fireball, Junior Dee, Jun 4 Shot, Lady Q, Machao, H-Man, Rankin Taxi, Hibikilla, Chehon, Ryo the Skywalker, and Rude Boy Face; duos and groups like Mighty Jam Rock, Megaryu, Ackee and Saltfish; and singers like Pushim, Kaana, Moomin, Minmi, Munehiro, and Pang are among the well-known performers who at various stages of their careers have achieved some measure of fame in Japanese dancehall culture. Most of these individuals were part of the underground dancehall scene before it boomed.

Stolzoff (2000) provides a useful categorization of the various performance styles, rarely discrete, in which Jamaican DJs and singers perform. These include, among DJs, such categories as the cultural Rasta, rude-boy Rasta, gangster/gunman, reality, slackness/loverman, comedian/gimmick, and all-rounder. Among singers there are culture singers, lovers rock singers, dancehall style singers, classic singers, combination acts, and sing-jays. While I will not elaborate on the specific meanings Stolzoff attributes to all these categories, Japanese dancehall artists may be similarly grouped, since most artists to some degree define their musical identities—including through their choice of professional names—in relation to Jamaican artists they admire.

The extent to which the performers may not be so categorized, however, is also significant. Japanese sound systems do play at their events a steady diet of Jamaican reality, cultural Rasta, and gangster/gunman tunes. However, few Japanese DJs perform in any of these styles, which do not very well reflect Japanese sociocultural, economic, or political circumstances. Jamaican reality DJs tend to express concern about crime, hunger, and political corruption in Jamaican society (a testament to dancehall's local sensibility); the cultural Rasta voices a revolutionary Afrocentric rhetoric that does not obviously accord with the Japanese situation; and the violent machismo that the gangster/gunman romanticizes seems at odds with life in a comparatively safe Japan. Just as Jamaican DJs must sometimes excise Jamaica-specific lyrics when recording dub plates for Japanese sounds, Japanese DJs have avoided performance styles that do not much reflect the presumed sensibilities of their Japanese audiences. This, of course, is less the case when Japanese DJs travel to Jamaica, New York, and London, and feel the need to adjust their performance style to fit what is expected by Jamaican audiences there. Papa Bon, who discusses below his travels to and performances in Jamaica and New York, illustrates this point. I suspect that one of the reasons why Mighty Crown's victory in 1999 was so surprising to many Jamaicans was because it required deep commitment to learning reggae ("tune") in archival depth; to developing a sense of which tune to play based on audience mood; and to learning and wielding dancehall's subculturally particular patois in the bawdy, adversarial manner ("argument") needed to defeat their rivals. When a Japanese MC does not just get by in patois, but also uses it to ritually question the heterosexual competency of his Jamaican rivals, or to flirtatiously offer "Japanese baby" to his Jamaican female audience members, it is somewhat at odds with assumptions about Japanese civility, as well as with the relative civility actually found in dancehall in Japan.

A category of deejaying worth commenting on here is the slackness/loverman mode. In Jamaica, the loverman is the DJ who proclaims his ability to attract women, his prowess in bed. When such sentiments enter into the realm of the explicitly erotic, they become "slack." In Jamaican society, "slackness" generally refers to moral misconduct of many kinds: a politician's failure to provide for his constituents, for instance, or utility companies' shutting off water and electricity frequently and without notice. Especially as used within, as well as by social observers commenting on dancehall culture, "slackness" can also be an emphatically pleasurable openness about matters of sex (while remaining within the limits of Jamaican heterosexual norms). This is an openness both on the part of the DJ, who is specific about what he likes in a woman, and on the part of the woman in the audience whose intentions to attract male attention are similarly clear (such as through erotic dress or, in the case of the small number of female DJs like Lady Saw and Makka Diamond, their own slack lyrics). Slackness within the dancehall, as a certain forthrightness about matters of sex, rather than cause for condemnation or shame, is celebrated: in the skill of the artist able to speak about such matters in an artful way, in reveling in the pleasures of courtship and sex. (Of course, some outside dancehall may have difficulty seeing the artistry involved when DJs—who are not all equally talented— describe women and sexual acts in blunt anatomical detail.)

Among Japanese DJs, slackness tends toward *sukebe* (the mischievously lewd), and is less frequently in the realm of *gehin* (the vulgar), thus readily meshing with traditions of popular humor in Japan. In this way, slackness in Japan is not so seriously about phallic empowerment in the genuinely self-impressed way that it is among slackness/loverman Jamaican DJs. The host of one Shibuya dancehall event I attended was an older man, perhaps in his mid-forties, who appeared onstage in a series of outlandish outfits. One of these was an ostrich outfit, in which the black, feathery body of the ostrich began at the man's crotch, with the bird's neck angled upward so that its head reached the level of the man's chest. While many Jamaican women outside dancehall feel insulted by the vulgar machismo in much slackness/loverman music, young Japanese women at events like the one in Shibuya might only giggle at this silly man.

The Japanese DJ's slackness, in fact, is sometimes linked to another category of DJing, the comedian/gimmick. Veteran DJs H-Man and Rankin' Taxi are among those who often perform in this mode. An example of this light-hearted reggae is H-Man's "Aketemo Kuretemo (Day in, day out)." In the song, H-Man describes his addiction to reggae music, one that afflicts him waking or sleeping. He is giddily tormented by lyrical possibility, of the creative potential that inheres in "connected words, connected sounds":

> *Aketemo aketemo kuretemo kuretemo*
> *Asa kara ban made regee tsuke*
> *Anata ni au no mo Watashi ga aru no mo*
> *Ima kono shunkan sono okage*
> *Aketemo aketemo kuretemo kuretemo*

Hiru de mo yoru de mo regee DJ
Aketemo aketemo aketemo aketemo
Tsugi naru tobira o mata akete

Day in, day in, day out, day out,
From morning until night: addicted to reggae.
In meeting up with you and just being around too,
Right at this moment, that's what it's about.
Day in, day in, day out, day out,
Doesn't matter if it's day, doesn't matter if it's night:
   I'm a reggae DJ.
Day in, day in, day in, day in:
Open up again [the possibilities of] what comes next.

Of all the performative modes that have made their way from Jamaica to Japan, perhaps the one that has arrived most intact is the lover's rock singer. These men sing in candy-voiced falsetto, with little explicit sexual content, about their undying romantic love for individual women. Probably the most popular lover's rock singer is Moomin. In addition to his talents as a vocal artist, the international power of love songs, and the fact that he is heavily promoted in *Riddim* (owned by Overheat Communications, of which Overheat Records, Moomin's label, is also a subsidiary), Moomin's success might be attributed to the appeal to the Japanese of his soft singing style, as well as to his music's similarity to that of such Jamaican artists as Jimmy Cliff.

NATIONALISM AND AUTHENTICITY IN JAPANESE REGGAE

While Japanese reggae artists adopt a broad range of themes and performance styles, a number of Japanese reggae songs bearing a strong theme of national pride have emerged, especially since 2000.[3] This theme affords perspective on the constitution of an authentic Japanese reggae, and the political stakes involved in this effort.

One of the ways in which Japanese reggae artists celebrate Japanese cultural distinctiveness—as seen in foodways, local cultural differences, national treasures, and even, for one mischievous DJ, instant ramen and the so-called shower toilet—is by linking it with the natural world. In the music video for Munehiro's "Japaniizu" (Japanese), the female singer announces that the song is dedicated, "to all Japanese Muffins / Yeah, Yeah! / Nippon! Nippon!" Munehiro is dressed in kimono with a parasol, spotlit in red against a black background. Yellow and green spotlights appear, which, combined with the red, complete the Rasta colors. The word "Japanese" appears in katakana[4] script, similarly spotlit in red, yellow, and green. This use of color literally highlights the Japanese through the Jamaican. Its riddim decidedly upbeat, the song is pitched in cultural naturalist qua nationalist terms:

> *Shiki ga irodoru yutaka na color*
> *Daichi ga umidasu minori no aka*
> *Mada mada utsukushii shimaguni kara*
> *Wakai ibuki ga hanatsu pawaa wa mugendai . . .*
> *Taishi idaki habatakō sekai e*
> *China Korea Asia*
> *Te o torimukaō heiwa e*
> *Jidai ga nagaretemo*
> *Uketsugō roots and culture*
> *Saa, mazu wa kono basho kara*
> *Nippon! Nippon!*

> Rich colors of the four seasons,
> Red of the harvest that the earth bears.
> From an island country, still beautiful
> The unleashed power of the breath of youth is infinite . . .
> With ambition, let's fly into the world—
> China, Korea, Asia,
> Let's join hands, facing peace.
> Even as time goes by
> Toward roots and culture,
> Yes, it starts from this place—
> Japan! Japan!

Especially during the roots boom, but even now, reggae music is closely associated with celebrations of the natural (for instance, reggae is most popularly regarded as "summertime music"). This song couples the beauty of the Japanese natural with that of the Japanese national, celebrating "an island country, still beautiful," resplendent in all its colors. Such an appreciation becomes a base from which Japanese can engage the international— in this song, China, Korea, and the rest of Asia. These celebrations of the Japanese natural are nearly de rigueur in patriotic Japanese reggae. Miki

Dōzan's "Japan Ichiban" (Japan, Number One), for instance, describes the natural beauty of Japan in "the springtime bloom of cherry blossoms / nights of full moons in the autumn skies / beautiful scenery that makes the heart dance."

Munehiro's song calls for an "original nation" to renew itself—ironically, through a return to its traditions. This is expressed in gendered terms in her video, most explicitly evidenced by her wearing kimono (which young Japanese women generally do not do very often now, except on special occasions). In "Nishi Muku Samurai" (Samurai facing west), Ryo the Sky-walker employs the same gendered logic, this time inflected through a masculinist reference to samurai. Making explicit how gazing westward often invokes self-orientalization, he specifically references the topknot (*chonmage*) and the sword (*kata*) as instruments of a revalorized Japanese masculinity moving confidently into the West. (This self-orientalizing anticipates my later discussion of how nihonjinron and jibun sagashi, in their aspects as internationalist returns to essentialized national selves, are compatible with each other, despite the time that separates their appearances.) Dōzan's "Japan Ichiban" is among the many other songs bearing this samurai theme. He laments how Western society became enamored of the sword and the topknot just as they were discarded by Japanese. In "Appare Japan" (Honorable Japan), Hibikilla's invocation of the samurai is less ambiguous, referring to Japan as a civilization of "the samurai fighter," and to the sword as "Japan's pride." However, in what may be a reference to the United States, and to Japanese society's imagination of itself as an emissary of postwar world peace, he says: "But there is pride also in throwing away the sword / Those good people over there, they still can't lay it aside?" If "those good people over there" are indeed Euro-Americans, this reference places the song on the list of patriotic Japanese reggae in which the West figures prominently. In "Appare Japan," the distinctiveness of Japan emerges out of numerous influences, including China and the United States.

> *Chūgoku kara kanji mananda*
> *Kagaku to igaku wa oranda*
> *Our emperor from kudara*
> *Shogaikoku e wasurenu kansha*
> *Sono jūnansa ga hanpa nai*
>
> We learned kanji from China,
> Science and medicine was Holland,

Our emperor from [the ancient Korean kingdom of] Kudara.
Don't forget to thank the various foreign countries—
That flexibility is excellent.

Significantly, given the discrimination against Koreans in Japan, this song celebrates the controversial possibility of the Korean provenance of the imperial line (Watts 2001). Japan is the beneficiary of a writing system from China and of sciences from the West. However, in most of these songs the West is cast in more negative terms. Dōzan's "Japan Ichiban" song comments on what is for him the weirdness of looking at Japanese commercials and fashion magazines and seeing only foreigners, of Japanese aspiring to be like the actors they see in Hollywood films. Like Ryo the Skywalker, who commands his "Japan crew," in patois to, "se [say] yu proud to be yellow," Dōzan calls for Japanese to recognize the absolute beauty of the color of their skin.

The song continues:

> Machigai nakatta Meiji Ishin
> Mazukatta no wa ato no hōshin
> Yugande nakushita aikokushin
> Conpurekkusu o toriharaō
> Nihon wa subarashii kuni mo hito mo

> The Meiji Restoration was not a mistake.
> What was bad was the path taken after that:
> Distorted, spoilt patriotism.
> Let's destroy our complex.
> Japan is a wonderful country, its people too.

The Meiji Restoration, which brought Japan out of a long period of seclusion from the outside world, was a first step toward Japan's becoming an international power. This in itself, and the imperial institution that was "restored" to power in 1868 as a symbol of national unity, are causes for patriotic celebration. However, Dōzan adopts a familiar postwar national rhetoric in which the noble patriotism of the Japanese people is exploited by its warmongering leaders. Assuming continuity between the third and fourth lines, this path of military colonialism is discreetly Western: Japan's inferiority complex toward the West led to Japanese leaders' competing with this West, in Western ways, with ruinous effect.

Even more explicitly critical of the West, and of America particularly, is Nanjaman's poetic, musically subdued yet politically unambiguous "Born

Japanese." He sings of Japan as a land of ancient samurai, of a people who fight with all their heart, of a people with *yamato damashii* (Japanese spirit). Japanese fly into the world, Nanjaman quietly intones, in search of something important. They look outward because they sense something amiss at home, as shown in the many people who work hard (a good thing in itself), but only out of an excessive concern for money; in the *usokusai* (reeking of lies) faces of politicians on campaign posters. In the spirit of jibun sagashi in its aspect as flight from the petty economics of life in recessionary Japan, Nanjaman—in a gesture similar to those of Ryo the Skywalker in "Nishi Muku Samurai," and Munehiro in "Japanese"—encourages his listener to look across the ocean, to escape in a single bound this flawed Japan. But the international, and the West particularly, are fraught with moral danger:

> *Amerika*
> *Minna akogareru jiyū no kuni*
> *Amerika*
> *Dakedo Indian o koroshite ubatta Amerika*
> *Kokujin o dorei ni shite ita Amerika*
> *Nihon ni genbaku otoshita Amerika*
> *Otoko to otoko ga kekkon suru Amerika*
> *Iraku ni misairu otosu Amerika*
> *Seigi no mikata no tsumori no Amerika*

> America,
> The free country everyone yearns for,
> America.
> And yet, it is the America that killed and robbed Indians,
> The America that enslaved black people,
> The America that dropped the atomic bomb on Japan,
> The America where men marry men,
> The America that drops missiles on Iraq,
> The America that is supposed to be the friend of justice.

America's offenses around the world are not only of the past; indeed, unable to lay aside the sword, its oppression registers in more recent times in such conflicts as the second war in Iraq.[5] These offenses do not only evidence themselves around the world, but also at home, including in heteronormative terms, given the designation of America as a (clearly sinful) place where men marry men.

In these songs, then, Japanese reggae artists sing and deejay against a Western, and specifically American, hegemony that, despite its destructive nature, makes the Japanese yearn blindly for America. Even with the recent Korean wave (*hanryū*)—the surge of popularity of Korean culture in Japan and elsewhere in Asia (see Hanaki et al. 2007)—it is still remarkable to hear a Japanese artist acknowledge with pride the strong possibility that the emperor's ancestors came from ancient Korea, as well as to hear China acknowledged as a significant source of present-day Japanese culture. The proud invocation of "yellow skin" in Miki Dōzan's and Ryo the Skywalker's songs provides a rare, explicit commentary on race in Japan (here vis-à-vis the international). Nanjaman evocatively articulates postcolonial affinities between American Indians, blacks, Iraqis, and Japanese.

However, despite these insights, this nationalistic line of Japanese reggae is problematic. It embraces Asia with little acknowledgment of Japanese militarism and colonialism throughout the region. Dōzan's song refers to past Japanese misconduct, but not very specifically, and only to quickly absolve the Japanese public of responsibility for the war. Without directly acknowledging the past, the celebrations of yamato damashii, the desire for an ambitious Japan to embrace its Asian brothers on Japanese cultural terms (as is heard particularly in Munehiro's song) sounds eerily similar to the rhetoric of the Greater East Asia Co-Prosperity Sphere, a colonial initiative to unite Asia under Japanese leadership. These songs support Koichi Iwabuchi's (2002) argument that recessionary Japan's popular-cultural embrace during the 1990s of an essentialized, backward Asia—orientalized in this way much as Japan positively orientalizes itself as the naturally resplendent land of the samurai—restores prewar rhetoric of a privileged Japanese nation as being in a unique position of leadership over its Asian neighbors.

I am not saying that Munehiro or any of the other artists are making secret calls for Japan to recolonize East Asia. Their celebrations of Japan are to be more immediately understood as an effort to constitute Japan as an intimate point of departure and therefore a safe place for return from the alluring, but at the same time forbiddingly alien, global (a theme that recurs throughout this book). My point is only that given a lack of specific discussion, however uncomfortable, of how the Japanese colonial legacy is still intensely of issue throughout Asia, calls for Asian unity centered proudly on Japan run the risk of appearing self-serving. Such calls seem too easily to represent the Asian political sphere as a unity most readily achieved with

Japan at its center, rather than what might be seen as an opposite reality, in which the Japanese center in recent history has actually been a source of regional discontent. This discontent has been voiced in debates surrounding the Japanese military's forcing so-called comfort women from Korean and other countries to be prostitutes for Japanese servicemen during the Second World War (Choi 1997; Min 2003; Stetz and Oh 2001; Yang 2008; Yoshiaki 2000); the visits of Japanese prime ministers to Tokyo's Yasukuni Shrine, where several war criminals are interred (Antoni 1988; Nelson 2003); and revisionist representations of Japanese colonial military aggression in Japanese schoolbooks (Barnard 2001).

In the end, this patriotic line of Japanese reggae emerges from feelings of national pride in the fifth period of Japanese reggae, following Japanese success in international competition. These feelings find a ready audience in many Japanese inside and outside the subculture. Living in a recessionary Japan, they are ready for a music that speaks to the possibilities of accomplishment overseas, accomplishments that must be marked as specifically Japanese (hence the traditionalist references to geisha and samurai).

This leads to another absence in most of these songs that is of concern in this book: that of Jamaica. Nanjaman does describe in "Born Japanese," for instance, how black Jamaicans were brought to the island after white people had killed off most the indigenous population. But in general, the Jamaican provenance of the reggae music through which these expressions of Japanese national pride take place is effaced. When Miki Dōzan sings that it doesn't do to defer too much to foreign countries, one wonders if he means to include not just America (in political terms) but also Jamaica (in musical subcultural terms).

The absence of the Jamaican in these songs, however, should not be a reason to miss the way this Japanese national sentiment remains significantly articulated vis-à-vis the "authentic" Jamaican. The (Japanese) nationalistic sentiment is appropriate to an authentic (Japanese) reggae, since it is common to hear Jamaican reggae musicians express a sense of pride in their own island country in nationalist terms. For instance, Munehiro mobilizes the expression "roots and culture"—a Rasta term that celebrates Afro-Jamaicans' material and spiritual situatedness in the soil, a sense of deep cultural history—with very similar effect in the Japanese context. Ryo the Skywalker admonishes Japanese men without symbolic topknots in a way that recalls the ridicule by Jamaican dreadlocked Rastas of non-Rasta Jamaican men as Westernized "baldheads." Nanjaman's homophobic sentiment is discreetly authorized by similar expressions in Jamaican dancehall; his annoyance at the dishonesty of Japanese politicians authenticates Japanese dancehall, given that Jamaicans make the same complaint about their politicians. The call for Asian unity and peace and love may be regarded as authentically (Japanese) reggae since it so directly corresponds to Jamaican reggae calls for pan-African unity and peace and love. The claims of the value of yellow skin are appropriately expressed through a music whose progenitors, also oppressed by the West, assert the value of their black skin.

In these ways, then, like the renderings of Japanese people as phenotypically white in Japanese manga, the Jamaican origin of Japanese reggae is rendered as a code that operates below the level of—and richly hybridizes—identification as Japanese. Despite Japanese reggae artists' lyrical and other performative moves to articulate reggae in specifically Japanese terms, in ways that largely efface Jamaica from the music, this Jamaican presence is felt in a generalization of political issues, symbols, themes, and rhetorical conventions expressed in Jamaican reggae, permitting them to be applied specifically to Japan. It is through a gaze toward and a careful knowing of the Jamaican—an instance of the broader Japanese gaze at the international, which many of the musicians mentioned above sing about—that reggae can be articulated as authentically Japanese. The formative experiences within the subcultural backstage tell a more complex story than the easy patriotisms that they give way to on mainstream stages. Next I discuss the personal experiences of two artists who have navigated this space in the process of learning, and obtaining the performative symbolic capital associated with, the Jamaican.

TWO JAPANESE DANCEHALL MUSICIANS

Papa Bon is one of many Japanese DJs whose lyrics cover a broad range of topics, from self-promoting bravado to messages of peace and love. Sticko at the time of my interview was a member of Mighty Crown; he is now a DJ with the group Fireball. However they differ from other dancehall practitioners, the two men's careers provide a fairly representative idea of the experiences of many male Japanese dancehall practitioners. These experiences include:

1 Bob Marley as the initial contact with Jamaican popular culture.
2 A rejection of and sense of alienation from mainstream, fast-track educational and professional culture in Japan.

3 Adopting a stage name drawing on that of an admired Jamaican artist.

4 Travel along the Tokyo–New York–Jamaica–Tokyo dancehall circuit described above.

5 Shock at witnessing Jamaican poverty on first arriving at the island.

6 A perception of Jamaicans as kind, strong, and cheerful, yet also tricky and aggressive, due to or in spite of their economic struggle.

7 The full awakening of love for Jamaican culture while in Jamaica.

8 Dismay at being misidentified as Chinese (called "Mr. Chin" or "Ms. Chin").

9 The Jamaican experience, particularly as inflected through Rastafari, as a medium for self-discovery and spiritual uplift less possible in Japan.

10 The application of skills acquired in Jamaica after returning to Japan.

11 Revaluating life in Japan, and oneself as Japanese, in relation to the Jamaican experience; a desire to share positive Jamaican experiences with other Japanese.

12 The desire to continue in the subculture despite economic and other hardships.

Of particular note are two sets of themes pertaining to a main concern in this chapter, and this book in general. The first pertains to my interest in this chapter with mapping the course that Japanese sound system members, singers, and dancers take in acquiring symbolic capital situated in Jamaica and New York—learning patois, acquiring new music, and a general immersion in the Jamaican experience—needed to help establish their reputations as dancehall artists (no. 4). The second pertains to themes in which elements like those found in the discourse of jibun sagashi (the search for self) are reflected (nos. 9 and 11).

PAPA BON

Takagi Hideaki—who uses the stage name of Papa Bon—and I met at the small Yokohama recording studio where, back then, he and other members of what would become the Mighty Crown Entertainment family worked. From there, we went to a restaurant to talk. Takagi is from Sapporo City, Hokkaido. He describes Hideaki and Papa Bon as two different people: a complete switch takes place once he assumes his DJ personality onstage.

About his music, he says, "I am very serious. I try to be [a] pure singer." I asked him about the relationship between his identity as Hideaki and his identity as Papa Bon. He laughed and said: "I'm not sure, because it was long ago. When I was just graduated from high school, I turned somehow [into] Papa Bon."

Papa Bon had been lead vocalist in his high-school band, and although the other members, who had nicknamed him Bon, quit the band to go to college and then look for work, he wanted to continue being a musician. He met a reggae DJ, who introduced him to the music; liking it, he decided to give it a try and thought about what his stage name would be. He kept Bon, and added Papa from the name of the legendary Jamaican DJ, Papa San. (The original name is interesting here for its exoticizing citation of the Japanese, returned now to Japan through Bon's adoption of this "Jamaican" stage name.) Papa Bon, he thought, was a good choice, because Hideaki would be an unwieldy name for "my Jamaican people and New York friends" to pronounce.

Bon studied economics at Hokkaigakuin University, graduating at the age of twenty-three. For the next two years, he worked part time, including at a musical instrument shop. He deejayed at various clubs throughout Sapporo, but he became frustrated about his options as a DJ in such a small city, where there was at the time no dancehall scene to speak of, and where he could get little information about dancehall. He felt that although Tokyo would be better, even that city would do little to help him develop his skills. He decided to use his savings from his part-time jobs to travel to New York, to improve his DJ skills through immersion in dancehall culture there.

"Everything was new for me," he said of his first few weeks in the city. One of the things that struck him most about New York was its diversity: he met black and Chinese people there for the first time, and he became good friends with an Argentine reggae fan. Quickly growing familiar with New York's dancehall scene, he met the members of Mighty Crown, rooming for a while with Cojie, who would become a Crown selector. He met a Jamaican producer who was interested in him as a Japanese DJ, and who encouraged him to perform at stage shows.

Bon said that when he first started out, it was very hard for him to "mash up the crowd." He recalled one event in the Bronx. He was speaking in English, but he stumbled and felt overwhelmed by the fact that he could not use Japanese. He simply stood onstage, speechless. "It was terrible," he

Papa Bon in 2008. Photo by Mighty Crown Entertainment.

said. When I asked him how the audience responded, he said, "They look like they worry about me." His friend advised him that in such situations he should act as if nothing had happened and never reveal his nervousness. He said that although he still gets nervous at major sessions, now that he is more comfortable deejaying, he tries to enjoy himself more. One of the things he feels he has particularly improved in is tune selection: like a skilled selector, he has become more sensitive about which in his repertoire of tunes he should perform, based on his sense of the audience's mood at any given moment while he is onstage.

Bon was bothered by the way many New Yorkers tended not to distinguish between Japanese and Chinese. He found that such people were more common in Brooklyn than in the "melting pot" of Manhattan. It is possible that the New Yorkers in question were Jamaican immigrants and Jamaican Americans, because he went on to say that his expectations, based on his experience in New York, about how his Japaneseness would be viewed in Jamaica were confirmed once he actually arrived there. "When they find that Japanese people, not Chinese people, they can't separate, you know, and call me 'Chin,' yeah . . . First time they call me like that, I thought what kind of person they are but finally I [got] used it."[6] (Bon's response seems like a reasonable irritation at being misidentified in this way; in chapter 5, I discuss how others' responses to this labeling can manifest themselves in more openly nationalistic terms.)

Bon went on to say that one of the things he appreciated about his time in Jamaica was the fact that he was often called upon to demonstrate his DJ abilities at unexpected times and in unexpected places. In Sapporo, Tokyo, and even in New York, his life as a DJ was confined mainly to dancehall venues. In Jamaica, however, dancehall was everywhere:

> My Jamaican experience is, anywhere, I can sing. Wherever. On the street, or house . . . If I sing with big voice at apartment, they don't care, also, on the street. I am wearing like this [gestures toward his clothing] so they recognize you are Japanese DJ so they want to kick some tune and I really love to sing in front of the people and kick some lyrics outside. Great thing, you know. I feel nice and they feel nice . . . One time I went to a Taco Bell . . . just Japanese friends and me. So, you know, the employe[e] said . . . "You smell . . ." I asked what you smell, so she said, she whispered me, "Weed, weed," because I'm just back from studio . . . So they go, "You a DJ, right?" So I said yes . . . So I start to sing in front of [them].

Papa Bon stayed in Jamaica for a year, during which time, relying on a network of both Jamaican and Japanese friends—Bon noted that young Japanese DJs are now flocking to the island to "pick up studio style, like me"—he recorded a CD and traveled across the island with a sound system, performing at a number of dances. At first he spoke and deejayed in patois, but later he opted for a mixture of patois and Japanese. It is this linguistic mixture—primarily Japanese, with Jamaican flourishes—that characterizes Japanese dancehall culture today (a development which most people I spoke with say began with Rankin' Taxi).

After his year in Jamaica, Bon returned to New York and, a few months later, to Sapporo. At the time of our interview, he had been in Sapporo for two years: the city served as a home base from which he traveled to perform in other regions of Japan. He felt frustrated about the situation in Sapporo, which had no reggae scene to speak of. He said that when he talked to people in a position to build up the scene there, they did not seem to understand what he was talking about, and he suggested that some resented his advice because they had not seen as much of the world as he has. (This treatment might be related to the suspicion with which Japanese who have spent a significant amount of time overseas are sometimes regarded.) He found the unwillingness of these individuals to take a chance on dancehall regrettable, because he felt confident that, if introduced properly, the subculture would blossom there (as indeed it did in recent years).

As is the case with even the most successful Japanese dancehall artists, it was difficult for Papa Bon to make a living from dancehall. Only in the summer could he make decent money. He estimated (at the time of this interview) that some of the bigger DJs like himself made around 50,000 yen (about $420) for single performances, performing up to three times a month in the summertime, but sometimes not at all at other times of the year.

> Wintertime is so terrible, so I got some part-time job [as a carpenter, construction work, maintenance] and pass over that terrible time. I don't like to deal with that kind of work . . . I keep on dealing with reggae music. It's so rough and hard, it has ups and downs.

Papa Bon felt that at 32, he was at a crossroad in his life, and he had to consider the possibility of stable, full-time employment. He said he would be happy to find work that allowed him to develop his love of dancehall music, to continue improving his English, and to keep meeting interesting people. He acknowledged that at the moment, however, it was difficult:

> Maybe this is time to decide . . . to get another job . . . Playing reggae music in Japan is so hard. Because there is no big deal, and we can't get big promoters so easily like regular music, like pop music. It is difficult to get big deals. So we have to think to survive in the market . . . I'm an only child and I just left my father and mother in my hometown, right? And [it's] time to get married, too. I'm over 30, you know, [I] have few chances to get married. So I . . . start thinking about my life. Really music is important for me because this is my hobby and something I put my energy into . . . If I [give up] reggae music, I am a hopeless person.

At the time of this interview, Papa Bon was struggling financially, given his desire to pursue reggae music. His story is similar to that of most dancehall artists, both male and female, who tend to be marginal in the Japanese socioeconomic order, where most people not only claim middle-class status but also take conventional paths toward that goal. In pursuing reggae music, Papa Bon has had to defer marriage and the economic security that comes with full-time work. In the discourses, explicit and otherwise, of the search for self (discussed more fully in chapter 5), this rhetoric—and reality—

of financial struggle for artistic self-realization is common. The issue of class emerges again in the next chapter, in my discussion of Japanese donnettes; in chapters 4 and 5, through the many practitioners of roots reggae and Rasta who criticize capitalism in Japan and overseas; and in the final chapter, vis-à-vis the links between class and ethnicity in the success of Mighty Crown.

MIGHTY CROWN AND STICKO

Sound systems are public-address systems run by a small group of men (sometimes women) who perform essentially three roles: MC, engineer, and selector. Cost-conscious promoters of international events are sometimes able to cover the travel and other expenses of only one or two of the sound's members, who comfortably assume all three roles. Masta Simon is Mighty Crown's MC. (All the members were in their twenties at the time of my interview with Sticko.) Simon controls the mike. He greets the crowd, pays respect to ("bigs up") important people involved in the event, and announces the tunes, often explaining to his Japanese listeners their meaning and relevance for Jamaicans. He punctuates the playing of each tune with exhortations for the audience to shout, jump up, and dance. Sticko is the engineer, whose primary responsibility is to ensure audio quality before and during the event.

Mighty Crown's selectors are Sammy T., who is Simon's brother, and Cojie. They select the tunes to be played throughout the event. The selectors file through the several crates of records placed behind the turntable, mixer, and other onstage equipment, laying them on the turntable, listening through their headsets to time one tune's succession into the next. The selector has to be able to find songs appropriate for a crowd's assumed tastes, the occasion of a given night, and the mood of the crowd at any moment, organizing tunes in sequences that manage crowd energy well. There is a division of labor among the two Mighty Crown selectors: Sammy T selects more contemporary dancehall tunes, and Cojie is very familiar with older Jamaican music. Another critical and continually challenging aspect of the selector's job is staying on top of what is popular among dancehall fans in Jamaica and, by extension, Japan, which requires gaining access to the countless recordings that the Caribbean island has produced over the past few decades.[7]

In many respects, certainly in its group structure, Mighty Crown is a typical sound system, but it differs from other Japanese sounds in a number of ways. First, having spent much time in Jamaica, its members are better able to speak patois than those of other Japanese sound systems. Several members of Mighty Crown attended an American school in Yokohama, where English was the main language, and all of them spent several years in the United States. Second, Sticko, the engineer, studied audio engineering in New York, although he started learning about sound system engineering informally, through advice from members of the earliest Japanese sound systems, and through trial and error. Whatever discernible effects this may have on the quality of Mighty Crown's sound, few other systems have this sort of formal training. Furthermore, for many sounds, dancehall reggae is only an occasional pursuit, a hobby; for Mighty Crown, it is serious business. Mighty Crown Entertainment today includes a clothing line and a record label. In addition to audio recordings, they also produce and sell DVDs of their events. The price of obtaining quality dub plates, as well as the other costs of maintaining Mighty Crown as a quality sound, is a financial burden which all the members are expected to share; that was the case even in the days when members had to work at part-time jobs outside their sound-system activities to support themselves. (Cynical observers suggest that this ability to acquire high-quality dub plates accounts more than anything else for Mighty Crown's success.) Other business endeavors revolve around the Mighty Crown name: several free dancehall papers (*Riddim*, *Strive*, and *Yokohama Reggae Times*) have close working relations with the sound system. As is generally the case in dancehall and other black urban musical cultures like hip-hop, Mighty Crown describes itself as a family or crew, in which established artists collaborate with and support the musical careers of their up-and-coming colleagues, often friends they grew up with. The Mighty Crown Family includes Papa B, Guan Chai, and the singer (as opposed to a DJ) Jing Teng. The final member of this family is the group Fireball, which has a musical (including vocals and riddim) and performance (a group, as opposed to the more common individual DJ) style with some similarities to the Jamaican group T.O.K. Fireball includes Jun 4 Shot, Criss (a singer), Chosen Lee, and Truthful (Sticko's name as a DJ).

While it would be instructive to provide profiles of all the members of Mighty Crown, here I will focus only on one, for purposes of economy and relative depth. Sticko is one of the three original members of Mighty Crown. When I interviewed him around 1999, he was officially the group's engineer, but he also regularly acted as its selector and MC. His speech bears the MC's swagger, whether in Japanese (among other Japanese), in patois (to me at Club Citta—he did not know me at the time but guessed I was Jamaican), or in urban American English (to me later on as a U.S.-based researcher). He was raised in Kamakura and attended St. Joseph's International School, a small Catholic school in Yokohama founded in 1901 by the Society of Mary (the school has recently closed). Sticko told me that unlike most schools in Japan (or the United States), where students spend only several years before moving on to a school at a higher level, students attended St. Joseph's from grade school all the way through high school. This created a sense of intimacy among the students, he said, many of whom helped develop his musical tastes.

In such an intimate space, trends spread quickly. This included underground music. Sticko said that he constantly heard house and hip-hop coming from the radios of the older students in the school lunchroom. "We been trekking on the world music scene I guess very naturally," he says. "It just sink in me, you know, and just listening to that stuff all the time."

It was there, where new music was precious symbolic capital, that Sticko first became exposed to reggae:

> I myself was always, like, searching for some different kind of music other than what I hear at school, too, you know . . . Then one day I checked the CD store. And I found this song, long dreadlock guy on the jacket cover. That was Bob Marley. And I never knew, I just . . . "Who is this guy dressing so . . . ," just followed that and listened to it.

Sticko and his friend's brother, who was also familiar with reggae music, began going every weekend to a club called Zema—which, according to Sticko, was the first dancehall reggae club in Yokohama (this was around 1990, the year before Mighty Crown was formed). He started going to events by Banana Size, one of the first sound systems in Japan, and by Junior Lee, one of the earliest local DJs, whose rapid-fire vocal style intrigued Sticko. For his school's annual rock show, he created a band with his friends and performed Bob Marley songs, with himself as lead singer.

However, Sticko's interest in reggae music centered not so much on roots reggae as on dancehall. He started obtaining tapes of performances by Jamaican sound systems like Stone Love and Body Guard. Although during this period dancehall reggae was still deeply underground, Sticko became aware of such Japanese DJs as Nahki and Rankin' Taxi, and of Taxi's sound system, Taxi Hi-Fi.

Sticko and his friends decided to start their own sound system. Trying to come up with a name, they thought of Turbo Crown, a Jamaican sound system whose tape they had heard and liked very much. Sticko continued:

> We were just looking at . . . some reggae record, right? And it was on the bottom in small letters, it said "Almighty," right, "Almighty God" or something was written on it. "Mighty, Mighty, Mighty's good, man." [He laughed.] Just like that. And we just made it up.

Mighty Crown had its first party, which was fairly well attended—about a hundred people—in part because the new sound system appeared with other, more established performers. From there they began looking for clubs where they could play regularly. They discovered a basement club in Yokohama's Kotobukichō area, which Sticko laughingly described as a "ghetto."

Sticko graduated from high school and decided to join Mighty Crown member Masta Simon, who had also attended St. Joseph's, to study in California. Sticko never attended any classes, however, preferring to select at various parties. In the end, he decided to return to Japan to attend college. However, he "didn't even get there" either and joined Sammy, who was already selecting in New York (where he met Cojie, the fourth original member of Mighty Crown). Sticko started selecting at parties himself and decided to go to an audio engineering school that Sammy had planned to attend, but was unable to.

Sticko took a spring trip from New York to Jamaica. (He said that the trip made him sure he had been right to study musical engineering. As a result of that trip, he felt overwhelmed by his need to experience the world beyond books; he said that becoming a musician was the only thing he wanted to do. For the first time, after that first trip to Jamaica, he found himself getting good grades.) Sticko stayed for a month near Montego Bay, one of the island's major resort areas. He went with Nanjaman, a well-known Japanese DJ (mentioned above) and a friend of his, who had been to Jamaica before and had friends with whom he and Sticko could stay. Sticko described his first impressions of the island:

> It was really shocking for me, the first time I saw the situation. You know. Out from Japan, New York, straight into Jamaica and see the old shacks, people living in there, so much kids running around . . . barefoot and all that, it was a real culture shock for me. But I didn't understand

why people, why they're so happy. They're really happy, you know. And when Nanja come the kids is all like, "Nanja, Nanja!" . . . It was so amazing for me. I was able to stay with them for a month. The space was really small . . . I was sleeping on the floor. I didn't really mind that you know 'cuz they were treating me so nice.

He described other Jamaicans' attitude toward him, a "rich tourist," as "aggressive." Sticko saw this aggression as stemming from economic hardship, which also informs the reggae music he loves so much. He was struck by the ambition of Jamaican people: "I just felt the power inside them to live their lives . . . They don't waste their lives . . . Everyone has a real set objective in life."

Sticko returned to New York, then after another two years, returned to Japan. There he continued his work with Mighty Crown. At that time, in the mid-1990s, the sound system had difficulty pulling in crowds. The effort to maintain a sound system was in itself expensive for the four young part-time workers.

Throughout the years we been saving up a lot to build our own sound system, right? And we were working just to get dubs, and all that. Most of the years throughout it was like that. And while I was in New York it was the same thing. Hustle. Go to school, hustle, you know. Slowly we started to pull [in] crowds . . . We just kept on struggling. We just build it one by one . . . First we started out from a small club . . . then we moved on to [Club 24], then we packed that place, then we moved onto Bodega and then moved on to Heaven. You know, we took each step, and we took it carefully each time . . . I just remembered it was really hard for me. I just remember I was always struggling. Didn't have no money . . . [One of my lowest points] was when I used to work as a painter . . . They don't only do painting. They do cleaning and all that too. Like for half year I did that stuff and like you can get 200,000 yen [about $1,800], right, every month, right, but . . . half of that goes to Mighty Crown. Every month.

Gradually, however, especially with its recent success overseas, the sound system became very popular nationwide. For regular juggling events, they commanded around $2,000, a figure that has probably escalated dramatically over the past few years; for sound clashes, they will charge more given the high costs of, for instance, acquiring the dub plates needed to defeat their rivals. Yokohama, because it is Mighty Crown's home base—that is where the sound's members grew up—is the center of dancehall culture in Japan, yet even in neighboring Tokyo, the sound can draw thousands.

At the time of our interview, Sticko had recently begun to shift focus from the sound system to his career as a DJ. It was in this context that he responded to my question about whether his trip to Jamaica had affected his perspectives as an artist.

> Right now I DJ a lot, I sing now too. I'm away from the sound systems a little bit . . . And as an artist what I feel is I just wanna be real. I just wanna be me. And that's what Jamaica's good about. They're them, you know. I'm an Asian born, Japanese, and my roots is down in here, and I realize that and my culture is as beautiful as their culture and their culture is as beautiful as mine, and I just love their culture and . . . when I show them the picture of Japan and stuff they love it too. And, I don't know, I just wanna be me as a Japanese. As a Japanese I see a lot of stupid stuff going [on] in Japan right now . . . All over the world . . . it's the same thing . . . The negativity, you know, the whole, I don't know . . . anger . . . and when I think of that I just wanna tell my people first what I felt, what I been through, what I saw, you know, so that they can see some, have a wider span of view, you know, and as an artist I try to do that because Bob Marley's music inspired me a lot and taught me what positiveness and how to live my life and how my life is precious, them type of stuff. It's funny that this Japanese culture didn't teach me anything like that but music from far in Caribbean taught me that . . . It's really funny to me. So I just really thank that I [came across] reggae music. Because this music really gave me, I don't know, taught me how to live.

The beauty of Jamaican culture, the insights afforded by Bob Marley's music, become a means by which Sticko recognizes the value of his Asianness, his Japaneseness, the beauty of his own culture. Interestingly, then, Sticko's assertion of his personal enlightenment overseas, one through which he is able to criticize Japan, dovetails into the rhetoric of Japanese national identity. On the one hand, there is Sticko as the member of this intimate collective known as "the Japanese." On the other is Sticko as an individual who must (temporarily) leave this collective in search of self-actualization. This is a tension which recurs in much Japanese fiction and non-fiction writing on travel to Jamaica, discussed in chapter 5.

EVENT STRUCTURE: JUGGLING, RUB-A-DUB, CLASH

Japanese dancehall events closely resemble their Jamaican counterparts in structure. There are three main kinds of events in which sound systems are central. Regular juggling (a sound system's playing a series of DJs' tunes recorded on the same riddims, or playing tunes that are thematically linked) starts around 10:00 p.m. Especially at this point, the tunes tend to be fairly mellow. If roots reggae gets much play at dancehall events, it is usually around this time. Crowd volume and energy are relatively low. Some people remain in the bar area having drinks and talking with each other; a few sway on the dance floor.

Gradually the venue becomes more crowded, and by just after midnight, the selectors have already begun juggling the most popular tunes, their most impressive dub plates. How long juggling continues depends on the length of the show, if any, that comes after it. If this is a major rub-a-dub event—the second kind of event, in which, again, live DJs and singers perform over riddims provided by the featured sound system—then juggling, rather than being an event onto itself, has basically served to warm up the crowd and ends soon after midnight, when the DJs and singers start appearing. If the event features only one or two DJs, then juggling continues deeper into the night, and the event reaches a peak around 2:00 or 2:30 a.m., when the DJs and singers begin appearing. After they have performed, juggling finishes out the night. Some audience members who have driven to the event leave around this time, but commuters stay later since the trains, which stop running just after midnight, start again around 5:00 a.m.

The third kind of event is the clash. A sound clash refers to adversarial selecting between two or more sound systems. The winner of this competition is the sound which succeeds in exciting the crowd the most. This is achieved through the MC's combative verbal prowess (or "argument"), tune selection and ordering, and dub plates acquired from the most popular Jamaican DJs. A panel of judges or a promoter, using audience response as a guide, decides the winner. Clashes are organized into rounds. In each round, sound systems take turns playing their tunes, with less and less time to do so as the rounds progress. During the last few rounds, the sounds only have a couple of minutes at a time in which to perform, driving the crowd into a fever pitch as only fragments of popular tunes are played. The Mighty Crown–Judgment event described below did not have the pitch of sound clashes in Jamaica. There, clashes can get extremely heated, with each sound routinely questioning the sexual orientation of the members of the competing sound, or suggesting infantilizing return to their mothers' breasts. This event, rather, was intended as a celebration of the sounds' recent international victories. Still, the event was structured into rounds, with the sounds expressing toward each other the kind of ritual antagonism typical of clashes. This clash was followed by a rub-a-dub session, featuring several of Japan's best-known DJs.

PATOIS IN JAPANESE DANCEHALL

I did not meet a single Japanese MC—or a selector or engineer, for that matter—who did not have at least some familiarity with dancehall patois. (Although they also appear onstage, engineers and selectors who perform in these strict capacities alone do not need to address the crowd during their performances and tend to be less familiar with patois than MCs are.) Patois is mostly confined to the stage: once away from it, the sound system members converse in Japanese, with occasional words or phrases in patois. At all the events, at least some elements of dancehall patois are used onstage; which ones, and how, depend on several variables. The use of dancehall patois effects the regular structure of the dancehall event in Jamaica and thus, by adopted extension, in Japan. There, dancehall terms may be placed into four categories: interjections, commands, interlude terms, and open terms.

MCs use interjections and commands while the selector plays or "runs" a tune. These are often common patois or English expressions routinely used in dancehall. Although many interjections are nonverbal and seem arbitrary and spontaneous, they always appear in the same situations and are pronounced in essentially the same way. "A-ha," "Uh-huh," "Well!" "Wooah-y!" "Yes [DJ's name]!" and "Yo!," for instance, are used while running a tune; the MC often exclaims, "Hol' on!" to indicate his recognition of the audience's excitement at a particular tune.

Commands are often directed at the selector, audience members, or live DJs waiting just off stage. "Come again!" indicates that the selector should play the tune again. "Come in [performer]!" is used to invite a performer onstage. "Bun [burn] fire!" means "Light your lighters!"—a form of audience support for the sound system. This term is originally Rastafarian, as fire is a spiritual purifier for Rastas. "Hol' up!" "Pull up!" or "Hol' on!" are used to stop the playing of a tune, a strategic move that excites the crowd, followed by playing the tune again (an act immediately preceded by "Come again!"). "Run dat!" or "Run tune!" is directed at the selector after the MC has finished introducing a song.

Interlude terms occur during breaks in the music, or when the volume has been lowered. These terms, and the interlude in general, often call attention to the event as an event. It is during this time that the MC thanks individuals significantly involved in the sponsorship and organization of the event, makes announcements about upcoming events, or reminds listeners of the purposes for which this event is taking place. For example, the Mighty Crown–Judgment event was, as noted above, a celebration of the two sounds' recent international victories; I also attended a couple of other events which celebrated the lives of Japanese dancehall artists who had tragically passed away. Among these interlude terms are "Big up [someone]!" "Big up yourself!" or "'Nuff Respect!" ("much respect"). Jamaicans as dancehall's progenitors are also routinely paid homage to using these terms: "Big up all a di Jamaican dem inna di house, seen? Yes, man, 'nuff respect."

Open terms are those found in patois in general, rather than being particular to dancehall. They are often heard there in part because they communicate ideas or feelings that emerge regularly from the music and in part, perhaps, because of the ease with which they can be mastered. Open terms can also be interlude terms in the sense that they often appear in the interlude period, when the MC's patois is most likely to manifest itself in relatively complex forms. "Yu si right about now . . ." is used to introduce a new tune, performer, or stage in the event. "Seen?" (Understand?) is commonly used in contemporary patois. Its usage in dancehall is derived from Rastafarian dread talk, where it reflects the value that Rastafarians place on wisdom and spiritual insight. "Yu nuh?" (You know?) is another easily mastered expression. "Yuh dun know seh . . ." (You've done knowing that . . .) is used to emphatically suggest, for instance, that it is not a matter of debate that the DJ being introduced is the greatest.

This list does not represent the full range of patois ability of Japanese MCs. Although a few are capable of little more, some, especially those who have spent much time in Jamaica, are able to employ a more fully socialized patois.

I have described the transnational paths that sound system members and DJs take to acquire the symbolic capital of dancehall, including Jamaican patois and dub plates. In the following section, I describe the Mighty Crown and Judgment Sound Station (whose members are Tucker, the MC, and Crush, the selector) clash-celebration, focusing on how the two sounds use this symbolic capital. They do so, I will argue, in ways ultimately intended to move the audience—and, discreetly, each other—toward an authentically local sense of participation in transnational dancehall culture.

EVENT: MIGHTY CROWN–JUDGMENT CLASH

Club Citta's floor is packed now, bodies close against each other in the cavernous space. It is only the first round, but Mighty Crown has just finished running one of its biggest dub plates, by Buju Banton. The crowd is still buzzing from the tune, and the brief humming silence that ensues ends when the selector, Sammy T, whose body has been cradled around his turntable, steps away and thrusts both index fingers triumphantly into the air. At that instant comes the music to "Ghetto Pledge," then the voice of Baby Cham:

> Mi haffi rate Mighty Crown whe hol' di faith
> Cah we haffi let dem music . . .

For most Japanese dancehall fans, Baby Cham is a DJ from remote Jamaica whose voice can be heard only on mass-produced CDs. Hearing the familiar, popular tune versioned to have Baby Cham utter the name, "Mighty Crown" (the original lyrics are: "Mi haffi rate every youth whe hol' di faith / Cah we haffi mek Jamaica feel proud"), the massive (the crowd) comes alive. At this moment Sammy T, expecting this "forward" (the massive's affirmation of the MC's performance), sharply rewinds the record, reducing the tune to a sped-up screech. He raises the needle. "Hol' on deh!" shouts Simon, the MC. Pleasantly stunned by the sudden interruption of the music, the audience recognizes the MC's recognition of their excitement and waits for his selector to run the tune again. But first, Simon, in skilled control of his musical supply, makes some demands. "*Reggae no suki dattara, chō, migi te, migi te!*" And then he repeats it in patois: "All who love reggae music, right hand inna di air so!" The other onstage members of Mighty Crown demonstrate; hands, and voices, rise in response. "Yo, a di fuss roun,' yu nuh, fuss roun'!" Simon says, reminding the crowd that more is to come.

Sammy T runs the tune again, this time more fully:

> Mi haffi rate Mighty Crown whe hol' di faith
> Cah we haffi let dem music flow

Wha Cham seh
Bun a fire pon a fool an pon a bait
Whe a walk inna battyman[8] crowd
Wha Cham seh
Di bigga heads a itch, di rich a get richer
Nuttin nah gwaan, mi well want a shower
A full time we show dem a who have de power . . .

Sammy lowers the volume and Simon speaks over the tune to introduce the final song of Mighty Crown's first round. Sammy runs the tune. After only the first line, the audience recognizes the voice of Bounty Killer, the king of gangster dancehall.

Look into my eyes,
Tell me what you see
You see Mighty Crown . . .[9]

The massive rumbles: another forward. The selector pulls up. Simon screams "Fire!" and lighters flicker against the dark. A woman in the audience raises her voice in saluting gunfire: "Plow, plow, plow!" "Come again," Simon says, "Final entry!" The selector runs the plate again. "Hey yo, yeh-low!" Bounty says in his signature greeting. He voices the sound system's self-appointed title, "Mighty Crown, the Far East Ruler." "Hey yo, yeh-low! Sammy T, Simon. Hey yo, yeh-low!" Simon informs the crowd in Japanese that Bounty Killer, though just done with his American tour, was still able to rampage across Japan on a recent tour here. He thanks Bounty Killer (presumably for coming to Japan) in Japanese (*kansha*) and in patois ('nuff respect), then continues with the tune.

The light dims, and the spotlight switches from the Mighty Crown left to the Judgment right side of the stage. Judgment's entry is preceded by a digitally fragmented, partially repeated sample of the patois expletive "bumboclaat," accompanied by audio effects that sound something like antagonists striking each other in a Chinese martial arts film.

Somewhere in the swirl of digital sound, a familiar voice emerges. "Hey yo, yeh-low!" Yes, like most other dollar-savvy Jamaican DJs, Bounty, playing no favorites, also recorded a dub plate for Judgment; in the low-key competition between the two sound systems, Judgment is already suffering a little. "Judgment Sound Station hot . . ." Bounty says. Along with his solitary selector and fellow MC, the Judgment seems isolated, compared to a half-dozen men onstage representing or supporting Mighty Crown. This onstage bodily support is a significant part of the sound's ability to win official clashes. When popular tunes are run, the audience feeds off the energies of the men onstage, who excitedly demonstrate their appreciation of their colleagues' musical skills.

In patois and Japanese, the two men take turns respecting and bigging up everyone involved in the event: Mighty Crown; the men ("di shotta bredren") and women ("di sexy gyal dem") who have come from all over Japan to attend this event; *Riddim Magazine*; Rankin' Taxi, "Japan's God-father of Reggae," who stands between the two sounds and whose equipment is being used at the event; "all a dem black people, big-up unnu self, seen?" After these introductions: "You see right about now? A Judgment time."

> *Ikkyoku me, kore wa*
> *kami no koto*
>
> This first tune, it's all about
> Divine issues.

He runs a dub plate, and the crowd goes wild. "Wooay!" screams the MC. "Wooay! Wooooooooay!" The crowd shrieks, and the MC sharply rewinds the record; the crowd's buzzing fills the abrupt silence. "Hol' on! Hol' on!" The MC cues up the record again, and Tony Rebel's "Jah Is on My Side" begins again, in biblical double entendre,

> Come, come, come,
> Judgment a come, come, come.

Despite Mighty Crown's ferocious start, Judgment looks up to the challenge.

Judgment completes its round and invites Mighty Crown to return to the stage: "Come in, Mighty Crown." There is applause, and the fractured, repeated voice of the ubiquitous Bounty Killer, accompanied by robotic droning, again declares Mighty Crown "the Far East Ruler." "Hey yo! Hey yo!" Simon repeats over and over, and the crowd starts to cheer. He declares tonight's event a party for the two recently victorious sounds, then proceeds to big up *Riddim*, the event sponsor, and several DJs and sound systems. Next he introduces Sticko, who will act as MC for Mighty Crown's next round. The crowd is still buzzing from Judgment's performance, but Sticko is in no hurry to work the massive over to his side. He starts with a few "nice and easy," sung (as opposed to deejayed) dub plates, warming the crowd to his sound, his presence. *"Yoshi,"*[10] he says, almost indifferently. But as the round progresses, the crowd gets hot. Sticko pounds his chest with an open hand. Into the mike he shouts, "Mighty Crown!"

Soon the event arrives at the point when each tune is played for only a few seconds. In these later rounds, even when audience reaction produces a forward—which in earlier rounds would be followed by fuller replaying of the exciting tune—Sticko moves on to a new tune. With this rapid selecting and, with the gradual move into contemporary dancehall—marked by more energized riddims and harsher DJ vocality—the crowd that had been softly stepping and swaying gently when the evening began is now jumping wildly about.

Many Jamaican dancehall tunes concern the DJ's wariness of those who resent his success. Sammy T, who had been selecting most of the night, had a stint as MC. He played a tune which included the line, "Dem a talk say a we dem wah kill" ("They're saying that it's us they want to kill"). "Think you can test Mighty Crown, nuh? Judgment?" Sammy T growls. "Think you can test us, Judgment?"

Sammy T ends Crown's round with a torrent of pointed fingers and verbal gunfire from the crowd. "Come 'cross," Sammy orders Judgment. His tone of voice and choice of this expression, rather than the standard, more polite "come in," is (only ritually) full of contempt. At this moment, the shattered "bomboclaat" and the name Judgment reverberate across the club to begin Judgment's next round. The Judgment MC, however, does not directly respond to this, only acknowledging the good vibes in the club and issuing big ups: "Remember, it's all about Judgment, yu nuh." He plays several dub plates; at this point, just about every major Jamaican dancehall artist has been represented. With the same rapid selection, big-name plates, emphatic forwards, and the MC's displays of his own delight, Judgment comes right back and has the crowd in its hands. Mighty Crown looks on from its shadowed half of the stage and nods and steps as well—but not as much, of course, as when it controls the mike.

The rounds are over, and Rankin' Taxi, who has been cheering the two sounds evenly throughout the night, takes over the mike. He asks the crowd in Japanese if they had a good time, and the audience signals its approval. "Mighty Crown!" some cheer. "Judgment!" cheer others. Taxi introduces

Ishii Shizuo, head of Overheat, who steps onstage. In his early fifties or so, he wears a baseball cap and red leather jacket. "Rankin' Taxi. Judgment. Mighty Crown. *Taose!*" (Get them!—presumably referring to rival groups everywhere). The audience applauds.[11]

Japanese Dancehall as Performative Socialization

Japanese (and Jamaican) sound systems use patois, dub plates by Jamaican DJs and singers, and other forms of subcultural symbolic capital as firepower against "sound boys" from the opposing sounds. To decouple the familiar voice of a famous DJ or singer from a familiar song to specifically celebrate the power of the sound system right in front of the audience affords the sound a certain phenomenological prestige. The power to bridge this gap between the culture's Jamaican stars and the casual Japanese fan provides the sound with a credibility that delights the massive. To hear Cham declare in a new version of a standard tune how highly he rates Mighty Crown, and to see Crown, a Japanese sound system, before one's eyes as Cham makes this declaration, performatively widens the field of international dancehall culture to encompass Japan, even while narrowing it to this place, this sound, this night.

This immediate siting of dancehall in the Japanese local, then, is significantly effected in transnational terms. Japanese sound systems in Japan are culture brokers, figures of instructive authority in the constitution of the Japanese dancehall as one node in the performative field of an international subculture. In line with the performative field—national or local in other analytical contexts—framed here in transnational terms, Japanese dancehall to date remains organically connected to the Jamaican international. This is shown in the stories of travel to Jamaica by artists like Papa Bon and Sticko. One dimension of the social politics of this field, then, involves negotiation of Jamaican difference. The acquisition and use of patois is one key resource in this effort, even as it is clear that, at times, onstage patois especially as used between international sounds like Judgment and Mighty Crown is well beyond the comprehension of most fans. (Few fans, for instance, will know the difference between "come in" and "come 'cross.")

At least two levels of socialization, then, are taking place: sound to fan and sound to sound. On the first level, the event unfolds as the sound systems' entertaining the fans. Patrons attend dancehall events not simply to hear reggae music, not simply to enjoy Japanese dancehall as a still-evolving thing unto itself, but also to partake in a Jamaican experience that helps define Japanese dancehall. This is achieved, for example, by bigging up Jamaican people, through the cross-cultural intertextualities of the dub plate, by adopting such utterances and gestures as the Jamaican rude boy's "Plow, plow, plow!" and burning fire. In these ways, the audience ritually, viscerally, comes to understand how this music ought to be consumed. Set roles are assigned for the sound systems and the audience, and the audience therefore has an exciting, manageable, yet important form of play through which to undergo its Jamaican experience. Part of this experience is understanding, achieving, and even exceeding the passion of Afro-Jamaican audiences, one that can be celebrated in the nationalist Japanese reggae discussed above. As an MC put it at one event I attended, "*Jamaikajin ni namerasenai!*" (Don't let the Jamaicans beat us!).

The sound-sound interaction is a second aspect of this "glocal" performative socialization. It is a ritualized means by which the members of both sound systems mutually construct and affirm their identities as dancehall artists. This effort unfolds not only in the immediate spaces of Yokohama or Tokyo dancehall clubs. It also unfolds—in an experientially deeper and more compelling manner than is the case for most fans—in the distant clubs of New York and Kingston, where Japanese sound system members, singers, and DJs like Papa Bon and Sticko have had to perform before Jamaicans, in the Jamaican language.

The two levels of socialization are not discrete. For less experienced patrons, not understanding exactly what is going as the MCs deploy their Jamaican musical and linguistic symbolic capital in sophisticated ways is the price of appreciating the dancehall experience. For these fans, listening to the MC's speech must be a little like attending an immersion course in patois, to be suddenly placed in New York or Kingston, among Jamaicans, watching two Jamaican sounds perform. Part of the attraction of these events is entry into an unfamiliar space and then having to learn it, having to navigate this environment unlike anything immediately outside the club's doors. Dancehall culture in Japan is authentic for Japanese simply because it is intensely pleasurably felt; this pleasure is partly one of gaining knowledge about the Afro-Jamaican. Performative citation of this Afro-Jamaican authority, however, ultimately services the authority of Japaneseness, seen here as the ability to consume Afro-Jamaican difference.[12]

As noted above, for sound systems like Judgment and Mighty Crown, familiarity with the nuances of Jamaican subcultural expression, and the subtle sense of fraternity between sounds as they mobilize this knowledge in onstage competition, discreetly effects their authority as cultural guides. This fits well with Bourdieu's (1984) appreciation of the power of symbolic capital—including the power to reproduce itself—as significantly residing in its unstated nature. For Bourdieu, those who are subordinated within a given social order often do not recognize the subtle ways in which those who have power exercise it over them. At this point, it might be more productive to shift the analysis from what is, after all, for fans and even serious practitioners the playful, pleasurable spaces of the dancehall to the relationship between dancehall culture and the societies in which it is rooted. (The language of "subordination" and "exercise of power," while to some degree appropriate to the ritual antagonisms of the dancehall, especially in Jamaica, seems heavy-handed compared with what is at stake in the broader social spaces beyond the dancehall.) There, another kind of misrecognition—that is, a lack of recognition—of power is foregrounded. Although there is a rhetoric of national pride in much of Japanese dancehall, and although there is a general social pride in the international accomplishments of groups like Mighty Crown, these performers are by no means part of the Japanese musical or social mainstream, declining as they have to pursue conventional education and careers. Dancehall itself, furthermore, is looked down upon as vulgar by many Japanese outside the subculture. This is shown, for instance, in the skepticism with which many donnettes, who are the subject of the next chapter, are regarded by potential boyfriends.

The kinships between dancehall artists in their respective countries, and dancehall's circumscription as a subcultural space, help to marginalize these judgments. Dancehall as transnational performative field is informed by multiple politics, values, and motivations that inform and help validate the practices of artists in any given node within this field. Despite the comfortable returns to Japaneseness that performers' success in international dancehall has brought about, the assumption of hegemony sustained through misrecognition of its power is by no means a foregone conclusion. Failure to acknowledge power, rather than working to sustain that power (as Bourdieu argues), potentially announces its limits.

3

Fashion and Dance
PERFORMING GENDER IN JAPAN'S REGGAE DANCE SCENE

After January 2002, when I completed the dissertation that this book is based on, a number of major developments took place in the Japanese dancehall scene. One of these occurred not in Japan, but at Pier One, an open-air venue in Montego Bay, Jamaica. This was Junko Kudo's victory in the national dancehall queen competition later in 2002. Unfortunately, I missed that event (I did see it later on DVD), but I was able to attend the competition two years later. By that time, in part because of the large numbers of international performers—especially Japanese—recently attracted to the event, it was no longer a national competition, but the International Dancehall Queen Competition. (In 2006, Japanese represented the largest non-Jamaican contingent of contestants.)

The twenty-six entrants in 2004 were predominantly from Jamaica, but the United States, Trinidad, Canada, Sweden, and Japan were also represented. The event was organized into four rounds. In the first, each performer would dance for about 40 seconds, to the same riddim that all the other dancers performed to. In the second, the field would be reduced to fifteen dancers performing for a minute each. In the third round, the field would be reduced to ten dancers; then it would be down to five.

Warm applause—rather than the outright surprise that seems to have greeted Kudo when she performed in 2002—greeted Kiyo Akiba. Akiba appeared onstage wearing a red dress with a fringed hem. The crowd grew louder as she hopped about the stage, thrusting her hips forward as she landed on the beat, one arm before her in something like a salute. Akiba suddenly rushed to the enormous, red and black speakers on the elevated stage, which were about twelve feet high, twelve feet wide, and only a couple of feet deep. "Miss Japan, be careful now," a woman onstage, one of the hosts of the event, cautioned. Akiba executed a move called a headtop: a headstand, her calves and thighs at right angles to each other, hips rocking back and forth. The speakers shuddered dangerously with her effort. The crowd buzzed for a few seconds afterward; it was the best showing up to that point.

Latesha Brown, a slender, eighteen-year-old Jamaican woman, impressed the crowd through all the rounds with excellent choreography. The crowd exclaimed in surprise as Maude "Momo" Francato, a white Canadian dancer, appeared onstage: she was very thin (the Afro-Jamaican ideal tends toward a more full-figured look). But Francato turned the audience around with some very skilled, well-choreographed dancing, and made it to the final round.[1] Akiba made it to the final round as well, dressed in the latter stages of the competition in a white jacket and white batty riders (short shorts, also known as "Daisy Dukes") with the two characters that comprise her given name written graffiti-style, one on each cheek.

At the end of the final round, before the announcement of the winners, there was a performance by several former dancehall queens, including Junko Kudo. Her long blonde hair highlighted with purple streaks, she performed in a lemon-colored, midriff-length blouse and lime-green batty riders. The crowd cheered loudly when, near the end of her performance, she moved each cheek of her buttocks, one right after the other (always a crowd pleaser); with that, she waved, smiling, and left the stage.

Ayanna Armsby, of African descent (I am not sure of her nationality, but she is based in New York), was voted best-dressed dancer. Kiyo Akiba, the Japanese entrant, finished third in the competition, winning $30,000 in Jamaican dollars (around $500 in U.S. dollars). Francato, the thin Canadian, finished second, winning $50,000 Jamaican. Brown, the eighteen-year-old Jamaican, won both the prize for best dancing and the overall competition; as the International Dancehall Queen for 2004, she won $100,000 Jamaican (over $1,600 U.S.).

In this chapter, I explore the politics surrounding Japanese dancehall divas' performances, specifically through fashion and dance, within the performative field of Japanese-Jamaican encounters like the International Dancehall Queen Contest. I argue that this encounter is crucially framed by cross-culturally relative notions of gender and sexuality, race and class—not only in Japan, but in both countries. I consider the extent to which divas and female patrons can use dancehall to assert a political or moral stance inflected especially in these terms. In doing so, it is important to note that reggae dance has moved beyond the underground in Japan, establishing a mainstream presence increasingly divorced not only from its origins in Jamaica but also from its subcultural status as an art form by—and, to some degree, for—women, despite the explicit way it is structured in male attention. Especially in this mainstream space, donnette culture strongly works to reinforce commoditized objectification of female bodies. In this space, the culture of the donnette sustains a gendered economy in which it is she who is most marginalized. The non-progressive nature of this mainstreamed culture is reflected in the fact that few of these women ever had or ever will have hope of joining the upper levels of Japan's professional ranks. Both as a reflection and a consequence of their involvement in dancehall, few have real opportunities for corporate professional advancement—especially when they are past their mid-twenties, by which time they are usually expected to have quit their jobs to get married.

Some might see the mainstreaming of reggae dance as evidence that there is, in the end, no safe place beyond capitalism's constant strategic recuperation of popular tactics (de Certeau 1984). While I would not state the case so strongly, I do see as quite limited reggae dance's potential to meaningfully undermine in broad social terms Japan's patriarchal limitations on women's educational, employment, and other opportunities. Reggae dance is limited because it is so saturated in consumption, and because of its status in the mainstream as mere vulgar play. However, many dancers most steeped in the subcultural underground still see reggae dance as an autonomous space in which they are able to express their womanhood in positive ways. Despite its commercialization, reggae dance in this space potentially represents a lived metaphor permitting women to tactically, pleasurably deconstruct the ideological strategies (including patriarchal and classist ones) taking place all around them. In this way, dancehall—

just by being a complex, gender-specific pursuit that brings many women together in the same spaces, engaged in the same cultural practices—potentially becomes a bodily metaphor socializing them into felt understanding of such forms of social hegemony.

This sense of dancehall as enabling a degree of gendered agency is informed by Japanese dancers' imaginings of black women as powerful. In this way, in addition to affording insight into gender and class in Japan, the performative field of the Jamaican-Japanese donnette scene provides insight into political constructions of blackness in the global context. Coming to terms with these issues of gender, class, and race in both places, as understood and enacted in transnational dancehall, represents for me one meaningful way in which Japanese divas' expressions of desire for agency—specifically to become powerful women—might be realized. This is through recognition of how racial, classist, and gender-based political domination as commonly experienced by Jamaican and Japanese donnettes, in their respective societies, is part of broader, global structures of oppression to which these non-Western societies both belong.

In exploring these issues, I discuss gender in the Jamaican dancehall, including the issue of homophobia, and masculinity in the Japanese dancehall. I then discuss gender in modern Japan, including the largely male fear that women's expressions of sexual independence as asserted through foreign cultural forms has long invoked. I link this discussion to the case of the commoditization of reggae dance. I then explore the transnational experiences of Japanese donnettes, focusing on the duo Dear Chicks and Jamaica's 2002 National Dancehall Queen, Junko Kudo. I then analyze a dancehall queen competition that took place in 1999 in Tokyo, using this event as a means of exploring the issues of gender, race, and class in Japan that emerge from the Japanese-Jamaican encounter.

Gender and Sexuality in Jamaican Dancehall

Men are the main agents of musical production in Jamaican dancehall culture. There are very few women in the ranks of producers, promoters, and managers, and especially in the onstage realm of deejays and sound system members. These gendered attitudes are reflected in dancehall lyrics. The lyrics assert male agency—in urban Jamaica, often circumscribed by reduced socioeconomic opportunities and by political and other forms of violence—through the instrumental triad of the microphone, the pistol, and the phallus. The objects of these fetishized instruments are, respectively, rival DJs or those (including politicians) who have committed offenses against the innocent (such as poor ghetto youth); the "badman" or those envious of the DJ's success (often, again, rival DJs); and women.

How do these gender attitudes play out in performative terms? Dancehall music and lyrics valorize male heterosexuality in four key ways: materialism, violence, slackness, and homophobia. Male dancehall practitioners weave around themselves a constellation of material possessions that helps signify their desirability as heterosexual men. Especially given dancehall liaisons with hip-hop, men's assertions of their heterosexual worth increasingly involve the symbolic capital of the brand name. Rhetorical violence is a second critical performativity of male heterosexuality in the Jamaican dancehall. Dancehall reflects the intense competitiveness brought about by the island's economic difficulties (Cooper 1997; Hope 2006; Stanley-Niaah 2004; Stolzoff 2000). It is one of the few opportunities many poor, black, young Jamaican men see for socioeconomic advancement, and as such is a highly competitive field in which one makes a name for oneself through verbal and musical combat. "Slackness," discussed earlier, is the third key performativity of heterosexual masculinity in Jamaican dancehall. Outside the subculture, it gives credence to respectable Jamaicans' complaints about the vulgarity of dancehall. Within the subculture, however, it is turned on its head, becoming a sly male declarative directed toward attractive donnettes. As used within dancehall's borders, the term is perfectly performative. That is, it is not so much a call for or a reference to actual sexual engagement as it is an aural (re)citation, a reiterative invocation of the idea of female and, by extension, male heterosexuality at their normative limits. Slackness helps meet dancehall's heterosexualizing imperative: the need for heterosexuality, like any form of identification, to perpetually bring into being its own condition as moral-only choice, to effect the impossibility of anything else.

A fourth, notorious manifestation of the heterosexual masculinity of dancehall is its pronounced homophobia (Chin 1999; Glave 2000; Williams 2000). Gay men and women are routinely demeaned and threatened with violence in much of dancehall music. The controversy surrounding the homophobia heard in these songs reached a fever pitch in the early-1990s when a tune by Buju Banton, then a teenager, reached the ears of gay-rights activists in the United States. In "Boom Bye-Bye," like many dancehall songs before and since, Banton expresses his desire for gay people to be executed, in this case by being shot in the head. Banton has since apologized, but tunes in which homophobic content is prevalent continue to be popular among many Jamaican dancehall fans. Hostility toward homosexuality is felt not only among dancehall audiences but also throughout much of Jamaican society. Like consumerism, violence generally, and slackness, homophobia makes incessant rounds, patrolling the borders of the heterosexual normative. Dancehall's incantational gay bashing perfectly reflects the idea of performativity as reiteration ritually effecting what it names: the abjection of the homosexual—the ground against which normative heterosexuality negatively brings itself into being—and the moral-political always already-ness of the heterosexual subject. "Battyman fi bun," chanted ad nauseam in dancehalls, both creates and sustains a moral universe in which "homosexuals should burn."

Masculinity in Japanese Dancehall

To what extent are these performed heterosexualities present in Japanese dancehall? Because much of the effort to create an authentic Japanese dancehall revolves around achieving parity with its Jamaican counterpart, a good deal of the foregoing discussion applies here. Both types of dancehall share, for instance, the common use of certain phrases; the idiosyncratically harsh vocal quality of Jamaican DJs like Buju Banton adopted by Japanese counterparts; displays of male bonding intended to excite and sway the crowd; male greeting gestures, like the vertical tapping together of closed fists; and the approving shouts of "plow, plow, plow," hand raised, with index and middle fingers pointed (primarily a male gesture). Among the noticeable differences among men in Jamaican and Japanese dancehall is that dance for men in the former setting is somewhat more common and rehearsed, while in Japanese dancehall it seems more spontaneous. However, inspired by such Jamaican dancers as the legendary Bogle and Ice, both recently deceased, a male dance scene has emerged in Japan. A dancer named Ivan is among the most celebrated performers on this scene. A troupe of female Japanese dancers headed by Ivan finished second in the World Reggae Dance Championships, in an otherwise all-Jamaican field of seventeen competitors performing in Kingston on Emancipation Day, August 1, 2009. Although male dancehall fashion in both Jamaica and Japan is influenced by the materialism of hip-hop style, male fashion in Japanese dancehall revolves less around Kingston raggamuffins' resourceful eclecticism and more around a more upscale urban chic. And though the mike is present, the gun and the phallus—in a Japanese society with little violent crime, where openly indecorous behavior is frowned upon—are less heavily referenced.

DJ and MC orality both in Jamaican and Japanese dancehall is a sign of masculine agency. Men speak; women are spoken to, and of. In Jamaica, DJs and MCs empower themselves through oral affirmation of Jamaican culture, and in Japan through spoken knowledge of it. Male MCs and DJs in Jamaica use this subcultural orality to reaffirm values held by the audience, and themselves become empowered in this way. This affirmation, expressed through the creative, exciting linguistic and musical codes of dancehall, readily becomes ecstasy. The same of course is true in Japan, but there men are also empowered by their ability to verbally bridge the cultural gap between familiar Japan and exotic Jamaica. This too becomes ecstasy, an aspect of which, I argued in the last chapter, is coming to understand the ecstasy of the Afro-Jamaican. Dancehall patois is de facto male-dominated symbolic capital, through which this emotionally powerful knowing can take place.

Viewed through Japanese MCs' rendering of the classed roughness of Jamaican male dancehall speech (which also reflects the class backgrounds of many male Japanese dancehall practitioners), subcultural language in its gendered and socioeconomic aspects also subtly makes it hard to regard women as properly belonging to the ranks of sound system members and DJs. The Japanese language employs honorific or humble verb endings, terms of address, and other markers that either suggest or make explicit the gender (and, more broadly, the social status) of the speaker and the listener. It is somehow unseemly for Japanese women to use the unrefined Japanese of the Japanese dancehall (unless their performances depend on a kind of transgressive humor). The formal and otherwise gender-specific language that women are expected to use contrasts with the male (read as permissibly informal, low-class, or vulgar) speech of Japanese sound system and DJ culture. I doubt that male MCs and DJs in Japan think much about their power of voice within the subculture in gendered terms. Yet the fact that most DJs and sound system members are generally and have for so long been men, both in Jamaica and Japan, is not a coincidence.

Another comparison between the performance of masculinity in Jamaican and Japanese dancehall is the attitudes expressed toward homosexuality. The antigay voices of Jamaican dancehall echo loudly in its counterpart in Japan. Comedic intimations of male-male love abound in Japanese film, television, and manga; the male characters in manga for girls are often rendered with a languid gentility; and a transsexual kick boxer from the Philippines had become something of a celebrity during my stay in Japan.[2] However, none of these examples deal with homosexuality explicitly as political identity; in general, homosexuality is rarely discussed in the mainstream Japanese media. Compared with Jamaica or the United States, homosexuality seems to be more tolerated, so long as it remains private and does not interfere with the individual's social obligations (McLelland 2000). While heterosexual Japanese may express their discomfort with, or even contempt for, homosexuality with expressions like *"kimochi warui"* (disgusting), the advocacy of physical violence against gays is comparatively rare in Japan. McLelland notes that mainstream Japanese opinion about homosexuality is flexibly mobilized according to the diverse prerogatives of that mainstream: a gay man, for example, can represent a threat to family life, but can also be a woman's best friend.

Given this relative openness toward homosexuality in Japan, the vehemence of the expressions of homophobia in Japanese dancehall startled me. This was so despite understanding how Japanese MCs' and, to a lesser extent, DJs' (MCs run Jamaican tunes; DJs make their own) condemnation of homosexuality in some measure reflects the familiar strategy of authentication through mimesis. One Japanese DJ, Haiman, recorded a song called "Okama fe dead" (Gays Should Die), in which he condemned gays and transsexuals, "wherever, whenever," to death, as "hopeless," unbearable to look at, their sexuality "nasty" (*kitanai*). (Couched in comic terms, the vehemence of the antigay sentiment is supposedly diluted, making it culturally and morally more accessible to Japanese listeners. This is one in the fairly narrow group of gehin—vulgar—songs that explicitly refer to genitalia and sex acts.) The following is how one MC—wagging and thrusting his index finger at the audience as he spoke—introduced Banton's "Boom Bye-Bye":

> Yo! Hol' on! Yo!
> *Ore wa yo, reggae suki wa yo!*
> *Toku ni kirai na mono ga hitotsu aru yo na!*
> *Soitsu wa, homo, okama, lesbian, dōsei aisha!*
> So, all who no like battyboy,
> Hand up inna di air now!

Me, I really love reggae!
There is one thing I hate especially!
And that is: homos, transsexuals, lesbians, same-sex lovers!

This culturally transferred, performative hostility toward homosexuality can be partly explained by the fact that many of these DJs and MCs, raised in a society where heterosexuality is normative, feel genuine contempt toward homosexuality. This rhetorical hostility might also be seen as an instance of a point I made earlier: not only does this hostility valorize the machismo of Japanese DJs and MCs, but it is also a sign of straight Japanese male subcultural ability to represent the significance of antigay machismo among Jamaican dancehall artists. The "role perfectionist" extremes (De Vos 1973) of this mimesis disclose themselves in their poor fit with the relative openness to homosexuality in Japan. That is, what is most immediately at issue for these artists is getting dancehall right, including its (originally Jamaican) homophobic sentiment, even if homophobia is a more charged issue in Jamaica than it is in Japan. Being openly gay, or even being rumored to be gay, can literally be a life-threatening situation in Jamaica; that is much less likely to be the case in Japan.

My argument for the partial Jamaican provenance of Japanese dancehall homophobia should be taken only for what it is analytically worth, one dimension of the gendered differences between Jamaican and Japanese dancehall. That this homophobia, whatever its cross-cultural nuances, is "only" performed does not make it innocent and should not obscure its enmeshment in a transnational performative field significantly characterized by male heterosexism. It does not absolve Japanese artists of a homophobia that, in my opinion, is ultimately their own.

Female Sexuality and Consumption in Japan

The Japanese media—like so many other institutions in the country, dominated by men—have long questioned the fidelity to traditionally female roles in different generations of Japanese women. Part the products of the media, part social reality, the so-called modern girls were young urban women employed in large numbers for the first time during the 1920s. They were deeply enamored of an American culture of consumption rapidly emerging at the time: "The Modern Girl was . . . interested in shaping the materiality of everyday existence . . . Not 'just looking' . . . [this] commodified woman [was] a customer in a newly rationalized consumer culture" (Silverberg 1991, 243). Fueled by the economic boom after the Second World War, this gendered forging of selfhood through consumption continues to be a powerful force in Japanese society today. Increasing numbers of urban women are defying the expectation that before they turn twenty-five, they will surrender their jobs as office ladies or department-store clerks, or in various other low-skilled positions to become wives and mothers. Working later in life, they sometimes live with their parents into their late twenties and thirties, in part to continue supporting their expensive tastes (Skov and Moeran 1995).

Today, much as was the case for Silverberg's modern girls, the various consumable interests through which women articulate their identities as young, adventurous singles come from foreign culture. Given Western modernity's now familiar encroachments into Japanese life, there is little controversy today about the many single women and housewives, for example, who take English lessons to partake of the culture of the English-speaking West. However, when Japanese women's engagement with the West is suspected of being sexual in nature, they become subject to moral scrutiny. Beyond sexual possessiveness, this scrutiny might be part of a more general anxiety about the cultural and political autonomy of Japan—many of whose cultural traditions are appreciated in gendered terms—in the face of Western power.

Karen Kelsky and Nina Cornyetz have described the Japanese media's sensationalizing interest in contemporary Japanese women's sexual relationships with Western men, including African Americans. Kelsky (1994) argues that Japanese women use these men to ethnoracially foreground and thus valorize Japanese womanhood. Cornyetz (1996) takes issue with this, arguing that the fact that some Western men and Japanese women get married is a sign of the progressive potential, as opposed to the primarily exploitative nature, of these relationships. Cornyetz further emphasizes the difference in social power and symbolic association between white and black men in Japanese women's liaisons with each group. Instead of the foregone conclusion of an exploitative gendered nationalism, Cornyetz calls attention to the value for Japanese of what I described earlier as performative thirdness, of self-consciously creating racially hybrid selves that referencing blackness (such as through tanning and dreadlocking) helps produce. Even where this racial hybridization is merely playful, it potentially upsets a racial order in which the Japanese identify with a specifically white West and devalue blackness.

Cornyetz offers some important qualifications of Kelsky's argument, which are relevant to my discussion of the Japanese encounter with Jamaican culture. This encounter, perhaps in a trip to the Caribbean island, has indeed introduced many Japanese to the realities—violence and corruption, complex humanities, neocolonial and neoliberal gutting—behind the music they love. It has led, in several cases I know of personally, to Japanese-Jamaican marriages, relationships in which a primary intent of exploitation can less easily be assumed. Distinguishing between the white and black partners of Japanese women, rather than grouping them as Western men, is also crucial for acknowledging the political, social, subcultural, and other factors that might differentially inform these women's interest in these men. Making this distinction creates greater room to consider the specific ethnoracial politics involved in Japanese liaisons with black Jamaicans— not just Western, or even just black, men.

Still, I want to examine Kelsky's argument further. For her, those Japanese women who seek out Western men only playfully "reiterate themes of dualism and exploitation which are out of step with the transnational theories seeking to uncritically celebrate the carnivalesque, creativity, anarchy and liberation of desire to be found in an 'orderless' postmodern world . . . [This] creativity hinges for its effect upon exploiting the dualist and essentialistic racial/national constructs that these same theorists want to dismantle" (Kelsky 1994, 475). I agree that it is important to problematize what is for many observers—including Japanese and many Western aficionados of Japanese popular culture—the easy, entertaining spectacle of Japan's "taking the best and leaving the rest" from around the world. The issue becomes particularly significant when one acknowledges (as Cornyetz explicitly does) that it is not just the powerful West that is being consumed, but also subaltern esunikku peoples whose opinions about first-world takings and leavings of their cultural productions have been structurally silenced.[3]

As citizens of one of the world's most powerful countries, the women of Japan's reggae dance scene, generally speaking, have a relatively large amount of time for a range of leisure pursuits. Reggae dance as one of these pursuits neatly, as well as deeply facilitates these women's self-identifications as young urban consumers. Marginalized as many of them are in the male-dominated Japanese economy, they are relatively free of the obligation to start working long before and continue working long after regular business hours. Yet their income as office ladies or as small-business, part-time, and "free-time" workers are far from negligible to the Japanese economy (Skov and Moeran 1995), given their numbers and their frequent status as single, childless adults, living rent-free with their natal families. These women have relatively more leisure time and disposable income to go clubbing, to spend money on dancehall fashion, to purchase the various media and other products related to reggae dance, and to take extended trips to Jamaica. While these women may be at the greatest risk, given their status as less valuable workers, of losing their jobs during Japan's economic downturn, in a sense, they are relatively well adapted—compared to male corporate workers—to navigate this new economic terrain. Lack of financial independence—relative to the financial independence they would have, if they had the same opportunities as men—is not, for most Japanese women, something new; it is not, furthermore, something much expected of them as women, in contrast to men, who are expected to be breadwinners. My sense is that the significant place of women in the discourses of the search for self, reflected in the large number of women pursuing artistic careers in places like New York (Adachi 2005) and in the many writings on jibun sagashi that cater specifically to women (discussed in chapter 5), has to do in part with the recognition that women in some ways are in the best position to actively embark on the self-reevaluations that the long recession has inspired. I would also add that much of this applies not only to socioeconomically marginalized women, but also to socioeconomically marginalized men like the working-class DJs and sound system members (especially in the earliest days of the movement) discussed above. These men, too, off the educational and professional fast track, have been able to make alternative lifestyle choices like dancehall culture.

In the next section, I discuss how dancehall social politics as constituted in Jamaica became resituated not only in the Japanese subcultural underground, but also now in the commercial mainstream. While I frame this discussion broadly, I pay particular attention to reggae dance. Like the modern girls of an earlier day, Japan's reggae dancers immerse themselves in a foreign culture, which subjects them to a moralizing scrutiny that doubles as desire for these women. Reggae dancers, however, immerse themselves in a third-world (albeit urbane), unapologetically erotic Afro-Jamaican culture, an immersion which—along with the responses to it—helps disclose the workings of gendered, class-based, national, and racial imaginings in contemporary Japan. In this way, I provide a mainstream context for my later discussion, more deeply situated in the subculture, of the lives and subversive potential of Japan's reggae dancers.

Media, Gender, and the Commodification of Reggae Dance

Dancehall during the initial period of my research had a small but solid presence in Japanese mass media. Free dancehall papers like *Riddim, Yokohama Reggae Times*, and *Strive* published articles and advertisements concerning local and Jamaican artists performing in Japan, upcoming club events, discounted flights to and accommodations in Jamaica, new albums, specialty reggae shops, and the like. The shops themselves are important sources of information about the dancehall scene (as well as the roots and dub scenes) in Japan. These shops, as well as some of the larger stores, offer fliers about events, back issues of *Reggae Magazine* (something of a collector's item), and books on such topics as reggae, Rasta, and marijuana. Videotapes of Jamaican movies like *The Harder They Come, Rockers, Countryman*, and *Dancehall Queen* can also be found there, as well as taped performances by major Jamaican artists as well as recent CDs of Japanese reggae events.

With the growth of dancehall has come a surge of entrepreneurial and commercial interest in the subculture, much like the one that occasioned the rise of roots reggae in the mid-1980s. Indicating a general progression from subculture to becoming part of the mainstream (a progression that might be roughly measured in terms of production cost), dancehall media now include websites, magazines, DVDs, music videos, and television programs.

WEBSITES

In the early days of the roots reggae boom, a number of Internet sites emerged, most of which were small operations, often run by individual fans. Jah Itagaki's Reggae Life website has been up almost since the popular advent of the Internet. The website has been a source of information on the reggae scene in general, including reggae-related news and events in Japan and Jamaica. As a measure of the growing popularity of reggae in Japan, this once-modest site now features advertisements from amazon.co.jp, Apple, Nike, and other major corporate players.

Another long-lasting website is Dancehall Sista's World. This site is part of a larger one run by a group called Ruff-Cut International, based in Kanagawa. Ruff-Cut was one of the businesses that emerged in the early 1990s as part of the roots reggae boom: its owners sold merchandise such as reggae CDs, DVDs, sweatshirts, T-shirts, jewelry, stickers, and incense. Its Internet presence remains largely centered on this commercial effort. Dancehall Sista's World, however, has been a major source of information on the reggae dance scene since its earliest days in the mid-1990s. The extensive website has archived photographs and articles about several years of the Dancehall Queen Japan competition in Tokyo, as well as about dancehall news and major reggae events in Japan and around the world.

MAGAZINES

In the mid-2000s, with the upsurge of interest in dancehall, *Rove*, a new reggae magazine, appeared on the scene. This magazine appears to be positioning itself to become the primary mainstream source of information about reggae music in the country, much as *Reggae Magazine* did during the first boom. As noted earlier, there are a number of other reggae magazines on the market, including Overheat's *Riddim* and *Strive*, free papers that have been an important part of the reggae scene for years. The emergence of *Rove*, however, seems to be directly in response to the recent popularization of reggae culture in Japan; the first seven of their thirteen issues to date are currently sold out. The other reggae magazines incorporate some articles on roots reggae but appear to be more focused on dancehall, given their deep historical roots in this particular aspect of Jamaican musical culture. *Rove*, perhaps because it is more of a mainstream magazine, seems willing to draw on a deeper fund of Jamaican music. It includes articles on Japanese and international dancehall, as well as on roots and dub music artists; events; fashion photo spreads; record reviews; record shop, restaurant, and club ads; and so on. *Rove*'s musical cultural depth provides the obvious benefit of broadening the potential readership to the older generation of reggae fans, and of providing more topics to write about each month. In addition to *Rove*, a number of major urban music, dance, and fashion magazines—including *Warp, Eyes Cream, Dance Style, Woofin', Juicy,* and *Luire*—between 2004 and 2006 alone ran special issues on dancehall in Japan and Jamaica. Drawing on her contacts in the Jamaican reggae scene, the music journalist Minako Ikeshiro published a "music book"—part book, part music magazine—called *Di Reggae Book* (2006) on the Jamaican reggae scene.[4]

Another new, major player on the reggae dance scene is One and G. This company's website has a registry of about 250 "All Japanese Reggae Dancers" who perform individually, as part of a pair, or as a group, offering brief profiles of each. One and G is clearly trying to brand the reggae dance phenomenon in Japan. In addition to a line of bags, shoes, and lingerie, One and G also has an affiliation with Playboy, through which it sells a line of the latter's accessories (earrings in the shape of the Playboy logo, for instance).

One and G has become something of a cottage industry centered around reggae dance. The company has produced approximately thirty reggae dance DVDs that are widely distributed through, for example, Amazon.co.jp and Tower Records. One set of videos spotlights some of the more accomplished dancers. Several of the videos are instructional. About eleven are of various stops on a 2005 One and G nationwide reggae dance tour, which went to Hokkaido, Fukushima, Hiroshima, Kyoto, Tokyo, and elsewhere.

As noted before, Sister Kaya was one of a few female roots reggae singers when this genre was most popular in Japan. Her production company, Sistren, has been involved in a number of projects focused on women in the reggae scene (Ohba 2000). In addition to producing all-female reggae events and an album of female roots reggae and rhythm and blues singers, she has also jumped on the bandwagon of reggae dance. One of her productions is the salaciously titled *X-Rated Japanese Reggae Dancers*. This video is worth some attention here, as the featured dancers speak about their involvement in reggae dance, as well as some of the hurdles they have had to face because of that involvement. (The names of Japan's reggae dancers, including those featured in the video—Naked Crew, Hard Core J, Love Milk, Mata Doll, Bashment, Earl Grey, Gran-Dee, and Ananasi—are also often salacious. This effect is emphasized by the sexual otherness that the foreign can so routinely connote in Japan, in this case the use of English names. At the same time, curiously, the impact of a sexually explicit name like Love Milk is slightly offset by being in another language. Other names, like

Bashment and Ananasi, are less sexually explicit and reference the Afro-Jamaican—in this case, respectively, the dancehall term for party and the infamous folktale trickster.)

In the video, each dancer responds to a series of questions, posed to all the dancers and appearing in patois on the screen. One question is: "Wat is dance fi you?" The responses include "*seikatsu*" (everyday lifestyle), a reflection of the all-consuming nature of reggae dance. Another question is: "Wa mek yu tun [turn or become] a reggae dancer?" Some women reported seeing Jamaican dance videos and becoming interested in this way; one woman said she had been familiar with hip-hop only, saw reggae dance, went into "culture shock," and decided she wanted to try it. A third question is: "Yu ever have trouble becoming a reggae dancer?" One group of women spoke about the circulation of "strange rumors" (*hen na uwasa*) about them. This is something I have also heard in my interviews. I chose not to ask about the details of these rumors, but the women appear to feel that the rumors are circulated by dancers jealous of their success. Other women talked about their limited time for sleep, given their pursuit of both work and dance. One dancer spoke about the various aches and injuries (*karada no koshō*) that come with dancing. She also laughingly described as most bothersome, as did several other dancers, the negative way in which reggae dancers have been unfavorably judged—for instance, by their boyfriends—because of the perceived impropriety (*tōhi*) of some of these "dirty" (*kitanai*) dance moves. A fourth question is: "Wa yu want fi do in di future as a reggae dancer?" Some women said that they simply wished to continue dancing and improving as long as they physically could, despite the disapproval of their loved ones. One dancer said she wished to continue simply because it was a profound expression of who she was as a person.

A common response to several of these questions reflected the women's belief that reggae dance perfectly captured the appeal, the heart of what it is to be a woman. The women described reggae dance as a great means of showcasing the beauty of a woman's body. They also consistently described it as a way of becoming empowered: the English word "power" was often used. One dancer said enigmatically that she wanted to start a revolution (*kakumei o okosu*) through reggae dance. In the quick-question, quick-answer format of the documentary interview, there was no further elaboration of this reply. Nevertheless, the women's belief that reggae dance gives them a way to express a sense of empowered womanhood appears key to the appeal of reggae dance in Japan, and it resonates with what some of my own interviewees had to say (which I will discuss further below). It also fits with the theme of toughness that recurs in fiction and nonfiction writing on Japanese travel to Jamaica, discussed in chapter 5.

As noted above, many of the women occupy what might be considered marginal, gender-specific positions in the urban Japanese economy: clerks in small specialty stores selling women's clothing and accessories, hairdressers, beauticians, dressmakers, and so on. The desire to become powerful women may be understood in terms of this marginalization. But none of the women linked the issue of power to their occupational status. In fact, I do not think that the women necessarily see themselves as marginalized because of their jobs; indeed, some happily chose to do this work. These occupations are close to, and even facilitate their interests in, the fashion side of reggae dance. Instead, the desire to become powerful women has more to do with the mastery of a very difficult set of subcultural practices that are specific to women, and from which men are excluded. Another dimension of this desire to become powerful women is the fact that reggae dance is specific not only to women, but to Jamaican women, whose strength some Japanese reggae dancers appear to view in specifically racial terms (I will discuss this point below).

Outside of the realm of dancehall cultural production to which Sister Kaya's video belongs, one recent, startling, but perhaps inevitable development in the mainstreaming of reggae dance in Japan is the use by several pornography companies of reggae dance's popularity to sell their products. One company, in addition to its regular offerings, has produced a line of at least eleven sex DVDs with reggae dance themes. The covers of some of these DVDs, which cost between 2,000 and 3,500 yen (between $18 and $32), proclaim that the acrobatic actresses featured are "real reggae dancers" (*honmono regee dansaa*) who are able to offer "excellent shake hip" to their sexual partners and viewers. Although proclaiming the appearance of reggae dancers specifically, one film is ambiguously titled *Black Dance*; subcultural nuance here is stripped away, replaced by an elemental imagination of the Afro-Jamaican dancehall as blackness, dance, and sex, with the Japanese women who embrace it as erotic creatures apart. Films such as these require no real knowledge of reggae dance on the part of the dancers, their onscreen sexual partners, or the men consuming the films. What are left are outfits in the color of the Jamaican flag, or in Rasta colors—and soon enough, not even that. The films are one source of the anxieties that reggae dance purists like those described above have about participating in a subculture that, while appealing intensely to their desire to become powerful women, also leads to the presumption among many that they are sexually available—as so much domestic and international discourse on Japanese women imagines them to be—in ways that they are actually not.

MUSIC VIDEOS

As dancehall has become increasingly mainstream, a number of artists have released albums with major record companies. For example, Papa Bon (whose career, happily, has taken off substantially since our interview) and Fireball have albums with Toshiba EMI; Ryo the Skywalker, Pang, and Mega-ryu with Avex Entertainment; Mighty Jam Rock and Minmi with Victor Entertainment; and Pushim with Sony. Far different from underground dancehall up to the late 1990s, music videos with high production value are now part of an increasingly corporatized Japanese dancehall. The range of visual styles, cross-cultural references, and ideology expressed are, unsurprisingly, extremely broad, even within the *oeuvre* of a single artist. Some are in the mold of the reggae artist as club player, surrounded by dancehall divas; others depict the artist sauntering moodily through the streets of Tokyo; and many are basically onstage performances featuring the artists in multiple costumes.

Given this breadth, I will focus on one video. If Munehiro's video (described in chapter 2) performatively naturalizes reggae as always already Japanese, Hibikilla's "Will" reflects a different strategy for the authentication of Japanese reggae in relation to Jamaica. "Will" opens with a broadcast on Irie FM (a Jamaican radio station) in which the announcer introduces listeners to a song he is about to air, by "the Japanese reggae entertainer, Hibikilla." The video depicts Hibikilla arriving at the Norman Manley International Airport in Kingston, casually dressed in jeans, a black T-shirt, and white baseball cap. Jamaican men confront him there, their expressions and gestures cajoling, presumably because he is a rich Japanese. These images are linked to the song's title, which conveys a message of survival, of overcoming: "Where there is a will," Hibikilla intones in English, "there is a way." Hibikilla is seen pulling his small luggage carrier through various scenes of Kingstonian life, and later performing in the countryside; Jamaican people in scenic settings are depicted in various postures of slow-motion repose. Filming the video in Jamaica foregrounds the island as the home of reggae music; Hibikilla's presence there authenticates his status as a dancehall artist in Japan. Being played on Jamaican radio, being appreciated by Jamaican listeners makes clear that this is real reggae music.

Perhaps the most nationally visible sign of the current vogue of dancehall in Japan is TV-Tokyo's television show *Ryūha-R*. The program, on the air since 2001, explores urban Japanese culture—including music, fashion, and dance—with dancehall reggae and hip-hop dominating. The fusion of the two genres, like the easy blend of dancehall and roots reggae in *Rove*, also speaks to the recognition that each of these musical scenes becomes more commercially viable linked to the other. As Americana, and more specifi-cally as African Americana, hip-hop remains a major popular-cultural phe-nomenon in Japan, and in some measure the mainstream (as opposed to subcultural) rise of dancehall has benefited from hip-hop's popularity (while I attribute this rise primarily to Mighty Crown's and Kudo's successes overseas, dancehall-to-hip-hop crossover artists such as Shaggy and Sean Paul have also played a role). Similarly, a mature hip-hop culture in Japan, the United States, and elsewhere has drawn upon the perceived rawness and difference of dancehall as a vitalizing force. With this mixture of elements, but with dancehall treated as a distinct subcultural phenomenon in its own right, *Ryūha-R*'s content is much like that of many of the magazines dis-cussed above. Japanese dancehall musicians like Miki Dōzan, Moomin, Pang, Megaryu, Boy Ken, and Hibikilla, and reggae dancers like Dolce Vita, Love Milk, and Junko Kudo have all appeared on the program.

Performing Femininity in Japanese Dancehall

The mainstreaming of dancehall reggae, then, has taken place in a number of terms. Key among these is its provision of a space for increasing numbers of young women to express a sense of gendered autonomy as well as to play. The victories of Japanese dancehall artists in international competition and dancehall's associations with the earthiness, naturalism, and spirit of over-coming of roots reggae are used to convey messages of national pride and renewal perhaps presumed to have a ready audience in recessionary Japan. Compared with other elements of Japanese reggae culture, reggae dance has very quickly entered the mainstream. This is so because it meshes well with ideologies and commercial strategies already in place in Japan, includ-ing those surrounding the objectification of women's bodies. One and G's links with Playboy, and the uses to which pornography companies have put reggae dance, illustrate this point.

Despite these commercializations, however, dancehall continues to be primarily an underground movement. It is not just a commercial phenomenon made by record executives, television producers, fashion-magazine editors, and music-video producers. As Condry (2006) notes for hip-hop, and as is true of dancehall in Jamaica, Japanese dancehall emerged—and continues to draw its vitality—from the interpersonally realized creativity of artists and fans. Moving away from the commercialization of reggae in recent years, I want to return, so to speak, to this underground. I will briefly discuss the sound systems, DJs, and singers as well as fans who are among the key players in this scene. I focus on women, exploring the subcultural and social politics that inform how these women perform, including as women, in dancehall culture.

Female Dancehall Artists

Because there are so few female sound systems, it is hard to generalize their members' attitudes toward some of the issues that preoccupy their male peers, such as homosexuality. However, at one event showcasing female talent in Japanese dancehall, the MC of an all-female sound system introduced an antigay Jamaican tune in a way reflecting the attitudes commonly expressed by the men. She said in Japanese that the next song was about "battyman," explained to her audience what the expression meant, then dismissed homosexuals in patois at the end of the introduction: "Guweh!" (Go away!). Chinatsu, a female MC who operates her sound system, Time Machine, alone, said that although she thought herself unusual in the sense that she was one of very few female Japanese MCs, and although a couple of male dancehall performers expressed disapproval of her as a female MC, she did not believe that her subcultural position and approach to the music as a woman was significantly different from those of the men. (I have not heard her make any mention of homosexuality in her performances; her Japanese, while energetic when she is before the mike, does not take on the roughness of the male artists.)

Among the well-known but comparatively few female DJs are Lady Q, Sister Mami, and Machaco. In general, female DJs' songs tend to revolve around topics not far different from those of the men, but romantic songs; songs about nature, unity, peace, and love; and comic songs (like those of

Lady Q) appear more consistently. I have never heard an antigay tune by a female Japanese DJ—such tunes are rare even among male Japanese DJs, as in general are songs dealing directly with sexuality. The unforgiving evaluations of male sexual endowments and performance by some female Jamaican dancehall DJs, similar to male Jamaican DJs' evaluations of women, is currently absent in Japan, especially since such explicit descriptions of Japanese women appear only rarely in tunes by male Japanese DJs.

Among female Japanese singers are Pushim, Kaana, Munehiro, and Minmi. As noted above, the roots singer Sister Kaya has initiated a number of projects promoting women involved in all aspects of the Japanese reggae spectrum. Reflecting the rift between dancehall and roots in Japan, one roots fan confided to me her belief that Sister Kaya, who has long been identified with roots reggae, was "confused" on account of her involvement in dancehall, perceived as a far cry from the naturalism and spirituality of roots reggae and Rastafari.

Fandom

Fandom is a slippery notion in dancehall culture. It usually implies some degree of separation between those who are artists and those who consume artistic production. When artists make it big, they often become part of an organizational structure of managers, assistants, and so forth who regulate public access to them, given their status as icons and money-making resources whose presence and time must be managed carefully. Fandom as a concept is analytically useful for me because it foregrounds what talents, skills, or knowledge are defined as valuable; because it affords insight into relations of social power, in which some have access to the resources to develop talent whereas others do not; and because often the artist iconically represents the aspirations of the fan, or something the fan (as a social being) deeply values. Many female fans of Takarazuka idolize the female actors who play the leading male role (otokoyaku) as women who achieve, on and in some cases off stage, a sense of independence that is conventionally considered the province of men (Robertson 1998).

With regard to such values in the context of my own research, I have already discussed MCs' representing to their fans the exotic difference of the Jamaican, a difference which gains its meaning in part from its situation in a Japan that still largely imagines itself as closed and homogeneous.

I have discussed the idolization of Nahki's enigmatic ("alien") presence as unlike that of other Japanese artists, one which resonates with a broader ethos of hybridized self-making in Japan. Fandom in Japanese reggae culture might be thought of in generational, regional, national, and cyber-spatial terms. It takes place within a shift from a generally older roots to a younger dancehall reggae scene, with all the associated tensions. The social analytic value of fandom emerges in regional terms on considering how the decisions of some roots reggae fans to move from the city to the countryside is informed by a naturalist appreciation of the Japanese rural that is both subcultural and, more broadly, romantically modern.

In the Japanese Reggae community of Mixi, a social networking site, fans' discussions of their favorite Japanese artists show how full-fledged and independent this "japarege" scene has become. The discussions are striking for the broad range of dancehall performance styles that are nationally represented, invoking fan appreciation in a wide range of terms: H-Man's deftly funny lyrics, the muddy quality of Rude Boy Face's voice, Papa Bon's complex rhyme schemes and rapid-fire delivery. These fans make very little reference, even in passing or by way of comparison, to the Jamaican scene, except for the very occasional comment that Elephant Man or TOK is someone's favorite "artist over there" (mukō no aatisuto). Given the vitality of Japan's reggae scene, the Jamaican market, according to the members of some Jamaican-based Japanese sound systems, is increasingly viewed as separate and is increasingly becoming marginal for many of the youngest Japanese dancehall fans who have only known japarege.

But what I want to address here is how the conventional line between artists and fans is not clear-cut in dancehall, as compared with many other subcultures. In a sense, the main way to be a fan of dancehall culture, beyond attending events, is by reading about reggae musical culture, buying a lot of music, or even purchasing the equipment needed to start a sound system. Many of the serious fans of dancehall reggae do all of these things as a matter of course; indeed, a couple of fans in Mixi's Japanese Reggae community jokingly described themselves as operating sound systems, except that they do so without audiences, alone in their homes. It takes only a few more steps to venture onto the stage as an artist. This is very different from the Takarazuka performers Robertson describes, who have to train from a young age at a very selective school. This thin line between being artists and being fans in reggae culture also helps explain the great growth in the number of Japanese sound systems in Japan. Therefore, much of what I have said about dancehall practitioners also applies to the fans, including both their valuation of the Jamaican as an instructive counterpoint to the restrictively Japanese and the sense of pride in J-reggae as a sign of Japanese international accomplishment.

This participatory egalitarianism largely derives from dancehall reggae's status as a product of the Afro-Jamaican popular (and is arguably rooted more deeply in the same ethos found in other forms of African diasporic musical performance). Dancehall culture at its most essential is really pretty essential: a couple of people play records and hundreds dance. Part of the reason for the recent rise in the popularity of reggae dance in Japan is that participation fundamentally requires very little. More than the audio equipment that is a key technological sign of dancehall's gendered separations, the body, ultimately, is the primary resource employed in this subculture. Much of the appeal, as discussed above, of dancehall reggae for Japanese women is that it calls for a new vision of their bodies, what they are capable of, what they are permitted to do, of who is beautiful. I have attended events in which fuller-bodied Japanese women dance onstage with an abandon not seen elsewhere in Japan. This perhaps problematically references the Mammy-esque idea of Jamaican women as always fuller figured; reggae dance, furthermore, as discussed above, readily belongs to the mainstream objectification of women's bodies. Still, in its primary aspect as subculture, reggae dance fosters an appreciation of a woman's worth not so much according to the ideals of feminine beauty found in the mass media and in commerce, but according to what the woman can do. The vast majority of dancers labor unknown in the subcultural underground, without much hope or desire of someday being discovered by those forces that police the line between fandom and genuine artistry. Part of the subversive potential in reggae dance, then, inheres in the women's recognition of dancehall as a site in which to achieve the pleasure of the gendered body performing beyond its limits, unaffected in these moments by the opinions of men, corporate Japan, or anything else.

Transnational Dancehall Sisterhood

However, one measure of commitment to the reggae dance scene is travel to Jamaica. In many ways, the Jamaican women whom Japanese dancers encounter there are seen as ultimate embodiments of empowered womanhood, one that significantly motivates Japanese participation in the subculture. But despite this respect, given the cultural, geographic, and economic gap between Japan and Jamaica, Japanese women must imagine the encounter in ways that manage these differences. I illustrate this situation by focusing on three reggae dancers: Saori and Kana of Dear Chicks, and Junko "Bashment" Kudo.

DEAR CHICKS

Despite the 250 women on One and G's registry, not many of the women who are part of Japan's reggae dance scene perform professionally. Those who do earn only small amounts of money each night they dance, and tend to characterize their dancing as a hobby. Reggae dancers generally appear during major rub-a-dub events. There is an annual Japanese Dancehall Queen Japan competition, as well as a bevy of more recent events, including One and G's tour.

Dear Chicks is one of the dancehall duos that performed regularly during the first two years of my research. I first met them with a female colleague in 1999 at a noisy, upscale, Asian fusion restaurant in Shibuya. Dear Chicks is comprised of two women, Kana and Saori, who were then both in their early twenties. When I asked how they chose their duo's name, they explained that they looked in the English dictionary for a word that had a positive, feminine quality, and came up with "dear." They looked for another word meaning "women" and liked "chicks." Saori said she learned about dancehall watching videos. She had prior dance experience, and had been dancing for a longer time than her partner. While she wanted to make a living from her dancing, Kana, who was then working part time at a hostess club, said she was thinking about taking a break from dancing for a year or so. Dancing was physically demanding, she explained, and she did not want to lose the pleasure she gained from it. She did not care so much about succeeding professionally but only wanted to dance for fun.

At one point in the conversation, my colleague, Kana, and Saori got to chatting among themselves. The conversation turned to the Jamaican movie *Dancehall Queen*, which many Japanese reggae dancers say first got them interested in reggae dancing. Kana said that there were parts of the film she did not fully understand, since she was not very familiar with patois. When I explained that the female protagonist used her secret identity as vampish donnette to pit the film's two male villains against each other, her face lit up in understanding and approval. "*Sugoi!*" she exclaimed. "*Okaasan tsuyoi!*" (Wow! Strong mother!). This perception of the strength

of Jamaican women is perhaps one aspect of Japanese women's identification with dancehall culture.

About a year after I first met them, Dear Chicks appeared in the first
edition of *Strive*, in a column called Powder Room Talk (Soma 2001). The
author is Emi, of Emerald Emiland, a clothing company which makes customized outfits for dancehall dancers. She writes: "To everyone who's read
up to this point! This magazine really reeks of men, so right around here I
showed up thinking I should try to perfume things up a bit" (Soma 2001,
36). She says she will interview Dear Chicks to get their impressions about
the state of dancehall fashion in Jamaica. Saori and Kana describe their
disappointment about the few major dances during their recent first stay in
Jamaica. However, things did not turn out too badly, because they were able
to meet Buju Banton and acquire a dub plate from him. Speaking presumably of the studio where the dub plate was recorded, Saori says, "I thought I
had to go with the vibes, and right there I took my shoes off and danced. I
can't come up with the words for that day . . . It was so moving, so exciting!"

Soma asks: "To wrap up, have your feelings as a dancer changed, or have
you come to feel that there's something you'd really like to do next?" Kana
responds: "The next time I go to Jamaica I want to perform in a show. Not
doing things according to standard: I want to dance in a way that expresses
my own enjoyment. Exciting the fans, getting them into it, everyone having
a good time. I really want to do it." Saori agrees. Soma mentions her own
experience in Jamaica:

> When I went to Jamaica, in the glitter period, when I went to the bath-
> room at indoor dances, I met a lot of sisters [*oneesantachi*] who were
> dressed in these colorful outfits, lined up before the glass, fixing their
> makeup . . . We exchanged makeup, praised each other's outfits, turned
> the powder room into a place for communication [*komyunikeeshon*]. I
> really liked going there. (Ibid.)

She observes that although the fashion of Jamaican dancehall continues to
be outlandish, simplicity and casualness are the new trends. The article
closes with a question to the reader: "What are you wearing to the dance
tonight?"

In describing their interactions with Jamaican women, Kana, Saori, and
Soma perform belonging within an international community of dancehall-
minded women. Soma's use of the term "oneesantachi" mobilizes a metaphor of sororal affinity; her use of the common English loan word "kom-

yunikeeshon" to describe her powder-room interactions with Jamaican women lends this endeavor an internationalizing flavor. It fits smoothly with kokusaika in its aspect as easy global exchange. If *Strive*'s Powder Room Talk is a written, remote performance of this gendered kinship, the Jamaican powder room itself becomes a proximal node in the transnational performative field of a gender-exclusive dancehall sub-community.

However, an analysis of the practices through which the powder room becomes the space of an encounter between Jamaican and Japanese women involves more than gender. With the notion of performative field, I want to invoke a broader, more complex politics that also potentially includes, for example, race, class, and ethnicity. The three women place themselves within a space understood until then primarily as a site of creative exchange between black Jamaican women, many of whom are poor. While the three women can comfortably discuss their presence there in gendered terms, it is politically more difficult to do so according to race, ethnicity, and economics. Jamaican women may indeed see the Japanese presence in the powder room in terms of a genuine sisterhood. They might also see it, however, as a sign of tourist and other consumptions from which poor, Afro-Jamaican women are generally excluded. This reality is difficult to represent in the breezy spaces of *Strive*'s powder room, in which good feelings between people (not a bad thing in itself) marginalize a heavier politics.

JUNKO KUDO

A few days after the 2004 International Dancehall Queen Competition, I visited Junko Kudo, Jamaica's National Dancehall Queen for 2002, at the residential complex in Kingston where she was staying. When I met Kudo, dressed that day in pastel colors, several things struck me. Although she spoke to me mostly in English, she sometimes used Japanese, as well as in patois, especially when imitating Jamaican conversation. In doing so, particularly in replicating the speech of Jamaican women, her voice assumes a playfully shrill tone. Her English has some interesting elements of patois to it. The "au" in her "because" sounds like the "a" in "car." "Can't" becomes "cyaa'"; and she uses terms like "rey rey rey," a Jamaican neologism meaning something like "and so on" or "whatever." Also, she is a terrific storyteller, wide-eyed and physically engaged in her re-enactments. As the interview progressed, I was impressed by the respectful honesty with which she spoke about some of the sensitive political issues mentioned just above, issues she generally raised without prompting on my part.

Kudo grew up in rural Aomori, in northern Japan. She became interested in dancehall as a student in junior high school. When she was thirteen, a popular musician, Kubota Toshinobu, released a song with a beat she liked very much; she later discovered that it was a reggae beat. Another early encounter with reggae came when she went to a festival where reggae and hip-hop were played. There was a man onstage, she said, who danced the entire day, and she was impressed not only by his energy, but also the reggae music he danced to.

Kudo decided not to attend college. She liked making things with her hands, and she decided to study how to make orthodontic devices. She did this work after finishing high school, and though the work was fine, she felt bored doing the same thing all day long. She did some research and, with a look of relived apprehension, described her surprise at discovering that people in her line of work tended to die soon. Then almost twenty years old, she moved to Tokyo to study hairstyling, another of her passions. She looked for a job in upscale Aoyama. In this trendy area to which many young women with her training flock, such work was difficult to come by. Luckily, though, she did find a job, so she was happy. She would work hard in the days, she said, and at night she would go to reggae clubs like Garan and Open in Shinjuku and Club Jamaica in Minato-ku. Even at this time, late in the roots reggae boom, she was not really thinking about dancing; she was still just listening to the music. Among all the clubs she visited, she described Shinkūkan, a club (since closed) near her salon in Aoyama, as having an especially great vibe for dancing. She went there every weekend, even when she was sick. It was this club, she said, that made her a dancer.

Kudo described first seeing reggae dancers in Japan, such as those performing on reggae nights in the Tokyo club Harlem, in the late 1990s. Despite her growing interest in reggae dance, she was startled when she first saw these women in their skimpy outfits. She described them as appearing "uncomfortable" (in a social sense, I imagine).

FIRST TRIP TO JAMAICA

Although she had never done reggae dancing onstage, Kudo's growing interest in this dance led her to travel to Jamaica in December 2000. In the familiar story of Japanese seeking to prove their mettle at the artistic source, she said she wanted to know "if my dance is okay in Jamaica or if I misunderstand reggae dance." Perhaps reflecting the Japanese tradition of artistic learning through apprenticeship to a master,[5] Kudo sought out Stacy, one of Jamaica's most acclaimed dancehall queens. She was not able to meet her on this trip, but decided to test her ability by going to a dance in Tivoli Gardens. Tivoli Gardens is widely considered one of the most dangerous neighborhoods in a country with one of the highest per capita murder rates in the world. Kudo said that her friends emphatically advised her against it, and that although she was afraid, she wanted "to listen [to the] real voice of Jamaican people." Upon seeing her about to perform, Kudo said, the Tivoli residents were skeptical about "Ms. Chin's" dancing ability, but they were shocked and greatly impressed when she showed them her moves. The next day, people she did not know, people who had not even been to the event, began approaching her and talking to her; word had spread.

2001–2: BASHMENT CREW

Returning home after this trip, Kudo started dancing professionally in Japan. She partnered with Satono to create Bashment Crew. Bashment Crew performed in the 2000 Japanese Dancehall Queen competition (won by Earl Grey; the 1999 event is described below). Kudo got a lot of work (though only a little money) in part, she said, because of her ability to incorporate some difficult moves that very few Japanese dancers, if any, were able to execute. She performed across Japan—in Tokyo, Nagoya, and Osaka—laughingly comparing the people of Osaka, where dancehall is presently very popular, with garrulous, expressive Jamaicans. Despite the image of girlfriendship that is projected in onstage performance in Japan, Kudo is frankly competitive. "We have badder style than them," Kudo said of Bashment Crew's rivals. "That's why they get jealous."

Kudo said that more than the athletic aspects of her dancing, she is most concerned with imagination: "Lay down, listen to reggae music, imagine . . . I imagine all the time." Other dancers, she said, started doing the headtop once they saw her doing it. As the scene in Japan continued to grow during this period, more and more crowds and more and more dancers began to appear. However, just as Bashment Crew had become very popular, Satono was injured, so Kudo decided to go solo. With this, she said, she felt she needed to mature even more as a performer.

After some deliberation and delays, she decided that she would perform in Jamaica's 2002 dancehall queen competition. She said that she was very

Junko Kudo. Photo by Nobu (ᴀᴠɢᴠsᴛ) / Rove.

nervous, concerned that if she did not do well, it would harm her reputation in Japan. She was also concerned about many Jamaicans' assumptions about who was or was not able to dance well. "Every Jamaican person say winey-winey thing [gyrating hips], dancehall queen thing is original Jamaica and ghetto, is not uptown," Kudo said. "Ghetto. Ghetto girl have real wine. No foreigner can do like . . . Jamaican people, everybody think. 2002, everybody surprised."

DANCEHALL QUEEN 2002

The sponsors of the Dancehall Queen Competition charter a bus to pick up competitors wherever they live in Jamaica, transporting them to Montego Bay. Like the powder room in Soma's narrative, this bus in Kudo's narrative represents a critical space of her encounter as a Japanese woman with Afro-Jamaicans. Kudo, again, was forthright, this time about the ethnic and racial frictions between her and the other women being transported to the competition:

When I went in bus, people was like "A wheh dis? Miss Chin, yu cyaa' tek dis bus, a no public bus. Dis bus go to MoBay, Dancehall Queen Contest. Yu cyaa come. Miss Chin, yu haffi go Halfway Tree . . ." They don't believe. And then the leader, a woman, she control the bus. She say, "No, no, no, no, no. This girl goin' enter." Everybody say, "A wha? But Ms. Chin cyaa' dance, Ms. Chin cyaa' wine. No, no, no, no, no, no, no . . ." At that time, just two years ago, but they don' understand Chinese and Japanese different. [Everybody] who have this skin [points to her skin] is "Ms. Chin" . . . They just don't know . . . I didn't really understand but I feel they don't welcome [me]. "Where can I sit down?" Scary . . . "How can I get friend?"

Soon the driver played a cassette tape. At the time, the Diwali riddim was very popular (heard, for instance, in Sean Paul's "Get Busy" and, later, Rihanna's "Pon de Replay"; Kudo tapped out the riddim perfectly across her body at this moment in her story). She continued:

Somebody say they wan' test me . . . "Chinese!" Somebody say, "No, no, say 'Japanese!'" "Yo, Japanese!" [At this point in her story, Kudo adroitly simulates from the seat of her chair the performance she gave to the women in the confined space of the bus]. "Heeeh!" "Oh, she know clap hands." . . . They find out I love reggae music . . . And then people try to know me. They wan' understand why Japanese can dance, why Japanese came here, why Japanese love reggae. Why Japanese *know* reggae. They don't understand why Japanese know reggae.

Once the women arrived at their hotel in Montego Bay, she was gradually able to break the ice, despite her communication difficulties. There were several women to a room, contributing, she said, to a sense of closeness among the contestants. She recognized one of the contestants from the previous year's competition from a videotape she had seen of the event. When Kudo told the woman this, the woman declared in surprise, "Junko seh Junko know mi face!" She also recognized a second woman from a tape of the 1998 competition, whom Kudo described as having "a big bottom" and as being "*kakkoi*" (cool). To help alleviate her problems communicating, one woman offered to translate to Junko what the other women were saying; although this in itself was less than helpful—the translation ran from patois to patois—she said she was grateful nonetheless because the attempt made her feel welcome. All the time, Kudo said, someone was with her.

While most Japanese in Japan might usually understand "Japaneseness" in a convergence of ethnic, racial, and national terms, this Japaneseness can be felt more specifically in racial terms in international spaces like Jamaica. Kudo's regard of the dancer's "big bottom" suggests an awareness of her own phenotypic difference from many of the Jamaican contestants. Kudo's narrative here closely mirrors a common motif found in the Japanese mass media, such as sports manga for youth, in which physically slight Japanese are intimidated by, but somehow work hard (*gambaru*) to prevail over, the ripped, hulking black and white athletes they compete against. It also fits the discourse of jibun sagashi, in its narrations of the challenges that the solitary self-maker, far from home, must overcome to achieve self-actualization. As another instance of specifically racial sensitivities that many Japanese have as they travel overseas, Kudo describes how, upon taking the stage early in the event to introduce herself, she heard the audience respond to what she imagined was for these observers the striking difference of her skin color. Another specifically racial observation had to do with height: Jamaican people, she said, including some of her competitors, were generally shorter than she had imagined: "but Jamaican people don't know Japan things, Japanese people don't know Jamaican things."

Kudo progressed through the rounds, impressing the crowd and making it to the final five. But she had exhausted all of her moves, she said, and was tired. Describing herself as an only child who did not have to fight any brothers and sisters for what she wanted, she described herself as "weak," as giving up easily. But then she realized that this was her last chance, that there was no coming back the following year. At this point in her narrative, Kudo again described a specifically racial anxiety upon observing one particularly athletic performer who had made the final round:

> Japanese don't have good . . . muscle. Different. Black people have . . . more, compared, I feel . . . I don't have long [legs] like Jamaican . . . I am fat girl in Japan but I don't really have a big bottom like . . . Jamaican people [laughs]. What can I do? Still a lot of contestant say, "Junko, do your best, do your best. You bad, bad, bad, bad. You the Dancehall Queen, you the Dancehall Queen."

In the end, she did give a great performance. Even before the announcement was made that she had won the competition, before she received her trophy from the former boxing heavyweight champion Lennox Lewis, many people in the audience were shouting, matter-of-factly, "Japanese, Japanese."

In the years since her victory, Kudo has become one of Jamaica's most popular dancehall queens. She has performed throughout the Caribbean, Europe, and North America, for the most part wherever there is a large Jamaican or more generally West Indian population. She has also, of course, performed in Japan. At the time of our interview, she had just returned from Japan (she presently spends most of her time in Jamaica). Given the dancehall boom there, under way already for about seven years at that time, she was startled by how frequently people on the street recognized and approached her. She now gives dance classes—the existence of reggae dance studios are another measure of the commercial growth of reggae dance—and recently released an instructional video.

I asked Kudo what her family made of her being a reggae dancer. She replied that at first they disapproved. But then she described showing her mother a tape of one of her performances. Seeing the enraptured look on the faces of the Jamaican audience members, her mother, Kudo said, was happy that Kudo's dancing could have that effect on people.

Sited in the powder room, on the bus, and in similar spaces, Soma and Kudo present initially contrasting representations of Japanese women's encounter with dancehall divas in Jamaica. In the Jamaican powder room described in the *Strive* article, the sense of sisterhood between the two groups of women is ideologically assumed; this is a space in which both groups of women are able to engage in subcultural exchange on a global playing field that is politicized primarily in gendered terms.

Kudo, describing the early part of her bus ride, conveys a somewhat different experience. She feels excluded from a cultural space constituted primarily for, and through the performative practices of, underclass Afro-Jamaican women. If in Soma's narrative Jamaican-Japanese solidarity seems given in gendered terms, in Kudo's narrative this solidarity is to be achieved through the difficult work of overcoming ethnic, national, and racial assumptions about each other.

This effort at solidarity, however, is not only complicated by Jamaican women's reflexive desire to maintain this space as recognizably their own (in my opinion an entirely understandable desire, given this scene's partial status as defiance of the pressures that Jamaican women particularly and intimately experience). Viewed in terms of a performative field whose social politics are also significantly Japanese, this effort toward solidarity is further complicated by that dimension of the Japanese desire for journey into the Jamaican that is not so much an effort toward cross-cultural solidarity, but also about Japanese cultural accomplishment. Minako Kurosawa as a graduate film student at New York University, directed a fine documentary on the lives of Japan's reggae dancers. Her 2007 film, *Born in JAHpan*, includes a profile of the five Japanese women—Harune, Juicy R, Hardcore J, Mishulan, and Crissy—out of a total field of twenty-five who performed in the International Dancehall Queen Competition in 2006. Mishulan, Hardcore J, and Crissy finished in the top ten; Crissy finished third. In the film, which captured the passion and commitment that the women bring to their dance, the theme of female empowerment strongly recurred (again, the English word "power" was often used). I was struck by the acute disappointment of one of the two women who did not finish in the top ten. Literally at the point of tears, she felt this disappointment as Japanese. While reggae dancers aspire for success on the Jamaican stage, this success, once achieved, is deeply felt as a Japanese accomplishment; if denied, it is personally felt, in this dancer's words, as "Japan's shame" ("*Nihon no haji da na*").

In addition to this woman's experience, as well as the stories of Saori, Kana, and the women in the Sister Kaya video, Kudo's story gives some sense of the personal investments that Japanese women have in reggae dance. I also want to describe, however, the ways in which this commitment manifests itself in onstage performance, its performative difference—despite its clear status as erotic dance—from the pornographic. In the following section, I describe the 1999 Dancehall Queen Japan competition in Tokyo. I offer this description to make ethnographically clear the level of skill that goes into these performances; the importance of fashion; audience interaction, including as differentiated in gendered terms; and the difference between these events and those taking place in Jamaica. Thereafter I analyze this event in each of these terms. I conclude by resolving the above discussion of reggae dance's potential as a means of gendered solidarity between Jamaican and Japanese women, as well as among Japanese women.

Dancehall Queen Japan 1999

Spicy Chocolate starts out easy, running some slower tunes but working its way to a harder sound as the night gets deeper and Shibuya's Vuenos grows full. Few people here, however, came to hear Spicy Chocolate, or even to hang out with dancehall luminary Rankin' Taxi, tonight little more than an audience member.

By around midnight the crowd has built significantly, and soon the club is filled. From the staircase leading upstairs, patrons vie for clear views of the stage below. The Spicy Chocolate MC, Bigga Raiji, reminds his audience—no more than two-thirds of which is male—that tonight's event is the 1999 Dancehall Queen Japan competition, the main showcase for dancehall divas in the country: "Nuff danca inna di place, y'know, ri-ight?" The MC goes on to name some of the dancers who will appear tonight. Although Dear Chicks was scheduled to perform, one of the dancers had suffered a slight injury just before the event, and the pair had bowed out. The following year, a dancer from another group had to pull out because of a hernia, and I heard of yet another dancer who had to perform solo for a while because her partner had suffered a hernia. Dancehall's acrobatic moves can take a high physical toll.

Bigga Raiji, a heavy-set man in his twenties wearing a Boston Red Sox baseball cap and an oversized FB (a popular brand among dancehall and hip-hop fans) T-shirt, greets the crowd in a raspy, excited voice. He holds aloft some brightly colored toy maracas and says that those who want one, who want to have a good time tonight, should "Say hoo-ooh!" The crowd obliges, and he distributes them in the front row. "Now," he yells in Japanese, "The first dancers, Cherish!"

The club darkens, musical effects are sounded, and before the lights come on again, two darkened figures enter the stage from the left. The lights return to catch the two women in mid-stride. They wear black midriff tops, tight black shorts, and black suede platform boots. Their backs sprinkled with glitter, the women's outfits are identical except that while the outfit of the first woman, who wears black fishnet stockings, seems made of cotton, the other's outfit has a more rubbery look and is lined, near the edges, with a black furry material. One wears a zebra-striped cowboy hat and platinum blonde wig; the other wears a black cowboy hat and purple wig. The other groups of dancers have similar variations in their otherwise identical outfits.

With the dancers now in full light, a deep male roar rises; whistles and "gunshots" issue, maracas rattle. The dancers position themselves with their backs turned to the crowd, slightly bent at the waist, waiting for the music. One long-haired young man in the front row, blowing a blue plastic horn, leaps close to the women; a slight, bespectacled man—wearing a dark suit and a plastic badge identifying him as a member of the event staff—approaches, also from the left of the stage. He says something to the young man, evidently warning him not to get too close to the performers, then exits.

Cherish's performance, as well as those of the other dancers to come, is a combination of moves most of which are found in Jamaican dancehall. These include standing erect with one's back to the crowd, hands behind the head, and jiggling one's buttocks while moving the hips as little as possible; standing on, for instance, one's right leg with the left raised straight upward and locked in place with the left arm; crouching on two hands and one knee, while the second leg is held aloft and swayed in the air; various pelvic maneuvers while on hands and knees or while on hands and the tips of one's toes; and crouching slightly and, with hands on thighs, moving the hips in a circular or vertical motion. Among the most complicated moves is the headtop (mentioned earlier), a headstand—or the more manageable shoulder stand—with legs aloft and horizontal, or bent while rhythmically moving the hips. As the high rate of injury suggests, these moves can be physically challenging; there are moments in many of the performances in which the dancers, losing the beat, must take the time to reposition themselves, or in which they abandon, with a smile, some of the more complicated moves after several attempts. There are periods in the performances in which one dancer stands or squats motionlessly, focusing attention on the other's dancing.

Each group performs for four or five minutes, during which time six or seven songs are played with the rapidity—moving quickly from one tune to the next—of a sound clash in its terminal stages. The dancers choose tunes according to the level of energy the tunes bring to the performances and according to whether they contain themes related to sex, gender, or dance. For example, Cherish chose songs like "Winey Winey" (again, the word in patois refers to moving one's hips in dance or sex); "Bedroom Bully," which celebrates women's initiative in the bedroom; "X-Rated," about sexually energetic women who "cyaa' done" (can't get done [enough]); and "Boom Bye-Bye," perhaps both for energy and for the celebration of female heterosexuality that condemnation of male homosexuality supposedly implies.

The second group, Natural Juice, appears dressed as pink and black "negatives" of each other: while one wears a black top and short skirt, both lined in pink fur, with a pink fur ball like a rabbit's tail attached to her bottom, the other wears a pink top and skirt both lined in black fur, with a black fur ball attached behind. Beneath the loose-fitting skirts, the women wear slightly oversized "underwear," color-coordinated parts of the costumes. Even in this sexually charged atmosphere, any exposure of private parts, such as by wearing sheer clothing, would be in very poor taste: the quality of the performance derives from the fashion and dance themselves.

When the woman in the mostly pink outfit comes close to the edge of the stage, back turned, the long-haired young man knocks the black fur ball back and forth with his toy gun. She does not seem to mind.

The third dancers, Donnette, appear in blue-and-white checkered midriff blouses, battyriders, and high black boots. One of the dancers dances on the ground and comes close to the edge of the small stage. The long-haired man blows his horn close to her face; while continuing to dance, the woman looks over to the left of the stage and says something. When she stands and turns, the man fires his toy gun with a loud "Plap!" at her behind, and the woman, still dancing, turns around briefly to glance at him. Later when the woman dances close to him again, one of his acquaintances, anticipating trouble, pulls him away from the edge of the stage.

During the performance, one of the dancers falls; the crowd cheers her back to her feet.

Donnette exits, the club darkens, and a brief intermission follows. At some point in the intermission, with the crowd shuffling, the long-haired man is displaced from his position in the front row.

The contest resumes. The MC announces Honey Butts (Kana said she considered them to have the best fashion sense in Japanese dancehall), who are dressed in white karate jackets—with their group's logo on the back—bound by a green belt, along with short black tights and high, black leather boots. Plastic marijuana leaves adorn the hair of one of the two women, fitting Banton's voice, which roughly intones, "Gimme di weed / Good ganja weed." Honey Butts executes—slowly, very carefully—the headtop move, and the crowd cheers not so much because it is sexy or smoothly done but because of its level of difficulty. In fact, one of the dancers loses her balance and topples onto her back; the other rushes over and dances with her to cover. A couple of young men in the front row laugh, not unkindly.

Love Milk, the fifth group, appears in neon-green bikini outfits, with skirts each essentially made up of two pieces of transparent neon-green plastic bound at the upper corners, and high leather boots, one pair black, the other pair white. Their performance is well synchronized and fluid, including a headtop by one of the two women, who has reddish-gold hair that hangs in two plaits down to her thighs. After their performance, a young man in the audience cries out in loanword English that Love Milk was "sexy," and Bigga Raiji repeats in Japanese, "They were sexy? No mistake."

He introduces the sixth dancers, Aatie Irie. This trio is dressed in glittering gold-colored tops and skirts, sheer legwarmers, and long black gloves. Each has donned distinguishing headgear: one wears a kind of glittering, golden beret reminiscent of the roaring twenties, the second a barrette, and the third a bandana. With the stage now full, one of the dancers dances to the extreme left, where Taxi, wearing a Marley T-shirt, sits. As she, oblivious to his presence, moves her hips in time with the beat, he in turn, watching the woman, cheerfully brings his maracas close to her behind and shakes them to the movement of her hips. At the end of their performance, the group throws colored streamers into the air.

The special guest is Time Machine, a sound system run by a young woman named Chinatsu (mentioned earlier). Offstage, she introduces the Fly Girls, a trio fully dressed in silver blouses, jackets, and pants. Chinatsu emcees over the music: "Hey! Hey! Hey! . . . Yes, it's all about Fly Girls, dedicated!" During the dance, each Fly Girl steps aside, drinks from a bottle of water as the other two dance, then slips seamlessly back into the fray while another takes a break.

After a brief intermission, all the dancers appear onstage. They do an impromptu dance to help the judges and audience members make their decision. Within and across groups, they dance to a couple of songs from the soundtrack of the film *Dancehall Queen*.

As they leave the stage, Bigga Raiji reappears and speaks in Japanese: "The winner is . . ." The music swells in anticipation. "The Kamikaze Promotion Dancehall Queen 1999 winner is: Love Milk!" Love Milk enters the stage looking really happy, jumping about excitedly as they are given a trophy; the woman receiving the trophy pumps it with one arm up and down in the air. Applause rises, the shrill cries of their female supporters in the crowd now prominent. The MC reminds the young woman to thank everyone, and she says *"Arigatō gozaimasu!"* into the mike, bowing deeply. One of the women poses for the cameras as she leaves the stage. She places one hand on an outward-thrust hip; with the other hand, she makes a peace sign while she flashes a big smile. Her partner playfully pokes her braided head to move her offstage more quickly.

Performativity, Performance, and Power in the Dancehall

The women performing in the 1999 competition did so within a transnational performative field dominated by Japanese (and Jamaican) men. The staff and audience were predominantly male, and the Spicy Chocolate MC was a man. Though not as obnoxious as the long-haired man, Taxi's playful shaking of the maracas close to the dancer's behind as she danced sanctioned this sexual objectification. ("Sanctions" may be too strong a word, though, since in dancehall this objectification is so fully assumed.) But despite how much male power saturates and structures this competition, a strong sense of female agency was also evident. The elaborateness of the outfits and the synchrony of the steps conveyed to both male and female viewers the sense that unfolding before one's eyes was the culmination of a process that only a few women had shared before. There was something going on behind the closed doors of the Japanese powder room that Japanese men were not privy to. The stage area had become a female creative space, and men were allowed only at its periphery; attempts to go beyond were met with the threat of expulsion. Male sexual desire was incidental to the art of fashion and dance that unfolded on the subcultural stage: there was no attempt to sexually excite the men outside the strict code of diva performance.

Song selection might be seen as another manifestation of claims to female agency in dancehall. A great number of Jamaican dancehall tunes treat women as sex objects, but many others celebrate women's initiative in the bedroom, as the DJ Shabba Ranks puts it, "left, center, and right." As much as one suspects that the male DJ's celebrations of women's sexual agency are accompanied by sly winks to his male friends, it is telling that a good number of the Japanese dancers specifically chose songs with such themes. As the Dear Chicks and *X-Rated Japanese Reggae Dancers* interviews suggest, many Japanese women are attracted to reggae dance because it represents an erotic performative code they can feel is entirely their own as women. Reggae dance has little to do with men per se; it is an endeavor in which the women can perform sexuality in a safe and enjoyable way without actually having sex with men. (In this regard, homosocial reggae dance is ironically conservative.) Reggae dance, furthermore, speaks through the performance of female sexuality to broader issues of gendered power, of which sexuality is only one element—as Kana's exclamation of "Strong mother!" illustrates.

During the contest, the sisterhood that Soma imagines between Jamaican and Japanese divas in Jamaica is perhaps sensed more readily, and as being deeper, in Japan, among Japanese women. Despite the personal frictions in the Japanese reggae dance scene, the participants are all Japanese, and they generally share all that comes with this common identification. Though usually drowned out by male cheers, the support of the sizable contingent of female audience members was loud and warm, particularly during the execution of difficult moves and with the announcement of the winners. Throughout the competition, these women looked with rapt attention at the details of the performers' dress and dance, much in the pedagogical spirit of predominantly male sound system culture.

The solo performances of the Jamaican donnette can present an image of spectacular autonomy both onstage and in the shadows away from the stage. Japanese divas in Japan, on the other hand, frequently perform together, and more exclusively in the stage's cheerful light. Two or more dancers onstage offer more to look at, in the way of creativity in dress and dance. Unlike her Jamaican counterpart, the Japanese reggae dancer in Japan, while indeed making some aesthetic claims to her individuality (Natural Juice's cottontails, Cherish's cowboy hats, Aatie Irie's headgear), generally accedes to friendly membership within a duo or group. Her participation there is defined by a group dependence, which, like clashing in Jamaica, is a much remarked-on feature in Japanese social life. Over the years, as many of Japan's reggae dancers think about competing in Jamaica, however, it may be that they are orienting their dance accordingly. This might help explain what appears to me an increasing number of solo performers in recent years. (In fact, Kiyo Akiba, the woman who finished third in the Jamaican competition in 2004, was one of the two women in the victorious Love Milk.) At the One Love Jamaica Festival in 2004, in addition to being surprised by the public nature of the venue in Yoyogi Park, I was also surprised to see the number of solo performers, some climbing up the scaffolding of the stage. This is an act which throws light on the dancer as an individual performer, in contrast to the girlfriendship emphasized in the Vuenos event (which was more underground, and in an earlier era). Back then, and still now, many considered the sight of a dancer performing alone, to use the word of one female fan, as a little *sabishii* (lonely).

Gender, Class, and Race in Dancehall

Feminist observers in Jamaica both celebrate and dismiss the power of the dancehall diva in effecting positive change for women. Those who praise these women see their spectacular celebration and control of their sexuality as empowering; others see the women as participating in an ultimately masculinist subculture, in which they are only accessories. The English literature scholar Carolyn Cooper (1997) views dancehall as a space in which women can liberate themselves from the puritanical, Anglocentric sensibilities imposed on a people of African descent. Anthropologist Norman Stolzoff, however, believes that "Cooper overstates her case about [dancehall's] liberatory effect for women . . . The popularity of slackness provided a new means to talk about sex, which to some extent exposed the contradictory attitudes about sex in Jamaica. Yet I would argue that . . . slackness never challenged the social hegemony based on men being the rightful owners of power in Jamaican society" (Stolzoff 2000, 105–6).

I agree with Stolzoff that slackness in itself does little to counter the broad structures of male dominance in Jamaican society. But perhaps he is reading what he, citing Foucault, sees as the marginal influence of slackness on "our fundamental relationship to sexuality as a field of power" (Stolzoff 2000, 105) more fundamentally than Cooper would have intended. That is, although he discusses throughout the book issues of race and class in Jamaican society, perhaps he represents here the social politics surrounding the expression of dancehall sexuality as being more singularly about sexuality and less about their Afro-Jamaican aspects than Cooper (and I) would be inclined to. Cooper is claiming a dancehall femininity that is empowering not only to the extent that it liberates women from men's marginalizations of them, but also to the extent that it subverts the neocolonial notions of feminine decorum on which this power is partly based. The political disenfranchisement of women in Jamaica is rooted not only in gender and sexuality, but also in class and race.

Terisa Turner redefines "the male deal" to refer to what she sees as a historical collusion between capitalist and sexist exploitation: "capital needs a male deal because it mediates class struggle by reassuring men that they have a stake in power relationships through their continued subordination of women" (1991, 70). Capitalist exploitation flourishes in part because working-class men have entered into a relationship with a capitalist system which, while exploiting them, also permits their own mitigating marginalization of women. What is at work in Jamaica is not only a capitalist system that marginalizes poor men and in turn poor women, but also a neocolonial, neoliberal system that marginalizes poor black men and in turn poor black women. By disclosing the oppressive conjunctions of colonialism and capitalism in Jamaican society, the Afrocentrisms that inhere in dancehall culture potentially permit Afro-Jamaican women to pleasurably interrogate in performance the triad structure—gendered, class-based, racial—of the male deal.

It is in this complexity that I see dancehall's greatest potential as a means of gendered liberation for Japanese women. In exploring dancehall as a performative field, a space in which the social politics of Jamaica and Japan converge and are complexly worked through in performance, it becomes evident that the political disenfranchisement not only of Jamaican women but also of Japanese women must be seen in the conjoined terms of gender, class, and race. With regard to gender, in Japan as much as Jamaica, dancehall is a space in which women must shrug off the fear of stigma if they are to embrace an art form that speaks to them particularly as women. With regard to class, Japanese women and men most deeply involved not only in dancehall but also in other aspects of Jamaican culture in Japan tend to occupy marginal positions within the Japanese socioeconomic order. Kudo worked as a hairdresser, for instance, and Kana worked for a while as a hostess.

However, class is relevant not only in the socioeconomic sense of the term, but in the moralizing one as well. Here class intersects discreetly with race: many of the women discuss how they are looked down on for their participation in this erotic form of so-called black dance. The potential of dancehall as a means to challenge gendered, socioeconomic hegemony might be seen in the way it has required women who love reggae dance to dismiss the puritanical standards of middle-classdom by which so many—in Japan, Jamaica, and elsewhere—historically have been judged. A historical aspect of Western discourses (both male and female) of non-Western women, including Afro-Jamaicans and Japanese, has been of both these women as sexualized, as unenlightened in gender political terms, situationally imagined as sexually passive (Japanese women as submissive geisha, black Jamaican women as victims of an exceptional black male sexism) and aggressively licentious (today's Japanese women as updated dragon ladies who consume foreign men, black Jamaican women as belonging to a naturally avaricious race). As such, both Jamaican and Japanese dancehall divas disregard demands that, as low-class women in the Western-dominated global moral order (relative to the purity that is discursively assumed of Euro-American women), they work extra hard to overcome these assumptions about them. They disregard the rules of bourgeois, gendered citizenship in many modern or modernizing non-Western nations, refusing to comply with imposed sexual ideals discreetly but significantly—and often illusorily—constructed as Western. In the Jamaican case, this Western is primarily colonial Victorian. In the Japanese case, it is true that Euro-America came to be seen, as discussed earlier, as a threat to the morality of young women. However, it also represented the standard against which Meiji reformers—who constructed the supposed lack of morals of Japanese women as the clearest sign of Japan's backwardness among advanced nations (Czarnecki 2005)—anxiously judged Japan's progress into the modern world.

Many of these women, especially the less famous dancers, can eventually quit the dancehall scene and, through marriage, re-enter life as "normal" Japanese women. Thus they may have little to lose in the long run. But the social price now, while they are dancing, can still be high, including difficulty in maintaining stable relationships with their families and significant others. Despite these challenges, hundreds of Japanese women are drawn to reggae dance. These numbers do not of themselves necessarily indicate a revolution of gender ideology in Japan, or in attitudes toward blackness encountered in Japan and beyond. In some ways, as argued above, they represent the way in which transgressive subcultural practices become absorbed into the masculinist, nationalist normative, and an enfolding of the stereotypical difference of the Jamaican into the familiarly valorized Japanese. But this process is never guaranteed. Among the growing number of performers with their various investments in donnette culture, both as performed here and as linked to the ethnoracial difference of the Jamaican there, lies the performative potential for an unsettling of gendered and classist hegemony in Japan. In the enactments of dancehall culture taking place all across Japan, as well as in the actual encounters with Jamaican women in Jamaica, there is always the possibility of seeing Afro-Jamaican women beyond their physical difference; of wishing to engage the social problems facing Afro-Jamaican women in ways that do not begin and end with the easy assumptions of a common sisterhood; of interrogating the homophobia heard in much of Jamaican dancehall; of apprehending Babylon in all its local and global guises; even of seeing, of a sudden, the conjunctions among all of these.

4

Body and Spirit

RASTAFARIAN CONSCIOUSNESS IN RURAL JAPAN

Although dancehall has established a presence all over Japan, even in rural areas, for the most part, its urban ethos confines it to cities. In contrast, Rastafari celebrates the natural world in ideological counterpoint to urban life. In considering how Rastafari has taken root in Japan, then, it might be productive to consider the Japanese imagination of the rural in relation to the urban. The countryside has long been seen as a main preserve of the traditional in Japan. Japanese folklore studies (*minzoku-gaku*), as exemplified in the early modern writings of Yanagita Kunio, has celebrated the rural—its customs, practices, and mythologies—as the site of a timeless national identity. But heralding this space as a wellspring of the emerging nation's strength simultaneously required its marginalization. The rural was celebrated by nationalizing forces centered in an urban modernity, which ironically represented the greatest threat to rural values. The state forces driving this urban modernity ultimately thought little of the rural— which, as it truly exists beyond reflexive modernity, is in many ways marginalized in the national imagination. This is apparent in everything from the growing state regulation of the lives of rural women (Tamanoi 1998) to the physical urbanization of the rural landscape.

In her exploration of Japan's anxieties surrounding its status as a modern nation, Marilyn Ivy (1995) discusses contemporary Japanese figurations of and yearning for *furusato* (hometown). During Japan's modern period, "the countryside literally became regressive, opposed to the 'progressive' powers of urban-based capitalism. Yet urban domination could not be sustained as such, but in time became open to the uncanny returns that such repression inevitably ensures . . . The furusato is, then, properly *uncanny*, because it indicates a return of something estranged under the guise of the familiar" (Ivy 1995, 107).

Today, the uncanny rural manifests itself not only as Japanese tradition in relation to Western modernity, but also in ways beyond both of their immediate discursive purviews. Japanese can leave the overly familiar West and Japan behind to seek fabulous new postmodern selves in the global. Their hybridized ontologies can be rooted in the earth of a rural natural whose history can be managed, including performatively, to permit such rootings. These ontologies can be raised from the depths of local mythological time, drawn from the wider spaces of the global, or both. They may come to constitute local celebrations of the Japanese nation, and possibly also—given the restless border crossings of the global—an interrogation of it (Buell 1994).

In this chapter, I argue that the Japanese use Rastafari in a number of ways, including to critique class difference, consumerism, and the colonial past of both the West and Japan. This critique is significantly sited in the cosmopolitan urban, where one is most likely to witness consumerism at its extremes, to see the greatest disparities between human want and human possession, to encounter the peoples of the West's and Japan's former empires. However, I focus on the ways in which Rastafari is sited in the rural, particularly the countryside imagined as a pure sanctuary from the modern urban. I argue that while Rasta is used to critique aspects of Japanese society and history, it is also used to valorize the premodern rural— ironically through a global cultural form that is significantly modern urban. This effort involves articulating Rasta as an unusual expression and so a vitalization of existing Japanese spiritual tradition—significantly including through performative practices in which the body is the means as well as its own spiritual end—and as such might be seen as one of the uncanny "returns" that Ivy describes.

In exploring these issues, I will first identify some key ideological and symbolic features of Jamaican Rastafari, describing as well the internationalization of the movement. I discuss the movement in Japan, situating it in relation to other manifestations of Jamaican popular culture in the country. I proceed to discuss the ideological routes through which several of my research participants came to identify with Rasta. I do so as part of my belief that rather than viewing the authenticity of Rasta in Japan in terms of its direct fit with its Jamaican counterpart, it is more productive to see how the movement's ideological and symbolic features are rearticulated according to Japanese sociopolitical prerogatives—which are elucidated in the process—particularly as they manifest themselves in regional terms. The chapter's ethnographic focus is on the members of a roots reggae band living and performing in rural Japan.

Rastafari in Jamaica

Rastafari is a messianic protest movement that emerged in colonial Jamaica in the 1930s. While Rastafarians are an eclectic group, they believe that Ethiopian Emperor Haile Selassie I is black people's returned messiah. Africa, the black person's true home, is heaven; Jamaica is hell. Repatriation is the black person's only means of salvation from the corruption of "Babylonian" Jamaica, a colonized metonym for the corrupted West (Chevannes 1994; Smith, Augier, and Nettleford 1960).

Below I identify some critical ideological and symbolic features of Jamaican Rastafari as an Afrocentric movement. By "critical features," I mean those attributes of the movement which, while not necessarily exclusive to Rastafari, are richly articulated with each other to give the movement its particular ideological valence. I use "articulated" in Stuart Hall's sense of the word—as the interlinking of concepts, values, and beliefs existing in "non-necessary" (Hall 1996, 144) relation to each other to create a new system of belief—in this case, one which manifests itself in a particular politicized imagination of blackness.

IDEOLOGICAL FEATURES

One critical feature of the Rastafarian faith is the gaze toward Africa. As noted above, Africa is heaven, and Jamaica hell. This gaze is by definition transnational, seeking out—as the gazer does—spiritual repatriation to the motherland. The gaze toward Africa can be linked to a second definitive feature of Rastafarian ideology: a critique of colonialism and capitalism. These are different names for the same disease—Babylonian oppression—that has torn black people from their homeland and thrust them into an oppressive New World. A third critical feature, related to the second, is condemnation of technological overdevelopment. Technology is a measure of Babylonian arrogance, its past and present means of enslaving African and other non-Western people.

Despite condemnation of Babylonian technology, Rasta is firmly grounded in the material world, and this constitutes a fourth ideological feature of the movement. This belief, unsurprising given the material poverty from which the movement emerged, manifests itself in the Rastas' cry that it is the lionhearted, not the meek who have been mentally colonized by the Christian faith, who shall inherit the earth. This aggressive posture toward Christianity leads to a fifth critical feature of Rastafari: valorization of wisdom as opposed to knowledge. Rastas condemn Christianity's attempt to mediate the black person's relationship with God, or Jah (the product of which is knowledge), demanding instead that each follower find Jah individually, deeply, and constructively (which is wisdom). This distinction also manifests itself in Rasta's skepticism toward academics, who are viewed as fools committed to reproducing the knowledge of Western man.

This fifth feature closely informs a sixth: multivalent identification with the movement. Because of the stress on personally achieved wisdom, and because the movement easily spans the religious, the sociopolitical, and the popular cultural, Rastafari even in Jamaica is a very open-ended phenomenon. Some Rastafarians wear dreadlocks, and others do not; some Rastafarians, but not others, smoke marijuana. Most Jamaican Rastafarians do not identify with any religious organization (although such organizations certainly exist). While almost all see Selassie as divine, a few have questioned this divinity, choosing to see him as only human. But rather than diminishing Selassie, humanizing him ideally affirms the divinity within every human being. In stressing openness as they do, these last two critical ideological features of Rasta—personally achieved wisdom and ideological valence—both undermine the authority of European Christianity and especially facilitate the Japanese appropriation of the movement.

A seventh ideological feature of Rasta, deeply implicated in all the others, is a valuation of the natural world. Sensing the sacred in the greenness of grass, in the grace of sunlit trees and of birds turning in the air, the ability to let these marvels suffuse one's being, nourishes the Rastafarian spirit.

(Here, as discussed in the introduction, the view of Jamaica as hell becomes ambivalent: while such a view of Jamaica is to be seen as a condemnation of the historical circumstances under which Africans arrived at the island, Rastas are also able to see this hellish place, in its phenomenological minutiae, as divine.) Rastas consume the sacrament of marijuana and engage in "I-tal" (natural) living to achieve spiritual closeness to the natural world, geo-racialized as black Africa; dreadlocks and an unshaven face mark the natural Rastaman.

An eighth feature of Rastafari is its use of a critical metalingustics. While English is Jamaica's official language, most Jamaicans speak patois, a creole combining various West African languages and English. However, given the relations of neocolonial social power that can inhere in language use, many Jamaicans see the use of patois as a mark of unsophistication, vulgarity, and unintelligence. The use of "standard" English is perceived by many Jamaicans as an indication of social grace, intellectual capacity, and accomplishment (Cooper 1997). Given the links between language and socioeconomic qua racial marginalization, Rastafarians see language as an instrument of black Jamaican oppression but also, potentially, of their liberation (Pollard 1980). They fashioned "dread talk" into "an argot whose linguistic patterns rejected the relationships of subordination and superordination found within the structures of words themselves . . . Through this often involuted discourse, the Rastas asserted their own power over history, for they believed that a diminutive discourse created the obsequious personality" (W. Lewis 1994, 287–88). Among the metacritical techniques employed in dread talk is the replacement of what is perceived as the negative elements of positive words by positive elements, in order to emphasize the words' positivity. "Understand" thus becomes "overstand." The opposite is also true: one should not be deceived into thinking that there is anything "uplifting" about "op-pression"; the word "downpression" is used instead. These inventions clearly have an element of play, one generally found in patois. But in the end, they are about the very serious business of calling attention to the ideological colonialisms that inhere in colonized people's use of the colonizer's language.

A movement founded by men, and one in which men are numerically dominant, Rastafari is deeply patriarchal. Male domination thus constitutes a ninth critical feature of in the movement. Historically, men have occupied the center of orthodox Rastafari's social and religious life. The religious leadership is generally male. Subject to a number of taboos, women conventionally do not share the chalice with men, nor do menstruating women prepare men's food. While Rastas generally struggle against neo-colonialism, then, Rasta women must also struggle against the patriarchal attitudes of Rasta men. But just as Rastafari empowers itself by appropriating elements of familiar Christianity (such as the notion of a messiah and the use of the Bible—interpreted properly—as a sacred text), Rasta women sometimes articulate their own worth not outside of the Rastafarian belief system they might see as in some measure oppressing them, but very much from within it. The Rasta celebration of creation becomes one of female procreation; understanding Babylon's attempt to destroy the black population through birth control and abortion clinics takes place not in abstraction, but directly through the bodies of black women. Despite the marginal place that women have historically occupied in Rastafari, many today are forcing a revaluation of their place in the movement. They are seeking to make clear the ways in which Rasta men and women must become equal partners in the struggle against their common enemies.

SYMBOLIC FEATURES

Rastafari in Jamaica is marked by a number of core linguistic and visual symbols that give expressive, including performative, substance to the above beliefs. Primary among the linguistic symbols is the term "Babylon." The name affords a sense of consistency to this immoral territory, despite the shifts over time in the construction of this space. In the early days of Jamaican Rastafari, Babylon referred to the white British colonial world. Over four decades after Jamaica's independence, Babylon today more powerfully invokes neoliberal capitalism and the global political machinations embodied in such institutions as the World Bank, the International Monetary Fund, and the Central Intelligence Agency (Black 2003).

In Rasta visual symbolism, the lion—like the Rasta colors of red, green, and gold, and the outline of Africa—is closely identified with the continent which Rastafarians see as their homeland. For devout Rastas, dreadlocks are an important embodied sign of natural connectedness to Africa, as they resemble the mane of the lion, the "dreadful" king of beasts. Some have argued that dreadlocks began when Jamaican Rastas saw pictures of the Mau Mau of Kenya, freedom fighters against British colonial rule who wore their hair in similar manner. The lion, when depicted with a crown on its head, and a cross, scepter, or staff with the Ethiopian flag secured in one of its front paws, invokes Haile Selassie. Images of Selassie himself, as a child or young man, in imperial garb or in military uniform, constitute another set of recurrent Rastafarian images.

Rasta truth is achieved, however, not only through the sign, but also in wielding it in performance. An important element of this performative effort toward Rastafarian truth is "word sound power." This concept speaks to the liberatory power of words, their aural capacity to move those who receive them. The very sound of words is powerful. "Word sound power" can manifest itself in reasoning sessions, during which Rastafarians philosophize spontaneously but intensely about issues of concern to them. Reasoning sessions—perhaps the definitive religious practice through which followers know—can develop in Rasta yards (loose affiliations of Rasta families and friends under one roof) and communes or during "groundation" ceremonies taking place during major events in the Rasta calendar.

Rastafari within and beyond the Diaspora

Much of Rastafari's international popularity has developed within the African diaspora (Campbell 1987). Rastafarians immigrating to Great Britain (Cashmore 1983), the United States, and Canada (Montague 1994) have used Rasta as a tool to resist the postcolonial and capitalist exploitation encountered in their new countries. Since the 1970s, however, it has been the United States, particularly its eastern seaboard, to which the majority of Jamaicans have been immigrating. New York is home to a large community of Jamaican Rastafarians, who have established craft shops, political groups, community centers, and numerous denominational "mansions" in the city. Hepner (1998) suggests that since Rasta immigrants live at a great distance from their Jamaican "homeland," in the very center of Babylon, Rastafari in New York is achieving an organizational density that the movement in Jamaica has notoriously lacked.

Borne on the waves of reggae's popularity, Rastafari has also reached Africa. As in Britain, Canada, and the United States, in Africa, Rastafari appears to retain much of its original racial political mission and spiritual fervor. The movement is nonetheless inflected according to local issues of power vis-à-vis race, ethnicity, other religions, class, and gender. Terisa Turner (1991), for instance, argues that the future of Rastafari in East Africa and elsewhere in the diaspora may depend on how successfully it links race, class, feminist, and other concerns. The ease with which many West African youth have come to accept Rastafari stems from the fact that it is informed by the same Christian beliefs with which they and their ancestors have been indoctrinated, even as they are critical of these beliefs in their aspect as instruments of Western hegemony (Savishinsky 1994).

Given Rasta's simultaneous identifications with and dissociations from Western culture (redemptive struggle in the heart of Babylon, liberation from Christianity through a Christianity-informed movement, resentment yet valorization of diasporic dislocation), and given its idealization of Africa, its spread throughout the diaspora is unsurprising. But all around the world, dreadlocks and other elements of Rasta style have been adopted by hippies, surfers, and hip-hop fans, few of whom are Jamaican or Rastafarian. As practiced in such spaces, the gap between these Rasta signs and their conventional, African diasporic, theologically particular signified grows wider. How does one understand the attraction of Rastafari and dancehall for non-African people? The internationalization of Rastafari has been driven in part by its concern with alienation, a globally common experience (Yawney 1994). This concern is expressed through the movement's "master symbols" (like Babylon) which, given the ambiguity that inheres in all symbols, bear rich potential for new cross-cultural meaning. William Lewis (1994) sees the "social drama" of Rastafari as harmlessly apolitical: Rastas tend not to participate in the Jamaican political process, which they regard as inherently and irredeemably corrupt. Yet the foreignness of Rasta, its philosophical similarities to Marxism (Rastafarians reject wage labor as a form of capitalist exploitation), and its advocacy of the oppressed all challenge many societies' sociopolitical status quo. Rastafari "assists in bringing about a consensual community. This in itself is empowering" (Yawney 1994, 79). For me in this chapter, what is important is not so much defining "Japanese Rasta," but rather seeing how these critical features of Rastafari are reworked in the Japanese context. (In the final chapter, I examine the implications of such reworkings for the possibilities of a Japanese Rastafari in terms of its relation to the diasporic movement.)

The symbols and reworked politics of Rastafari have manifested themselves in a range of locations beyond the geographic and demographic spaces of the African diaspora. Rasta has appeared among American Indians (Ullestad 1999), who use roots reggae to speak of their historical struggles as a people. It has also surfaced throughout Asia and the Pacific: Frank van Dijk notes the popularity of roots reggae in Australia and New Zealand. While many young Samoans and Maori there saw themselves more as fans of reggae music than as followers of Rastafari, a small number sought a deeper understanding of the religion, "including belief in the divinity of Emperor Haile Selassie and the return to the Promised Land" (van Dijk 1998, 194). Van Dijk suggests that one of the reasons why it has been possible for Rastafari to take root in the region—in 1986 a Jamaican denomination of the movement was established there—has been that Rasta shares a strong millenarian ethos with other religious movements: "since the introduction of Christianity in the early nineteenth century, identification with the lost tribes of Israel, for example, has figured in several religious movements emerging among the Maori" (ibid.). This curiosity about the lost tribes of Israel also manifests itself in Rastafari in Japan, which I discuss in the next chapter.

Rastafari and Jamaican Musical Culture in Japan

Rastafari has been transmitted to Japan, as it has around the world, largely through roots reggae music. Thus, I want to briefly locate Rasta on the spectrum of current Japanese interest in Jamaican culture. In many ways, if dancehall might be seen as representing one end of this spectrum, roots culture represents the other. As is true internationally, dancehall culture in Japan is informed by its urban orientation, speech-song styled orality, digital musical production, emphatic heterosexuality and consumerism, and, given these, its proximity to and liaisons with hip-hop. The culture of roots reggae and Rasta in Japan today, heir to the interest in roots reggae music that was most intense in the mid-1990s, is now more rurally based than in the past; musical production revolves primarily around live (non-digital) instrumentation; its participants tend to endorse "natural" living, which often includes the wearing of dreadlocks; and as a result, it has come to be closely related to a preexisting counterculture (or hippie) movement in Japan. Dancehall musicians usually reside relatively independently of each other in urban areas. Roots musicians, who are often older than dancehall fans and who are sometimes parents, tend to live in close-knit, rural communities.

In addition to fans and practitioners with an exclusive commitment to reggae music, some Japanese are part of this scene temporarily, nonexclusively, or otherwise provisionally. Fans in this group feel comfortable attending reggae music events in clubs that might also play hip-hop, rhythm and blues, J-pop, and other genres of popular music. I asked Overheat's Ishii what he made of the earlier boom in reggae culture in the 1990s, and he described it as "a big joke." While there was certainly a greater commercial interest in roots reggae—evidenced, for instance, in the number of people who attended Reggae JapanSplash and bought reggae CDs— only a small core of fans stuck with roots reggae once it slipped back under the radar of mass-media interest. With regard to practitioners, singers like Minmi, Kaana, and Pushim are largely or primarily identified with reggae, but they also record rhythm and blues and other forms of music to extend their fan bases.

The inflected nature of the reggae scene in Japan is also apparent in the existence of a number of Jamaican musical subgenres in addition to dancehall and roots reggae. The proximity of these other subgenres to dancehall and roots reggae may be thought of in terms of how the music is made. It might also be thought of in terms of the degree of sociopolitical commentary typically associated with the music. With this classification in mind, I focus on two of these subgenres. The first might be called "Jamaican instrumental music," and the second is dub. Jamaican instrumental music is urban Japan's live instrumental (as opposed to digital musical) take on a range of postindependence Jamaican music. Jamaican instrumental music might include roots reggae, but I treat this genre as a separate category since it is primarily musical and has little if any concern with the Rasta ideology usually found in roots reggae. Jamaican instrumental musicians who perform roots reggae, then, are interested in roots reggae primarily as music. In addition to roots reggae, they tend to focus on earlier genres of Jamaican music like ska and rocksteady. Among the performers in this group are bands like Home Grown, Dry and Heavy, Tokyo Ska Paradise Orchestra, the Determinations, and Yahoo. Instrumental ability takes center stage with these bands: they are acclaimed largely because of their skill in reproducing popular Jamaican music as well as in producing their own. For instance, Tokyo Ska Paradise Orchestra, a large ensemble of musicians, has deservedly enjoyed some international acclaim as an excellent ska band since the early days of roots reggae in Japan. Yahoo, another excellent band, is known for its fusion of roots reggae with a more pop-rock sound.

The second subgenre is represented by dub sound systems like Mighty Massa, Direct Impact, Jah Works, and Shandi I. If Jamaican instrumental music gravitates instrumentally toward Jamaican ska and roots reggae, dub gravitates instrumentally toward dancehall: the latter two are forms of electronica. Dub's ethereal, reverberating cool, however, is distinct from the jaunty, Jamaican folk-musical (and, more recently, hip-hop inflected) beats heard in contemporary dancehall. Many Japanese dub artists, closely informed as their music has been by its British Jamaican counterpart (these dub musicians travel to London to develop their knowledge of the music), also often oppose the perceived lasciviousness of dancehall. This is an antagonism shared by Japanese practitioners of roots reggae at the extreme end of the ideological spectrum of Jamaican music in Japan.

From digital to live, then, the musical-productive spectrum runs from dancehall and dub to Jamaican instrumental and roots reggae. From less to more politically conscious (at least by conventional association), the ideological spectrum runs from dancehall and Jamaican instrumental music to dub and roots reggae. While respecting roots people for their commitment to the natural lifestyle of Jamaican Rastas, dub followers sometimes noted that they prefer not to go to such extremes as abandoning city living altogether. They are somewhat critical of roots followers who bring their lifestyle—most dangerously emblematized by the consumption of marijuana—into Tokyo's public spaces. Still, because dub followers are among those most committed to Rasta ideology, where appropriate I will incorporate their experiences and opinions into my discussion in this chapter of the Rasta scene in Japan.

Whether dancehall or roots, dub or Jamaican instrumental, popular music in general dominates Japanese interest in Jamaican culture. It is hard to find anyone deeply involved in any aspect of Jamaican culture in Japan who is not also a musician. However, there are some nonmusicians with an artistic interest in Jamaican culture, including Rastafari. One is Kads Miida, a commercial artist with a broad repertoire, but whose work for much of the 1990s was dominated by his personal immersion in Rasta. Like many Japanese during this period, he traveled to Jamaica, wore his hair in dreadlocks, and lived among Rastafarian elders on the island to better understand their way of life. His hair now short and undreadlocked, his clothing urban casual, he believes that although he never truly could and does not now identify himself as Rasta, his Rasta-themed paintings, completed shortly after he left Jamaica, reflect his concern—one that unites all his paintings— with man's relationship with the natural world. He continues to paint live at many reggae events. Naoko Morioka, another artist based (at the time of my research) in Okinawa, is well known for her Africa-themed postcards. Although she does not paint Jamaica itself—unlike many of her friends, when we spoke, she had never been to the island—dreadlocked figures often appear in these works as part of her depiction of the continent as a profoundly spiritual place that is the ancestral home of all humanity.

Japanese Rastafarians

Dean Collinwood's and Osamu Kusatsu's (2000) paper, based on research conducted in 1986 and 1987, is the only academic work I have encountered on Rastafari in Japan. Employing a sociological model of deviance, the authors contend that the Japanese see in this lifestyle—with its stress on being close to the earth and living in natural simplicity—a way of becoming more profoundly Japanese. This is so because traditional Japan similarly values living in spiritual closeness to the earth. This basic hypothesis is borne out throughout my research. However, while the concept of deviance is productive in advancing this hypothesis, it fits my theoretical interests less well. Deviance considers Rastafari in Japan in terms of its distance from mainstream Japanese norms; I want to consider the ways in which Rasta, like many supposedly oppositional subcultures, might be seen as very much a part of the mainstream. Deviance, relatedly, tends to center on what is not normative within a given society, limiting an accounting of the fact that Japanese who dreadlock their hair and sing reggae music "deviate" specifically through a foreign, indeed an Afrocentric, cultural form. Rasta's provenance as a religious movement in the African diaspora will be important for my considerations in the final chapter of the potential of Rasta in Japan as more than just a lifestyle, but as a religion.

The great Japanese interest in reggae in the 1980s and 1990s helped create among a small number of Japanese not only an appreciation of the music but also a deeper interest in the religion behind it. This interest, especially in rural areas, became significantly linked to the preexisting counterculture movement in the country. Rasta, like the counterculture movement, includes a commitment to natural living which manifests itself in many of its adherents' decisions to live in rural areas, practice vegetarianism, consume marijuana, wear their hair long, and practice progressive politics. Given this kinship of ideology and subcultural practice, many hippies in the mid-1970s gravitated toward Rastafari.

In part due to the ways in which Rasta has merged with other movements, it is impossible to estimate the number of "Japanese Rastafarians."

The term itself is problematic: some individuals identify themselves as Rasta; others say they see their lifestyle as Rastafarian, or are well-versed in Rastafarian matters, but do not go so far as to claim to be Rasta. I did not meet anyone in Japan who claimed to believe that Haile Selassie is God—the definitive feature of the Rastafarian faith—without some qualification. The pursuit of Rastafari is as individualistic in Japan as it is in Jamaica, but it would still be fair to characterize Rastafari in Japan as far less cohesive as a socioreligious and political movement. Yet, as discussed below, Rasta in Japan manifests itself as a community, representing a rich symbolic method by which its followers explore, collectively and individually, the socioeconomic, political, historical, religious, and personal in Japan, Asia, and the world at large.

I want to use the term "Rasta-identifying Japanese" to describe the research participants whose lives I discuss in this chapter. The phrase is admittedly clunky, but at least it clearly indicates my concern with not representing Japanese Rastafari as something finished, as a given from which further analysis too easily proceeds; rather, the rooting of Rastafari in Japan is an ongoing process. I should note that while this exploration can manifest itself in such embodied terms as the wearing of dreadlocks, many Japanese wear dreadlocks but have little knowledge of or interest in Rasta. In such cases, dreadlocks are often an expression of identification with reggae music, or even just an effort at black cool without an interest in reggae. I do not consider these individuals to be Rasta-identifying Japanese. What is important in my use of the term is that with or without dreadlocks, and with or without appreciating or performing roots reggae, the individuals I do describe that way see Rasta as the primary ideological resource for leading and understanding their lives.

I generally use Rasta-identifying Japanese to describe only those individuals who, in spite of Rasta's individualism, regularly meet with other individuals for whom Rastafari plays a similarly important role in their sense of self in the world, and who regularly participate in Rasta-related events taking place across Japan. To return to the question of how many Rasta-identifying Japanese there are, I can say I have personally met throughout the course of my fieldwork about twenty-five people who meet these criteria. I strongly suspect that there are far more than twenty-five people who meet these criteria, since I have seen or briefly encountered scores of individuals whose appearance or rhetoric fit the bill. However, since I am not able to more deeply confirm that they meet the two criteria above, the information presented below is based primarily on the roughly twenty-five people I met and got to know well, who I can say with some confidence do meet these criteria.

Urban Perspectives on Rastafari in Japan

Japanese engagement with the movement is not homogeneous but is inflected in a number of terms. The region of Japan in which this engagement takes place is one such term. I do not want to get into a chicken-or-egg discussion, but different regions provide different resources for different kinds of identification with Rastafari. For example, urban areas offer relatively greater access to people and things Rasta, such as concerts, restaurants, and craft shops. Rasta-identifying individuals living in urban areas tend to appreciate Rasta primarily as a means of sociopolitically critiquing the world inside and outside Japan. They tend to pursue natural living only to the extent possible in these urban areas. I also found this use of Rasta as sociopolitical critique in rural areas, especially where Rasta was linked with the counterculture movement. However, Rasta in rural areas tended to be more strongly defined by a pursuit of a natural, sometimes communal lifestyle that did not always seem to be focused on sociopolitical critique. Where linked to this counterculture movement, rural Rasta was often global culturalist and somewhat less emphatically global political. By "global culturalist," I refer to a generalized interest in the indigenous cultures of Africa, Southeast Asia, and North and South America. By "global political," I refer to activist concern for international issues of social injustice, notably those revolving around American Indians and Tibetans.

In the following section, I present the cases of three Rasta-identifying individuals living in urban areas. I discuss how their encounter with Rastafari has afforded them a sense of personal growth understood as a coming into awareness of a range of domestic and international issues of social justice. These include concern with socioeconomic, ethnic, racial, and other forms of inequality around the world, often as linked to those of Japan and even as experienced in the lives of the Rasta-identifying Japanese. I consider the specific aspects of Rastafari that these individuals mobilize and work through in this process, including the use of patois and dread talk, critique of Babylon, consumption of marijuana as a challenge to the social order, and effort to re-imagine Rasta's black politics in Japanese context.

Although many Japanese dancehall people described their encounters with Rastafari in Jamaica as enlightening, these individuals tended to dissociate themselves from Rasta-identifying Japanese. While respectful of Jamaican Rastas and their beliefs, a number of dancehall practitioners expressed to me their feeling that it is inappropriate for Japanese to pursue this profoundly Afrocentric Jamaican cultural practice. Yet dancehall people, fully ensconced in urban Japan, have little contact with roots people, who tend to live in the countryside. Lines of tension between dancehall and Rasta were more clearly felt, then, between dancehall and dub followers. Dub musicians, who move with ease between urban and rural performance venues, were among the most strongly Rasta-identifying people I met in Japan, particularly in terms of their adoption of diasporic Rastas' international political consciousness. Many dancehall people, therefore, often decried dub musicians for their improper adoptions of Rastafari, including marijuana consumption that threatened to mar broader public opinion of dancehall. Many dub people, on the other hand, saw dancehall culture as crude, materialistic, and apolitical.

It is hard to draw any general conclusions about dub musicians, since this esoteric element of Japanese reggae is relatively small. But among the dub musicians I met, some clear patterns emerged. Their urban residence gave them frequent opportunities to travel to New York, Jamaica, and especially England, the international base of dub culture. They often had extensive personal and business contacts with Jamaican people in Britain. They were well versed in and passionate about the political issues of race and social class that concerned the British Jamaicans they had met, and they sought strongly to apply the Rastafarian critique of "Babylonian" oppression to Japan. Their identification with Rasta often extended to consistent use of patois influenced by dread talk, onstage and in the company of black Jamaicans like me. The dub musicians were among those who wrestled in the greatest emotional depth with their identifications as Japanese people in this Afrocentric movement.

FIRE

By the time of my two-month trip to Japan in spring 2001, I had known Fire (a pseudonym)—then twenty-six and an MC for an up-and-coming dub sound system—for two years. By express train, his home is only about an hour from a major city, but his community retains enough of a rural feel, with rivers and mountains nearby, to satisfy his naturalist inclinations. Fire grew up near a U.S. military base where, unlike most Japanese, he was in a position to become friends with black and white Americans, and with Japanese Americans. He had listened to a broad range of Western popular music even before his teenage years, having frequented many American clubs, discos, and CD shops. As he entered his teens, however, he started listening to more—in his words—"aggressive" music, such as punk, rock and roll, heavy metal, and hip-hop.

His first exposure to reggae came when, based only on its album cover, he bought UB 40 and Chrissie Hynde's rendition of the Sonny and Cher song "I Got You Babe" from a neighborhood shop having a close-out sale. He did not have a record player at home, so he went to a friend's house and played the album there. He thought the song was strange and did not especially care for its "*darui*" (listless) pace. But he was intrigued by it nonetheless because on the flip side was a version, which struck him as being similar to voiceless karaoke. The song, he said, would haunt him afterward, and he listened to it continuously. He asked his father, something of a connoisseur of black music, about this reggae music. His father gave him a tape by Bob Marley, and soon Fire was introducing his friends to reggae. He had been playing many different kinds of music at parties since he was fifteen, but soon after his introduction to reggae, he began playing this music almost exclusively.

Fire believes that his taste for aggressive music before he discovered reggae was a direct reflection of his troubled youth. "Jah know everyting, what I did. Nuff trespass, nuff sin," he said. "I-an-I was a gangsta, man, rude boy, man." He said that he then wore his hair in dreadlocks and smoked marijuana less as a Rasta and more as a rude boy.

When he was around twenty, after one of his frequent trips to England, where he had gone to pursue his interest in Jamaican culture, he was arrested for marijuana possession. He spent about three months in jail. He believes the severity of his sentence was a reaction to his interest in Rasta, and he uses the experience to critique Japanese apprehension about difference as a preemptive means of social control:

> I don' criticize that. I don' complain about that because after that experience I get know nuff tings and I have learned nuff tings, good tings and bad tings. Good tings is nuff a di bredren inna my family and my Empress, yu know, love I, and pray fi I to get out, yu know, and how every-

body worry 'bout me, care about me, tink about I, and I feel really love from di bredren dem, you know. So as I really feel say I haffi take care a our bredren . . . Bad tings is how wicked is Babylon system. Dem man ya bloodclaat [a Jamaican expletive] dirty! You know. Unfair, very unfair, because dem know me is likkle bit different from di other person dem . . . I man jus,' you know, tek herb to hol' a meditation. Irie. Dem thinking this man likkle bit different, you know. Because di first time when mi deh inna police station, I don,' I don' give up man, I didn't give up . . . I just reason di Babylon dem say, this is herb, natural ting. It good for di cancer. It good fi di cancer, good fi di asthma, I explain about dat. Dem never care 'bout that obviously. Di people dem tink that this, this, this people dem dangerous . . . I have a strictly different opinion of that they have heard before. That is the reason why them like, you know, put mi inna jail longer than other person . . . It's not good for my parents and family and friends because them waiting fi dem come out so I jus' surrender dem say, "I was bad," yu nuh . . . That was very very good experience. I give thanks Jah [claps his hands together] still. I jus' give I-ses [praises] to the Holy One . . . I have learned lot of the things, and I am able to know where I am, where I am coming from. . . . and Jah tell mi seh you better inna jail to reason yourself, know yourself.

This extended quote gives a sense of Fire's ability, similar to that of several other Japanese I met, to speak a more or less fully socialized patois (Fire speaks patois better than most Japanese, though). By "fully socialized," I mean that he learned his patois not only from films, books, and other such sources, but by spending time among Jamaicans—in his case, in Britain. I am often struck by how intensely many Japanese interested in Jamaican culture want to learn patois; they are much less interested in standard English or other Western languages. Seen from one perspective, patois and Jamaican culture, like Said's (1979) Orient, are forms of a subjugated knowledge: knowing Jamaica facilitates domination over it. But from another perspective, it is possible to see as positive the fact that people like Fire value a small island's language as something worth knowing. This is in contrast to the way in which many Westerners—and even many Jamaican people—see patois as deficient, broken English, rather than a language with its own inherent value as the lingua franca of the majority of Jamaicans.

However, Fire in this quote is speaking not only in patois, but also in dread talk. This is shown by the use of such terms as "I-man" (I), "I-ses" (praises), "Babylon," and "bredren" (brethren). "Empress" communicates a particularly Rastafarian respect for his girlfriend (I do not think he was married at the time, and I do not know this woman's race, ethnicity, or nationality). While Fire used patois and dread talk with me most of the time, my sense of this particular conversation was that his use of this subcultural speech was intensified, given the heavy reasoning he was doing. It is only appropriate to use dread talk to describe his growing appreciation of Babylonian oppression and narrow-mindedness, of the love his family and friends showed him, and of himself as a person, since these were all achieved through Rastafari.

Fire also said that as a result of his "controlled and dominated" experience, he did indeed enter into a more mature relationship with Rastafari. After leaving jail, he went on to create his sound system. He felt the need to warn his friends about the medical and legal risks of marijuana use, especially given how strictly it is prohibited in Japan:

> Every man, every woman, every creation eat food fi survive, even the bird, insect, whole animal eat food. But they don' addict fi di food, man. Food is fi life. I-an-I bun herb, fi carry on di life. So some a di man smoke herb fi fulfill dem temptation, you understand, you know [in a low, insinuating voice], they want herb, they want herb. Fulfillness. Like di some a di pickney [children] dem, some a di women dem want sweet cake, sweet cake, can't stop, tings like that, man, addictive. You know, so, I-an-I need a food, but that's for the, enough, fi carry on, like, *energy*. So I smoke herb fi energy. You know, I don't smoke herb like di pickney dem eat candy, more candy, more chocolate. Some a di bredren, when mi look 'pon some a di bredren, man, like pickney, man, want more chocolate. You understand . . . This is Japan man, so you have to . . . balance . . . When you go Jamaica, when you go, like, Amsterdam . . . as much as you want, man, but this is Japan. And when you look 'pon di world, when you look 'pon Babylon, dem getting *rough*, man, and di bredren must know about that. Lotta bredren gone a jail, you know, lotta lotta bredren man, even I . . . As I experience say, I'd like to warn di bredren dem. Don' kill youself! . . . Don' waste your life.

In Fire's troubled past, an engagement with Rastafari was largely restricted to marijuana use. When this troubled past came to a climax with his imprisonment, it brought about a more positive relation with Rastafari. Rasta provided him with a set of discursive tools with which to criticize Japanese resistance to difference, and to criticize what Fire sees as his acquaintances' own careless use of the herb. This critique, which makes addiction to marijuana both juvenile and feminine, suggests Fire's adoption of patriarchal Rastafari attitudes to women (despite their elevated status as empresses).

BROTHER TAFFY

The course of Brother Taffy's (a pseudonym) identification with Rasta is in many ways similar to Fire's. Brother Taffy, too, is a dub musician. In his thirties at the time of our conversation around 2001, he spoke to me in patois, English, and Japanese. While in the company of his Japanese friends, or when he speaks to them over his cellphone, his Japanese can assume a surly, bossy toughness. When he speaks to me, however, his expressions sometimes evince a searching sensitivity, even a sense of anguish.

At the time of our interview, we were leaving his urban home in his vehicle, heading toward the hills. He was taking me fishing. We had met a couple of times before, but this was our first opportunity to talk at length. Much of Brother Taffy's understanding of Rastafari is informed by his early experience with what might be termed class difference in Japan:

> I-an-I house is, was shack. One time typhoon come. I-an-I roof, gone! So, later [sings a line from a Mighty Diamonds song], "I need a roof overhead!" You know? An' my family was poor so we had to go out shack so because . . . very small shack . . . My parents and grandparents and me and my younger brothers living together. So situation no good. My parents think about future but they don't have enough money so she have to borrow money . . . So my mom was pub manager . . . Gamble town. And cycle race there . . . When finish last race, final race, four o'clock, two minutes, you know, a lot of gambler go down to station. My mom's corner was near the station. Lot of drunkard and Mafia, Japanese Mafia, yes, *yakuza*, and bad man, so I-an-I [home town train station] has four mafia office and one right wing office. Dangerous, man.

Although a cousin and a younger brother as well as several of his childhood friends became members of the *yakuza*, and although he was twice scouted by the crime syndicate, Taffy did not join. He was nonetheless troubled in his youth: like Fire, he describes himself then as a "rude boy." He struggled academically; he claimed that none of his classmates liked him because he was a bully. "*Yowai mono ijimenai*," he says. I interpreted this to mean "the weak don't bully": by bullying, he would not be perceived as weak and would not himself be bullied. He smoked heavily, sniffed paint thinner, did drugs, and rode with *bōsōzoku* (motorcycle gangs).

To enter high school, Taffy had to study intensely for the first time in his life. For four months he did little else, and because of this and the other difficulties he was experiencing, he said, at fifteen, his hair turned completely white. When he entered high school he reverted to his rude-boy ways, and his hair turned black again.

Brother Taffy thought about his childhood poverty, his residence in the ghetto, the many Koreans living there, the heavy yakuza scouting in the community. He reflected on this neighborhood's location near heavy industrial facilities, an electric transfer station, and a military training ground (all prime targets, he notes, in case of war). He linked all these to the fact that he is burakumin, a member of Japan's outcast community.[1] He likened *hinin* (nonpeople, as they were known during the Tokugawa period) to black slaves. "I-an-I forefather, Japanese slave," he said. "We have slavery . . . like black man." He explained how his burakumin forefathers, among other discriminations they faced, were used by the emperor to plant rice with little compensation, like black slaves on American plantations. Restrictions were placed on the burakumin diet: rather than the choice portions of the cow, he said, they could eat only its innards.

Today, it remains common in Japan for the families involved in marriage negotiations to conduct background checks on their prospective son- or daughter-in-law. One of the main possibilities investigated is whether this person might be burakumin. Despite his mother's opposition, Taffy decided to leave his neighborhood to prevent his future in-laws, who are not burakumin, from discovering his ancestry. Now married, he remains very anxious about this possibility.

In addition to connecting his experience as a marginalized person in Japan with that of blacks throughout the diaspora, he also uses Rasta to more generally critique Japan's relationship with the West. Japan, he says, is "mixed up." He thinks Japanese are "killing themselves" by adopting Western-style mass consumption and production, describing his country as "a money-making factory" that needs to "cool down." "I wanna be spiritual [in] everything," he said, "but I live inna Babylon, inna concrete jungle situation. Now depression in Japan. Soon come inflation. This is Babylon system in Japan." In addition to the uncritical adoption of Western economic values, he sees the spread of signs in English—he points them out as we drive through the city—as evidence of Japanese acceptance of Western cultural imperialism. He considers this especially unfortunate because he believes that Japan's admiration of the white West is largely unreciprocated. He relates a story in which he is greeted by a white man he had never met before while walking on a street in London. "*Konnichi wa. Arigatō,*" the man said—and then, "Fuck you, Japanese." Taffy believes the man might have been reacting to recent news concerning Lucie Blackman, a white British woman allegedly murdered by a Japanese man in Japan. "Maybe white people don't like Japanese," he suggested.

Taffy suffers from depression and visits a psychiatric hospital as an outpatient, after a brief stay there two years earlier. He attributes his difficulties in part to the stress he feels trying to find a way for himself as a Japanese man who so deeply identifies with Afrocentric Rasta: "I was astray because Rastaman culture is black man culture." He recognizes that as a Japanese person, he was expected to be "Buddhist or something," but "I'm Rasta. But why Rasta, I don't know. This is Jah guidance." He sees a universality in Rastafari that helps explain Bob Marley's international popularity: not unlike Marley's, Taffy's blood is "ghetto blood." But the same ghetto identification that so powerfully links him to Bob Marley and Rastafari stigmatizes him in Japan. "I was rude boy so I smoke spliff and I was sometime pusher and street gang, my family and I'm Rasta, I'm singer." A vivid look of despair fills his eyes and then instantly recedes. "I want to be black man. I want to be black man. Everytime."

Wanting to be black for Taffy is not so much about belonging to a biological group. It is not just the self-hybridizing play of parlor-tanned skin and temporary dreads. For him, the stakes in this mission of self-making through blackness are higher and more deeply felt than for most Japanese. The desire to be black is the earnest fantasy of escape from the hardships he faces given his actual identity as burakumin. He is of ghetto blood, the descendant of "Japanese slaves," has been a rude boy. The possibility that others may discover his secrets torments him. While each of these helps justify his right to Rastafari, all combined entitle him less to Rasta than would the singular sign of black skin. He wants to be black because blackness would entitle him to the spiritual comforts that come with being Rasta, which would in turn mitigate the possibility that his world might collapse about him at any time. Yet Brother Taffy continues down this road of a Rastafari that offers him no guarantees. He has at least found in it a means of discreetly speaking his burakumin identity into fuller being, one otherwise relegated in Japan's public discourse to the status of the brutally unsaid.

RASTA AND INJUSTICE: POLITICAL ACTIVISTS

Taz (a pseudonym) was introduced to me by a friend who had met him at a gathering sponsored by an organization advocating for migrant workers' rights. One rainy night in 1999, the three of us sat in Taz's small, suburban Tokyo apartment, drinking the tasty chicken and potato soup that he had prepared for us, and eating crispy, store-bought *gyōza* (dumplings stuffed with spicy minced pork). We drank beer through the night and listened to Burning Spear, watched documentaries, and talked.

Taz, then thirty-seven, and his apartment, are Geertzian nightmares of the highest order, the kinds that choke thick description on its own ambitious tongue. Briefly, then, he wore a tight army jacket over a white T-shirt, on the front of which was printed the communist hammer and sickle. The arms and shoulders of the T-shirt were torn apart and pinned back together. His black jeans were ragged. He wore high black leather boots and big silver-framed glasses, behind which his eyes swam, magnified. A few parallel lines were etched horizontally into the stubble on the side of his head. The hair on the top of his head was swept up high; at the back, it grew long. Two or three of these long strands were matted together, the thickest one brown near the end. His hairdo thus combined the styles of mohawk and dreads.

The décor of the apartment reflected the broad range of Taz's political concerns. The walls were covered with photographs of Haile Selassie, Bob Marley, the Dalai Lama, Marx, Engels, Lenin, and others. He later explained that he did not really idolize any of these figures: as a political activist, he was only curious about how they were able to garner the support of the masses. Despite his general ambivalence toward the leaders, he said that he liked what he had heard about the Dalai Lama, especially what he had seen of the monk's relationship with the people of Tibet during a visit to the country a decade earlier. He said he had reservations about Gandhi—who, Taz believed, in insisting on nonviolence, was in effect telling his followers to "just die." Taz's apartment looked like a small video shop: his shelves were crammed with hundreds of videocassettes of various news programs and documentaries on topics ranging from Hitler to the American military presence in Somalia. Two huge banners adorned his bedroom: one showing

Bob Marley, and the other Che Guevara. Motorcycle and bright red construction helmets, and rows of black boots lay about the room.

Taz shares with Taffy a strong sense of his present political self as a product of his "ghetto" upbringing. He showed us photos of his hometown, complete with many dilapidated buildings, in Toyama prefecture, which he cheerfully described as *"ura Nippon"* (backside Japan). He shares Taffy's and Fire's deep frustration with what they view as Japanese intolerance of difference, which he expressed for a time earlier in his life through punk music. He played a Northern Irish punk band's rendition of a Marley song, "Johnny Was." He explained that he often cried listening to this song, about a man consoling a woman over the death of her son. Like that man, he, too, felt overwhelmed by all the distress in the world, so far beyond his ability to change as an individual. He said he has come to wed the class-conscious anger of Japan's punk subculture with that of Rastafari.[2] Like Fire and Taffy, Taz believes that Rasta gave him a way to articulate his disaffection with social inequality not only in Japan, but in the world at large. He said that while he has long understood capitalist exploitation, Rastafari, through its use of the term "Babylon," gave him a concrete way of thinking about it. "At first I thought my position and Bob Marley's position were different, so I really didn't care for his music that much." But then he studied Rasta more deeply, saying that he "first came to understand the soul of Rasta, the soul of Bob Marley, the soul of Burning Spear at about nineteen." He felt that while most hit songs tap into superficial, easily sold ideas, Marley's music was serious and deep. It is in this kind of music, Taz believes, that there is greatest potential to effect social change.

He came to see the political and economic problems of Jamaica, Africa, Asia, and South America as separate neither from each other nor from his concern with Japan's imperial history: all were manifestations of a Babylonian system of global economic oppression. Even compared with other urban (as opposed to many rural) Rasta-identifying Japanese like Taffy and Fire, Taz does not do much to forge a Rasta identity based on any religious practice or lifestyle. Yet Rastafari is the principal guide for his ideological and political life. He feels that all of his beliefs as a political activist are contained in a famous speech by Haile Selassie imprinted on one of the many T-shirts he makes as a hobby. In the speech, Selassie declared that until domestic and international race-based inequality are "finally and permanently discredited and abandoned," humanity would always be at war.

Our mutual friend and I stayed until close to midnight; once we reached the bus station, we realized the buses had stopped running. The rain was pouring now, and no taxis were passing. I decided to call for one on my cellphone.

Taz glared incredulously at the phone, then looked at me. Switching to English from the Japanese he had used most of the evening, he said, "That is Babylon!"

Rural Japan: The Counterculture and the Esunikku

In the urban context, then, Rasta is largely understood as a means of speaking to one's personal experience of and sense of disaffection with inequality and intolerance in Japan and overseas. The rural represents another space in which Rasta ideology is articulated. Here, Rasta intersects with another global cultural form significantly rooted in the countryside: the counterculture movement. This Japanese movement in many ways reflects its counterpart in the United States. Individuals who are part of this scene wear tie-dyed clothing and long hair, and play American folk music; among younger fans, New Age music is more in vogue. Activists' criticism is directed against the American military presence in Japan as well as the imperial institution, as a symbol of authoritarianism domestically and of Japanese colonialism throughout Asia. Ecological awareness and holistic communalism are embraced, in contrast to consumerism. The counterculture movement in Japan, as in the United States, is concerned with such causes as freeing Tibet from Chinese occupation and preventing the strip mining of Big Mountain, in Arizona, to protect the environment of the local Native Americans. The movement's followers are often interested in the religious cultures of these regions, as well as those of East India; American hippie interest in Japanese culture, particularly Zen Buddhism, facilitates links with the U.S. movement. The American poet Gary Snyder, whose writings are strongly influenced by Zen Buddhism, has visited a small mountain village in Nagano prefecture where several Japanese families steeped in the counterculture movement have settled.

Most of the residents of this village are rural Japanese whose families have lived there for a long time. But over the last couple of decades, several families who are part of the counterculture movement have moved into the area; many of these individuals knew each other previously. They live in the upper elevations of the remote mountainside in hand-built, sometimes solar-powered houses. According to some of these newer residents, although their children attend the local schools, the older residents' unfamiliarity with the counterculture lifestyle has occasionally led to strained relations with the newer residents. This lifestyle is characterized by anything from interest in the music of Jimi Hendrix to fascination with Native America (there is a sweat lodge built near one of the houses, several of the homes feature Native American architecture and décor, and the bookshelves of some of the newer residents are stacked with works about American Indians).

Countercultural concern with other cultures around the world, such as those of Native Americans, has come to include an interest in Rastafari. Until recently, a dreadlocked African American man lived in the mountain village with his Japanese wife and their two children. Another dreadlocked man, the Japanese drummer for a roots reggae band, still lives there with his wife and two of his children. A third man there showed me pictures of himself from about twelve years before, when he too wore his hair in dreadlocks (his hair remains long), and spent time in Jamaica in order to develop his appreciation of Rastafari. He supports himself in part by making African drums, a skill taught to him by the African American man who used to be his neighbor. Bob Marley's image recurs around the town, with a painted portrait of the musician displayed outside one family's house; many of the families have some of his music.

Much of the Japanese interest in Rastafari, then, especially in rural areas, appears linked to the counterculture movement as one aspect of a broader interest in world culture. Since at least the late 1980s, in both rural and urban areas, the discursive and stylistic movement known as the ethnic—esunikku—has taken interest in world culture to its extreme. A discursive and stylistic category onto itself, the esunikku mixes into one big stew everything considered ethnic—that is, nonwhite but, significantly, largely without Chinese and Korean cultural elements (maybe too much history there).[3] Enter one of Japan's many rural or urban ethnic shops, and you will find American Indian dream catchers, baskets, and beads; Ghanaian wooden sculptures, *djembe* drums, and xylophones; posters of Bob Marley and Ras Pedro's famous "Rasta Baby" painting; Tibetan prayer flags; Nepalese wrist and ankle bracelets; bronze Shiva sculptures, Parvati paintings, and saffron saris; jade pendants from Thailand; and Peruvian crystals and fabrics.

In August 1988, a ten-day event called *Inochi no Matsuri* (Festival of Life) was held at a ski lodge in Nagano prefecture. Based on the book later published to document the event, and based on feedback I gathered from those who attended, the event seemed to revolve around Native American and other forms of spiritualism, antinuclear protest, ecological activism, advocacy of the legalization of marijuana, and other forms of counterculture-identified activism. It also included some elements from Africa and the African diaspora, such as reggae performances. Inochi no Matsuri is held every twelve years, and I attended it in August 2000, at another ski lodge in Nagano. This event seemed to include all the elements of the one in 1988 and perhaps more, drawing not only on the energies of the Japanese hippie movement, but also on an esunikku sensibility that had come to maturity in the intervening years.

Surrounded by mountains, the resort area was littered with brightly colored tepees and tents. The main activities took place over approximately six square miles. About 2,500 people reportedly attended. There was a large area with dozens of tents and stalls in which vendors sold arts and crafts from around the world. In one section, some of the residents from the Nagano town described above sold produce they had harvested from their own farms. Mobile restaurants selling dishes from Egypt and Ghana were stationed about the grounds. Many people were dressed in brightly colored, loose-fitting, tie-dyed or hemp clothing; Japanese women lounged on the grass in the traditional costumes of peoples ranging from Native Americans to North African Bedouins. Japanese dreads moved through the crowds. One dreadlocked man, holding a staff decorated in Rasta colors, displayed a sort of bamboo shrine on which was carved about three hundred dreadlocked heads. (He told me the viewer was free to associate the figures with Rasta, Hindu sadhus, Australian Aborigines, or Buddha. He also said that once he had carved a thousand heads he would sell the shrine or give it away to a temple.) There were chants by North and South American Indians and sadhus, American folk songs, and performances by reggae bands. Taiko drums and Okinawan *sanshin* (three string; an instrument related to the samisen) took their place beside sitars and didgeridoos. The noise of performances from other, faraway stages, the steady drumming of djembe—it seemed every other person had a djembe—distantly flavored the air. In the evening, a half-naked performance troupe, their bodies powdered white, slithered up and down the scaffolding of the main stage, glaring eerily at the audience as a huge ensemble of musicians, featuring two female dancers in blond wigs, played acid jazz. The festival ended with a rave concert.

One Ghanaian man chatted quietly with the many people seeking him out about his drumming. He went to perform onstage, and while drumming a woman walked up to him to take his picture *"Dame!"* (Don't!) he barked. The woman hurried away. Once offstage, he expressed to me his profound irritation at being in this sort of place, where he felt Japanese people had so little difficulty in stirring his culture, which meant so much to him, into this seemingly senseless stew. The following day, however, the creator of the bamboo shrine said he enjoys this kind of scene for the same reason: because it brings together so many cultural elements. However, most of the older people I spoke with who had also attended the 1988 event said that this one simply left them numb. These different positions bring up a tension that I will discuss in the final chapter. This is the tension between the desire of many Jamaicans to preserve the particularities and intimacies of Jamaican life among Jamaicans where it is most deeply felt, and the feeling of many Japanese that Rasta is merely one element in the broader, exhilarating cultural diversity found outside Japan's borders.

Reimagining Spirituality: Rural Dreads

As discussed earlier, urban Rasta-identifying Japanese tend to use the movement to criticize what they see as class-based social injustice in Japan and overseas. This is also true to some extent of rural Rasta-identifying Japanese. But perhaps more than in the city, rural Rasta is expressed not only in personal spiritual and political terms, but also in familial and communal ones. An aspect of Japanese identification with Rasta that helps distinguish it from the counterculture and the esunikku involves intimate knowledge of the Jamaican Rastafarian worldview and religious practices. This knowledge begins to mark out the possibilities of an individual's identification with the movement. But what are these possibilities? What are their limits? For these individuals, is knowledge of Rasta the same as belief in it? How relevant can Rasta—an Afrocentric spiritual movement, a religion originating on a tiny island on the other side of the world—be for Japanese people?

During my first research trip to Japan, I made my first visit to Kyoto, one of Japan's ancient capitals, famous for its many major temples and shrines. I visited a few of the best known of these, including Ryōanji Temple. Founded in 1450, the temple belongs to the Rinzai sect of Zen Buddhism and is most famous for its *karesansui* (dry landscape) garden composed of fifteen rocks. Visitors, after their obligatory count of the rocks, imagine what the landscaper must have had in mind when he arranged the rocks as he did. The temple grounds are meticulously landscaped; as is the case with most Buddhist gardens, there is a sense of the landscapers' having exercised enormous control over every corner of the grounds, from the profusion of flowers and plants to their chromatic spread in space. Nature is made to seem itself, even as this appearance fully stands as an expression of human control.

Along one of the cordoned paths guiding visitors on precise routes through the temple grounds, past shaped kinships of trees and the sound of water flowing over rocks, stood a sign that read (in Japanese and English):

> We need your cooperation [in maintaining] this time honored temple. This Ryōanji temple is a cultural property. Please comply with the following requests:
>   1 No smoking [in] the precinct, except in the designated smoking area.
>   2 Do not step on the moss. . . .
>   3 Do not enter the private area[s], partitioned by a bamboo pole or a rope.
>
> —Ryōanji Temple

Nature as experienced today in Japanese Buddhism is cultural property. This property belongs to everyone, and thus to no one. No hand can touch it, except that of the state charged with its care. The natural is experienced from this remove. Buddhist naturalism is complex and deeply culturally informed; over the centuries, its meanings have come to be fully given. (Shintō too represents a historically deep, politically invested, perhaps even politically compromised imagination of the natural, given Shintō leaders' complicity in Japan war time effort.)

But Rastafari returns nature to its condition as the unknown. It is reclaimed in blackness, a profoundly usable idiom of the enigmatic natural. Rasta in Japan has little to do with Haile Selassie as divinity. He is significant to most Rasta-identifying Japanese to the extent that they respect his significance to Jamaican Rastas. This respect, such as is performatively demonstrated when his name is called upon during the use of marijuana, is a kind of proxy for a direct belief of one's own in the divinity of Selassie. The spirituality of Rasta-identifying Japanese has less to do with a belief in Selassie's divinity and has more to do with reclaiming the Japanese natural, imagined as a tabula rasa on which to rewrite one's supposedly timeless and natural (though actually profoundly historicized and acculturated) self. It is an uncanny return through the Afrocentrisms of Rastafari to a vitalized spiritual self.

The lives of Ras Seek, Ras Tanki, and Ras Tibby (all pseudonyms)[4] reflect these concerns with articulating a Rastafarian religious identity free of the weight of Buddhist doctrine. Ras Seek is a roots singer who was in his mid-thirties when I first met him, in 1998; not long after that, he got married and moved with his new wife and baby to a small town on the Izu peninsula. There, he says, he feels very much in his element. Once as he drove us home from a concert in Tokyo, I noticed that he was quiet and seemed very tense; only after he had left the city did he seem more relaxed. At that point, he said that the police often pulled him over because of his beard and dreadlocks.

Seek traveled extensively in his twenties, including stays in Jamaica, England, and Ghana, where he met many Rasta brethren. He stayed for several months in the famous Rasta community in Shashamane, Ethiopia. He is a member of the Twelve Tribes denomination of Rastafari, and until recently he published a free paper that featured the speeches and writings of Haile Selassie; profiles of Jamaican musicians; and his own musings on Rastafari.

Seek was the eldest son of a Buddhist monk, and according to tradition, Seek was to take his father's place in the monastery when he passed away. Seek had studied Buddhism at a university in Kyoto, but over time, he grew disaffected with the religion. He began to study the religious traditions of other countries. Drawn to reggae's powerful beat, he grew interested in Rastafari and decided he would not follow in his father's footsteps. When his father passed away, a monk friend of the family took over the monastery until Seek's younger brother was prepared to take on this responsibility himself. At first his brother did not understand Seek's decision, but he eventually became more supportive. Seek says, however, that because of this decision, "maybe I made my mother cry."

Ras Tanki is a reggae singer, twenty-five in 1999, the year I met him. Like Seek, he wears his dreadlocks long, down to his lower back. He speaks very comfortably in patois and dread talk, using such expressions as "sight-up" (see), "trod" (walk), and "in this time" (now, nowadays). He says in his youth, he was always searching, describing himself as having a very spiritual bent from an early age. His search took him through a period of drug use. He developed an interest in Rastafari and grew his hair in dreadlocks. In

1994, he visited Jamaica for the first time. During this visit, he struggled to become Rasta, and believing himself a fake, shaved off his dreadlocks. He describes this as the single most important act of his spiritual life. He went to *nyabinghis* (gatherings of Rastafarians) all over the island. At one such event, everyone present was asked to remove his or her tam to reveal that all were true Rastas. The "bald" Tanki caused a great stir. The other attendees were furious at his presence, searching roughly through his scalp for the number 666 (the mark of the devil). He spoke to the crowd from his heart about his struggle to realize his Rasta self; they relented and came to accept him. He became a student of the late Augustus Pablo, the well-known dub musician and Rastafarian.[5] Tanki regrew his locks, and even though he realizes he must mature more fully into the movement, he now declares with certainty: "I am Rasta."

Tanki also confirmed my suspicion that Japanese interest in Rastafari can come out of a sense of dissatisfaction with the Shintō and Buddhist traditions. He described how Buddhism has become a very formalized religion in Japan, although in its earliest days, it was "just Buddha moving," with people drawn to his spirit. He says this while discussing his effort in Japan to maintain his spiritual connection with Rastafari despite being away from Jamaica, the implied link between the two statements being that the trappings of formal religion are not necessary to maintain an elevated spirituality. A holy man in a holy land is holy enough, but a holy man in "Babylon" is truly holy.

Ras Tibby lives with his wife in mainland Okinawa, in a rented house in a seaside village. In his early forties in 1999, effusive, an experienced traveler, his mind constantly searches for cultural connections between Africans and other peoples around the world (a common tendency among many of the dreads I met). He was curious, for instance, about the fact that an Indonesian instrument he played was so similar in form and sound to the African kalimba. He notes that the Aborigines he met in Australia described themselves as African, and questioned why it was that China, to whose influence Okinawa's lion-shaped *shiisaa* sculptures has been attributed, has no lions itself (hence the possibility of an African connection). Just over five feet tall, Tibby described how the village children, when he went outside with his locks flowing freely (he described his feeling of pride as he did so), followed him, calling him by the name of a local mythological creature who is tiny, with long hair and an impish red face. All of these examples are meant to suggest the mysterious universality of Africa and Rastafari.

Tibby also talked about his stay in Jamaica in 1998, where he was supposed to have met Mutabaruka, one of Jamaica's most respected Rastafarians. He missed him, but he did have a chance to study with the late Mortimo Planno, another Rasta famous in part for initiating Bob Marley into Rastafari. As opposed to Tibby's decision to study with Planno, many Japanese in Jamaica turn to Dr. Bagga, an herbalist who became well known among Japanese dreads with the publication of *Synchro Vibes* (Keita 1993)—a book written by a Japanese man who traveled to Jamaica and learned Rasta medicinal techniques from Dr. Bagga. Tibby is put off by Japanese dreads who flock to Dr. Bagga just because they read about him in this book. He described his confrontation with an older Japanese dread who told Tibby not to title himself "Ras" Tibby because he believed Tibby did not understand Rasta. He expressed his intense dislike of the idea of a "Japanese Rastafari," feeling that all Rastas are Rastas.

Ras Tibby is annoyed, similarly, by the search of some dreads for the origins of the Japanese people among "the Japanese" of today. He believes such a search, if really necessary, must take place among the Ainu, the indigenous people who occupied Japan before the arrival of Korean and Chinese settlers. He also said he was not fond of communal life, because it is exclusionary. Many of these remarks seem intended as criticisms of the elder who told Tibby he did not understand Rasta, as well as those associated with him. I discuss this group presently.

I have discussed the range of ways in which several rural Japanese have articulated their identifications as Rastafari. In all three cases, Rasta was a way to revitalize their spiritual lives. Rasta revealed for Seek the staidness of the monastic life laid out before him, one he felt compelled to reject. For Tanki, Rasta gave him a vision of himself as a solitary Japanese Rasta buoyed with a spiritual energy that institutionalized Buddhism lacked. For Tibby, the African blackness of Rasta seemed to have set down roots around the world, including in rural Japan, where it enigmatically surfaces in the form of Okinawa's mythological creatures and its shiisaa statues.

While most Japanese pursue their Rasta identifications individually or within their own families, in the next section I focus on one group of Japanese dreads who formed a Rasta yard using those found in Jamaica as a model. Just as Japanese dancehall artists put into practice the skills they learned in Jamaica in the effort to site Japan within the broader performative field of international dancehall, these Rasta-identifying Japanese seek to root Rasta in Japan by creating a space, a Rasta yard, which localizes in performative practice the life experience they gained in Jamaica. But also, just as the endeavors of Japanese dancehall artists in Japan must ultimately be appreciated as sited in local terms (even while these endeavors importantly invoke the gendered, socioeconomic, and other politics of both societies), the quotidian performativities of the Rasta yard must not simply be judged by their fidelity to the Jamaican, but must be most immediately understood according to local social politics (even while they may be seen as complexly invoking the politics of both places). Thus I first discuss the town, Yoshino, in which this yard is located, in order to give a sense of the communal, historical, and religious ground in which Rasta has taken root. I then discuss the yard as a space, the residents' daily lives and embodied subcultural practices, and an annual festival—all in order to understand the range of ways in which the dreads root their global cultural identifications as Rastafarians in the Yoshino present and, more deeply, in its imaginarily uncanny rural past.

Yoshino

Yoshinoyama (Mount Yoshino) is a small community of about 700 residents in Nara prefecture. The community is part of Yoshino-chō, with about 10,800 residents. Yoshino is well known for its rich local culture. The name evokes for many Japanese as well as Americans the image of cherry blossoms, a variety of which (*yoshinozakura*) is named after the town. Yoshino is quiet for most of the year, its businesses, often on the top floor of three-story homes (the lower two used as living quarters and warehouses, respectively), less fully staffed. For the most part, only a small trickle of hikers and tourists pass through. In April, however, when the mountain ranges surrounding the town blossom into clouds of pink, the trains to Yoshino Station and the cable car running from the base of the mountain, where the station is located, up to the town are in constant operation. The usually empty parking area, about the size of a football field, is crammed with buses and other vehicles, and the narrow winding streets fill with hundreds of visitors. Several large inns (*ryokan*) serve these visitors, and the restaurants, gift shops, and stores selling handmade candy lining the narrow, tarp-shaded main street do a thriving business. Many visitors come for the *kuzu* (arrowroot) products for which Yoshino is also known.

Yoshino's rich political and religious history is also well known. Emperor

Go-Daigo fled from Kyoto to Yoshino in 1337 and set up a rival southern court, which survived until 1392, when it succumbed to Kyoto's northern court. Go-Daigo himself died in 1339 and is interred at Yoshino's Nyoirin-ji Temple. Mount Yoshino is the site of the Kimpusenji Temple complex, which includes the Zao-dō Main Hall, headquarters of the Shugen Honshū sect of *Shugendō* (Miyake 2001). Shugendō is a form of mountain asceticism found only in Japan, mixing Buddhism with the practices of pre-Buddhist ascetics. Legend has it that the religion was founded by the priest En-no-Gyōja on nearby Mount Ōmine. Zao-dō is 34 meters tall, making it the second largest wooden edifice in Japan,[6] and it is one of several structures and artifacts throughout Yoshino that have been designated national treasures. The temple complex plays an important role in the life of the community. Among the annual events (*nenchūgyōji*) that the temple organizes is the *kaeru tobi* (frog jump) festival, which takes place every July 7.

As one among many small Japanese towns that try to survive by seeking a distinctive place for themselves on the map of national and even international tourist interest, Yoshino's star has risen even more in recent years. In April 2002, a major travel magazine, *Tabi no Techō* (Travel Notebook), ran a special feature on the town. More significant, however, is the fact that officials from Nara prefecture and Yoshino lobbied UNESCO to designate a number of pilgrimage sites, and the routes connecting them, as a World Heritage site. Mount Yoshino and nearby Mount Ōmine are included. Banners placed all around town advocating this designation declared, "*Yoshino-yama o sekai isan ni*" (Toward Mount Yoshino as a World Heritage Site). The effort came to fruition on July 1, 2004. As part of Kimpusenji's yearlong celebration of the UNESCO designation, hundreds of Shugendō practitioners from all over Japan convened at Zao-dō to pray for world peace. Three sculptures of *gongen* (incarnations of Buddha, or bodhisattvas) housed in the hall were displayed to the public for the first time in four hundred years. This event was advertised in part with a flier headed with the words: "*Yoshino kara sekai e. Sekai kara yoshino e*" (From Yoshino to the world. From the world to Yoshino).

YOSHINO DREADS

Yoshino is also home to a roots reggae band, eight of whose ten members are dreads. Most have their own homes, some in Yoshino and some beyond. However, when the band performs frequently, especially in the summertime, those members living furthest away often stay in the house of Takuji, the band's oldest member and main lead singer (all names given for Yoshino dreads and family members are pseudonyms). And regardless of the performance schedule, band members visit the house year-round for extended periods of time. For example, in spring 2001, in addition to Takuji, his wife, and their baby daughter, who live permanently in the house, one band member was living there with his two children, and another with his wife and two children. The house is open not only to band members and their families, but also to acquaintances.

Yoshino dreads seem to be not just fully integrated into the Yoshino community, but indispensable parts of it. Describing the town's initial reaction to his friends' dreadlocks, Saiji—he is the only one of the band's two members who does not wear his long hair in dreadlocks—said that the townspeople, unfamiliar with Rasta, were only curious. Other than the dreadlocks, Saiji continued, the men seemed "normal" to the townspeople, and so the locks never became much of an issue.[7] Another factor was that Takuji and Masato especially have long been respected members of the community. Cousins, the two men grew up in Yoshino, know everyone really well, and profess a deep love for their hometown. Masato told me that he never appreciated Yoshino so much as when he returned there from his travels around the world. Takuji-san's mother owns a craft shop; Masato and his wife own and operate one of the major inns in Yoshino. Thus the men are important members of the business community. Masato also enjoys some regional renown as a potter: he has been featured on local television—dreads and all—as one of several noteworthy artists in the area. Furthermore, both men participate in two of the town's most important annual events. They are central to the organization of the kaeru tobi event. and are also involved in *hanami* (viewing cherry blossoms), given Masato's and his wife's ownership of one of the inns, which become very busy during this season.

THE RASTA YARD

Like the dancehall, the Rasta yard represents a space in which Yoshino dreads are able to perform their identities as followers of a transnational Jamaican movement, in ways that are informed by the sociocultural and political life of Jamaica (and the broader global for which this Jamaica is to some degree a metonym), and that valorize the rural Japan in which it is situated. About seven years ago, in India, several of the band members began talking about the idea of creating this yard. The lead singer's rented house came to be used for this purpose. The house is modeled after Rasta yards in Jamaica, where several members have stayed for periods of time lasting from about one to six months. The Japanese author of *Synchro Vibes* describes Dr. Bagga's yard in Jamaica, where he stayed for some time: "Of the people who stayed at Dr. Bagga's house, who were family members, relatives, friends? . . . Dr. Bagga even took in and raised children who were not related to him, so it was one great extended family of humanity" (Keita 1993, 8). Rasta embraces this open, "traditional African" family structure, in which people live in extended—as opposed to isolated nuclear—families. One of the men drew two lines on the ground representing the Japanese social situation as one in which groups of families live their lives parallel to each other, without much contact with each other. He then drew a circle representing Rasta, illustrated by the Rasta yard, as inclusive of all people.

The yard is located near a spot where big purple, blue, and white hydrangeas bloom in the summertime. A path that runs off the road leads to a flight of steps made out of earth and logs; the house sits at the top of the steps. Outside the old but well-maintained house, damp clothes and bunches of *yomogi* (mugwort) dry on a line in the sun. Piles of chopped wood are stacked in a shed and covered with a blue tarp.

The house's sliding door leads to a small entryway where shoes are removed; the entryway opens up into the living room. Near the far right corner of the living room sits a large, low, round table surrounded by about eight sitting cushions (*zabuton*) placed on the tatami-covered floor. Between the table and the entryway is an old-fashioned wood stove used for cooking as well as to heat the uninsulated house in the winter. Two outer walls run behind and to the right of the table; to the left is an area the children usually occupy while eating.

To the extreme left of this area is a wall on which hangs a large poster of Hindu deities, as well as a large framed photograph of a seated Haile Selassie. A long, white silk cloth rests on top of and hangs evenly along the sides of the frame. Beneath the picture are statuettes of Hindu deities, and below that a photo of Bob Marley in performance. On a stand resting against this wall sits a sort of miniature Hindu shrine, and behind that a small replica of the same Selassie painting. On the stand also sits a television, which the children watch only very occasionally, as well as a videocassette recorder and stereo equipment. Near the stand is a telephone, with a big wooden box where visitors can place coins to pay for their calls. Continuing counterclockwise, completing the circle that began with the entryway, next is the kitchen area. The entire area described so far—entryway, living and dining room with unofficial play and eating areas for the children, and the kitchen—is about twelve by nine feet. This area is also decorated here and there with a large photograph of the lead singer and his daughter, a *sumi-e* (ink and wash) painting by one of the band members, a couple of hanging guitars, other paintings with Hindu motifs, a tie-dyed banner, and Rasta-colored (red, green, and yellow) fliers for past events in which the band has performed.

A corridor runs from this main space through the center of the rest of the house. On the left side of this hallway is a washroom, where laundry is done and the residents bathe; inside the washroom is a picture of two smiling Ethiopian women. Beside the washroom is a lavatory. A sign (for visitors) near the toilet reads (in Japanese): "Water for toilet here." Also near the toilet is a series of tiny faded sketches of a couple in various, labeled sexual positions. On the right side of the hallway—along whose wall sits an oversized ten-thousand-yen note, upside down—is a big storage space. On the door to this room, which runs the full length of the corridor, is a picture of African women carrying big jars of water on their heads. The hallway ends in two bedrooms, a smaller one to the left, and a larger one straight ahead and to the right. The permanent residents use the smaller room, and long-term guests use the larger. When there are many overnight visitors, they sleep packed closely on the floor of the living room.

As the interior of the house attests, then, there is an easy flow of the many elements of global culture that comprise the residents' international experiences. Rastafari occupies the center, most obviously shown in the naming of this space as a Rasta yard, the central place of the Selassie photographs, the Rasta-colored fliers of the band's performances, the picture of the Ethiopian women (and, less directly Rastafarian, the African women carrying jars of water). With regard to the upside-down ten-thousand-yen note, Jamaican Rastas make precisely the same symbolic gesture with Jamaican currency to disparage the capitalist worship of money. Yet the Indian (the Hindu poster), the specifically African (again, the picture of the women with the jars), and the Japanese (the sumi-e painting) are not to be overlooked. They reflect an effort to construct a space in which the men's given identification as Japanese becomes linked to a desired identification with a global that is most specifically Jamaican Rastafarian, but also African, Indian, and potentially, richly, anything else. This given identification as Japanese is given not only because they are Japanese, but also because all these elements are ultimately to be sited in the ground of the Japanese rural.

But who are these individuals? How do they lead their daily lives as people, as a community? How is the Rasta yard—as a local siting within the broader field of international Rastafari—and the Rastafarian way of life that the yard stands for, constituted as such in daily practice? Diet, dreadlocks, and medicinal practice are three embodied and interpersonal means of realizing Rastafari. Participation in the annual kaeru tobi event represents a fourth, in this case annual, public ceremonial instance of this effort.

The band members ranged in age from the early thirties to the mid-forties around 2000. As musicians, they play a happy brand of roots reggae, in which most of the men take turns on the vocals. Their songs reflect such themes as the joys of the Rasta lifestyle, the beauty of nature, and the importance of recycling. While they perform year-round, traveling from one countryside venue to another in a large van, most of their performances are held in the summer. The band members earn little from their performances, and they engage in various part-time work. Takuji sells antiques at open-air fairs and markets in Kyoto and Nagoya. Three other band members—Hayato, Aran, and Keiichi—work with Masato and his wife at the ryokan. Masato and his wife, who supervises the staff and works in the reception area of the ryokan, perform in another, smaller reggae band. Hayato, Aran, and Keiichi perform various tasks in the maintenance of the ryokan, which is very busy in the spring. Their work continues throughout the year, however, in order to prepare for the busy season and also to tend to the few customers trickling in at other times. Saiji is an artist and paints for a living, and Aitarō works occasionally for a lumber company. The others are engaged in similar work in and around nearby Osaka.

Almost all the members are married, and the women staying at the yard—most frequently Keiko, who is Takuji's wife and who has a daughter with him, and Naemi, Keiichi's wife, who has a son and a daughter with him—work together taking care of the children. They were very polite to me, usually the only adult male at the yard in the daytime, given my status as a visitor to the house and my primary association with the men. On my second visit, I was taken aback by how much more at ease with me they seemed compared to the first trip, greeting me not only with the requisite civility but also with genuine warmth.

While the women, like the men, tended to wear ethnic or tie-dyed cloth-ing, often with accessories carrying Rastafarian motifs, they did not seem as Rasta-oriented as the men. None wore her hair in dreads. The women, curiously, seemed relatively indifferent toward Rastafari, an attitude most clearly expressed to me by Ras Tibby's wife Sayumi, during my stay in Okinawa. Tibby and I had been talking about Rasta, and then he went away briefly, leaving me with her and the two people who had driven me to meet her and Tibby: Naoko Morioka, the postcard artist, and a male acquain-tance. I asked Sayumi how she felt about Rasta, and she declared her in-difference toward it. Naoko playfully interjected to declare that men are "weak," and that they labor to find meaning in life. Women, on the other hand, "overstand" these things. Men struggle to live ideologically in the world; women live sensibly in it. Tibby returned; he said that sometimes he looked at Sayumi and felt that even though she was ambivalent toward Rasta—sometimes saying dryly, "What is Rasta?"—he suddenly realizes that she too is Rasta. As Tibby said this, Sayumi remained silent. The women at the Yoshino house demonstrate a similar attitude to Rasta, al-though they are less pointedly indifferent than Sayumi. They seemed gener-ally at ease with communal life and with their responsibilities, although Keiko once told me a little ruefully that she wished she could travel with the men as frequently as she once had, when she was a backup singer for the band. She felt that now she could not go with them that often, since she had to take care of the children. She also expressed her slight unease at times when her husband's dreadlocks attracted attention.[8]

The men usually begin returning from work around eight o'clock, and even if they will retire to their own homes for the night, they often have dinner at the Rasta yard. However, the wives and children of these men usually have dinner at their own homes. This routine corresponds with the tendency of working men in Japan to hang out with their male colleagues after work, leaving little time for family life. The Yoshino men take seats around the low, round table; Takuji usually sits in the corner. A cassette— almost always reggae, often their last performance—plays in the back-ground. As the men enter the house, they always greet those already seated in the Jamaican style, tapping right fists vertically, then head on horizon-tally, and sometimes raising their fists to their chests. As or after they complete this routine, they say, "Ya-man," a common expression among Jamaican men.

The meals, cooked and brought out by the women, are almost exclusively vegetarian. Beer is never served—which is unusual for large male gatherings in Japan—and the men consume alcohol away from the house only on ceremonial occasions. These dietary restrictions reflect Rastafarian proscription, and reflect one means by which the Rasta yard is interpersonally and bodily constituted as a spiritual, as well as a mundane, place. These "Ital" (natural) meals include soba noodles, fish, salads, *iri genmai* (toasted brown rice), stewed vegetables, apples, kimchi, white and light brown rice sprinkled with sesame seeds, store-bought or home-made jam, and miso soup. Drinks include hot tea and coffee, iced tea, and apple juice. After serving the men, the women sit in the eating area for the children, and as they feed the children, they themselves eat. If there are no children about, the women eat at other available spaces around the table.

Conversation at the table remains very generalized. Despite the symbolic critique of capitalism in the form of the inverted bill, the deep reasoning about Jah and Rastafari, and about national and world politics, common among diasporic Rastas, is missing among the Yoshino dreads. My careful attempts to elicit talk on these matters were met with brief, perfunctory replies, nor did these issues emerge of their own accord. This reluctance is part of my sense of Rastafari among some rural individuals as more global cultural than global political. (This is not to say, however, that Rasta in Japan is without efforts toward theological complexity, as discussed in the next chapter.) The attitude in these gatherings was defined more by an effort to reinforce the homosocial bonds (Roberson and Suzuki 2003) of shared experience—as co-workers, members of the same band, neighbors, fellow travelers, and friends—through the metaphor of Rasta. While not precisely matching the movement in the diaspora, then, this use of Rastafari becomes a way for these individuals to situate their collective encounter with the world outside Japan in terms that are most meaningful to them.

Eventually the conversation dies down; the men—intricately tapping their fists together—return home or stay over for the night.

DREADLOCKS AND MEDICINAL PRACTICE

In addition to diet, dreadlocks represent a second bodily means by which Yoshino dreads site global Rastafari in the rural Yoshino present, here through a reimagination of the town's religious past. Masato showed me a rendering of En no Gyōja, the founder of Yoshino's Shugendō sect, who is usually represented with a beard and long hair down to his waist. "He is Rasta," Masato said to me, with a smile. Like the long-haired, mythological figure with whom children in Ras Tibby's community associated him, En no Gyōja's "dreadlocks" as playfully linked to that of Jamaican Rastas send the roots of Japanese Rastafari mysteriously into the local past. If this appreciation of Rasta is rooted in the rich soil of Shugendō's past, and if the trunk is Yoshino in the here and now, then Jamaica and Africa are branches that reach more broadly into the global. As the house's prominent Hindu décor attests, Indian culture—which figures significantly in the counterculture scene in Japan, the United States, and elsewhere—represents another branch, playing a critical role in the men's Rasta identifications. Several band members have traveled to India, as noted earlier; Takuji says that he was in some ways more impressed by the subcontinent of India than by the small island of Jamaica. Other members compare Rastas to Indian sadhus, the Hindu ascetics who, like Rastas, wear their hair long and matted. Dreadlocks, then, enigmatically site a range of global spiritual traditions as well as those of the local past in the present, within the individual and collective bodies of the Yoshino dreads.

Medicinal knowledge and practice is a third embodied means of situating international Rastafari in daily local life. One day, the band was scheduled to perform in Gifu prefecture, several hours by car from Yoshino, and Takuji invited me to ride along. After breakfast, the group set out from the home of another of the band members where the group's van, emblazoned with the band's name in Rasta colors, was parked. The dreads stopped by a convenience store and then hit the road for the main leg of the trip.

We settled in for the long ride.

The air in the van grew hot and sleepy.

Sirens sounded close by.

A chilled, alert silence filled the van. Every head was thrust to the nearest window. We looked around and found the vehicle: a firetruck.

We watched the truck roar by. Silence again. And then, everyone burst into laughter.

Hayato was seated closest to me, and we talked for most of the trip. In his late thirties, his English was curiously flavored with Italian, which he speaks fluently, having lived in Rome between 1989 and 1995. His father, married five times, fled there after the Second World War as a failed kamikaze pilot. Several of Hayato's comments revealed an intimate familiarity with Rastafarian ways of thinking. Marveling at the scenery outside, he would suddenly scowl at the way technology brutalized the natural landscape, seeing a tortured female figure in the antennae-filled hills rolling by. Then he began nodding off to sleep. Or rest, he would say, because Rastas never sleep: to be asleep is to be dead. He said he never dreams, because dreams are illusory and pointless. Only when awake does one have agency over one's life. This recalls many Jamaican Rastafarians' belief that true Rastas never die, that the kingdom of heaven is not in the sky but here on earth.

Hayato shared with me some of his deep pharmaceutical knowledge, which he says he gained partly from his father, an acupuncturist. He also gained some of this knowledge from his contact with Japanese Rastas who had been students of Dr. Bagga, himself an advocate of the use of aloe to aid in the functioning of the lymphatic system. Hayato described how at eighteen, he had used chemical sprays to deal with his asthma, and said how much he is against such remedies now. He said that Aitarō's friend died about six years ago from a heart attack brought on by use of one of these sprays. He prefers *shizen ryōhō*—natural therapy—which he considers safer and more effective. He recommended the use of dried, shaved, and crushed mugwort to help wounds to heal; a cabbage leaf placed on the forehead or lime rubbed on the skin reduces fever. *Biwa* (loquat) leaves when warmed and placed upon a wound for ten minutes take impurities away from the blood. He produced a blue medical kit that he carried with him everywhere, and took out an antibiotic spray as well as *mogusa* (moxa), used by acupuncturists to stimulate pressure points in the body. He broke off a flake, placed it on a spot on the back of his hand, and lit it. He showed how his hands and arms were marked by the mogusa burnings he endured to overcome his asthma.

Aran, with whom I would also speak at length on the ride to Gifu,[9] as well as the other band members, had similar burns across their bodies and were intimately familiar with the information Hayato was sharing with me. The men have made their bodies into instruments with which to link, through application of cross-cultural pharmaceutical knowledge, Rastafarian and Eastern identifications. The enactment of acupunctural and Rastafarian medical techniques upon their bodies, and the resulting marking of the bodies—coupled with dreadlocks and the group's communal consumption of natural food—ground attenuated global selves in local practice.

KAERU TOBI

The dreads' participation in the kaeru tobi (frog jump) festival represent another, less everyday means by which the dreads performatively realize their Jamaican Rasta identifications. The festival, held in 2000 just before the Gifu trip, is based on the story (of which there are several versions) of a man who cursed at a local deity out of his hatred of Buddhism. The annoyed deity sent a gigantic bird, which suddenly transported the man to the edge of a remote cliff and left him there. A priest passing by delivered the man by transforming him into a frog. The priest carried the man in this transportable form to Kimpusenji Temple, where other priests returned the man to human form. The story is seen as illustrating the power and graciousness of Buddhist priests. In the kaeru tobi festival, a young man dressed in a frog's costume is transported via *taikodai* (the taikodai looks like a portable shrine, but its main compartment accommodates a large drum as well as a drummer). The taikodai is carried all over the town by several men, before finally being taken to the temple to participate in a Shugendō ceremony.

On the morning of the event, Takuji asked me if I wanted to participate, and although I was not sure what the exact nature of that participation would be, I agreed. He took me to the ryokan and we entered a room where the dreads were moving their massive locks about as their partners helped them get dressed in traditional matsuri (festival) wear. Masato offered to help me get dressed, and it was only then that I realized I had been invited to help carry the taikodai through the streets of Yoshino.

When everyone was dressed, we went out and got into a van, which drove us to a local restaurant; there we ate at no charge. Next we drove to the building where two taikodai were located, a smaller one for children and a larger one for us. The smaller taikodai was similarly designed, with long poles running along the sides for its bearers to grasp, except that, sensibly enough, this smaller one had wheels. Nearby, a young man with plucked eyebrows was being fitted into a frog costume, and the drummer was also close at hand.

The children charged ahead with their taikodai, and soon it was our turn. One of the dreads ritually offered me sake. The taikodai, I was told, was properly borne by about twenty-five people. There were roughly fifteen of us; of this group, nine were band members, including seven dreads.

A clacking sounded—first slow, then rapid. We heaved upward the taikodai, with the frog man above and the drummer inside, and set it on our shoulders. It was heavy, but after a few steps it felt manageable. We stepped out of the facility, turned, and walked down the street, the men's chanting punctuated by drums.

After we had walked for a few minutes, the weight seemed heavier. Near the end of this stage—there would be about five in all, with short breaks in between—we came to a stop, shuffling from side to side, while thrusting the taikodai violently up and down in the air. We repeated after the leader of the procession, "*Ugokase yo! Erai yacha!*" (Move it! You are great!) while the frog man pranced above. Finally we set the taikodai down. We had stopped before one of the town's several temples. Women approached us with wet towels, water, small cans of beer, and lemon drinks. A small group of onlookers had gathered there, and photographers shot pictures of us from a distance.

Masato led the procession in its final stages. We set the taikodai down when we arrived before the elevated Kimpusenji Temple. Down the crowded main road, a procession of Shugendō priests approached, accompanied by the sound of conch horns. With great difficulty, we hoisted the taikodai up a long, steep flight of steps leading to the temple steps. Before hundreds of onlookers, we shuffle-danced while chanting and jostling the taikodai about, and then for the last time, with much relief, we set it down.

The sense of accomplishment the taikodai bearers shared was deep and real. Dreads told nondreads and nondreads told each other, "*Otsukaresama*" (You worked hard, good job). Dreads did the same among themselves, adding the three-step fist motion.

The focus of attention shifted to the massive temple. A wooden walkway led to a short, broad flight of steps leading up to the temple and was intersected by a second walkway, running parallel to the base of the stairs, to form a cross. At the end of the longer walkway—the bottom of the cross—the frog man crouched immobile, head low. Scores of monks dressed in animal (perhaps deer) hide, with tiny black discs on their shaved heads, flanked each side of the stairs. On the elevated landing, before the doors leading inside the temple, were several television cameramen, as well as rows of seated Shugendō and civil-servant dignitaries.

Soon the frog man traveled to various points of the cross, where several monks were positioned. The monks performed a series of rituals upon him, and two monks removed the head of the costume. This revealed not the young man with the plucked eyebrows, but an elderly man with bristling gray hair. He disappeared among the monks to the right of the landing, and the monks sounded their conches. The ceremony's end was announced over the public-address system. With a stir, the large, mostly middle-aged and elderly crowd began to disperse.

History, Repatriation, and the Glocal Body

I have argued in this chapter that one broad way of characterizing the ideological uses to which Rastafari has been put in Japan is in urban and rural terms. In the urban context, Rasta-identifying Japanese like Fire, Brother Taffy, and Taz use the movement to criticize class difference, ethnic difference, and consumerism, as well as the uncritical adoration of the Euro-American. Brother Taffy and Taz particularly position their own working-class backgrounds as a definitive aspect of their Rasta identifications through which they are able to criticize Babylonian corruption internationally and domestically. Brother Taffy uses Rastafari to voice his disaffection with ethnic discrimination in Japan, and Taz links his Rasta identifications with his activism in support of the homeless.

But criticism of social inequality in Japan, and the ways in which it is linked to Western imperial and capitalist power, can be shown not only in what is consciously verbalized, but also in performative habit. In this way, for instance, Brother Taffy's critique of Western power might be seen as rendered not only through expressions of disdain toward the blind Japanese desire to learn English, or toward the preponderance of local street signs in English. It might also be seen through the very rendering of this critique in a patois regarded among many in the West (including many Jamaicans) as unworthy of the status of a language of study. This aspect of critique of the West is relatively unselfconscious. That is, Taffy and others did not choose to learn patois as opposed to English; rather, the decision was an extension of their subcultural identifications and international experience. It is still criticism, however, and more potent precisely because of this unselfconsciousness. In this way it further illustrates that the primacy of the West in the Japanese imaginary of the international cannot be so easily assumed (Hendry and Wong 2006).

While rural dreads also voice criticism of Western and Japanese hegemonies, it is in these habitual terms that their critique is most fully evident. And it is in this discreetly performative behavior that the subversive potential of the Yoshino dreads' participation in the kaeru tobi festival emerges. Their very presence as dreads at a rural Japanese festival interjects signs which complicate easy, conventional readings of this event as a traditional Japanese event. However, I want to argue that, ultimately, the effect is of a Rastafari that makes the familiar mystical in a way that valorizes that familiar, and hence secures the dreads' place in their community.

Time is an important aspect of how this takes place. There are two dimensions of the Jamaican Rasta imagination of history. One is hermeneutic; the other is memorial. The first view of history sees it as a biblical past that guides recognition of the present, in which contemporary events constitute a realization of the word of God. The second view of history invokes a glorious, African past, one which existed before enslavement and to which Jamaican Rastas seek return. The truths buried in history, then, are inscribed in the Bible, Selassie's published speeches, and other sacred texts; they are also heard in the nearer voice of diasporic memory. Both imaginations of history converge on Ethiopia, an ancient biblical land that stands as a metonym of the Africa that black Jamaicans' ancestors left behind.

The past for Yoshino dreads might be seen in similar terms. In the next chapter, I will say more about the first past, that constructed through a reimagination of writings on ancient Japanese history. My discussion at that point will necessarily be linked to the second, memorial past. For now, I wish to offer some comments only about this memorial past, in the context of the Yoshino dreads' participation in the kaeru tobi festival.

While for Jamaican Rastas, the remembered homeland is unambiguously Africa, for Yoshino dreads and many other Rasta-identifying Japanese, there are the secondary (though ontologically crucial) homelands of Jamaica and Africa, and the primary homeland of rural Japan. Pilgrimages to or simply imaginings of Jamaica and Africa help bring Rasta identifications into being; such imaginings are resolved, however, in the homeland of the Japanese rural.

Dread participation in the kaeru tobi festival is a performative working through of the memorialized past of this rural local. Like the African diasporic memorial past of Jamaican Rastas, this memorial past is one to which Yoshino dreads here and now imagine themselves as generationally linked. As furusato, it is the past of parents and grandparents and great-grandparents, and so on down the line, as well as their cultural practices, like kaeru tobi, lived vitally in the present. (The hermeneutic past, on the other hand, while also imaginarily ancestral, is both more sudden and more remote. Rather than an immediately generational, discretely interconnected, communally intimate past, this hermeneutic past is one suddenly realized around current events that are teleologically projected into a redemptive future.) Like Jamaican Rastas who reject bourgeois orthodoxy for an imagination of the African premodern, Japanese dreads who participate in the kaeru tobi festival engage in a temporal regression (performatively registered in the present progressive) from modern urban Japan. Through Jamaican Rasta—a primary metaphor for all global ethnic groups' religious encounters with the natural world—Yoshino dreads embrace Shugendō tradition not so much as followers, but rather as a familiar local enigma which thereby uncannily accords with exotic, global Rasta. "From Yoshino to the world. From the world to Yoshino."

Jamaican Rastas, "born" in Africa, want to return there to recover their natural, spiritual selves. Yoshino dreads are a step ahead of the game: they have been repatriated all along, even before they left Japan. Their travels provide them with performative resources, including the symbolic corpus of Rastafari, through which to celebrate the fact that their journey begins as well as ends in the promised land of the local. Masato commented that he greatly appreciated Yoshino, including all its rich traditions, once he returned from his travels, more so than he had growing up there. Through diasporic Rastafari, then, Yoshino dreads inflect and thus vitalize their claims to a local Shugendō tradition that has already articulated a relationship with the natural qua spiritual in a rich and meaningful way.

The Yoshino dreads, of course, did not offer to explain to me the symbolic significance of their presence at the festival. In the improvisational, cross-culturally hybridized play of signs evident at the event, such a logic, if it exists, will not present itself in an obviously sanctioned way. But it is too easy to say merely that a group of dreadlocked Japanese men (and one Jamaican anthropologist) in traditional festival wear carrying a man with plucked eyebrows who pranced around on a taikodai while dressed in a frog suit can have no hope of making sense. In an effort at reading this event, I feel that the best place to begin is with the blunt presence of these signs, the utter and uncompromised way in which they are proffered to spectators. Indeed, I do not think Japanese audiences there know how to read these signs, except from this same starting point: that they are simply there, and thus in some way they always already make sense. I try to imagine how the dreads imagine the audience imagining them, the meanings both they and the spectators might be able to construct out of the stark fact of their dreadlocked presence. Such readings, to be plausible, have to be readily intuited from these starkly given signs, from a shared cultural knowledge— even if not consciously recognized as such.

What is readily apparent to all is the playful unusualness of both the frog man and the dreads. They are not of the everyday; they are manifestly from someplace else. In this sense, they are visibly travelers, not only across the town on this day, but also across the wider spaces of the global and the deeper ones of mythological time. It is ontological travel magically, festively put on display. My sense of the shared reading of the dreads' and the frog man's participation in the festival is as a celebration of the local natural which returns, via the global spirituality of Rastafari, estranged from its origins and yet still strangely sensible to them. The local-global-local narratives of the dreads' travels and that of the frog man are both tales of spiritual journey, whose meanings revolve around individuals (dreads and frog man) taken beyond the familiar boundaries of themselves into the larger, more dangerous, but ultimately redemptive world of the natural qua spiritual. Both dreads and frog man perform their return to familiar existences after confronting something spiritually beyond their original selves. In doing so, the known (Shugendō, these men who grew up in Yoshino, the frog man in his original form) is dramatically valorized as it is juxtaposed against, but weirdly in accordance with, the unknown (Rastafari, the difference of the dreads, and their and the frog man's having been away). The readily apparent difference of the dreads and the frog man, then, are compatible signs of an odd beyond that is ceremonially made to belong. This naturalizes Rastafari locally, in a way that facilitates the dreads' Rasta identifications, and in a way that ultimately valorizes the local world in which the dreads lead their daily lives.

Even as they have been returned to their former selves, the dreads remain marked by their time in spiritual transit. Locks mark this return from an encounter with global spirituality. Liminality somatically lingers, worn as the fantastic signs of spiritually naturalized selves. Seen in these terms, the frog is not so much a privileged passenger of the taikodai-bearing dreads. He is, rather, an uncanny brother, one whom the dreads are positioned to guide toward repatriation into his natural self.[10] By accompanying this local figure so conspicuously before so many witnesses at the festival, the dreads help secure their own return home.

5

Text and Image

This chapter explores Japanese writing, as well as accompanying images, on Japanese encounters with Jamaican culture. I focus on two sets of writing. The first is a body of non-Rasta, Japanese writing whose authors assert—as Jamaican Rastas claim for the Jamaicans—that the Japanese are the true ancient Israelites, and thus provide Rasta-identifying Japanese a resource for authenticating their Rasta identifications. The second is fiction and nonfiction writing about Japanese travel to and residence in Jamaica. Unlike previous chapters, where the performances examined have been more proximally oriented, in this latter set of readings, I am not immediately concerned with the performers (the authors) themselves. I am more concerned with their literary representations of "the Japanese," writ large, and cast in relation to Jamaicans. The kaeru tobi festival might involve understanding the dreads' playful reconstitution and reaffirmation of the local identifications that they and their "audiences" share; similarly, I wish to argue, the writers of these texts mobilize ideas about Japaneseness that they share with their readers. One of these shared ideas is of the world outside Japan as a challenging space in which Japanese selves may become actualized, a self-actualization readily returned to the rhetoric of national accomplishment. Today, this effort, distinguished in part by its unfolding within a time of prolonged recession, is significantly realized through travel abroad, including to third-world countries like Jamaica. Contemporary representation of travel in these terms belongs to a broader discourse of jibun sagashi, or "the search for self."

Jibun Sagashi: "The Search for Self"

The search for self has been an important term in Japanese public discourse since the early 1990s. It speaks to the dissatisfaction many people have come to feel about their lives, and to their desire to bring what they consider their true selves into fuller being. There have been over fifty book titles in which the term appears, to my knowledge the earliest of which, significantly, was published in 1992. There are many more books that directly and otherwise invoke the concept of jibun sagashi but do not use the term in the title. A search of titles in which the term appears therefore does not capture every work in which the concept is significantly invoked. Still, these works do give a sense of the breadth of ways in which jibun sagashi is employed, and its status as a consumable effect of the turbulent times in which it emerged. The facts that some of these works deeply explore the search for self as a concept and that others only superficially invoke it are both indications of its current appeal. These works might be grouped into four overlapping categories: self-help, scholarly works, youth and education, and travel.

The first category, self-help, is by far the largest. Some works in this category mobilize an array of psychological tools to help the reader lead a more fulfilling life. They use the search for self as a guiding principle according to which readers' self-actualization as human beings might be achieved. Examples of titles in this category are *One's Own Psychology: An Invitation to the Search for Self* (Enomoto 1998), *Search-for-Self Therapy: Let's Start from the Discovery of Small Joy* (Koike 2002), and *Workbook of the Mind: A Search-for-Self Communication Guide that Anyone, Even Alone, Can Do* (Kokoro no Waakubukku Seisaku Gurūpu 2006). Many of these books are presented in gendered and professional terms. For instance, several of the works in this first category belong to a series by one publishing company (Popuraa Sha) called The Journey into the Search for Self. These books are geared pri-

marily toward young women, encouraging them toward social indepen-
cence. A number of other books in the category are geared toward men
(Nakamura, Nakamura, and Inoue 1997); some speak particularly to the
lives of corporate workers (Fujie 1995). One of these works, titled *The Book
to Read When Work Goes Badly: The Ultimate Advice on the Search for Self*
(Ogawa 1998), speaks to the sense of malaise that has come to pervade the
lives of corporate workers in the recessionary era. Closely related to the
category of self-help is that of moral education, in which the author deline-
ates a set of values that readers are to aspire to, in the search for their better
selves (Ōmori 1997). In some cases, this instruction comes from venerable
celebrities, such as singer Akiyama Satoko (1994).

A second category of readings is scholarly works, including evaluations
of the careers of various authors, that use jibun sagashi as an organizing
theme. These include such books as *Theorizing the Feminist Novel: Female
Authors' Search for Self* (Watanabe 1993), and *The Search for Self: The Collected Fiction of Kawazoe Hitoshi* (1995). The third category is youth and
education. There is a great deal of overlap between this category and the
first, self-help. Here the advice is being given not only for the benefit of the
reader, but also for those, such as parents and educators, who are charged
with the upbringing of young people (Ōgon 1998; Ōsumi 2001). Such writings often start from the premise that many young people in Japan today
are troubled. This is in keeping with the highly publicized incidence of
murders in Japan during the 1990s and 2000s committed by Japanese
youth.

The fourth and final set of readings is the one I am most concerned with,
especially where it overlaps with an interest in discontented youth. It includes writings on travel. I discuss these further below, viewing as I do
much of the fiction and nonfiction about travel to Jamaica as of a discursive
kind with this fourth category of writing.

SOCIAL AND HISTORICAL CONTEXT

But first, how might these works and their mobilization (including their
opportunistic use) of the discourses of the search for self be placed in social
and historical context? If use of the term is not the only means by which to
judge whether the concept is in play, then what elements or conjunction of
elements might indicate its presence? How is jibun sagashi a product of its
times? In what follows, I identify three aspects of jibun sagashi's particular

sociohistorical valence: the serious consequences of recession on Japanese society, the Japanese desire for individual self-actualization, and writing as a technology of self-making.

RECESSIONARY JAPAN AND THE "LOST GENERATION"

Since the bursting of the economic bubble in 1991, and with the increased openness of the Japanese economy to the forces of neoliberal capitalism, Japan has experienced a steady economic decline. There is a pronounced sense that Japan is in crisis (Yoda and Harootunian 2006). The vaunted system of lifetime employment has become decreasingly viable for many corporations that have encountered hard times. Japanese youth have been among the most affected by these developments. Zielenziger (2006) speaks of these young people as a "lost generation." This appellation is problematic, along the lines of Woronoff's *Japan's Wasted Workers* (1983) or Generation X. These terms lump together huge groups of very different people according to their supposed status as victims of a social present beyond their control.

However, the term does convey the very real sense that the powers that be, viewed as responsible for improving the situation of each new generation, are indeed failing. Many young people are unable to pursue increasingly unavailable—and perhaps what they come as a result to consider as overvalued—corporate careers, moving rather from one temporary job to the next as *furiitaa* (free timers). Japan has been gripped by one sensational story after the next of the brutal murder of Japanese students by their alienated peers, most notoriously the 1997 case of Shōnen A, a fourteen-year-old boy from Kobe who killed an eleven-year-old boy and a ten-year-old girl. Although not precisely a new phenomenon, *hikikomori* (shut-ins), like furiitaa, have emerged as prominent social archetypes in the recessionary period. Japan has an astoundingly high suicide rate (over 30,000 annually for several years now, out of a population of 125 million). With so many women deferring marriage and childbearing later and later in life (Orenstein 2001), the birth rate is declining, shrinking the number of future taxpayers who will have to finance Japan's enormous public expenditures.

THE JAPANESE SOCIAL AND THE GLOBAL INDIVIDUAL

These recent developments have occasioned the need for new life perspectives. However, jibun sagashi, one discursive attempt to address this need, is not an entirely new phenomenon, as it may be linked to a group of similar ideas that have long circulated in the Japanese public sphere. The neuropsychiatrist Okonogi Keigo (1981) introduced the term *moratoriamu ningen* (moratorium people) in the late 1970s to describe what he perceived as Japanese youth's increasingly delayed entry into social adulthood. The mass media provides so many choices for consumption, Okonogi argued, that only ephemeral engagement with them becomes possible, promoting a similar attitude of disconnection from the responsibilities of adulthood. *Shinjinrui* (new breed) is another term that was in vogue for a while. The term suggests a generation utterly apart from its forebears, a generation of self-centered youth who, born after 1945, have known only the affluence of the postwar era. A similar, recently explored term—one close to jibun saga-shi—is the notion of *ikigai* (Mathews 1996, 718), "that which most makes one's life seem worth living." Mathews posits three aspects of the cultural shaping of "the Japanese self": one that is unconscious; one over which the individual believes he or she has little control; and, directly important to understanding ikigai, one that the self is aware of and actively seeks to shape. Ikigai, usually understood in terms of "family, work, or personal dream" (ibid.), is what motivates this shaping of the cultural self. It is possible to see jibun sagashi as in part a discursive manifestation of this third domain of self-shaping. In it, the individual makes choices from "the cultural supermarket" (ibid.)—at home and overseas—in an effort to achieve a fulfilled selfhood.

Many of these terms, whose prominence has been orchestrated to a significant degree by the mass media, reflect concern about the place of personal desire and personal agency in relation to social obligation. Such concerns emerge at times when individual aspiration, given broader domestic and international developments, easily becomes (or is profitably made to become) of issue. In this way, moratoriamu ningen and shinjinrui are to be related to Japan's postwar prosperity, one which many older Japanese believe is making the new generation soft and self-centered. I would suggest that jibun sagashi as discourse (as opposed to as personally lived) is part of this lineage of terms that express a tension between the Japanese social and the Japanese individual in the modern world, and that the regular emergence of such expressions indicates the depth and persistence with which this tension is felt.

Unsurprisingly, this sense of the individual in the modern world is often framed explicitly in relation to the West. For instance, I have already mentioned the modern girls (*moga*) of the 1920s, who many men in the media construed as having an unhealthful, selfish fascination with Western popular culture (Silverberg 1991). But as I also suggested earlier, jibun sagashi might be significantly distinguished from such previous discourses by the fact that it is articulated not only in relation to the West, but more fully vis-à-vis the world at large. In the Japanese media today, *kokusaika* (internationalization) has largely been cast as a problem, given the increased—though still marginal—presence of foreigners from the third world arriving in the country (Lie 2001). However, in its element as consumable difference, kokusaika as hypothetically linked to jibun sagashi happily offers fresh perspectives in lifestyle design from all over the world. This includes the encounters with the Jamaican that are the focus of this chapter.

WRITING AS A TECHNOLOGY OF SELF-MAKING

Autobiographical writing, never a purely personal project, is always ideologically shaped by the moment in which it takes place. Both before and after the Second World War, left-wing and progressive groups helped organize movements that encouraged the masses, including students and female workers, to write about their everyday lives (Figal 1996). These movements were motivated in part by an effort to challenge state nationalism and to promote social egalitarianism. *Jibunshi* (self-history), linked to these earlier efforts, refers to a movement in autobiographical writing that grew especially popular with the death of Hirohito, the Shōwa Emperor, in 1989. A collective remembering of the Shōwa period (Tamanoi 2000) that ended with Hirohito's death, jibunshi also became an individualist, commercialized enterprise in which everyday people were taught, through "conferences, advertisements, regular publications, culture center activities, and extension courses" (Figal 1996, 925), how to write their personal histories.[1] If the popularity in jibunshi was critically linked to the end of the Shōwa period, and if moratoriamu ningen and shinjinrui are products of postwar prosperity, jibun sagashi as a mass-media phenomenon represents a similar writing of the individual self onto the pages of recessionary Japan. In this way, it becomes evident that it is not only the individual who is being written about, but also Japanese society itself. In many of these writings, Japan becomes both point of departure and destination in the search for self. That is, it is often Japan that the dissatisfied, searching self eagerly leaves behind; Japan is also the safe haven, the conclusion to which these searching selves often seek to return.

This metaphor of travel and safe return is not incidental. A key way in which jibun sagashi manifests itself is in the autobiographical telling of the stories of Japanese youth traveling overseas. Of particular interest are the narratives of young people traveling not as part of a large tour group, but as individuals braving the world alone. While these young people often rely on networks of Japanese people in the places they travel to (Goodman et al. 2003), travel as represented in jibun sagashi is fundamentally defined as a solitary effort toward self-discovery. This endeavor often comes to fruition through engagement with another culture.

In 1961, Oda Makoto, then a recent graduate of Tokyo University who had travelled to the United States on a Fulbright scholarship, authored a travelogue entitled "I'll Give Anything a Look" (Nan de mo mite yarō). The author describes his travels across the United States, Asia, Europe, and the Middle East (Oda 1961). The book became an enormously popular best-seller, selling hundreds of thousands of copies in its first year and becoming "a cultural phenomenon" (Suttmeier 2009, 64). Japanese travel overseas until 1964 had been limited to travel the Japanese government deemed of national importance; with the liberalization of international travel that year, many Japanese youth embarked on the kind of shoestring travel (binbō ryokō) around the world that Oda described. Citing reviews of Oda's book, and linking it to the emergence of the postwar leisure industries in Japan, Suttmeier argues that the travelogue was popular largely because its author's representations of his intimate encounter with the West—including his romantic liaisons with white women and his witnessing of racial discrimination in these countries. These helped to create a sense of national pride in a postwar Japan that could now recognize that the idealized West was flawed. Like much of the rest of the world, the West was available to Japanese consumption, to an "ethnographic" gaze that often doubles as domination. These themes are reflected in my discussion further below of Japanese writing on travel to Jamaica. Yet while Oda's book may be most productively framed by the sense of national pride that came with Japan's postwar emergence as an economic superpower, the more recent writing on Japanese international travel is also often informed by the realities of Japan's new social and economic struggles. While Oda's account of his solitary travel throughout the world positioned him as the roguish hero of a recovering nation, the lone, global self-searchers of the present day often leave Japan to escape the restrictiveness of a powerful nation in decline. The third world is often represented as a space in which this sense of restrictiveness can be overcome.

An early example of the more recent travel writing that has popularized this solitary travel is the popular series of books by Sawaki Kōtaro that began with *Shinya Tokkyū: Honkon, Makao* (Midnight Express: Hong Kong, Macao; 1986). In this series, the author—whose journey begins when he decides to quit his job as a sarariiman—describes his travels to such destinations as Hong Kong, Macao, the Malay Peninsula, Singapore, India, Nepal, China, Turkey, and Greece. Sawaki's experiences were made into a film, and Japanese television has subsequently aired many programs featuring Japanese youth traveling the world alone, in pairs, and in small groups (not counting film crews). One of the most popular of these, a long-running fixture on Sunday evenings, is *Sekai Ururun Taizaiki* (Homestay in the World), which features Japanese youth traveling to remote parts of the globe, usually among indigenous people, where the Japanese spend an extended period of time living, eating, and dressing, sometimes scantily, as the local people do. A book bearing the name of the television program and subtitled *The Moving Search for Self as Told by Twenty Travelers* (*Sekai Ururun Taizaiki* 1998) depicts the experiences of twenty Japanese young people in Canada, China, England, Finland, Hungary, Iceland, Indonesia, Italy, Jordan, Malaysia, Mongolia, Peru, Russia, Thailand, and Vanuatu. Another example, Yoshikawa Hideki's (1999) *Bankoku Jibun Sagashi no Ringu* (The Ring of a Bangkok Search for Self), is a collection of stories about Japanese kickboxers living in Thailand. The group includes a young woman, an aging fighter, and a young man who forsook his career as a corporate employee to fight. As I will discuss in my analysis of Japanese writing on travel to Jamaica, such works often use overseas experiences to reflect upon Japaneseness similarly inflected in gendered, generational, professional, and other terms.

Writing Japanese Rastafari

The first body of literature I want to examine in considering how the three factors that help define jibun sagashi also bear on Japanese identifications with Jamaican culture centers on the notion of the Japanese as the ancient Israelites. Jamaican Rastas read the Bible, the words of Haile Selassie, and several other sacred texts for the Afrocentrisms they believe are contained within them—hidden, in the case of the King James Version of the Bible. Similarly, some Rasta-identified Japanese dreads read this "Japanese as ancient Israelite" literature because it seems to privilege the Japanese movement and its followers as the chosen people. This, again, is a claim that Jamaican Rastas make on their own behalf.

I first met Tanki on my last day at Inochi no Matsuri. He said he could drive me to his home and then to the bus station, from where we could travel together to Tokyo, where he had some business to take care of. As he drove his small van home through the Japanese Alps, he talked about the mysterious connections he saw between Rasta and Japan. He described an ancient tribe that had come from Israel to settle in Japan. In those ancient times, a struggle for imperial power developed between the newcomers and another group that had arrived earlier from the Asian mainland. (At some point, the newcomers gained power; Tanki suggested that Japan's royal family is descended from this group.) The newcomers were able to travel from mountain peak to mountain peak in a single line, walking on air instead of climbing up and down valleys. But then Buddhism was instituted by Babylonian authorities to alienate the people from their power. Buddhist monuments were built over holy sites, and the Japanese people have come to lose their sense of connection with their Judaic past. Tanki posited Rastafari in Japan as a remnant of this connection. (Here, again, is the sense of Rasta as disaffection against Buddhism that I first suspected as I walked through Ryōanji Temple.)

Tanki appears to have received many of the ideas he was sharing with me from the elder dread who criticized Ras Tibby for his use of the title Ras. This elder evidently got these ideas from the popular literature mentioned above. I first became aware of this literature through Ras Seek. As a former monk in training who had read broadly on religiosity in Japan, he had become something of a mentor to me in my explorations of Japanese Rasta. (Seek prefaced his recommendation that I investigate some of these works with the statement that he himself did not necessarily accept their claims as true.)

In their 1995 study, Goodman and Miyazawa place the Japanese imaginings of Jewish people in historical context. They note that early Japanese nationalists, at a time when Japan felt threatened by Western political and military power, represented the Jewish people as members of an occult group out to undermine the Japanese nation. After the Second World War, some Japanese identified themselves as the chosen people, a move that might be seen as making Japan's victimization into a sign of its people's uniqueness, intended to mitigate Japanese suffering in the immediate post-war era. The current literature, assailed by the international Jewish community as anti-Semitic, rehashes stereotypes of some Jewish people as "fake Jews" who are bent on global domination. The best-known contemporary exponent of this line of thought is Uno Masami (1985, 1995), whose best-selling books on the topic were very popular in Japan in the 1980s and into the 1990s. Uno claims that the United States is run by a shadow government of Jews who seek the destruction of the Japanese nation.

In contextualizing this most recent literature linking the Jews to the Japanese, Goodman and Miyazawa see significance in the fact that this new wave of anti-Semitism emerged in the early to mid-1980s, coinciding with a nationalism in ascendancy largely due to Japan's economic success. Prime Minister Yasuhiro Nakasone had much to do with this rise in nationalism, seeking as he did to create an ethnically proud Japan that had a prominent place among the nations of the world. His infamous assertion that blacks and Mexicans had brought down the "intelligence level" of an ethnically and racially diverse United States was meant to stand in contrast to a homogeneous and therefore powerful Japan with a rightful position of leadership in the world. The notion of a syndicate of American Jews resentful of Japanese power helped explain Japan's struggle to reach its rightful place in the international order. Goodman and Miyazawa further suggest that the scapegoating of Jewish people in Japan became easier with the deepening malaise—given the sacrifices needed to sustain the Japanese economy—among the middle class.

Many of the writers who have produced this literature have been Christians, including Uno, a fundamentalist minister. (The very few Japanese who are Christian, however, do not typically hold these views.) These authors manifest the hatred and simultaneous embracing of Jewish heritage seen in Christianity elsewhere. Resentment of supposed Jewish supremacy coexists with admiration of, and a desire to supplant, this supremacy. In *The Ancient Israelites Will Rise Again in Japan* (1995), Uno distinguishes between the Sephardim, the true Jews who fled Babylon and came to Japan, and the Ashkenazim, the fake Jews who seek to rule the world. He provides supposed evidence that the cultural artifacts and practices of the true Jews have been assimilated into those of the Japanese of today, who are their descendants. The *mikoshi* (portable shrine) used in Japanese festivals, for instance, is derived from the ark of the covenant, which itself is located in Mt. Tsurugi, in Tokushima prefecture, on Shikoku. Other writers similarly argue that the Japanese people's Judaic past has been variously interred in rural Japan: "King Solomon's mines are said to have been unearthed at

Mount Tsurugi on the Island of Shikoku. A stone engraved with Hebrew letters is reported to have been discovered on the isle of Awaji. The village of Shingo in Aomori prefecture is identified as the site of the grave of Jesus, who is reported to have migrated to Japan after his brother James was mistakenly crucified in his place" (Goodman and Miyazawa 1995, 6–7).

Like the links between international Rasta and local Shugendō tradition, the mysteries of the ancient Jewish diaspora are interred in the Japanese local and made into potential resources for the assertion of uncanny Japanese selves. Whether portraying the Jews as local ancestral selves or as global villainous others, these Semitic representations, Goodman and Miyazawa assert, constitute a strategy through which the Japanese claim for themselves a privileged place in the world, one situated deep in the heart of Western Christianity. (This might be yet another example of the strategy, often found in nihonjinron, of making Japan unique through its embodying Western ideals more ideally than the West.)

Without mentioning Rastafari in Japan, the authors indirectly shed light on what motivates the move toward Semitic affinity among Japanese practitioners of Rasta:

> Unlikely as it may seem, the history and theology of the Black Hebrews provide important perspectives on the Japanese experience. Black Judaism is one of many responses to the dilemma of black existence in the twentieth century. At least eight black Jewish sects originated in Harlem in the period from 1919 to 1931 ... Seventeenth-century speculation on the fate of the Ten Lost Tribes was an integral part of the Protestantism that became the religious tradition of the slaves, and the view that the Negroes are really the Hebrews of the Bible thus derived from the slaves' own Protestant religious tradition . . . A sociological study of the black Jews found that . . . their Jewish identity moderated their feelings of powerlessness, normalessness, and anomie. (Goodman and Miyazawa 1995, 62–63)

For Japanese dreads who seek to authenticate, deepen, and sustain their identification with a movement born on a faraway island, and who are citizens of a country which manifests in so many ways feelings of "powerlessness, normalessness and anomie" in relation to the colonial and modern West, it is difficult to ignore the discovery of a particularly Japanese literature which posits—as Jamaican Rastas do in their own Semitic identifications—that Japanese, including those who identify with Rasta, are descended from the ancient Israelites. However, Rasta-identifying Japanese lose sight of the fact that the emergence of both instances of Semitic identification are linked by a common Afro-Asian immersion in, and a desire to contest, Western hegemony. Instead, they see in this connection multiple uncanny, identity-authorizing conjunctions between self and other: between contemporary selves and ancient Judaic others, between contemporary and ancient imperial selves, between contemporary domestic selves and contemporary foreign (Jewish, Jamaican) others.[2]

Rasta-identifying Japanese do not explicitly invoke the term "jibun sagashi" in their adoption of these writings. However, their efforts at creative self-making through adoption of the "Japanese as ancient Israelites" literature is significantly informed by the sociohistorically particular discursive economy from which jibun sagashi emerged. This is shown in the three interlinked terms identified above. One is fairly straightforward and implied in much of this discussion: if writing is a technology of self-making, then reading writings on individual or collective self-making (the Japanese as the chosen people) helps effect similar, more particularly framed efforts toward this end (the chosen Japanese people, or person, as Rasta).

The second way in which this literature is interlinked with the notion of jibun sagashi is its emergence out of recessionary Japan. Many Japanese who identify with Rastafari do so out of a sense that the lives conventionally prescribed for them are restrictive, deepening that sense of middle-class malaise that Goodman and Miyazawa describe. (Again, this "Japanese as Jews" literature was very popular well into the 1990s, as the social effects of the recession were being felt more and more intensely.) When the usual benefits of middle-class life, such as lifetime employment and being part of financially stable families, are no longer available, the cost of that life—for men, time with their families; for women, the absence of meaningful educational and professional opportunities—does not seem worthwhile, and alternatives like Rastafari appear more viable. I have met a number of Rasta-identifying Japanese who say they have decided to live in the countryside precisely to avoid the demands and pressures heaped on them in urban settings. While there are some Japanese dreads who might be described as comfortably middle class, and who consume Rasta as a new, interesting lifestyle among many other affordable lifestyles, most Japanese I met who pursue Rasta in the greatest depth can hardly be viewed in these terms. The literature on the Japanese as Jews helps justify, albeit in a speculative way, identifications with a Rastafari that represents, much as it does in the

Jamaican colonial and neoliberal context, one personal, politically enriching means by which to come to terms with the pressures of life in recessionary Japan.

The international context to which Jamaica belongs points to the third way in which the adoption of the chosen people literature by Rasta-identifying Japanese is part of the same discursive climate as that of jibun sagashi. This adoption and the ends to which it is directed belong to broader contemporary Japanese valorizations of the global (including, but not limited to, the West) as a key space in which personal aspiration is to be directed. However, as I have discussed in this and preceding chapters, this search for actualized selfhood through the international, although often constructed in counterpoint to conventional social obligation, references not only the authority of the international as that which transcends the Japanese, but also the authority of Japaneseness as the imperative to root the international in Japanese soil, on conventionally Japanese terms. In this case, it takes the form of liaison with an Afro-Jamaican religious culture that is made meaningful for Japanese by citing diasporic Semitic identifications by both Japanese and Jamaicans, and through rooting not only Western (Jewish) but also non-Western (Rasta) religious identifications in the soil of the traditional local.

Nonfiction about Travel to Jamaica

A second example of Japanese textual liaisons with the Jamaican through which the discourse of jibun sagashi might be considered are writings on Japanese travel to Jamaica. As noted earlier, the boom in interest in Jamaican culture led to several works of nonfiction about Jamaica. Books like *Jamaica and Reggae A to Z* (Tokyo FM 1997) describe a wide range of aspects of Jamaican culture and society, but particularly those having to do with reggae music or Rastafari. Often filled with cartoonish drawings, photographs, and maps, these books provide brief entries on archetypal Jamaican figures like rude boys, folklore, famous musicians, sightseeing spots, nightclubs, and local products, as well as Rasta, dancehall, and patois expressions. Yvonne Goldson, a Jamaican author living in Japan, compiled *Jamaika-go o hanasō! Patowa-go handobukku* (Let's Speak Jamaican! Patois Handbook; 1998), a patois-Japanese-English guide that also includes discussions of male-female relationships in Jamaica, typical Jamaican meals, and the nuances of so-called Jamaican time. Most of these books include entries on the history of the island, Rastafari, reggae music, and travel around Jamaica. Many provide detailed information—including addresses and phone numbers—of nightclubs, restaurants, record shops, and similar establishments in Japan as well as Jamaica where Jamaican culture can be experienced. *Reggae: Jamaica's Wind and Light* (Tagawa 1985), features a brief essay on reggae's diffusion beyond the island and its status as world music. This work, essentially a picture book, presents familiar images of Jamaica as a blue-skied, sandy, verdant space peopled by shirtless children and aged dreads. One comes away from many of these books with an overwhelming sense of the textual and pictorial renderedness of Jamaica as an object of knowledge. African America—a key locus of Japanese consumption of the cultural production of the African diaspora—is chiefly considered as a part of a geographically expansive, predominantly white United States. Jamaica, in contrast, is a small island with a postcolonial history of only a few decades. In many of these works, then, Jamaica more readily emerges as a clearly circumscribed, fully knowable space.

Other nonfiction describes the writers' personal contacts with the island. A common theme uniting many of these works is the writers' sense of Jamaica and Jamaicans as bad, but still vitalizing and endearing. Ōga Tamanosuke's 1998 book, *Jamaika ga suki da!* (I Love Jamaica!), is an account of two travelers—the writer and Saitō Izumi, a photographer—who visit the island. Saitō, a newcomer to Jamaica, asks Ōga what he liked about the island on a trip two years earlier. Ōga is uncertain how to respond:

> "Hm. Ah . . . Got it. It might be that, I love Jamaicans."
>
> "Jamaicans, are they such good people?"
>
> "No way, they're bad people. I mean, sure, there are good Jamaicans. But the bad bunch, they've got a certain appeal."
>
> I couldn't explain that appeal. So I changed the subject. (1998, 8)

When Saitō reveals that what he most wants out of the trip is to take photographs for an exhibit in Japan, Ōga asks in alarm if Saitō imagines Jamaica to be like such scenic places as Hawaii or Phuket. Saitō admits that he does, and Ōga urgently explains that things are very different in Jamaica. If he simply points his camera at someone, Saitō will be asked for money, perhaps by one of the many Jamaican men who carry knives. If in such a case Saitō fails to surrender his money, he might be killed and both his money and his camera taken. Yet for Ōga and Saitō, Jamaica is—despite this badness and the unpleasant experiences they have—an addictive, exhilarating place.

Kimoto Yuko (1994) represents Jamaica in similar terms. But her anxieties about being in Jamaica stem from, and are greater because of, the fact that she is a woman. In *Honjama Jamaika*, whose tone is chatty and frank, she describes her three trips to Jamaica, each one taken with a different female Japanese traveling partner. Kimoto is struck by the constant efforts of the Jamaican men she meets to cheat her and her companions and to get them into bed. But even so, she cannot dislike these men. She also writes that there are many bad men in Jamaica. But these bad guys, she says, are "much, much more interesting than good guys" (1994, 11). Kimoto uses the adjective *warui* to describe the badness of these men; she says explicitly that the theme of her book is to determine whether Jamaican men are warui as opposed to *zurui* (sly, cunning). Like Ōga, she writes that "explaining this difference is difficult." But soon after she seems to conclude: "if they were zurui, I would not have gone to Jamaica three times" (1994, 11). Jamaican men appear to be bad in a way that only makes one "smile bitterly"; this badness is not often malicious, and it even has a certain charm. The "badness but goodness" of the Jamaican experience is apparent in Kimoto's description of riding on the back of a motorbike with a male Jamaican friend (the sexual innuendo is hard to miss). She remembers the "terrible pleasure" of the bike speeding roughly over pebbles, the harshness of the wind in her ears. Somehow in those moments, she writes, she feels able to live life intensely pleasurably. Jamaicans live in a violent country:

> Their way of having fun is violent. Riding without a helmet, pebbles, squalls, muddy roads, and darkness, every bit of it was "scary" for soft, civilized me . . . When you get past the feeling of being scared, you trust the pebbles and the squalls and the darkness; you even come to enjoy them. Once you fully undergo this process, your way of living sharply changes. (ibid., 116)

The Jamaican experience can be violent and terrifying, but pleasurable because it provides Japanese travelers a way to live intensely beyond their "soft, civilized" selves.

One Love Jamaica was written by Yamakawa Kenichi (1993), about his return to Jamaica for the first time in a decade. The language of this book is more introspective and less frequently incredulous than those by the other two, younger authors. Yamakawa, nearly forty on this trip to Jamaica, has returned to the island not in search of excitement. He has already sought to live as fully as he could the life of a "rude boy," only to conclude that "I was not a real Jamaican rude boy. I had some place to return to. No matter how much I loved reggae, it was not my culture" (1993, 7). His return to Jamaica was instead inspired by the need for spiritual renewal, as a number of his friends in Tokyo had passed away. His Jamaican experience is defined by another kind of loss, a sort of "imperialist nostalgia," except for tourists: the dreads whom he had befriended ten years before had retreated into the hills to avoid the many travelers flocking to the island. With bittersweet satisfaction, he thinks they left because "they were disgusted with tourists like me, stained with the poison of Babylon" (86). Despite this sense of being displaced in this new Jamaica, the island is still for him a vital, energizing place: "Europe, America, Japan continue losing life (*seimei*). But Jamaica breathes" (119–20).

Fictional Accounts of Travel to Jamaica

In many of these nonfiction works on Japanese travel to Jamaica, then, the selves searched for are ones that are tougher and more vital than they can become in Japan. The international does not just represent a space that must be negotiated in a tough-minded way in order for Japanese to become master reggae musicians and dancers. It is also a space in which achieving a toughness beyond the Japanese is an end in itself, valued on its own terms. These tougher selves are realized through an encounter with the badness of Jamaicans, through the hardships of Jamaican life, through its experiential primitivisms. Ōga and his traveling partner are at once traumatized and stimulated, made savvier global travelers by their run-ins with Jamaican menace. "Soft, civilized" Kimoto is exhilarated by this menace in a way that is nothing short of transformative. In search of spiritual renewal, Yamakawa retreats from Babylonian Tokyo to "breathe" in Jamaica. The search for a tougher self is a powerful element in much Japanese fiction about travel to the island. In the remainder of this chapter, I will discuss two such works.

ISLAND OF STARS AND REGGAE
The first is the 1985 novel *Hoshi to regee no shima* (Island of Stars and Reggae), also by Yamakawa Kenichi. This book tells the story of a writer named Kuwahara Reiji, who travels to Jamaica to finish writing a novel. He

had been working on the novel in Tokyo, but when his motorbike, his prized possession, is stolen, he decides to leave the city. It is not a Tokyoite who steals his bike, he decides, but Tokyo itself. He feels that Tokyo deprives him of his creative energies, and that Jamaica will invigorate him.

Throughout the novel, Reiji is presented as an aloof consumer of the Jamaican experience. He is the untraveled Japanese reader's ideal of the cool, in-charge Japanese globe-trotter who knows how to handle the natives, who are always trying to exploit him. He constantly walks away from or turns his back on Jamaicans who irritate him; in contrast, these Jamaicans, who depend on tourists like Reiji for a living, are quick to seek reconciliation. The Jamaicans of this novel are beggarly (one man offers to guide Reiji for a fee to a bank in plain sight across the street); in spite of Sticko's perceptions, unambitious ("It was okay not to do anything . . . Living only is okay. If my heart beats, if I breathe, that is enough. That's the Jamaican way" [Yamakawa 1985, 127]); and hopeless (Jamaica in this novel is essentially a state of despair).

Staying at a hotel in the resort town of Montego Bay, Reiji is befriended by a Rasta musician and meets his dread friends at a bar. But after a few minutes, Reiji stalks out of the bar, annoyed by the men who spoke of Japan as more Babylonian than New York, and who found similar fault with the expensive hotel where Reiji is staying. Dean, one of the dreads, rushes after him, calling out to him. Hands in the pockets of his jeans, spitting in disgust, Reiji continues walking. When the dread catches up, he tries to pacify Reiji, who complains that even though he was made to pay for all the men's food and drink, they said not a word of thanks: "Aren't Rastas the same as beggars?" (ibid., 30). Dean recoils, challenging Reiji to repeat the remark. Of course, Reiji does, then asks how Rastas who so despise Babylon can accept food and drink from one of its citizens. Dean explains in a long and impassioned speech that it is taken for granted that the person in the group with the most money pays. He implores Reiji repeatedly to take back what he said—to return his dignity as a Rasta, which Reiji now fully possesses—so that he will not have to lose his new friend from halfway around the world. As the dread waits,

> I looked at moonlit Dean's woolen hat, his white T-shirted shoulders. Because in the dark, I could not see black Dean's face very well. From across the street came the sound of waves. Here and there, frogs too were crying with voices like crickets.

I slowly sighed. And then I spoke.

"I was wrong, Dean. I take it back."

We walked once again, shoulder to shoulder. (ibid., 31)

Reiji's long, heavy sigh could be read in a number of ways. Perhaps it indicates a period of cooling down and embarrassed reflection on how he might have misread the situation, a recognition of the cultural difficulties involved in such relationships. An apology after this moment of reflection thus becomes deeper, more sincere; walking "shoulder to shoulder" seems to restore a measure of equality between the two men. But the fact that Reiji is in no hurry to apologize the way Dean was, and the fact that this relationship is clearly based more on Dean's need for Reiji than on Reiji's for Dean, suggest otherwise. The lazy attention to environmental detail—the frogs with voices like crickets, the sound of the waves—holds the reader, and Dean, in suspense as Dean waits to find out if his dignity is to be restored. The fact that "black Dean's face" is unseen also dehumanizes him: coming after his impassioned plea, this reference may be meant to evoke in the minds of Japanese readers a sense of Dean's humility, a faceless anguish with which blackness is too readily associated in Japan.

Reiji grows closer to Dean and another dread musician, Junior, and the three make plans to work together to smuggle ganja. A deal goes sour, however, and the three men are captured and imprisoned. Reiji is soon released on condition that he never return to Jamaica, but not before he is beaten by the police. Reiji's humiliation and unconditional expulsion serve primarily to signal a closure to his Jamaican experience, a familiar literary device in which the desire to be close to blackness is resolved by black people's extreme transgressions against the desiring protagonist.[3]

As Reiji's departure from Jamaica nears, the signs of his ever having been there are erased. The reader cannot miss the sense of dismissive transience that defines the latter stages of Reiji's Jamaican experience. Linda, Dean's girlfriend, tells Reiji that the police came and took all his possessions, except for his manuscript: while his material life in Jamaica has been obliterated, the story which he came to Jamaica to write—significantly set not in Jamaica, but in Japan—remains intact. Yamakawa's narrative of Reiji's Jamaican experience falls away around the metatext of life in Japan. On the day of his departure, Reiji thinks: "I would not land at this airport a second time. There was just no need to come again to this abominable island that killed [Dean]" (ibid., 229). But while in flight, Reiji discovers Dean sitting next to him, in disguise. Now known as Michael Ralphs, Dean explains that through the influence of a powerful music executive whom he had managed to place in his debt, Junior's release has also been secured. Dean and Reiji have a glass of wine as they toast their future together. *Island of Stars and Reggae* ends on this happy egalitarian note. But the ending does little to dispel the sustained contempt toward Jamaica that runs through the novel, a contempt which fosters the image of a tough, experienced international traveler that Japanese readers are supposed to be able to identify with.

In many ways, *Island of Stars and Reggae* and *Rastaman Vibration*, by Jah Hirō (1991), are very different works. Where Reiji's profound disdain toward black Jamaicans might be seen as an exercise of first-world privilege, Hirō presents his protagonist's travel to the island in politically progressive terms. *Island* is written in the self-involved first person; *Rastaman Vibration* in the heatedly ideological, omniscient third. *Island* is an easily consumed, pocket sized, 242-page book filled with glossy, tourist-friendly color photographs; *Rastaman Vibration*'s 365 pages are packed with sometimes difficult language, interspersed with a meager half-dozen black-and-white drawings. Reiji is more or less the same at the end of *Island* as the Reiji who arrives in Jamaica; the self Hirō's protagonist searches for is much changed by his Jamaican experience.

But in other ways the two novels, both by and about Japanese men traveling to Jamaica, are quite similar. One point of comparison recalls John Russell's (1991a) assertion that Japanese represent blacks either as people to be identified with, given the discontent with Western hegemony that both blacks and Japanese feel, or as people to be looked down upon, in the Japanese effort for parity with the West. The latter strategy appears more consistently in *Island*, and the former is more typical of *Rastaman Vibration*. However, both essentialize Jamaican people as cheerful, tough, and positive, and at the same time deceptive, criminal, and beggarly. The novels share a preoccupation with Afro-Jamaican skin and body odor; both feature protagonists irritated by Jamaican dismissiveness toward their specifically Japanese identities; and both focus on reggae and Rastafari to the near exclusion of other aspects of Jamaican social life.

In the remainder of this chapter, I focus on *Rastaman Vibration* as a fictional instance of the search for empowered Japanese selfhood in the world beyond the safe confines of Japan. The desire of Gorō, the protagonist, for this empowered selfhood is shared by many other Japanese who have traveled or imagine traveling overseas. Gorō's self-actualizing awareness of global suffering represents a (remote performative) working through of Japaneseness in its aspect as anxious insularity. This Japaneseness is often directly framed in relation to Afro-Jamaicans. Thus, I want to use my discussion of this novel to continue exploring Japanese social identity through encounters with the Jamaican, including—as Reiji's gaze at "black Dean's face" illustrates—vis-à-vis race. I focus on four themes through which Japaneseness is represented in Gorō's search for global, politically actualized selfhood: Babylon and its discontents, regular Japanese as the markers of Gorō's tougher self, Jamaican views of Japanese, and Japanese views of Jamaicans. Before I get to these themes, I want to provide a brief outline of the novel.

RASTAMAN VIBRATION

Gorō, the main character, is a middle-aged man who, at the beginning of the novel, is a manual laborer employed at a Tokyo construction site. As the novel progresses, Gorō's circle of friends comes to include Bongoman, whom he met as this Jamaican Rastafarian was playing drums on the sidewalk; Rie, who becomes his girlfriend; elderly Mr. Yamamoto; Sabu, a Japanese dread; and Take, a misfit teenaged member of a motorcycle gang.

Gorō and several of these friends flee Tokyo after Sabu attacks a cruel policeman for abusing a homeless man, and they travel to a commune where friends of Sabu live. From there they go to a volcanic island to attend a festival. During the festival, cries are heard that the police have raided the island and are coming after Sabu. The police find Sabu, encircle him, and then grab him. During the ensuing melee, Bongoman, who Gorō has met again by chance at the festival, is shot. "Gorō," he says, "come closer. Go to Jamaica. You will come to touch the past and present of the third world, seething like a crucible. Meet your Rasta brothers, travel together. You too will know the god, the beliefs, the dreams of Rasta. From there, your own true life will begin" (Hirō 1991, 161).

Mandated in this way to venture into the heart of blackness, Gorō travels to New York. After a brief stay there, he travels to Kingston—what might be, according to Furuta, a taxi driver and another of Gorō's friends, "the world's most barbaric city" (ibid., 200). Gorō is ready to fulfill his mandate in what he himself describes as a city where survival is paramount. After about three months, his hair has grown longer, his skin has darkened, and, to his delight, Jamaican people take him less frequently for a Chinese.

He becomes friends with a local ganja dealer named Jim, then himself becomes involved in the ganja trade. He reads the Bible, curses Babylon, and smokes much marijuana with his Rasta friends. Soon, however, Gorō begins to feel vaguely out of place in Jamaica, and he returns to Japan. Still, he comes to see the Rastas as modern-day Christs who preach peace and love to the world. He opens an I-tal food shop with Rie in the countryside, where he becomes a missionary of sorts, sharing Rasta's message with the youth of Japan.

BABYLON AND ITS DISCONTENTS

Rastaman Vibration begins in Tokyo, moves to the Japanese countryside and then to New York and Jamaica, and finally returns to the Japanese countryside. These spaces are rendered in more or less explicitly ideological terms vis-à-vis Babylon. The development of Gorō's lived understanding of the hard world beyond Japan—his toughness—begins with the recognition that his unhappy life in urban Japan already links him to the other Babylonian outposts he will soon venture into. The section in which the main action takes place in Tokyo is entitled "Babylon." Unsurprisingly, then, Hirō's Tokyo is a dark place of despair, with low-waged workers who benefit little from Japan's high-powered economy; slavish commitment to the rhythms of capitalism; homelessness; the aural and physical assaults of motorcycle gangs, the yakuza, and the police; overcrowding; and pollution. "Outside, summer's smell of hot air and exhaust filled the space about the concrete. With a sickened feeling Rie hurried toward the subway station. She felt like she was wandering in a sea of depersonalized, suited figures spat out from the surrounding buildings" (ibid., 23). Furuta's discontent is similarly explicit: "three years after leaving college, two years after starting to drive taxis, the grime of living was soaking into every crevice of his body" (ibid., 20). Gorō himself is characterized early in the novel as a lonely figure, the last to leave the emptied, somberly lit construction site where he works, declining opportunities to socialize with his friends.

The countryside, which will become the place where Gorō will choose to set down roots at the end of the novel, is depicted as a refuge from this corrupt space. At one point in the story, soon after the friends have fled Tokyo for the countryside, Furuta and Gorō draw water from a nearby well. As they do so, Gorō, undergoing a transformation that the reader has not been entirely privy to, drinks some of the water, saying, "God (*kamisama*), thank you for this clean water. Please send down your divine punishment to the Babylonians who try to destroy nature, even in the very recesses of the mountainside" (ibid., 87).

Later on, I discuss how various characters are referents against which Gorō might measure his personal political development. However, I want to note how one character affords an ideologized sense of the value of the Japanese rural. At the festival on the volcanic island, Gorō meets a local youth who had traveled the world as part of a circus troupe based in Denmark. When Gorō asks the young man why he had returned home, he explains:

> The island called me back. About two months before . . . near Paris, I was called out to and stopped by some black people on the roadside selling badges, all lined up. They were strange, with their hair like rope. They asked me if I was Japanese, and when I nodded, they handed a leaflet to me . . . It was a guide to this island's festival. *My* island. The mountain sending up smoke, the jagged coast, the grassland pasturages . . . the forest. Like lightning, nostalgic scenes raced through my mind, tears overflowed, spilling out. Those black people with their mysterious faces asked why [I was crying], and when I explained, [they said] it was Jah's guidance. They said the island was calling me back. I quietly agreed. After twelve years I returned to the island, and as a greeting of repatriation I offer the bough . . . of my overseas experience as a clown to the gods and spirits of the dead that I've missed so much. (ibid., 124–25)

The youth's story mirrors Gorō's own imminent journey into and return from the international. The youth himself represents one of many possible encounters with the global reseeded as local self. The quote is interesting in its use of the figure of the humble yet enigmatic Rastas—who, precisely as people on the fringes, are emissaries of the young man's repatriation to Japan. Just as the Yoshino dreads offer up the spectacle of their internationalized selves to local Shugendō tradition during the kaeru tobi festival, so does this young man offer his lived domestication of the international to the spirits of his island.

Gorō's arrival in New York City represents his own first step, under Bongoman's mandate, into the very heart of Babylon. Gorō finds New York a lurid place, full of random violence.[4] In a letter to Furuta, he describes it in a way befitting Bongoman's designation of the city as "Babylon," biblically vile: it is a place of homeless people, junkies and pushers, cross-dressing prostitutes, and porn shops. One particular downtown street concentrates these elements intensely enough to "make one feel like vomiting. But it also feels like training before going to Jamaica. Seems like it's even more incredible over there" (ibid., 175).

The "becoming tough" theme becomes more pronounced once Gorō arrives in Jamaica. The island is the main stop on Gorō's slumming tour. It is the place where he is to consummate his self-making through consumption of third-world malaise. In his first letter to Rie from Jamaica, he presents himself as a naive foreigner constantly being imposed on by the locals for one favor or another; he is not happy there. "Everyone's totally black, their looks are ill-intentioned, fire-gutted ruins are all about, and every day, I really regret having come to this horrible place" (ibid., 202). Over time, however, he becomes acclimatized to the Jamaican way of life, and he is able to write Rie in another letter that he is becoming "merry," "tough," "savage" (ibid., 203).

Feeling that he has gone as far as he can in his toughening Jamaican experience, Gorō eventually returns to Japan. But again, he decides to live not in Babylonian Tokyo, but rather in the countryside. Like the young man Gorō meets on the volcanic island, like the Yoshino dreads, like the dreads who adopt the "Jews as Japanese" literature, Gorō the international traveler comes to rest in the Japanese rural. In thinking about how Gorō's toughening travel speaks to ideologies of Japaneseness, what comes into view is Hirō's interpretation of Japan—home to Hirō's presumed readership—as comfortably assimilating the foreign and so discreetly celebrating itself. This recalls the rhetoric of furusato, of rural hometown and the Japanese countryside in general as a safe retreat from urban modernity (as well as from the Babylonian international, in this case). Such constructions of the countryside serve as a reminder of the potentially conservative affinities between jibun sagashi and nihonjinron. As a novel with certain ideological commitments, furthermore, the book is flawed in ways that I have already suggested and will discuss further: its racial objectifications, for example, and its very theme of toughening through slumming. Still, the story of Gorō's search for self in the third world sheds light on a sense of unhappiness among many Japanese that is based in socioeconomic terms, an unhappiness that upsets the notion that the Japanese, even in the recessionary era, are a homogeneous, middle-class people. It sheds light on the easy rhetoric of Japaneseness as an insular people thinking and doing alike, on the idea of Japanese as necessarily possessing or aspiring to

Western-based forms of power and prestige like that of Reiji's high-handed tourism. By representing, albeit imperfectly, Gorō's encounter with Jamaica, other potential sociopolitical articulations of Japaneseness come into view, one traveler at a time.

REGULAR JAPANESE AND GORŌ'S TOUGHER SELF

Several figures facilitate Gorō's toughening in his journey through Babylon. If Japanese like Sabu, the dread, and Jamaicans like Bongoman are agents of Gorō's toughening Jamaicanization, then this process is marked by his growing distance from regular Japanese. Rie, his girlfriend, is one such person. Gorō details his exploits in his letters to her, and in a brief letter back, she writes that she thinks he is going mad. She would like to visit Jamaica, which seems like an incredible country, but because like most Japanese she does not have Gorō's toughening experiences, she thinks Jamaica is frightening.

During his stay on the island, Gorō discovers Take in Kingston. Take decided to come to Jamaica after talking to Bongoman. When he and Gorō first meet on the island, Gorō is taken aback by Take's dizzying Japanese, by how out of place he seems there. Gorō, who seems to have forgotten his own first days in Kingston, laughs with Take at some visiting Japanese businessmen who weep at how horrible and dangerous this city is, with its frightening black people and its prison-like atmosphere. Gradually Take too, in his own way, becomes accustomed to Jamaican life. Employing cartoonish visual stereotypes of blacks, but transposing them onto Take's face, Hirō writes: "big-eyed, thick-lipped Take was deeply tanned, and if only he were quiet, he would make a magnificent Jamaican rude boy" (ibid., 244). The reader, gazing at Take, becomes better able to imagine not only the possibilities for Gorō's assimilation—as a middle-aged Japanese man—into the Jamaican, but also his limits. While young Take happily accepts Jim's invitation for sex with Jamaican prostitutes, for example, Gorō declines.

Gorō has his own indulgences, however, including his involvement in the ganja trade, getting into gunfights and smoking marijuana. But before he leaves Jamaica, he performs various acts of charity for the victims of a recent hurricane. Also near the end of the novel, at a small gathering of dreads, he is offered marijuana. Unlike past occasions, this time he declines. As a precondition for his return to Japan, he must wash his hands of the sins he has had to commit in his effort to achieve Jamaican toughness. In these ways, he becomes better able to reclaim his moral self as originally shaped in Japan.

These acts signal that he has not gone completely native (thank goodness he never actually shot anyone in those gunfights) and so can be returned to the fold of Hirō's Japanese readership. Here again, as with Sticko's narrative, Jamaican distance from Japan allows a critical perspective on Japaneseness, but in a way that ultimately reaffirms the value of that Japaneseness.

JAMAICAN VIEWS OF JAPANESE

Bongoman is the main figure in this novel through which the author is able to offer a Jamaican critique of the Japanese condition. In a letter to his son, Bongoman describes Japan as a mysterious country and writes how impressed he is with its people's beauty. As someone who has traveled throughout the third world, he is also impressed by Japan's wealth, low incidence of theft, and general peacefulness. He continues:

> There are also many temples and shrines that worship God. The temples of the other Asian countries are always crowded with worshipers, but in those of this country there are few people about . . . It's a lonely sight. The people here are strongly present-oriented, lacking interest in the past and future. Within this country's prosperity, with people and cars moving busily about, one can feel keenly something broken. In any case Jamaica, where there live poor people who believe in and love God, is a country of the exact opposite feeling. (ibid., 64–65)

This passage supports my earlier suggestion that many Japanese interested in Rastafari like Gorō (and Hirō) see Shintō and Buddhism as lifeless state religions, and in Rastafari the possibility of spiritual revival. This theme is developed further when Bongoman, wandering across Japan, encounters a Buddhist temple. Though awed by the sense of "Asian mystery" surrounding the place, he cannot understand the existence of a temple which took admission fees from tourists: it is wrong, he thinks to himself, "to make God into some thing to be gawked at" (ibid., 70).

At the temple, he meets a young monk in training who is fascinated with Rastafari; the monk professes to Bongoman his love of Bob Marley. He also expresses his dissatisfaction with Buddhism, which, so much unlike Marley's music, he sees as insufficiently engaged with the misery of the world. Bongoman advises the young man that even though he should remain true to his feelings, a deep search into his self and the social problems that so concern him will direct him the right way. But simply by having such a pure spirit, Bongoman says, the young monk "will become enveloped in the light of Jah" (ibid., 73). The young man brightens, and Bongoman finishes, "Ya man. You're a magnificent Rastaman" (ibid., 73). With the polemical clarity typical of this novel, Hirō uses the exchange between Bongoman and the young novice to criticize what he (or at least Gorō) sees as Japan's moribund spiritual life. Yet even as the young man seeks escape, Bongoman encourages patience. He expresses a deep respect for Buddhism and sees it as compatible with his own religious tradition.

Although in this brief meeting Bongoman encourages the novice to embrace Buddhism in Japan, he ushers his older protégé, Gorō, into America and Jamaica. Gorō's experiences there force him to deconstruct his Japanese identity. One aspect of this deconstruction is the previously mentioned Jamaican tendency to see Japanese people as Chinese-Jamaican, despite Gorō's numerous and irritated attempts at clarification. In one of his early letters to Rie he writes: "There is one thing I don't like. That is being called 'Chin, Chin.' 'I'm not Chin, I'm Japanese': this feeling just rises up in me. Even when I shout, 'I'm Japanese,' they say back, 'Here, Japanese and Chinese are the same thing'" (ibid., 201). Even after Gorō has supposedly become used to being called Chin, he writes to Rie: "I, Gorō, though singled out as 'Chin,' am still in Jamaica." Linked to the next sentence—"For the most part I have gotten used to Kingston's rough and tough lifestyle." (224)—overcoming this label appears to be an unexpected but important dimension of his achieving Kingstonian toughness.

However, when a small boy—who, when Gorō indicates he does not want any of the iced candy the boy is selling—yells "Chin!" and sticks his tongue out before running away, Gorō still winces at the label. "Hmm. Still Chin?" he muses sadly. This experience prompts explicit recognition of the nationalistic register of Gorō's irritation at this label: "Being called [Chin] bruises . . . Gorō's Japanese spirit [yamato damashii]" (ibid., 247).

In any event, the final resolution comes through the reconciliatory voice of Rastafari:

> "Hey, Chin," an old . . . Rasta on the roadside called out.
> "I'm not Chin. I'm Japanese!" The old man's eyes widened at Gorō's angry voice.
> "Come here. I want to talk to you."
> The man began gently preaching to Gorō, who had sat beside him. Gorō resignedly listened.
> "Even though you are Japanese, you mustn't get angry when you are

called 'Chin.' Just as we black people's roots are the same, whether American or Jamaican, Asian people are one. In the beginning, when God created the earth . . ."

From there the Bible lecture continued for almost an hour. After that, whenever he was called Chin, he resolved not to resist. (ibid., 247–48)

It is clear from the phrase "resolving not to resist" that Gorō remains ill at ease with being labeled "Chin." While suiting Gorō's global politics, while given weight by the fact that it is being offered by an elder dread and in a kindly spirit, the comparison between African Americans and Jamaicans as black people, on the one hand, and Chinese and Japanese as Asians, on the other hand, is not appreciated. Gorō listens "resignedly" to the dread, whose story textually fades into ellipsis. The story promises to be as long as stories go—beginning as it does in the biblical beginning. More than anything, Gorō feels pained by the fact that his deep identification as Japanese has in this space lost the relevance it has in Japan.

In this regard, the author's use of the term "yamato damashii" is interesting. It is understandable that Japanese like the fictional Gorō (and the Japanese reggae artists I interviewed) would want to be properly identified by the country they are from. This shock of realizing that one's primary identifications as shaped by home mean little in a new space overseas, or are radically altered according to that space's social politics, is a common experience, not one unique to Japanese. But the nationalist register of yamato damashii mobilized against being identified as Chinese invokes the negative attitudes many Japanese hold toward Chinese. It invokes the legacy of Japanese colonialism throughout Asia, a legacy that is an immediate cause of the tension between the two people. While there is politically progressive potential in Japan's recent embrace of the non-Western world (even though this happens mostly in the mass media or interpersonally outside Japan), this embrace also potentially reinforces the notion that the lines of global power run only between West and non-West, between those raced as white and those raced as not.[5] As with Munehiro's song, in the spectacle of Japan's romances with the Afro-Jamaican, and in these great, self-actualizing leaps into the global, a nearer landscape of regional frictions is quietly passed over. While there is much that is potentially progressive about jibun sagashi as an encounter with the world outside Japan, its conservative nature is clear in the ways that the self searched for is divorced from these postcolonial tensions.

Gorō's feelings about himself as Japanese—and therefore his ability to survive Jamaican cultural difference, poverty, and ethnoracial insensitivities —not only present themselves in his reactions to Jamaican views of Japanese, but also in how he (and Hirō, the author) as Japanese views Jamaicans. The political correctness evident in much of *Rastaman Vibration* do not extend to the apparently overwhelming need to communicate to the uninitiated just how *black* black people really are.

> "Will you give me a ride to Osaka? Give thanks." [Bongoman] grasped the man's hand firmly with his large *black hand*. (ibid., 67)

> [While drumming,] Bongoman's naked *black chest* glistened with sweat, his white dreads dancing in the air. (130)

> Homeward-bound Jamaicans crowded the waiting room. Children especially, dressed in their best, made light-hearted merriment. Little girls with curls bound with ribbons of primary colors. The figures of suited little boys—their mothers pushing carts bearing huge stuffed toys— walking as though dancing. The merriness of Caribbean people overflows . . . White tourists could be seen in the corners as though made tiny, overwhelmed by the power of *black skin*. (191)

> When he exited [the baggage claim area] he was utterly surrounded by beggars and vendors. Gorō shrank back at the *black faces* of the crowd. (208)

> The man snatched up and pocketed the money, and with a long *black finger* pointed to the road. (249; emphases added)[6]

Black Jamaicans are read in much of this novel like a collection of body parts: black hands, black chests, black skin, black faces, black fingers. In the third quote, blackness is made into a force with which Gorō politically identifies, one which keeps white people, so to speak, in their place. But then as he arrives in Jamaica, as described in the fourth quote, the limits of this political identification are disclosed in the way he instinctively shrinks back—not only because he is suddenly surrounded by so many people, but also because of their blackness. In spite of his intellectual embrace of blackness, one he needs in his search for a politically enlightened self, Gorō remains fearful of it.

All the quotes above are instances of a discrete fetishization of blackness, with the exception of the third, which is collective and enveloping. Stereotypes about overpowering black body odor are another way in which this collective, enveloping blackness is fetishized in the novel. Hirō describes Gorō's entry into the main floor of a Brooklyn sound system event: "The underground floor, with a black crowd of several hundred people jostling, was full of the smell of perfume and sweetish-sour body odor, and Gorō felt dizzy" (ibid., 188). Black body odor is a manifestation of black potency, one that threatens to overwhelm the delicate senses of the Japanese. Blackness is not impure matter out of place (Douglas 1978), but rather situates the pure matter of a Japaneseness that, unbearably, is. But blackness is not an impurity exactly; rather, it is a kind of positive energy. The following quotation, from a description of another sound system event, this one in Kingston, makes explicit this theme of blackness as positive energy:

> The heat of the sound system set ablaze the crowd in the square. From perspiring black skin came wandering a smell like burnt wheat flour. "The smell of Jamaica." Wherever he went, in that smell, Gorō felt the energy of Jamaican people; somehow it was a good feeling. It was a feeling of being alive. (ibid., 270)

The remark is couched in positive terms, a celebration of the black earthiness and vitality that Gorō came to Jamaica to discover. In contrast with his dizziness in the Brooklyn reggae club, in this second encounter, near the end of the novel and after many harrowing adventures, he is able to appreciate this smell as a sign of the vitality of Jamaican people. The ability to make such a claim signifies the fullness of Gorō's Jamaicanization.[7]

The preoccupation with black body odor is informed by the tendency of Japanese writers to employ blacks (and other foreigners) to refer to aspects of human physiology deemed inappropriate for public discussion. The funk emitted by all human beings when they dance in hot, crowded places becomes among black Jamaicans, given the primitive energies attributed to them, a sign of the natural endowments that bless as well as curse them. A certain note of self-congratulation is to be heard in these supposedly positive reclamations of black stereotypes. The writer is to be commended for presenting as a sign of vitality, goodness, or whatever, the unfortunate "fact" of black body odor. The stereotype of black people as having powerful body odor, however, remains unchallenged. Well-intentioned attempts to articulate positive comparisons with the other are often flawed by the limited discourses concerning these others, by the unwillingness to create more thoughtful ones, and by the fact that the other has been imagined as such.

Searching for Self in the Third World

Rastaman Vibration and other stories of Japanese travel to Jamaica significantly mobilize the three discursive elements that inform jibun sagashi, identified earlier in the chapter. The first was a reckoning with the social consequences of a recession that has deeply affected Japanese from all walks of life. Since Tokyo is the center of the Japanese economy, it is unsurprising that the literary imagination of a dysfunctional Japanese capitalism should be centered on this city. Both Yamakawa and Hirō, accordingly, construct Tokyo as a place which subordinates human well-being to the rhythms of capitalism—a city which steals life. A second aspect of jibun sagashi reflected in these works concerns the effort to navigate the Japanese social in relation to a desire for individual self-actualization, a process that has come to embrace not just the modern West, but the world at large (although, as with the esunikku, to the exclusion of postcolonial East and Southeast Asia). The characters and authors in the works of fiction and nonfiction explored here decide to leave the familiar behind, rejecting state and other demands that they lead recognizable lives. Instead, they choose to search for something of the real world beyond "soft, civilized" Japan, a search that often takes them to New York City and ultimately to third-world Jamaica. There, encountering bad Jamaicans, they become tougher, wiser global travelers and thus more confidently Japanese.

The third perspective on jibun sagashi concerns its performative aspect, specifically its use of writing, and less technologically, storytelling—including autobiography—as modes of self-making. By "its performative aspect," I mean how these publicly consumed narratives, in representing the actualization of fictional selves, cite not only the authority of that which lies outside Japan (the real world), but also, ultimately, the authority of Japaneseness. Even as they appear to challenge Japaneseness, these stories remain informed by and cite a persistent, authoritative vision of Japan as the necessary point of return. Storytelling is always reflexive, not only in the sense that it reveals something about the storyteller or the protagonist, but also in the sense that, as a construction of both storyteller and audience, it reveals something of the social values linking the two. Not only the character's presently known self, not only the self being searched for, but also the rhetorical codes through which these are expressed must be to some degree familiar to both writer and reader.

With regard to reflexivity, although I have been careful not to assume any equivalence between the attitudes of Gorō and those of Jah Hirō, it might be helpful to say something about the author in relation to this text. I met him at his modest mountainside home in Chiba. I had read only part of the novel at that time, but I felt that I should meet him anyway since I would soon have to return to the United States. He seemed like a nice man. He was not well at the time and was coughing heavily throughout our conversation. He talked about his life, his sense of estrangement from what he saw as the apathy of so many Japanese around him, how much he loved Bob Marley's music (a huge painting of the singer adorns his living room), his visit to Jamaica. He showed me a photo album with pictures of himself from this visit, of himself ten years before as the owner of a then well-known, but now closed Jamaica-themed establishment in Tokyo. He had also taken some artistic color photographs of Jamaican people while in Jamaica, and offered me any one that I liked. I chose one picture of a dark-complexioned young man, a cigarette stuck raffishly between his lips, wearing a white tam and a white shirt, with a red wall behind him. The photograph for me somehow captured what young men looked like at that time, in the early 1980s, when Hirō had visited Jamaica and I had left for the United States.

He admitted that writing the novel took a great deal of political energy out of him. Now he said he was tired, and even though he was still a fan of reggae music, he had moved on to other things, like writing about his two dogs, whom he loved very much. I met his wife, who was also very nice, and the three of us walked their dogs through the quiet streets of the mountain-side community. Afterward, he drove me back to the station—not before giving me a lot of *senbei* (rice crackers) to take back with me—in time to catch my bus to Tokyo.

What could we say to each other if we should meet again, now that I have read his novel? Who was this man I had met, and how had he seen me? How should I see him?

My discussion of Hirō's as well as Yamakawa's fiction has not been intended as literary criticism. I have been concerned with the performative terms through which Japanese search for self and in the process articulate Japaneseness. But my feeling as a reader—including as a Jamaican reader—is that both novels, whatever their intentions or merits, suffer from having too easily acquiesced to old discourses. These discourses do not fully enough imagine the humanities of those represented, of those who consume these works, nor, crucially, the circumstances of these figurations and consumptions.

6

Jamaican Perspectives on Jamaican Culture in Japan

In this book, I used dancehall, roots reggae, and Rastafari subcultural performance to explore gender, class, ethnicity, and other aspects of social
identity in Japan. I argued that these performances may be productively
framed vis-à-vis Western notions of blackness in the global context, and by
the particular situation of blackness in present-day Japan. I explored the
onstage efforts, particularly musical and oral, of sound system members
and deejays to forge a recognizably Japanese dancehall out of the Jamaican.
I also explored how the fashion and dance of Japanese donnettes spoke to
the cross-cultural construction of gendered power in the reggae dance scene
and to gender in Jamaican and Japanese society at large. I considered how
Rasta-identifying Japanese seek to phrase diasporic Rastafarian notions of
body and spirit in terms that root the movement and its followers in the
context of rural Japan. Finally, I examined the discourse in Japan of the
search for self through a body of writing that posits the Japanese as descendants of ancient Israelites, and in fiction and nonfiction writing—including
verbal and visual images—about travel to Jamaica.

   With the notion of performative field as a theoretical center, I therefore privileged a cross-cultural, multi-sited approach to understanding the Japanese adoption of Jamaican subcultures. These subcultures are becoming in many ways less explicitly associated with their Jamaican origins, especially within the broad base of the newest fans. Many of these fans are unfamiliar with Jamaican reggae. Reggae dance is showing signs of becoming just another form of Japanese erotica, distanced from its Jamaican origins. An older generation of dancers complain that a good number of the many newcomers to the scene, unconcerned with its Jamaican cultural nuances, have reduced reggae dance to a kind of go-go dancing. Maybe Rasta-identifying Japanese—at least those inclined to look—will find some spiritual core for a distinctively Japanese Rastafari that is as vital for them as Selassie is for Jamaicans.

Still, engagement with Jamaican sources, especially among the smaller group of practitioners on whom I focused in this study, remains an important part of Japan's Jamaican subcultural practice. The use of patois and the acquisition of dub plates from famous Jamaican musicians by members of Japanese sound systems gives Japanese dancehall an energizing, exoticizing connection with its Jamaican counterpart. Japanese dancehall queens still watch Jamaican video recordings and travel to Jamaica to learn the latest fashion and dance in the country, as well as to prove their own mettle there. Mighty Crown became especially famous after the group's victory at the 1999 World Clash in New York, where the Japanese sound defeated a field of Jamaican competitors. Rasta-identifying Japanese and the protagonists of works by Jah Hirō, Kimoto Yuko, Yamakawa Kenichi, and others search for spiritually deeper, more politically aware, tougher, and more vital selves by traveling to Jamaica.

I took the multi-sited perspective I did in part to be attentive to the global politics of cultural consumption and reproduction that are not always explicitly discussed in the consuming country. The fact that they are not always discussed does not necessarily mean they are absent or irrelevant. Again, especially among practitioners, silence on these matters— constructed as the private labor that goes into artistic becoming—can mask the fact that in terms of performative field, in cross-cultural political terms, easy Japanese adoption of another culture cannot always be assumed. Analyzing the very effort by Japanese artists to link the Jamaican and the Japanese is at least as important—both in immediate theoretical terms and within a broader progressive intellectual politics—as is the assumption that domestication is always already achieved. This is so even where this assumption is meant to show respect for the viability of the Japanese scenes as independent of the Jamaican. Despite the sensitivities that underlie it, this assumption can ironically work to marginalize the subaltern voice—which in this case is not Japanese, but Jamaican.

In this final chapter, I begin by summarizing my observations about how Japanese engagement with these Jamaican subcultures can be a lens through which to view the dynamics of social identity in Japan today. I discuss gender, religion, class, and domestic ethnicity, not so much as reflected in particular subcultures, but rather across them. I also discuss nation and race, aspects of social identity that become especially salient in the international context. Indeed, a primary purpose of this chapter is to resolve my discussion of global racialism in the Jamaican-Japanese encounter in internationalized Jamaican subcultures. I do so largely through exploring Jamaican responses to Japanese engagement with Jamaican culture. I argue that exchanges between Jamaicans and Japanese give evidence of three key discourses of race in the global context: the colonial-modern, the postcolonial, and the global postmodern. While I focus my analysis on global blackness, these three discourses, which I can discuss in only a preliminary way here, might be used as a way of thinking about Afro-Asian encounters such as those presented in this ethnographic study.

Jamaican Culture and Social Identity in Japan

GENDER AND SEXUALITY

As is the case among Jamaicans, the Japanese most deeply involved in producing roots reggae and dancehall music, as well as Rastafari, tend to be men. Thus these musical and religious scenes provide a foreign—and therefore both unusual and deeper—means of homosocial bonding, which is a characteristic of many arenas of both male and female life in Japan. For the Yoshino dreads, Rastafarian practice offers a code through which to enact their sense of solidarity as men. Membership in the predominantly male sound system culture is understood in familial terms, that sense of fraternity which is dramatically exhibited onstage—most notably in sound clashes. In this fraternity, denunciation of gay people, especially gay men, is a means of asserting one's heterosexual masculinity.

Despite—or perhaps partly because of—the male dominance of reggae and dancehall musical production, there are clearly demarcated spaces for women in these subcultures. Reggae dancers perform onstage the values of womanly togetherness. This homosocial bonding is extended by Japanese women overseas to Jamaican women, who represent the possibilities of an international, collective female strength as well as that of the individual woman. This is reflected in the careers of people like Junko Kudo, who performed in Japan with another woman but solo in Jamaica, in accordance with the performative conventions (and, as I have suggested, the individualist survivalism) found in Jamaica. The donnette provides one model for the erotic, cosmopolitan, of-the-moment "cos play"[1] of womanhood, what is through dancehall fashion and dance a clearly defined role which young urban Japanese women can adopt in their search for creative means to celebrate their identifications as such. For those so inclined, the donnette also provides a means of performing a seemingly transgressive sexual initiative. In this way, reggae dancers may be linked to various "bad girls" (Miller and Bardsley 2005), such as moga, who have captured the Japanese imagination over the decades.

However, I would not overemphasize this transgressiveness, sexual and otherwise. Many of the women who enjoy reggae dance do so, I have argued, because it has come to be structured around a culturally familiar—and in that sense, conservative—female homosociality, despite tensions between some dancers. Also, there is evidence in Japanese dancehall generally of a decidedly nontransgressive celebration of national identity and accomplishment. The spectacular rise of donnette culture in Japan over the past few years has revealed not only the conventional readiness with which the foreign is linked with hypersexuality—in this case, through the effaced referent of black women's bodies—but also, simultaneously, the facility with which corporate Japan is able to commodify this sexuality recognizably, and thus profitably, as Japanese. (While within the international reggae dance scene, this Japaneseness is ethnically and nationally distinct—as shown in the view of one Japanese contestant in the International Dancehall Queen Contest in Montego Bay that her defeat was "Japan's shame"—it becomes an unmarked heterosexual normative in the Japanese mainstream.)

With regard to gender in Rastafari in Japan, I met several women who strongly identify with the movement, sometimes independently of a male partner. Still, there is a general sense that Japanese women support their husbands' identification with the movement but often do not feel any personal need to become deeply involved. Comparing Rasta-identifying

Japanese women thus generalized with Japan's dancehall donnettes, the latter group may be more readily seen by those outside the subculture as "bad girls." The only publicly visible transgression of the former group is interest in a foreign subculture—which might manifest itself in the women's decision to dreadlock their hair, but which also, more happily, requires the women to behave with a certain reserve. These Rasta-identifying women are not exactly bad, then, because despite the strangeness of their engagement with Rasta, in some ways this engagement can be brought into line with discourses of chaste, traditional Japanese womanhood. I became acquainted with one dreadlocked woman, for instance, who wanted to become a Tibetan Buddhist nun. Even though inflected through the global religions of Tibetan Buddhism and Jamaican Rasta, this aspiration fits easily with the traditional image of Japanese women as chaste and pious. Rasta-identifying women often reside in the countryside, like most Japanese wives, living at home while raising their children. Their expressed indifference for the apparently contrasting scene of reggae dance may also be generational: donnettes who are part of the newer dancehall scene tend to be in their teens or twenties; women interested in the earlier reggae roots scene tend to be in their thirties and older, and so presumably more likely to be married.

RELIGION

The adoption of Rastafari in Japan provides an opportunity to consider the nature and state of religion in the country. This adoption reflects the discomfort some Japanese feel about a Japanese religious life that is less about fervor or morality and more about the pursuit of material benefit, as shown in the purchase of amulets to ensure safety in traffic and success on exams (Reader and Tanabe 1998). The practice of Shintō and Buddhism for most Japanese is a matter of social occasion. Shintō and Buddhism are mostly associated with the ritual celebration of a range of major annual life-cycle, and other, events: this includes the use of Shintō rituals at weddings, for instance, and Buddhist ones at funerals. Thus it is telling that, despite the fact that Rasta is a tradition that comes from halfway around the world, its Japanese practitioners have chosen it as suiting their spiritual and other needs better than what they see as the institutionalized utilitarianism of Buddhism and Shintō. In fact, Rasta's origin in a remote part of the world discreetly facilitates the fuller pursuit of this religion in personal terms, relatively free of international communal judgment (although Rasta-identifying Japanese sometimes pass judgment on each other's identifications with the movement).

Both the flexibility with which many practitioners identify with Rastafari in Jamaica, and by extension in Japan, and the flexibility with which Japanese pursue religious life generally raise questions about whether Rastafari in Japan is actually a religion. If "religion" means a theologically codified, ritually expressed imagination of the divine shared by a group of people, Jamaican Rastafari is clearly a religion. Thousands of followers have developed ritual means of expressing their belief that Haile Selassie is God. Although there are not many Rasta sacraments, there are definite ones surrounding, for instance, the consumption of marijuana and the wearing of dreadlocks; and although Rasta ideology and practice are largely individually pursued, there are various gatherings—in such places as yards and communes, as well as at such events as nyabinghis—where religious belief is collectively and ritually reaffirmed.

The most important element of Rasta faith in Jamaica—belief in Selassie's divinity—is not a major part of Rasta in the Japanese context. There are Japanese like Brother Taffy, who expressed to me his belief—shared by a very small minority of Jamaican Rastas—that Selassie's divinity exists "only" in conjunction with his humanity. But few other Rasta-identifying Japanese would see Selassie as divine even in these terms. While in Jamaica the cry "Jah Rastafari!" affirms Selassie's divinity in "word sound power," the same cannot exactly be said of this proclamation as is used, for instance, among the Yoshino dreads. For them, it serves as a reminder for those who have traveled to and communed with Jamaican Rastas of those experiences, and for all as a fetishized sign of knowledge of the Jamaican Rastas' powerful appreciation of this divinity. Fetishized, but not superficial: this aural sign mystically links the Japanese here and now to the world beyond, both geographically and spiritually. "Jah Rastafari" as invoked in this Japanese here and now can produce, as it does in Jamaica, feelings of joy, freedom, communion with one's brethren, and—this is where the question of Japanese Rasta's status as religion becomes tricky—a sense of spiritual closeness to the natural world. This spiritual closeness, even though divorced from direct worship of Selassie, might nevertheless be described as religious.

So given this tricky question of spirituality, is there a "Japanese Rastafari"? I suggest that this depends on where one places the emphasis: on "Japanese" (in this case, Japanese Rastafari would be definable in some key way as apart from the African diasporic movement) or on "Rastafari" (fundamentally centered, as it is in Jamaica, on the figure of Haile Selassie: Ras—the Amharic word for prince—Tafari became Haile Selassie I at his coronation in 1930). To the extent that Rasta-identifying Japanese travel internationally to commune with diasporic Rastas and are accepted into this larger community, and to the extent that they take that sense of communion with them back to Japan and work to sustain it, they are nominally members of the original religion. They are "Japanese *Rastafarians*," or Rastafarians who happen to be Japanese. How fully part of the diasporic movement Rasta-identifying Japanese are—given the ambiguous attitude many have toward Selassie, and, more important, the potentially negative effect that this ambiguous attitude may have on their relationship with diasporic Rastas—is a question that I, as a researcher and as a non-Rastafarian, am not in a position to answer. It can be answered only by the individual in his or her relationship with the community.

However, considered beyond its relationship with the Jamaican movement, and viewing religion in its aspect of possessing a coherent spiritual doctrine, I suggest that "*Japanese* Rastafari" is not now a religion. It is possible that a movement based on Rastafari—for instance, one which searches through Japanese history as mythologized by writers like Uno Masami—could come to articulate a doctrine of the divine independent of Haile Selassie. At the moment, however, no such doctrine exists. What we have are some Rasta-identifying Japanese who muse about Rastafari's rooting in the ancient Japanese past vis-à-vis Shugendō and a crypto-Japanese Judaism. It is possible to see such musings—particularly on Shugendō—as Japanese instances of a more broadly, mysteriously global Rasta (that is, of a Japanese *Rastafari* like the one Tibby advocates). However, to the extent that the musings are not or cannot be easily shared with Jamaican Rastas—particularly the idea of the Japanese as the chosen people—they are part of a *Japanese* Rastafarian belief system that remains unformed. Its formation has not occurred partly because of the uncertain—but surely alienated—relationship such a Japanese movement would have to diasporic Rastafari.

Whether *Japanese* Rastafari will ever come fully into being is an open question. To do so, it would have to overcome at least four obstacles. The first is the present small size as of the movement. The second is the deep foreignness of Rasta's presence in Japan. Despite its followers' lack of interest in proselytizing, or generally in engaging in coordinated political action; despite its nonviolent spirit; and despite the ways it shapes itself as Japanese, it would initially have to contend with mainstream apprehension about its foreign origins. The third challenge is that many Japanese attracted to diasporic Rastafari's call for unity, peace, and love may be unwilling to accept a Japanese Rasta that theologically incorporates an anti-Semitic literature (assuming that a *Japanese* Rastafari were to take this particular doctrinal path, and despite current practitioners' filtering out of the anti-Semitic element). The fourth obstacle concerns the sustaining of a *Japanese* Rastafari over time. There is a tendency toward discrete generational identification with the movement in Japan. Most of the Rasta-identifying Japanese I spoke with indicated that they would allow their children to decide for themselves whether they would follow Rasta. (This is in sharp contrast to the Jamaican case, where socialization of children into the Rasta faith is considered no less than an act of survival in Babylon.) While Rasta in Jamaica has become a pervasive social reality, in Japan it is a matter of personal choice, a choice that presented itself most potently during a particular period—from the mid-1980s to the late 1990s—in Japan's social history. It remains to be seen whether a *Japanese* Rastafari gains force under a new, or related, confluence of circumstances; whether another version replaces it or comes to exist alongside it; whether Rasta in Japan continues to be, as Tibby hopes, essentially the same as that of the diaspora; or whether it simply fades away. In any case, it is an interesting example of the long historical process through which the Japanese have sought to accommodate religious traditions like Buddhism and other foreign cultural forms in ways that suit their particular needs and sensibilities. Rasta constitutes one possibility of Afro-Asian, cross-cultural fertilization out of the many made possible in a globalizing Japan.

CLASS, ETHNICITY, AND NATIONALITY

It has been often remarked that most Japanese identify themselves as middle class: wealth is more evenly distributed in Japan than in most other industrialized nations. The demand that males, regardless of class, study hard to get into good high schools, where they study hard to get into good colleges, from which they can get good *sarariiman* jobs at good companies is made possible by a rigorous meritocracy which grants social rewards to those who have earned them. "Rewards" and "earned," however, are qualifiable terms: some Japanese men do not see working long and difficult hours for a company, however prestigious, or being able to spend only a few hours a week with their children, as rewarding. Many Japanese roots musicians and some dancehall practitioners have criticized this system because they believe it produces and maintains significant class-based inequities in Japan. Those who, like Taffy and Taz, grew up poor areas; the many male dancehall artists who work as furiitaa well into their twenties, and who thus have little hope of conventional middle-class lives; and the many reggae dancers who hold marginal jobs such as hostesses and hairdressers are living examples of this view. By applying Rasta's capitalist critique to Babylonian Japan, many reggae practitioners and Rasta-identifying Japanese criticize the very limited options available for those who choose not to submit themselves to the rigors of, or who are unable to find a place in, corporate Japanese life.

Despite the common idea of class homogeneity in Japan, I would argue that the very fact that so many people identify as middle class demonstrates the existence of class consciousness in Japan. Such a consciousness exists as an awareness of the pressure to be middle class. It also exists as the stigmatization felt by those—like the homeless, on whose behalf Taz advocates—unable to achieve middle-class standards of living, or by those who have voluntarily removed themselves from the grinding cycles of work-hard, spend-hard capitalism. In the early years of my research, before dancehall took off, none of the performers I met, some of whom were already well into their forties, had full-time jobs. This is significant because even now very few people can make a living only by pursuing their creative interests in reggae music. Most performers then worked part time, or ran small businesses. Even the most successful performers, like the members of Mighty Crown, for many years worked part time doing odd jobs.

As is the case elsewhere, in Japan, class is closely related to ethnicity. Japanese public discourse imagines ethnicity, like class, not to be an issue in Japan, yet it is in fact an important dimension of social difference there. Taffy's status as burakumin is inseparable from his ghetto upbringing and his childhood poverty, as is the case for the ethnic Koreans he grew up with. Of course, one could argue against the designation of burakumin as an ethnic group, since genotypically and phenotypically the burakumin appear to be as Japanese as anyone else in the country. They may be said to be able to partake of Japan's culture and nationality as fully as any other Japanese. However, many mainstream Japanese *imagine* that the burakumin are somehow different from them, and the burakumin are in turn intimately familiar with the restrictions that this imagination of them places on their lives. To the extent that ethnicity involves a group's historicized sense of its

The Yokohama Reggae Sai in 2006 was a festival in honor of Mighty Crown's fifteenth anniversary. Photo by Mighty Crown Entertainment.

social difference from a mainstream group, burakumin may thus be considered an ethnic group. However one chooses to characterize the burakumin, Brother Taffy and others use roots reggae to interrogate the myth of class-based and ethnic homogeneity in Japan, even if they feel they must do so—given the great social costs they face—in secrecy.

The local management of Mighty Crown's international success provides another perspective on dancehall's situation in Japan vis-à-vis class, nationality, and ethnicity. The Yokohama Reggae Sai (Festival), held on August 5, 2006, was a celebration of Mighty Crown's fifteenth year together. This event, featuring an array of Japanese reggae performers affiliated directly and otherwise with "the Mighty Crown family," could be seen as a culmination of the vogue of dancehall culture in Japan. In contrast to the small nightclubs of Japanese dancehall's early underground years, over 30,000 fans filled the sunlit expanse of Yokohama Stadium to capacity. As a manifestation of the national pride in Japanese dancehall at this moment, several people in the audience were waving the Japanese flag. One person waved a flag that was Japanese on one side and Jamaican on the other. Another wore a shirt with the green and yellow colors of the Brazilian flag: different countries, similar colors, same difference.

At one point, a video message appeared featuring several major Japanese and Jamaican celebrities. The martial artist Yamamoto "Kid" Norifumi; the actors Ishii Masanori, Kubotsuka Yōsuke, Asano Tadanobu, Suzuki Sarina, and Takenaka Naoto; and the Jamaican deejays Ninja Man, Assassin, Sean Paul, and Damien Marley took turns paying tribute to Mighty Crown. The retired sumo wrestler Konishiki also appeared on-screen to celebrate the sound. Then he told the crowd to wait, that he would be right there. Soon Konishiki was ambling in person down the long walkway that extended through the wildly cheering audience.

Sumo wrestlers are really interesting to me because of the ethnic transvestism I mentioned earlier. Sumo wrestlers traditionally take on professional names: Konishiki, Akebono, Musashimaru, Asashōryū. These four wrestlers—who have achieved or come close to achieving the status of *yokozuna*, the highest level in the sport—are not ethnically Japanese. Konishiki, ethnically Samoan, was born in Hawaii; Musashimaru is Samoan by birth but moved at an early age to Hawaii; Akebono is Hawaiian; and Asashōryū is Mongolian. The use of names, dress, and rituals associated with sumo, many of which are rooted in indigenous Shintō practice, not only helps make any match these wrestlers participate in culturally appropriate, but also helps to regulate the non-Japaneseness of the foreign wrestlers. By "regulate," I do not mean that the distinctively Japanese names, dress, and rituals associated with sumo conceal the background of the foreign wrestlers: most fans know which wrestlers are foreign, often just by their physical appearance. Rather, the standardized form of each match routinely disciplines the non-Japanese body—that is, submits it to Japanese cultural standards that this body must aspire to. The sight of the non-Japanese body submitting itself to and citing the authority of a Japaneseness reiteratively sustained through the sumo match enforces that authority. It also potentially undermines it, especially when the non-Japaneseness of successful foreign wrestlers is foregrounded in a way that becomes difficult to manage (as was the case with Konishiki's conflicts with the Japan Sumo Association).

Two of Mighty Crown's members, the brothers Sammy T and Masta Simon, walk a similar line: they are Japanese citizens of Chinese descent. The theoretical zero-sum game—according to which phenomena like reggae in Japan must be either ideologically laden or superficial, either about a heavy politics of identity or simply play—is revealed as pointless given the range of purposes and strategies according to which the two men and others in the public eye who are not considered regular (Yamato) Japanese manage this aspect of their social identities. This management, of course, depends on which ethnic group is involved, mainstream Japanese attitudes toward this group, and how the individuals are positioned in the public eye.

These possibilities might be considered as located along a sort of continuum of ethnic outness for those not considered Yamato Japanese. At the "out" end of the continuum are those whose public claim to fame is that they are not Yamato Japanese, like those who, given that their ethnic difference manifests itself phenotypically, appear in Japanese television commercials and print advertisements. Next along the continuum of ethnic outness are those like the foreign sumo wrestlers described above: everyone knows they are ethnically different, but their ethnicity is circumscribed by their visible commitment to a particular performance of Japaneseness. Further along this spectrum are the various performers and athletes Lie (2001) writes about, who only rarely discuss their "non-Japanese" Asian, Euro-American, or African American heritage, or who even conceal it to pass as mainstream Japanese. While many Japanese may know that these individuals are of foreign descent, this fact is not generally discussed in public, in order to "protect" the celebrity in question. At the opposite end of the spectrum are people like Brother Taffy, who feel the need to keep their burakumin identity hidden, given the intense stigma associated with it.

In public performative terms, Sammy T and Masta Simon are Japanese nationals. The 1999 victory of their sound system is celebrated as a Japanese victory, perhaps one of the globally successful "Japanese 'muffins'" Munehiro dedicated her song to. Their onstage speech has a striking roughness to it: men are sometimes addressed as "*omaera*" (you all, or "unnu," in patois), women are "*oneechan*" (literally sister, but in this context something like girl or, in patois, "gyal"). These terms may be intended to approximate the rough language of Jamaican rude boys, but they ultimately register as very casual, working-class Japanese speech. Sammy T and Masta Simon routinely pay verbal respect to Jamaican dancehall but go on to assert that Japanese reggae is great as well.

But although they are nationally Japanese, as ethnically Chinese, the two men can also performatively claim a position on the continuum of ethnic outness in Japan. Their particular location might be somewhere between the first and second position. The first position, again, is an openness about, even a reveling in, ethnic difference. The second is placing no

Mighty Crown in Yokohama's Chinatown. Left to right: Masta Simon, Cojie, Sammy T, and Super G. Photo by Hiroto Sakaguchi / Rove.

particular weight on the well-known fact of one's ethnic difference, given performative prioritizations of Japaneseness. Masta Simon and Sammy T do not generally identify themselves onstage or in the media as ethnically Chinese, but at the same time, they make their Chinese descent a key part of their extensive marketing of the Mighty Crown name. The fliers for their events often feature a stylistically sinicized Roman script. The logo for their clothing line, Nine Rulaz, for instance, features a dragon curled in the shape of the number 9. The Nine Rulaz website gives various reasons for the choice of number 9: it is the sum of the numbers in the area codes for Japan (081) and Yokohama, home of Japan's largest Chinatown (045); and in China, the website notes, it is considered a lucky number.

During a telephone interview, I asked Masta Simon about the significance of his Chinese heritage as a member of Mighty Crown. He said:

You got some people who got mixed blood. You got Americans mixed with Japanese, Japanese mixing with Jamaican. You know? It's who you really are. That's what I think. Because some people are afraid to say, talk out their heritage. But we're different, because God made all of us. There's a reason why you're here, there's a reason why I'm playing reggae music, too. It's all about expressing myself.

His Chinese heritage, then, is part of his social identity; this heritage, Japaneseness, and many other things make him the full human being that he creatively expresses through dancehall. Masta Simon's and his brother's ethnic identifications appear ideological not so much because they celebrate this heritage in opposition to a Japan that circumscribes domestic ethnic difference, but more because the men use their Chineseness as one position from which to engage the difference of Afro-Jamaican dancehall. (Their Chinese upbringing has afforded them access to the international—including attending an international school where English was the main language —that most Japanese lack.) Successful in this effort, they are able to valorize a Japanese dancehall in which the hybridizing signs of their Chineseness can comfortably, playfully, and recently very profitably coexist.

The Politics of (Knowing One's) Place

As Mighty Crown's star has risen since its 1999 victory, the members' status as Japanese artists has been occasion for tension in international competition. This tension sheds light on a set of subcultural politics significantly different from those found in Japanese dancehall. In Japan, Japanese sound systems involve audience members and each other in validating Japanese dancehall as a space within the broader field of international dancehall culture. In international competition, the transparency of this effort cannot be assumed. Jamaican sounds, in the ritual attempt to ridicule their competition, demand that Mighty Crown quit complaining about being blackballed since winning in 1999. They declare that Crown is no real rival because Jamaican audiences are no longer impressed by Japanese people speaking in patois. While these expressions are rhetorical and not necessarily felt offstage, Jamaican sounds have also complained that Crown and other comparatively wealthy Japanese sounds are driving up the price of dub plates.

Masta Simon of Mighty Crown aptly noted that in his international shows, he encounters two basic kinds of Jamaican responses to the Japanese presence in dancehall: some Jamaicans see this presence as a sign of Jamaican cultural accomplishment, and others see it as an intrusion. This tension is also felt in the donnette scene. The recent renaming of the Jamaican dancehall queen competition as an international event encapsulates this tension. On the one hand, the change from national to international is a measure of the heightened global status of this "ghetto" dance. On the other hand, it marks for underclass Afro-Jamaican women the partial or potential loss of a space that is thus no longer their own. Speaking to the more infamous of these frictions between Japanese and Jamaican dancehall artists, Masta Simon told me that Bounty Killer, long one of Jamaica's top DJs and a judge in World Clash, gave to Bass Odyssey the title that Crown and the vast majority of the audience believed Crown had won. Masta Simon said there was a blog entry in which the writer claimed Killer had stolen the title from Crown. Masta Simon said Mighty Crown had nothing to do with the blog post apparently a source of irritation for Killer.

In some interviews, Killer has declared his strong support of Japanese dancehall, but he has also voiced his annoyance and outright anger about the Japanese presence in Jamaican dancehall culture. In an online BBC interview, he responded to questions about a 2003 sound clash in which he scolded Jamaican sound systems for letting Japanese beat them.[2] In the interview, rather than retreating from his earlier remarks, Killer picked up where he had left off. He wondered why Mighty Crown, a Japanese group, was so taken with dancehall culture and why its members were speaking in patois; he suggested that these artists stick to other, more appropriate pursuits, like karate. Masta Simon himself has downplayed the Crown-Killer affair:

> It's not like we don't respect Bounty Killer . . . It's the words that he said. I guess he didn't mean it that way. But it sounded that way . . . There are certain things we gotta stand up to. I know that Killer rates us still as a sound, you know, pushing reggae music. He's a good person too. But . . . we don't beg no friend, Killer don't beg no friend. One day, time will tell, you know. Maybe shake hands . . . But it's the least right now.[3]

Masta Simon said he still plays Killer tunes, even though Killer has not recorded any new dub plates for Crown for several years.

A conversation I had with a Japanese woman, a photographer who has lived in Jamaica for over twenty years, provides another example of the ethnic and racial (as well as, in this case, gendered) tensions that can surface when Japanese encounter Jamaicans in Jamaica (as opposed to in Japan, where these tensions are often effaced in the discreet effort to make dance-hall self-evidently Japanese).[4] She has objected to the sexualization of Japanese women in Elephant Man's song "Chiney Ting." She temporarily posted on her website a translation of the lyrics of this song, which featured Elephant Man encountering two Japanese women. The women declare their intent to have sex with Jamaican men because "they are black and strong / an' di anaconda whe' long" (they are well endowed). The photographer believes that songs like these create the potential for embarrassment (or worse) for Japanese women who come to Jamaica as dancehall fans but who are unversed in the linguistic nuances of the patois and English phrases used in the subculture. (As an example, she describes Japanese women asking Jamaican women in the powder room about the meaning of the word "anaconda.")

Many Jamaicans doubtless share Elephant Man's and Bounty Killer's opinions of Japanese, but these views speak to the complexity of the ways in which different nonwhite peoples imagine each other. The complexity of these cross-cultural imaginings might be highlighted in this case by questioning to what degree the photographer's concern about Japanese women ought to be extended to Jamaican women. (Here too it becomes clear how the easy communication and sense of sisterhood of Soma's powder room are far from givens.) On the one hand, some people (not necessarily the photographer) might argue that Jamaican women generally are in a better position to defend themselves against Jamaican men than Japanese women are, given their greater familiarity with Jamaican culture and society. On the other hand, the possibility that Jamaican women might be better able socioculturally to navigate sexual objectification by Jamaican men does not mean that they should have to do so. Also, a sudden concern about one song's sexual objectification of Japanese women, when so many other songs objectify Jamaican women, runs the risk of appearing to privilege the sexual integrity of Japanese over Jamaican women. Perhaps a more constructive approach to the issue (one that I doubt the photographer would disagree with) would be for dialogue between Jamaican and Japanese women about their shared stake in dancehall subculture (in the way begun by Soma in her *Strive* article).

Jamaican Perspectives on Jamaican Culture in Japan

It is clear that the dancehall scene in both Jamaica and Japan is influenced by the growing Jamaican awareness of the Japanese presence in the subculture. The broader Jamaican response to Japanese interest in Jamaican culture, beyond that of Jamaican dancehall practitioners and fans, might be characterized in several ways. These include, of course, surprise. Even in the early 2000s, most Jamaicans were unaware of the Japanese interest in Jamaican culture. The tide began to turn with Mighty Crown's victory in New York, and perhaps even more with Kudo's more high profile victory in Jamaica. Crown won in the relatively esoteric space of sound system culture, which receives little attention from the mass media; Kudo's victory was reported in the Jamaican newspapers and broadcast media. One commentator in the chatroom of a Jamaican reggae website, puzzled by this Japanese interest in reggae, wrote: "What the hell is going on?"

Once at the airport in Kingston, I overheard a conversation between two Jamaican men about the Japanese interest in reggae. One of the two observed how little Jamaican people appreciated the enormous cachet of Jamaican culture in Japan and around the world. Pride, then, discreet in this case but often also explicit, is a second reaction. Savigliano (1995) notes that the Japanese are marked as a kind of exceptional other whose interest in a given foreign cultural form—in her case, the tango—is a measure of the great extent of its global popularity. Jamaican culture, similarly, must have traveled very far indeed to have attracted the attention of the Japanese, of all people. This global reach is especially significant since dancehall, the music of the Jamaican ghetto, is so profoundly local. Japanese victories in Jamaican dancehall help to validate dancehall in Japan; equally, in Jamaican debates about dancehall's vulgarity, Japanese involvement is a sign of the music's international power, and therefore of its domestic value.

A kind of negative pride is a third response to Japanese interest in Jamaican culture. Implied in Bounty Killer's annoyance at Mighty Crown is the feeling that by doing what Jamaicans do, this Japanese sound devalues dancehall as a particularly Jamaican form of expression. Killer obviously believes that only Jamaicans can exhibit the passion and the deep cultural knowledge required to play Jamaican music right; in fact, as part of his tirade against Mighty Crown, Killer listed some of the great Jamaican sounds throughout the history of the subculture that, in his opinion, Mighty Crown could not compete with.

A fourth Jamaican response might be framed in terms of the effort needed to situate the Japanese presence within the existing postcolonial Jamaican social order. Since the small East Asian presence in Jamaica has historically been Chinese, many Jamaicans assume that Japanese visitors are Chinese. Elephant Man's song, Japanese fiction and nonfiction about travel to Jamaica, and my interviews with Japanese artists who have traveled to Jamaica all bear witness to this assumption. (As slight evidence that things might be changing, however, a Chinese Jamaican colleague described to me encountering a black Jamaican man who, given Jamaicans' growing knowledge of the Japanese presence on the island, assumed that he was Japanese.)

The Japanese presence in Jamaican dancehall, especially in the case of Japanese who stay on the island for long periods of time, also raises issues surrounding racial body politics in postcolonial Jamaican society. Some of my friends have suggested that Kudo, although a great dancer, was helped by what they called her "exotic" appearance. Wondering how Jamaica's national dancehall queen could be Japanese, these individuals link Kudo's victory to the preference of many Jamaican men for "browning" (lighter-complexioned Afro-Jamaican women) over darker-complexioned women. Kudo and the many Japanese women performing in what is now Jamaica's International Dancehall Queen Contest do so in a predominantly black postcolonial society in which blackness has historically been viewed in ambivalent terms. I asked a female friend with whom I attended the competition in 2004 what she made of Kudo. She spoke as a Jamaican woman deeply ambivalent about the offering up of the bodies of Jamaican women to the raw gaze of such competitions. Kudo, she replied, somehow made it all seem less "disgusting." For my friend, the visible difference of Kudo's body made the profanity of dancehall dance no longer just about the sexual objectification of the bodies of Afro-Jamaican women. She had less reason to be personally offended because the objectified woman's body was no longer just like her own.

A fifth response is outright anger. Some Jamaican Rastas who have heard about the existence of the Japanese movement have complained that it seems to be divorced from religiosity. Another source of anger surrounds the accusation of cultural theft. The Japanese seem to have joined European, Chinese, Indian, Syrian, Lebanese, and other ethnic Jamaicans, higher up on

Jamaica's "pigmentocratic" socioeconomic order, as well as white Americans and Europeans, in the cultural exploitation of the island. There is a sense in which this is evidence of more of the same, another moment in the long history of theft of the cultural productions of black people, usually by whites, but in this case by Japanese. Jazz had its Paul Whiteman, rock and roll its Elvis Presley, roots reggae its UB 40, hip-hop its Eminem; now dancehall has its Junko Kudo and Mighty Crown. Relatedly, mixed-race people such as Bob Marley and Sean Paul, rather than the darker-skinned artists who otherwise dominate Jamaican music, are often more easily accepted in Euro-American markets.

Many scholars argue that culture empirically belongs to no one, that cultural nationalism can be dangerous, and that black people's unwillingness to accept whites (and Japanese) imagined as emissaries of this continued "cultural theft" can be unfair. I count myself among these scholars. I do think it is unfair to assume that any given Japanese person in Jamaica is out to "steal" Jamaican culture. However, these arguments are often accompanied by only marginal, if any, concern about the socioeconomic structures under which black peoples have sometimes been illegally deprived of their creative intellectual property. (Although culture belongs to no one, even academics exasperated by what they consider intellectually naive claims to the contrary can recognize the de facto authority of the Western legal notion of intellectual property, and the wrongness of cultural theft in these terms when it does take place.) When black people's exclusionism is consistently, and sometimes quite heatedly, more an issue than the structural reasons behind this exclusionism; when the irritating rancor of these subaltern voices discreetly comes to justify Western academia's silence on these issues; when those who even try to address these issues are immediately suspected of intellectual naiveté, academia loses credibility as the impartial arbiter of these debates.

A final response pertains to opportunism, in the best sense of the word. During one televised interview with the Jamaican ambassador to Japan, the interviewer asked what the Jamaican government was doing and should be doing to take fullest advantage of the cultural links between Jamaica and Japan. Jamaicans recruited by the Japanese embassy in Jamaica are now traveling to Japan as part of the Japan Exchange and Teaching Program; this and other educational programs also represent important possibilities for greater reciprocity in Jamaican-Japanese cultural exchange. I received an e-mail from a business student at the University of the West Indies who was working on a project to create a Japanese-patois dictionary; I have also heard from small record distributors asking how to tap into the Japanese market. These efforts dovetail into the argument by Japanese fans and practitioners of reggae that their tourist dollars and fees for dub plates help stimulate the Jamaican economy.

The Jamaican and Japanese economies are about as different in power as those of any two countries on earth. Yet the two countries are similar in that the culture industries of both have much "soft power" around the globe. Manga, anime, sushi, sports, and films help drive the economic juggernaut that is Japanese popular culture, one that has gone some way toward offsetting the effects of a recession now approaching its second decade. Reggae music, and the tourist industries that surround it (the national airline, hotels, cruise ships, beaches, clubs, annual concerts, and so forth), have helped keep the Jamaican economy on its feet, if barely. A small corrective for the economic difficulties facing Jamaican society, then, might be recognizing and more fully exploring the economic potential of not only Japanese but also a broader international interest in dancehall reggae (in addition to the already recognized interest in roots reggae). This would ideally be coupled with awareness of the tendency to privilege Jamaica's culture industries over other areas of the island's economy in dire need of development. It would be coupled with sensitivity to the fact that very little of the profits generated by the culture industries trickles down to the public in the form of social services, partly because of the neoliberal economic structure to which the owners of many of the businesses associated with these industries increasingly belong. It would be coupled with recognition of the extreme difficulty of asserting economic independence in the face of first-world governmental and corporate power. Visitors drawn to Jamaica's music, for instance, assume that their spending helps the island's economy. This is true to some extent. But many major hotels in Jamaica belong to multinational corporate chains that do not necessarily have much investment in Jamaica's economic development. This is symptomatic of a Jamaican economy many of whose private, and even public utility, companies are being displaced by foreign interests.

But all this said, a combination of efforts like those of the UWI student's Japanese-American patois dictionary; the development of organizations like the Sound System Association, which works to protect the legal and financial interests of Jamaican artists; and events like UWI's 2008 Global Reggae

Conference and the Reggae Academy Awards—in which Jamaican and international musicians, producers, scholars and fans of the music recognize, support, and basically acknowledge reggae's spectacular (and spectacularly profitable) internationalization—might be a self-sustaining palliative for some of the island's economic difficulties. As some of these examples suggest, then, it is not only as uninvested arbiters that academics might engage Jamaican popular culture, but as participants interested in helping people whose works our own as scholars benefit from.

Japanese Dancehall in the Western Media

As discussed in the example of Jamaican tourism, the global cultural economy to which dancehall belongs involves not only Jamaicans and Japanese but also the West. As noted earlier, Western representation, such as the increased visibility of Jamaican dancehall artists on MTV and in hip-hop magazines, has had a bearing on the rise of dancehall in Japan. Over the past few years, a few European and American media outlets have weighed in on the cross-cultural interactions between Jamaicans and Japanese.[5] I mention such works here because this reporting often directly takes on the global cultural politics between Jamaicans and Japanese that is my main concern in this chapter. For purposes of economy, however, I discuss just one such work.

The cover of the August 2002 hip-hop magazine *Vibe* advertised an article on the dancehall scene in Japan with the words: "Wannabes: The Weird World of Japanese Dancehall Fanatics." Inside, the article is prefaced by the following words: "The sun is not the only thing rising in the East: Reggae music is having a huge renaissance in Japan. But when obsessive Japanese fans fake a Jamaican accent, lock their hair, and tan their skin, is the fascination with black culture going too far?" (Dreisinger 2002, 131). This introduction immediately questions the authenticity of Japanese fans of reggae music. The words "weird," "wannabes," "obsessive," and "fake" and the image of Asians with tanned skin and dreadlocked hair index a contemporary Orientalist imagination of Japanese people as inscrutably crazy others.

The article raises the question of the "Elvis effect," in which black popular culture is appropriated by whites (here, by Japanese) for broader international consumption. "Where is the line," Dreisinger asks, "between cross-cultural influence and cross-cultural theft?" (ibid., 134). For Drei-singer, the propriety of Japanese dancehall artists' and fans' adoption of Jamaican culture seems to turn on the question of whether the Japanese acknowledge their sources and have in a sense paid their membership dues, such as by spending time among Jamaicans. Noting how linguistic differ-ence, such as that between Jamaican patois and standard English, can give voice to a marginalized people's resistance, Dreisinger asserts that a young Japanese woman who "lived in Kingston or Flatbush for a while . . . might have a more authentic claim to the language, like a white kid from the projects who tosses ghetto slang. This is something that most young Japa-nese reggae fans, who've never met an actual Jamaican, can't claim" (136). Dreisinger uses her conversation with a Japanese hip-hop group to consider the "unsettling" possibilities of the future of black music in Japan: "Instead of giving props to KRS-One and Rakim, several crew members say they discovered hip-hop via Japanese, not African-American, acts. Asked if they think there's something uniquely African-American about hip-hop, they fall silent. They can't understand the question" (138).

While I greatly appreciate the author's sensitivity to the politics of ap-propriation, I struggle with some aspects of her argument. A certain unpro-ductiveness, a kind of intractability often sets in when analysis of any group's engagement with another's culture is based on what in the end is an irresolvable moral politics of authenticity. Debates about who has a moral right to the music, and how that right should be exercised, do little to challenge the exclusion of black people from the benefits of their cultural productions. This is significant especially because Dreisinger's argument seems in part based on an effort to challenge this marginalization. She appears to link the possibilities of an appropriate Japanese engagement with reggae very closely to the fact that Japanese did not create the music. As weirdo, obsessive, and fake wannabes (I should note that these might not be Dreisinger's own words), the Japanese might even have a special obligation to demonstrate their respect and understanding of the origins of these musical genres. But what does ignorance about African American hip-hop make the men in the hip-hop group above? (This ignorance fits with my sense of mainstream dancehall reggae today, based on fan discussion in Mixi's "Japanese Reggae" chatroom—in which there is little discussion of Jamaican artists.) This is a consequence of the cultural "blending and clash-ing" (2002, 138), as Dreisinger herself notes, in contemporary global culture. This is not to say that all is fair game, because it is manifestly not. For me, however, only so much can be accomplished by getting Japanese to "big up" the original masters (although this is always nice, an important sub-cultural formality). Even with such expressions of indebtedness, the basic structural marginality of black musicians remains unchanged.

My own inclination is essentially to "allow" Japanese to continue doing what they have been with the music. I say this not because I think they do or do not have a right to, but simply because they can, and will. At the same time, more efforts might be made to encourage Jamaican musicians to develop the organizational means like those discussed above, by which they will be able to benefit more from the popularity of Jamaican music in places like Japan. It might be more productive to identify and pursue strategies whereby Jamaican musicians also "can, and will."

Global Racial Performativity

I have argued that ideas of race—and specifically blackness—both discreetly and explicitly inform Japanese engagement with Jamaican culture. In conducting this research, I have been struck by the range of ways in which blackness, as encoded in Jamaican musical and religious culture, is understood in Japan. I will end by bringing together my discussion in this book of the racial dimensions of Jamaican culture in Japan. I discuss what the manifestations of the flexible metaphor of blackness discloses about the idea of race in a global context, not only in the African diaspora qua West but also beyond.

Global race might be viewed as constituted in at least three major discursive terms: the colonial-modern, the postcolonial, and the global postmodern.[6] While these three, mutually informed discourses are admittedly quite broad, at least they bridge the even broader cleavages between West and non-West, first world and third world, diaspora and non-diaspora. They do so because they are defined by the geohistorical flow of ideologies of race between all these regions, thus presenting the possibility of alternative discursive formations, like the Afro-Asian, that are not contained within each side of these divides. I very briefly discuss each of these discourses in turn, focusing on the performativities of blackness and discussing how they are revealed in this research from both the Japanese and the Jamaican perspectives.

THE COLONIAL-MODERN

The specifically Western idea of race emerged at the nexus of several, mutually informed forces and conditions that define modernity. These include the Enlightenment concern with technological and scientific progress; the development of a capital-based world economy; the emergence of the nation-state; a growing sophistication of the technocratic apparatus of social control; and the combination of the forces of industrialization, urbanization, and the mass media. Colonial modernity speaks to the profound degree to which race and colonialism are both the products of and influences on the modern experience. Each of the above aspects of the colonial-modern condition can be readily seen in racial performative terms, in racial ideology realized on the level of the represented, regulated, racialized body (Foucault 1988, 1995; Stoler 1995, 2002). Depending on the society, period, and demography in question, black slavery creates certain needs: to regiment productive bodies in terms of fieldwork, artisanship, and housework; to control through terror; to segregate potentially dangerous bodies; to organize bodies in ways that ensure the proper distribution and withholding of resources; and to inculcate and measure acquiescence to an order in which only a few, regardless of color, can have much investment. This management of the enslaved African body turns most immediately on the sign of blackness. Those invested in the institution of slavery and in the postemancipation subjugation of peoples of color displayed racialized bodies in many ways: from the staging of black bodies in Western exhibitions and museums (Lindfors 1999) to the circulation of daily cultural commodities caricaturing black people's physical features (Goings 1994; Nederveen 1992). These representations, performatively routinized, rendered the colored body as object, as abject, in their regular, systematized assessments of black bodies in slave auctions; in displaying the body of Sarah Bartman, called the Hottentot Venus, on Western stages; and in the kinky, quotidian consumption of "Nigger Hair" chewing tobacco.

In this book, the colonial-modern discourse of race has emerged in a number of ways. From the Japanese perspective, it appears in the iconic kinship that Rasta dolls and related artifacts share with Mammy, Sambo, Memín Pinguín, and Dakko-chan, artifacts which belong to a global symbolic and political economy in which black bodies are readily rendered as objects to be consumed and displayed. The discourse appears in the calls of some Japanese MCs for their audiences to match or exceed the energies imputed to black Jamaicans, in anxieties about the athleticism of Jamaican dancehall divas. It emerges in the vivid attention that Japanese authors who write about travel to Jamaica pay to the black skin, body odor, and collective energies attributed to Afro-Jamaicans. From the Jamaican perspective, it emerges in ethnoracial stereotypes of Japanese as martial artists and geisha. Both the ideas of blackness in the Japanese imagination and the ideas of the Japanese that have captured the imagination of Jamaican and other non-Western people are in part localized instances of the exoticizing gaze of colonial modernity.

THE POSTCOLONIAL

Despite the negative racing of African, Amerindian, Asian, and Pacific Island peoples by the forces of colonial modernity, these peoples have historically engaged in bodily practices that resist this negative racing. Revolts and escapes by slaves are the extreme manifestations of a subversion which, as smaller daily acts—work slowdowns, feigned misunderstandings, tasks accomplished imperfectly—are necessarily obscured throughout colonial history (Scott 1985). In their more explicitly performative dimension, the daily acts include ridicule of the master, drumming, and the subterfuge of capoeira (Lewis 1992) and other diasporic martial arts. The postcolonial, then, as the second major modern racial discourse, refers to the ways in which colonized peoples have negotiated the forces of colonial-modern hegemony (Fanon 1967). This includes not only resistance seen in absolutely progressive terms, but also the reality of an ongoing need to negotiate colonial-modern ideology in, for example, the form of educational and political institutions.

In my research, the postcolonial discourse of race has emerged—in the Japanese gaze toward the Jamaican—in DJs' use of dancehall reggae music to assert a sense of pride as "yellow people," in identification with Rastafari seen as resistance against colonialism and its legacies. This colonialism is not only Western hegemony over blacks and Asians, but also Japanese hegemony over East and Southeast Asians. However, as an example of how postcolonial efforts at, in this case, Afro-Asian identity can return to the regressive colonial-modern, these connections are sometimes expressed through essentializing ideas of black people as tough. This toughness, despite its positive associations, stands in primitivizing counterpoint to the Japanese as soft and civilized. From the Jamaican perspective, suspicion that Junko Kudo won her dancehall queen competition because she was Japanese speaks to the ethnoracial tensions present in the articulation of national identity in postindependence Jamaica. Many Rastafarians, as I have noted above, have raised doubts about the choice of "Out of Many, One People" as the motto of a nation in which most people are black, recognizing that some segments of Jamaican society remain wedded to a colonial-era privileging of nonblack or lighter-complexioned people.

THE GLOBAL POSTMODERN

The third global discourse of race that emerges from my research is the global postmodern. Historiography might be a good place to begin thinking about postmodernism and the academic debates that have come to surround it (Jenkins 1997). On the one hand, postmodernism has been credited with bringing about a politically progressive end to an enshrined male, Eurocentric history. On the other hand, postmodernism's claims about the end of history in general, about the impossibility that any writing about the past could transcend the text's political situation in the present, seem less progressive for subaltern scholars whose own histories are finally being recognized. It may be that much of the concern about framing race in postmodern terms has arisen out of the latter sort of reading (Thomas 2004). Whatever the truth of the matter, to characterize race—like postmodern history—as contingent, as a "floating signifier" whose meanings shift over time and place, appears to approach a position from which the suffering of raced people might also be considered contingent (Jhally 1997).

Postmodernism has relatedly been read as a playful erasure of the past in ways which effect depoliticized, or problematically repoliticized, possibilities of consumption. Rastafari, both as a historically deep and ideologically complex form of anticolonialism and anticapitalism and as a religion, becomes reduced to roots reggae music, the fashionable difference of dreadlocks, and the consumption of ganja. It becomes impossible to view the wearing of dreadlocks and the use of marijuana for what they are among committed Rastas, that is, as actual sacraments; those who claim to be devout are seen as the merely addicted. Jamaican deejaying and sound system culture becomes nationalized as Japanese. Reggae dance is taken beyond its specifically Afro-Jamaican female origins—with all their gendered, economic, and other politics—and is resituated vis-à-vis the experiences of Japanese women. Then reggae dance moves again, from subcultural underground to the mainstream, where it becomes yet another instance of the commercialization of female sexuality in Japan.

To highlight these contemporary understandings of blackness (as encoded here in Afro-Jamaican culture), I identify the global postmodern as a third discourse through which racial performativities are understood today. The global postmodern is the unmooring, transnational circulation, and reseeding of local cultural production, and the racial and other politics involved in this process. The concern of African diasporic peoples about their effacement from the cultural forms they produced, on the one hand, and the sense that all is apolitical fair play, on the other hand, is one dimension of the global postmodern in these contested terms. The global postmodern is a process, as well as a debate about that process. My use of the term is meant to shed light on the ways in which global cultural adoption is not simply a foregone conclusion, but often also a highly contested process.

The global postmodern is also distinguished by its formation under the auspices of contemporary globalization, that set of forces under which neoliberal capitalism has come to establish its apparent supremacy today (Lewellen 2002). Given the efforts of globalization theory to speak to this new reality, this theory has generally displaced postmodernism as the predominant paradigm in the social sciences today. However, like the three global historical discourses of race, these two academic discourses overlap in important ways that further define my use of the term "global postmodern."

One such overlap is the centrality of late capitalism to both discourses. Both postmodernism and globalization theory emerged out of a neoliberal capitalist world in which a greatly expanded range of commodities increasingly satisfies more than humans' basic needs, more fully becoming means to express social selves. The global becomes the final space that these forces of late capitalism reach across to diversify and expand productive capacity and markets. Global consumerism today is distinguished from those of the past by the sophistication of the articulations of commodities' extramaterial value, and by the intensity and pervasiveness of its effects (Jameson 1991; Lyotard 1984). Among these global consumerisms are those associated with racial difference (Hall 1997a, 1997b), including that shown in Japanese consumption of the Afro-Jamaican: dancehall CDs and magazines, dance instruction DVDs, dub plates, tanning and hair salons, trips to Jamaica, Blue Mountain Coffee, custom-made reggae dance outfits, and so on.

A second, related overlap pertains to an issue raised above. This is the tension generated by the late capitalist dissociation through the mass media of cultural forms from their sources of origin. Again, issues of cultural authenticity are not exclusive to the present. Nevertheless, this issue has had particular resonance in both recently emergent discourses. In the case of postmodernism, it has been expressed in the easy, playful consumption of subaltern difference—and the questioning of that consumption. One view is that identities are ephemeral, and all is fair, pleasurable, depoliticized play. Another view is that this consumption is precisely political; that is, the social political circumstances under which the opinions of cultural originators are structurally marginalized.

A third overlap centers on the accelerated development of the media and other forms of technology, which has qualitatively changed how subcultural identifications take place around the world. Cable and satellite television, CD and DVD players, the Internet, and so on bring cultural material from distant Jamaica all the way to Japan, and from Japan to Jamaica. This has stimulated interest in how such postmodern developments have created new possibilities of hybridity and play (Appadurai 1986, 1996; Featherstone 1995; Featherstone, Lash, and Robertson 1995). Globalization theorists—including anthropologists—have also been interested in how people themselves, through the decreased costs of international travel and the diversification of travel destinations, move across and create new networks throughout the global landscape (Ong 1999). Among the ways such networks reveal themselves is as transnational fields of subcultural performance, including those initiated under the influence of the mass media described above. For instance, Japanese women watch the film *Dancehall Queen* and become interested enough in dancehall culture to travel to Jamaica, where they interpersonally encounter Jamaican dancehall divas for the first time, viewing each other in part in racial terms.

Global postmodern performativities of race emerge in a number of other terms in the context of this research. Fundamentally, they have to do with the Japanese encounter in Japan with a Jamaican music increasingly severed from its ethnoracial sources. From the Japanese point of view, this is illustrated not only by the easy adoption of reggae music not necessarily to celebrate the Jamaican but to celebrate a Japanese nation going through hard times. This severing of Jamaican culture from its human sources largely takes place according to a domestic Japanese politics of the international. While Japanese public and academic discourse on kokusaika (internationalization) link global economic reality and cultural imaginary, the usage of this term arguably tends toward the former. Kokusaika is generally used to account for the neoliberal economic circumstances under which migrant workers from as far away as Africa and South America are now physically in Japan. On the other hand, while analyses of postmodernism in Japan, too, have coupled global economic reality and cultural imaginary, it has perhaps been discussed most fully in terms of the latter. The global postmodern, linking as it does both the former (the neoliberal economic) and the latter (cultural imaginary), provides room to consider the relationship between the fear of the embodied presence of foreigners and playful indulgence in the mass media's representations of these disembodied others. Jamaican culture transmitted through the mass media is greatly welcomed by many Japanese, but perhaps less so a large number of real Afro-Jamaican "raggamuffins inna Tokyo City."

Japanese youth travel to and take up residence in countries all around the world as part of a search for creatively actualized selfhood. Like jibun sagashi itself as contemporary mass-mediated discourse, the desire to travel to Jamaica to learn about reggae music at the source is significantly constituted in global postmodern terms. Travel to the island is not in the service of immediate material needs, unlike other migrations from one part of the world to another. Rather, it is part of an extramaterial search for creative self-fulfillment, or sometimes simply an escape from the conformity of life in Japan. From the Jamaican perspective, global postmodernity in this case presents itself as the challenge of understanding a dancehall culture that has suddenly become hybridized by the Japanese presence. Japanese reggae dancers appear in songs and videos by Jamaican DJs; Japanese sound systems like Yellow Choice hold Kingston dances patronized by both Jamaicans and Japanese. Jamaicans have to reckon with the presence of the nearly 200 Japanese who have come to Jamaica (mostly Kingston) with the expectation of staying a long time, perhaps permanently. (This is the other side of many "search for self" narratives that, given their Japanese audiences, assume a return to Japan.) Unlike the majority of Japanese in the music business who visit Jamaica with clear intentions to return to Japan, these individuals are Jamaican residents. Selector Nari of Kingston 5 Productions, for example, has lived in Jamaica for several years and plans to stay indefinitely. This is part of his effort to network and position himself as a conduit between the Jamaican street and the international reggae communities in the United States, Europe, and Japan. Mad Dawg International —three Japanese and two Jamaicans living in Jamaica, New York, and Japan—uses the diversity of its members as one way of distinguishing itself from many other Japanese sounds on the dancehall scene. One of its selectors, Shige Bam Bam, resides in Jamaica and wishes to live there indefinitely. Measuring himself not in relation to Japanese sounds but rather to Jamaicans, he dreams of becoming famous in Jamaica, one measure of a successful realization of his desire to deeply understand Jamaican music.

This entrenched Japanese presence in Jamaica is welcomed by many Jamaicans who appreciate the Japanese love for Jamaican reggae music, and who see it as an opportunity for an unexpected international fraternity. However, in structural socioeconomic terms, it also raises Jamaican anxieties about the island's vulnerable economic position in a neoliberal economy dominated by the first world. In time for the Athens Olympics in 2004, Puma, an athletics apparel company, introduced a "Puma Jamaica" line of athletic and leisure wear. This line was linked to the urbane vibes of dancehall reggae and the mellower ones of roots reggae, and to Jamaica as a legendary producer of some of the world's greatest track and field athletes. The Japanese market, experiencing at just this time its great boom in dancehall reggae, was part of this successful campaign, and Puma athletic wear is a noticeable part of the dancehall look in Japan today. The appeal of the Jamaican, prominently including its flag, is branded by a multinational corporation in ways that were necessarily more profitable for the company rather than for the island (Mussche 2008). Seen more positively, however, the Puma Jamaica line also now stands as one reference point in future efforts to leverage the international popularity of Jamaican culture more fully to Jamaican benefit.

Having presented these three major global discourses of race evident in the Japanese encounter with the Jamaican, some disclaimers are in order. First, these discourses should not be taken to imply a strict chronology, with the colonial-modern first, then the postcolonial, and finally the global postmodern. That would suggest that postcolonial constructions of blackness emerge only after the colonial era, around the mid-twentieth century (or, in Latin America, as early as a century and a half before that), when many colonies became independent. In fact, postcolonial discourses of blackness have existed since the earliest days of colonialism and slavery. Relatedly, I am not interested in using this scheme to label in singular terms any manifestation of global race—that is, categorizing Rasta as only colonial-modern, postcolonial, or global postmodern. Which discourse takes center stage can simply be a matter of analytical focus; however, any manifestation may be productively seen vis-à-vis all three discourses. Therefore, Rastafarian constructions of blackness might be examined in colonial-modern terms if what is of immediate concern is the ways they resonate with colonial-modern ideas of blackness as primitive and close to the earth. If what is of immediate concern is Rasta in its most self-conscious aspect, as Afrocentric resistance, then a postcolonial framework for analyzing those global discourses of blackness to which Rasta belongs might be in order. And if what is of immediate concern is how Rasta has moved beyond Jamaica to be transmitted via commercialized reggae music to faraway Japan, then a global postmodern analysis of the flexible metaphor of, in this case, Rasta-encoded blackness may be more appropriate. The point, however, is that it might be even more productive to think about how any invocation of blackness might involve several of these discourses at once. The postcolonial is often the site of appearances of the colonial-modern (such as Gorō's aspiration to black toughness as a means of communing with his oppressed Jamaican brethren); the global postmodern mobilizes both the colonial-modern (for instance, through contemporary commodifications of Rasta that reference black visual stereotypes of an earlier day) and the postcolonial (the consumption of Rasta resistance through roots reggae CDs).

Second, by identifying these global discourses of race, I am not valorizing any one or the other. I am not endorsing, for example, viewing race in global postmodern terms. Rather, I am identifying global postmodernity as one key discursive term under which many people around the world have in fact come to understand blackness.

Third, I wish to acknowledge that this text is complicit with the three discourses of race it purports to analyze. I write about the colonial-modern from within a discipline making use of many intellectual and methodological conventions that are precisely colonial-modern renderings of other peoples; as a Jamaican whose concern with race in this study without doubt emerges from having been born in postcolonial Jamaica, and from being a black man living in the United States; and as someone whose arguments about the relevance of race are situated in a global postmodern world of increasingly frequent claims about the irrelevance of race.

Finally, I wish to recognize that the domestic and regional premodern constitute a necessary starting point for the ethnographic understanding of race at any given time or in any given place around the world. I hesitate, however, to include it as a fourth global discourse of race. While it is important to appreciate the similarity of the experiences of those low in caste and racial hierarchies (Takezawa 2005), caste for me is fundamentally different from the Western idea of race. The latter is an account, as caste is not, of biologically based differences across all of humanity. In contrast to caste as a socially endogamous system, race as a classificatory scheme bases its authority on the purportedly suprasocial science of biological heritage. While the premodern might not be included with these three modern discourses of race (according to my understanding of race as a modern concept), it still crucially informs the other three (as these three do each other). From the Jamaican perspective, Jamaican Rastafari represents a postcolonial return to a premodern Africa that is the true home to all black people. From the Japanese perspective, Brother Taffy engages with Rastafari in postcolonial terms that link modern race (African slaves) to premodern caste (burakumin). The Yoshino dreads use global postmodern Rastafari—a Rastafari that arrived in Japan primarily on the commercial currents of roots reggae music, and whose specific Afrocentrisms (such as seeing Selassie as a black divinity) are performatively managed—to revel in Yoshino's premodern Shugendō tradition.

Conclusions

These three global discourses of race represent one means of deconstructing an imagination of race seen only in Western and non-Western terms. As discourses, they move across these spaces and become meaningful in local, sociohistorically situated terms. They suggest possible alternative discourses to undo this Eurocentered binary. The Afro-Asian emerges as one of these alternatives, to the extent that the African, the Asian, and their intersections are significantly constructed in racial political terms. The long-distance Japanese gaze at the Jamaican, then, as well as the return of that gaze, represents an Afro-Asian challenge to assumptions about the West's unique power to define how nonwhite people are to understand themselves and other nonwhite peoples. However, even as an instinct toward postcolonial kinship partly defines the Jamaican and Japanese imaginings of each other, they are also defined by Western colonial-modern ideas of each other as primitives and exotics. The Jamaican-Japanese encounter as one contemporary example of the Afro-Asian foregrounds a neoliberal economic system that dominates both the Jamaican "sufferan" and furiita in Japan but it is also a way in which Japanese, by consuming Jamaica, become more fully, and quite happily, part of this structure.

Given the complex possibilities of articulation that inhere within these three broad discourses of global race, constructions of Afro-Jamaican blackness in Japan have shifted considerably in the decade of this research. During this period, reggae music in Japan went from a period of decline in the earlier popularity of roots reggae to a more recent intense interest in dancehall. Even as roots reggae has long been globally commodified, the image of Rastafari that is such an integral part of this music remains linked in Japan and elsewhere to a postcolonial imagination of blackness as a struggle against colonial and capitalist oppression, a certain primitivist naiveté, the love of nature, closeness to the earth, and a deeply spiritual desire for world peace. This vision of Jamaican blackness was somewhat more common in Japan from the mid-1980s to the late1990s than it is now. With the subsequent popularity of dancehall culture in Japan, the image of Afro-Jamaican blackness in the public consciousness has come to include images of the raw, savvy, hypersexed ghetto dweller; the rude boy; and the reggae dancer. Rasta then and rude boy and donnette now are all aspects of an archetypal repertoire of international black representation that are more or less fully fleshed out depending on the historical moment, depending on what arrangement of ideas about blackness in the world today best speaks to the time and the place.

These dynamic representations of Jamaican blackness in Japan, just like those of Asianness in Jamaica (today, no longer just Chinese, but also Japanese), indeed make explicit the value of ethnographically situating global performativities of race, nation, and ethnicity in time and place. In the past, ethnoracialized Jamaican subcultures were defined according to the colonial-modern, the postcolonial, and the global postmodern as experienced primarily in Jamaica. These subcultures expanded to include a broader Jamaican diaspora, in places like New York and London. Today they include countries farther afield, like Germany and the Netherlands. They also include Japan. Japanese practitioners of reggae and Rastafari travel between Japan and Jamaica, reshaping the multivalently politicized performative fields of an Afro-Asian encounter. A reasonable place to start an analysis of other, similar Afro-Asian encounters is by considering some of the things both regions have in common. One is a colonial legacy. A second is reckoning with this legacy. A third is the pleasurable illusion of having moved past it, even if the conjuring of this illusion traps both peoples in the same place. But given global postmodernity's aspect as a working through of the colonial-modern and the postcolonial, other global discourses of race are certain to emerge; old ones may re-emerge, to be newly recognized.

Introduction

1 At that time's rate of exchange, each locker cost just under two U.S. dollars.

2 I am not the first to produce such a title to describe reggae in Japan: a brief, anonymous article appearing in *The Economist* on the first reggae boom in Japan referred to it as "Trench Town East" ("Reggae Music" 1994).

3 British punk was heavily influenced by the reggae music of Jamaican immigrants to England. See Hebdige 1979.

4 In the late 1950s "Japan's Teen Queen" Michiko Hamamura recorded a popular calypso tune entitled, "Banana Boat Song." Calypso enjoyed a period of popularity in the United States during the late 1950s. Hamamatsu's popularity may be connected to this popularity of the music in the United States, where she has performed. See Hosokawa 1997.

5 The URL is http://www.overheat.com/riddim.

6 Masta Simon in a telephone interview I conducted with him on April 21, 2007.

7 This information is from the website of the Jamaican embassy in Japan: http://www.jamaicaemb.jp/japan/index.html, accessed September 22, 2009.

8 Shinjuku and Shibuya are commercial areas in central Tokyo.

9 A sarariiman (salaryman) is a male white-collar worker. Office ladies are female office workers, who usually have part-time, low-level jobs they are expected to

leave when they marry. See Ogasawara's ethnography (1998) of gender and power in the corporate workplace.

10 The work of Victor Turner (1982, 1987; Turner and Bruner 1986), who wrote extensively on sociocultural performance and its embeddedness in the quotidian, has closely informed my understanding of performance. For Turner, performance does not simply mirror society but can also actively foment social change. As process and creative play—provinces of the weak—performances also potentially threaten social authority whenever they take place, offering as they do what Turner calls alternative "designs for living" (Turner 1989, 24). Whether secret or public, performance is also liminal: it variously disrupts social routine, redirecting the flow of daily life. Cultural performances are reflexive in the sense that they potentially provide performers and audiences with new, if ephemeral, perspectives on their social lives. They help these individuals "reflect back on themselves, upon the relations, actions, symbols, meanings, codes, roles, statuses, social structures, ethical and legal rules, and other sociocultural components that make up their public 'selves'" (1987, 24).

11 Judith Butler (1993), drawing on the work of J. L. Austin (1975), Jacques Derrida (1988), and others, has written about the structures of power that can underlie the performance of social identity. I am not as invested as Butler is in the details of Lacanian psychoanalysis. There are, however, aspects of her general argument that I find very relevant to my own research. The main one is her discussion of the distinction between "performance" and "performativity." Performance refers to a situated body of acts, for which the performer is assumed to be more or less responsible. It is not unlike the relatively agentive notion of performance that Erving Goffman offers in his classic treatise, *The Presentation of Self in Everyday Life* (1959). Performance in this work is largely understood as an individual machination, influencing how others read one's self through "the art of impression management" (Goffman 1959, 208). Performativity, however, refers to those more broadly historicized, power-saturated, depersonalized discourses which inform socially appropriate behavior—such as those surrounding gendered norms in a given society, of particular concern to Butler. These actions, in turn, through their (re)citation of the historicized authority of these norms, come to reassert the value of the norms. Performativity refers to "reiterative and citational practice by which discourse produces the effect it names . . . The reading of performativity as willful and arbitrary choice misses the point that the historicity of discourse and, in particular, the historicity of norms . . . constitute the power of discourse to enact what it names" (Butler 1993, 2, 187). This distinction between performance and performativity will serve as one theoretical base for my discussion of gender in the Japanese dancehall.

12 By "race," I refer to social, political, and cultural self-identifications and ascriptions of otherness emerging from Enlightenment attempts to scientifically classify all of humanity. By "blackness," I mean how such self-identifications and ascriptions of otherness are based in beliefs about the biology of peoples of sub-

Saharan descent. In this way, blackness, like race generally, can function in two ways: as sign (skin color, for instance) and signified (a politicized ethos of selfhood and otherness that emerges from these expressions).

13 I say "partly" to acknowledge other relevant factors, such as Japan's (ideologically overstated) ethnoracial homogeneity. What some would see as racist regard for blackness, others might construct, in light of this homogeneity, as a natural, harmless desire to feel out and play with the novelty of blackness. This latter position is dubious, however: the myth of ethnoracial homogeneity, created through the silencing of internal difference (Ainu, Okinawan, outcaste burakumin [hamlet people], Korean, Chinese), is used as a socioculturally particular (and therefore, supposedly, innocent) way to understate the offensiveness of objectifying black people.

14 Representations of black people as hypersexual and savage, like renderings of Japanese people as "white" in comic books, might also be seen, for instance, as a function of the interplay in much of Japanese popular culture between the (Japanese) mundane and the (non-Japanese) fantastic (Napier 1996). The meanings that underlie the spectacle of blackness in Japan also emerge as functions of an objectifying gaze that is culturally sanctioned by the regarded's status as a thing to be looked at (*misemono*). The dehumanization of blackness in Japan further depends on the fact that there have historically been few people of African ancestry living in the country. For me, however, none of this absolves Japan of responsibility for the harm these representations create.

15 On the one hand, African America has long been a global standard-bearer for civil rights advocacy and other forms of resistance against Western hegemony. The African American civil rights movement inspired other social movements not only within the United States, but also throughout the African diaspora and around the world. But on the other hand, part of the attention to the African American case comes precisely from African America's situation within the United States and the Western world at large. Largely driven by this long situation in the center of international capitalism, representations of the African American experience have been disseminated globally. Jazz music throughout the twentieth century was stereotyped internationally both as black primitivism and as an ultimate sign of the American modernity that many other countries aspired to (Atkins 2003). African America thus becomes a regression that is also progressively modern, a hegemony and its own antithesis. That it is white America that has long profited and continues to profit from this irony may be a sign that in many ways structural racism—seen in conventional terms here as white corporate profit from black cultural production—has not significantly changed. Still, given that the twentieth century's most dominant genres of international popular music—jazz, rock and roll, hip-hop—had their roots in African America (as well as Jamaica, considering roots reggae and the deep Jamaican influence on the birth of hip-hop), and given the expressions of resistance heard in much of this music (including as inflected in local terms), the stability of this racism is not guaranteed.

1 The Politics of Presence

1 It would be impossible to describe in this restricted space the differences in racial demography, and their various causes and effects, in the extremely heterogeneous societies of South and Central America. In general, however, these countries have had a smaller percentage of black people than that found elsewhere in the second group of countries under discussion. This makes clear the importance of how racial demography can both inform and be informed by the performance of nationhood (Askew 2002). The iconic status of the female, mixed-race samba dancer bodily announces and thereby makes Brazil's claims to be a racially and ethnically egalitarian society (Browning 1995). Many Latin American societies, such as Cuba and Argentina, encouraged immigration from Europe as part of a deliberate project of "whitening," and thus supposedly advancing, the postcolonial nation (Helg 1990). These are among the hegemonic discourses that a number of black power movements emerging throughout Latin America have sought to challenge, often in performative terms (Hoffman-French 2004, 2006).

2 See Nassy Brown (1998) for a discussion of one of Britain's oldest black populations, the Liverpool descendants of African seamen who arrived in England during the eighteenth century. See also the work of Wright (2003) and Campt (2004) on the experiences of Afro-Germans. Essed (1990) and Wekker (2006) have conducted research on blacks in the Netherlands.

3 Today *jinshu* is used to refer to race as biological endowment, and *minzoku* is used to refer to ethnicity as a people's sense of belonging, based on such things as cultural practice (usually in contrast to those of other groups). Historically, however, the terms have not been so clearly distinguished, with some intermixture of meaning; see Weiner 1995.

4 See Kurokawa (2004) on the hula for a similar discussion of a genre of performance that came to be consumed and reproduced both as exotic and, given its initial reception in Japan largely through Hollywood films, as American.

5 See Tierney (2002) for more on the governing institutions and practices— including the scrutiny of non-Japanese who train to become sumo wrestlers— that frame foreign participation in the sport.

6 Black male members of the U.S. military traveling throughout Asia participate in a military machinery that has been a primary instrument of American Orientalism. But as Cornyetz notes in her critique of Kelsky's paper, discussed later, black and white men often occupy different places despite their shared identification as Western men.

2 Music and Orality

1 Dub music has come to have a particularly powerful presence in Britain's music scene.

2 See also Gilroy 1993, Leland 1992, and Manuel and Marshall 2006.

3   The journalist Minako Ikeshiro confirmed what were originally my only vague impressions of contemporary Japanese reggae, especially since 2000, as "conservative." I thank her for encouraging me in this way to more fully pursue this route. I am also much indebted to my colleague Shinichiro Suzuki, of Kwansei Gakuin University, for introducing me to a number of songs with this theme, including several discussed here.

4   Katakana is one of the two syllabaries used in the Japanese writing system.

5   As another example of indictments of ongoing American global oppression, the Okinawan duo U-Dou and Platy in some of their music criticize America's ongoing military presence in the prefecture.

6   Most Japanese people I spoke with who had traveled to Jamaica told me that they were taken to be Chinese. Until the recent surge in Japanese tourism to the island, the small (less than 1 percent) East Asian population in Jamaica has been almost exclusively Chinese.

7   Mighty Crown's membership has changed over the past few years. As of this writing, Sticko is no longer a member of the group. As mentioned, he remains a member of the Mighty Crown family as part of the group Fireball. In addition to Sammy T, Simon, and Cojie, Mighty Crown now includes Super-G, who is Japanese, and Ninja, who is Jamaican. The latter deepens Mighty Crown's skills at juggling (as opposed to the more antagonistically structured clash).

8   A derogatory term for a gay man.

9   The original lyrics, from the tune "Look," begin, "Look into my eyes, tell me what you see. / Can you feel my pain? Am I your enemy?"

10 This means something like, "All right, then."

11 No winner seems to have been announced; both sounds have reportedly gone on to claim victory in the event.

12 Here the (re-)cited authority in Butler's (1990) work reveals itself to be complex, never singular or absolute. Depending on one's perspective, this authority can be Jamaica as a subcultural source. It can also be the referent, Japaneseness, that shapes dancehall in the country into something recognizable to fans there.

3   Fashion and Dance

1   Francato also entered the competition in 2005 and 2007. She won the event in 2007, when forty-eight dancers competed, including representatives from such countries as Austria, Germany, and Estonia. Although she was a crowd favorite throughout the event, Francato's victory prompted a few members of the audience to throw bottles onstage. While it is not possible to know what motivated these actions, speculation is that it was because a non-Jamaican had won. Possibly reflecting that sentiment, the distraught second-place winner, Kadian Reid of Montego Bay, who also had much audience support, reportedly declared, "She can't even wine" (Wright 2007). ("Wining" refers to the erotic movement of one's hips.)

2   These examples raise a host of issues that are important in themselves, concern-

ing as they do the construction of homosexuality in Japan as functions of race, nationality, and ethnicity.

3 Despite Cornyetz's and Kelsky's relevance in these ways to the issues of race, gender, and consumption that I discuss in this chapter, their specific discussions of the relationships between black men and Japanese women, and of male-dominated black musical subculture as a means of Japanese male phallic empowerment, are less immediately relevant here. This is for reasons I have already discussed: from the few numbers of Jamaicans in Japan to give interpersonal charge to these imaginings, to the deflection of the intense machismo of Jamaican dancehall into the realms of humor. Afro-Jamaican sexuality as reworked in Japan, included in that third set of countries I identified in chapter 1, more fully occupy the spaces of the mass media. This has been especially evident in recent years, as dancehall—though still primarily a subcultural movement—has moved a few steps into the mainstream.

4 Among the rare academic, Japanese-language monographs on the topic, also see the anthropologist Shinichirō Suzuki's Reggae Train (2000), an ethnographic study of reggae in Jamaica.

5 This trend is evident in other aspects of Jamaican culture that Japanese are interested in. I discuss later Rasta-identifying Japanese who have traveled to meet and spend months studying with such Rasta and roots reggae figures as the late Mortimo Planno, the herbalist Dr. Bagga, and the late roots reggae musician Augustus Pablo. Japanese who travel not only to Jamaica but also to other parts of the world pursuing various artistic interests often behave in a similar way, seeking out recognized authorities in the subculture in question for guidance on how to pursue an art form or spiritual practice. This approach, I suspect, reflects an informal extension of the traditional attitude toward learning reflected in Japan's *iemoto* system. In this system, families, including artistic houses, are organized in relation to a main house dominated by an elder who trains his eldest son (or a substitute) to follow the art form more or less as the elder, and his forebears, practiced it. (This ethos, which Atkins [2001] discusses in the context of Japanese approaches to learning to play jazz, may partly inform the perception of the Japanese as an imitative people.) The dancehall and Rasta cases appear different from that presented in Yoko Kurokawa's (1997) study on hula schools in Tokyo, since the study of hula seems much more structured and more explicitly follows iemoto organizational principles. A network of assistants—who go on to start their own branch schools—often train lower-level students, with a smaller number of advanced students actually studying with a master; Kurokawa describes this as typical of the Japanese. However, despite the way in which the case of reggae dance appears looser, the basic iemoto approach is evident. Junko Kudo and other dancers have established their positions as reggae dance authorities not only through videos but through schools of their own. Perhaps in time this first generation of reggae dancers will give rise to subsequent ones in stricter iemoto fashion; this partly depends, of course, on the continued popularity of reggae dance in Japan. In

this way, then, I might refer to a point that I made earlier about Japaneseness bearing within it tension between the modern and the traditional, between ideology and exigency: rather than seeing this apparently iemoto-inflected approach as a sign of the application of a system that is Japanese, I want to look at how cultural ideas like iemoto are strategically deployed in contemporary Japan, where, for example, the discourses of jibun sagashi call for more informal, more individualized approaches to global cultural learning.

4 Body and Spirit

1 Burakumin came to exist as a cohesive community when a series of laws in the early 1700s formalized discrimination against them. Members of this group traditionally were leather workers and grave tenders or held similar jobs that brought them into contact with animal products and dead bodies. Such contact is considered polluting in Shintō belief, which subjects burakumin to social ostracization. Although a law has since been passed officially ending this discrimination, burakumin continue to be ghettoized in certain parts of Japan.

2 Punk emerged out of a similar sense of class-based discontent in Britain, and was deeply informed by the musical and other cultural influences Jamaican immigrants brought with them to the country. See Hebdige (1979).

3 Too much history, or one that inspires different handling: see Koichi Iwabuchi's (2002) discussion of "Asianism" in Japan.

4 "Ras" is a title used among Rastafarians generally. The three men here identify themselves in this way: I have changed only the second word in each man's name.

5 Pablo passed away in 1999, the year I met Tanki. Tanki described Pablo's passing as extremely difficult for him.

6 The great hall of Tōdaiji Temple, also located in Nara prefecture, houses the Great Buddha and is said to be the largest wooden edifice not only in Japan but in the world.

7 One elderly neighbor discreetly asked how many people were living at the house; I said I was not sure. I suspect that however normal they might be considered despite their dreadlocks, the dreads' living arrangements strikes some neighbors as unusual. If this has caused any openly negative judgment, however, I saw no evidence of it.

8 Perhaps some comparison between the donnettes in the last chapter and some of the more strongly Rasta-identifying women like Sayumi is in order here. Those in the latter group tend to be slightly older, in their thirties and beyond, and thus more likely to be married, living some distance from big cities like Tokyo. For these women, the world of dancehall is far away; indeed, some who grew up on roots reggae have never even heard of dancehall music. For both groups of women, travel to Jamaica represents a key way to validate Jamaican cultural identifications and practices, like roots reggae singing and dancehall dance. For donnettes, upon return to Japan, such identifications are generally sustained in urban areas. For Rasta-identifying women, it is rural Japan, imag-

ined as a space in which the roles traditionally expected of Japanese women are most fully realizable. Most Rasta-identifying women I have met are almost by definition able to speak deeply and feelingly about Rasta ideology, including its role as a critique of social injustice overseas and in Japan. However, while male Rasta-identifying Japanese tend to have a more self-consciously politicized and religious connection with the movement (perhaps partly because of high-profile male role models like Bob Marley), for female Rasta-identifying Japanese, the movement tends to be a matter of lifestyle. This includes their lives as rural wives and mothers, the most readily available model through which they are able to identify with the movement, but one inflected through the cosmopolitan difference of the Afro-Jamaican. While the women's engagement with Rasta in these terms might be read as comparatively light, since it is not always explicitly ideological in original Rasta terms, it is serious in the way it discloses gendered tradition as a mythology ever subject to performative reimagining.

9 Aran, in his early thirties in 2001, spent two months in Jamaica while in his twenties. He spent most of the time studying at Dr. Bagga's home. He was struck by how Jamaican people were poor like him and his present family—his twenty-six-year-old wife, and his eight-month-old baby and year-old child—but nonetheless happy. That experience, he said, affected him positively.

10 Perhaps this is true not only for the dreads, but also for me as a black Jamaican.

5 Text and Image

1 As another example of this general self-expression, in this case on the level of the text itself, Kinsella (1995) has argued that young women use "cute" hand-writing to challenge conventional, homogenized forms of inscription and in so doing express a sense of their individual difference.

2 The appeal of this literature for some Japanese dreads appears to have little specifically to do with its anti-Semitic rhetoric. For what it is worth, none of my research participants expressed an attraction to this literature in these specific terms. The appeal seems to have more to do with the fact that the writers of these works, who probably know nothing of the dreads' existence, articulate religious historical perspectives on Japanese identity that the dreads are able to suggest validate their Rasta identifications. This literature should be seen as an instance of Japan's identification with the Jamaican through ambiguous knowl-edge of it, rather than necessary belief in it. It should also be noted that some dreads, like Seek, have expressed reservations about this literature. I suspect that Tibby's expressed dislike of the notion of a "Japanese Rastafari," his belief that all Rastas are Rastas, was intended as a criticism of the adoption of these works by some Rasta-identifying Japanese.

3 See, for example, Oates 1990.

4 New York exists as a vivid place in the Japanese imagination of the global (Ezaki 1987; Takeda 1999; Yoshida 1979). Several articles in the *New York Times* (Adachi 2005; Ekman 2002; Prasso 2006) comment on the many young Japanese

—a large number of whom are women, less bound than men to their jobs—who have immigrated to and live in New York, including its downtown area. Part of the Japanese social imagination of New York City is as a haven for artists and proving ground beyond the confines of Japan. But just as New York may be the epitome of the cosmopolitan first-world in the Japanese imagination, it also exists, as Hirō's novel shows, as an intensely racialized, ghettoized space, a city with many, often dangerous black people (Takeda 1999). As the stories of many Japanese reggae musicians illustrate, part of the Japanese interest in New York is that it is home to several black musical subcultures. In addition to dancehall, these include hip-hop (Adachi 2005; "Fifty Yen?" 2003) and gospel (Christian 2000), subcultures that have enjoyed much popularity in Japan.

5 The fictional Gorō, though, is somewhat sensitive to these politics, having read an article on Rastafari written by his friend Furuta, and having met a Thai traveler who is discriminated against by American immigration authorities while Gorō as a Japanese travels freely.

6 Yamakawa's Reiji also constantly refers to the blackness of Jamaicans: "my shoulder was tapped, and when I turned around, there was the face of an utterly *black*-faced girl" (1985, 19); "on both sides of the streets, *black*-skinned Jamaicans overflowed" (48); "the boy's checkered shirt was torn here and there, and his lustrous *black* skin peeked out" (88); "at that moment, right before me, a *black* hand was extended [through the car window]. Without thinking, I pulled back" (116; emphases added). Yamakawa too uses the shock of blackness to evoke—"naturally," in the minds of his readers—fear, criminality, abjectness, and other characteristics alien to the Japanese self.

7 Yamakawa also describes Reiji working his way through a crowd of people milling outside a recording studio: "I walked, as though swimming, through hot air filled with the smell of the body odor of black people, and went inside the studio" (1985, 176).

6   Jamaican Perspectives

1 "Cos play"—short for costumed play—is a Japanese subculture in which participants dress in the costumes of characters found in anime, video games, live-action children's television programs, and elsewhere. Since it is a subculture in its own right, I am taking a bit of liberty by using the term to refer to the idea of the "costumed play" of a Jamaican reggae dance scene in which fashion plays such an important part.

2 The link to this interview is no longer available.

3 I contacted Bounty Killer's management agency to request an interview with him about the dancehall scene in Japan; the agency said he was unavailable as he was recording at the time.

4 According to Japan's Ministry of Foreign Affairs, there are now over 180 Japanese residents in Jamaica. See http://www.mofa.go.jp/region/latin/jamaica/index.html (accessed July 27, 2009).

5 This includes a twenty-five-minute documentary produced by the BBC (http://www.bbc.co.uk/1xtra/tx/documentaries/japanesedancehall.shtml; accessed July 27, 2009). The documentary begins: "Japan. A country of tranquility and temples. Of Zen gardens and geishas in kimonos. A culture known for its strict rules and order. Where its people are placid and polite. But hang on a minute: There's more to it than that . . . Welcome to the other side of Japan, and its current love affair with dancehall." The narrator wonders throughout about the contrast between tranquil Japan and the down-and-dirty music of dancehall reggae. Indeed, what animates much of the general Western interest in Japanese engagement with Jamaican music is an imagination of Japanese and Jamaicans as two exotic others who, given their status as such and given the discrete way each is figured in the Western gaze, surprise observers by interacting with each other. That these two people would have anything to do with each other is surprising since they, and the Western stereotypes associated with them, have been figured as discretely, and singularly, as functions of this Western gaze.

6 See the work of the anthropologists Yasuko Takezawa (2005) and Ruth Frankenberg (1994), who have articulated schemes with some similarities to this one in discussing the question of the universality of the race concept and white American women's narratives on whiteness, respectively.

Adachi, Jiro. 2005. "How Q Found Her Groove." *New York Times*. January 30.

Akiyama Satoko. 1994. *Aisuru Koto mo Manabu Koto mo: Akiyama Satako no "Jibun Sagashi" Ron* (Love and Learning: Akiyama Satoko on "The Search for Self"). Tokyo: Mikasa Shobō.

Allison, Anne. 1994. *Nightwork: Sexuality, Pleasure, and Corporate Masculinity in a Tokyo Hostess Club*. Chicago: University of Chicago Press.

Antoni, Klaus. 1988. "Yasukuni-Jinja and Folk Religion: The Problem of Vengeful Spirits." *Asian Folklore Studies* 47 (1): 123–36.

Appadurai, Arjun. 1986. *The Social Life of Things: Commodities in Cultural Perspective*. Cambridge: Cambridge University Press.

——. 1996. *Modernity at Large: Cultural Dimensions of Globalization*. Public Worlds, vol. 1. Minneapolis: University of Minnesota Press.

Askew, Kelly Michelle. 2002. *Performing the Nation: Swahili Music and Cultural Politics in Tanzania*. Chicago Studies in Ethnomusicology. Chicago: University of Chicago Press.

Atkins, E. Taylor. 2001. *Blue Nippon: Authenticating Jazz in Japan*. Durham, N.C.: Duke University Press.

——, ed. 2003. *Jazz Planet*. Jackson: University Press of Mississippi.

Austin, J. L. 1975. *How to Do Things with Words*. William James Lectures 1955. 2nd ed. Cambridge: Harvard University Press.

Barnard, Christopher. 2001. "Isolating Knowledge of the Unpleasant: The Rape of Nanking in Japanese High-School Textbooks." *British Journal of Sociology of Education* 22 (4): 519–30.

Basch, Linda G., Nina Glick Schiller, and Cristina Szanton Blanc. 1994. *Nations Unbound: Transnational Projects, Postcolonial Predicaments, and Deterritorialized Nation-States.* Langhorne, Pa.: Gordon and Breach.

Baudrillard, Jean. 1994. *Simulacra and Simulation.* Translated by Sheila Glaser. Ann Arbor: University of Michigan Press.

Befu, Harumi. 1992. "Symbols of Nationalism and Nihonjinron." In *Ideology and Practice in Modern Japan,* edited by R. Goodman and K. Refsing. London: Routledge.

Belson, Ken, and Brian Bremmer. 2004. *Hello Kitty: The Remarkable Story of Sanrio and the Billion Dollar Feline Phenomenon.* Singapore: Wiley.

Benedict, Ruth. 1946. *The Chrysanthemum and the Sword: Patterns of Japanese Culture.* Boston: Houghton Mifflin.

Benston, Kimberly W. 2000. *Performing Blackness: Enactments of African-American Modernism.* London: Routledge.

Bestor, Theodore. 2004. *Tsukiji: The Fish Market at the Center of the World.* Berkeley: University of California Press.

Bilby, Kenneth. 1999. "'Roots Explosion': Indigenization and Cosmopolitanism in Contemporary Surinamese Popular Music." *Ethnomusicology* 43 (2): 256–96.

——. 2000. "Making Modernity in the Hinterlands: New Maroon Musics in the Black Atlantic." *Popular Music* 19 (3): 265–92.

Black, Stephanie. 2003. *Life and Debt.* New York: New Yorker Video. Videorecording.

Bourdieu, Pierre. 1984. *Distinction: A Social Critique of the Judgment of Taste.* Translated by Richard Nice. Cambridge: Harvard University Press.

Browning, Barbara. 1995. *Samba: Resistance in Motion, Arts and Politics of the Everyday.* Bloomington: Indiana University Press.

Buell, Frederick. 1994. *National Culture and the New Global System.* Baltimore, Md.: Johns Hopkins University Press.

Butler, Judith. 1990. *Gender Trouble: Feminism and the Subversion of Identity.* New York: Routledge.

——. 1993. *Bodies That Matter: On the Discursive Limits of "Sex."* New York: Routledge.

Campbell, Horace. 1987. *Rasta and Resistance: From Marcus Garvey to Walter Rodney.* Trenton, N.J.: Africa World Press.

Campt, Tina. 2004. *Other Germans: Black Germans and the Politics of Race, Gender, and Memory in the Third Reich.* Ann Arbor: University of Michigan Press.

Cashmore, Ernest. 1983. *Rastaman: The Rastafarian Movement in England.* London: Unwin Paperbacks.

Chang, Jeff. 2005. *Can't Stop, Won't Stop: A History of the Hip-Hop Generation.* New York: St. Martin's.

Chevannes, Barry. 1994. *Rastafari: Roots and Ideology*. Utopianism and Communitarianism. Syracuse, N.Y.: Syracuse University Press.

Chin, Timothy S. 1999. "Jamaican Popular Culture, Caribbean Literature, and the Representation of Gay and Lesbian Sexuality in the Discourses of Race and Nation." *Small Axe* 5: 14–33.

Choi, Chungmoo, ed. 1997. "The Colonial Women: Colonialism, War, and Sex." Special issue. *Positions* 5 (1).

Christian, Nicole. 2000. "For Japanese, Gospel Music Sets Spirits a Bit Freer." *New York Times*. September 18.

Clammer, J. R. 1997. *Contemporary Urban Japan: A Sociology of Consumption*. Studies in Urban and Social Change. Oxford: Blackwell.

Clifford, James. 1997. *Routes: Travel and Translation in the Late Twentieth Century*. Cambridge: Harvard University Press.

Collinwood, Dean W., and Osamu Kusatsu. 2000. "Japanese Rastafarians: Non-Conformity in Modern Japan." *The Study of International Relations* (Tokyo: Tsuda College) 26: 23–35.

Condry, Ian. 2006. *Hip-Hop Japan: Rap and the Paths of Cultural Globalization*. Durham, N.C.: Duke University Press.

Cooper, Carolyn. 1997. *Noises in the Blood: Orality, Gender and the "Vulgar" Body of Jamaican Popular Culture*. Durham, N.C.: Duke University Press.

———. 2004. *Sound Clash: Jamaican Dancehall Culture at Large*. New York: Palgrave Macmillan.

Cornyetz, Nina. 1996. "Fetishized Blackness: Hip-Hop and Racial Desire in Contemporary Japan." *Social Text* 41: 113–39.

Creighton, Millie. 1995. "Imagining the Other in Japanese Advertising Campaigns." In *Occidentalism: Images of the West*, edited by J. G. Carrier. Oxford: Clarendon Press of Oxford University Press.

Czarnecki, Melanie. 2005. "Bad Girls from Good Families: The Degenerate Meiji Schoolgirl." In *Bad Girls of Japan*, edited by Laura Miller and Jan Bardsley. New York: Palgrave Macmillan.

Dale, Peter N. 1986. *The Myth of Japanese Uniqueness*. New York: St. Martin's.

de Certeau, Michel. 1984. *The Practice of Everyday Life*. Translated by Steven Randall. Berkeley: University of California Press.

De Vos, George. 1973. "Achievement Orientation, Social Self-Identity, and Japanese Economic Growth." In *Socialization for Achievement: Essays on the Cultural Psychology of the Japanese*, edited by George De Vos. Berkeley: University of California Press.

Derrida, Jacques. 1988. "Signature Event Context." In *Limited, Inc.*, translated by Samuel Weber. Evanston, Ill.: Northwestern University Press.

Dikötter, Frank. 1992. *The Discourse of Race in Modern China*. Stanford, Calif.: Stanford University Press.

———, ed. 1997a. *The Construction of Racial Identities in China and Japan: Historical and Contemporary Perspectives*. Honolulu: University of Hawaii Press.

———. 1997b. Introduction. In *The Construction of Racial Identities in China and Japan: Historical and Contemporary Perspectives*. Honolulu: University of Hawaii Press.

Doak, Kevin. 2001. "Building National Identity through Ethnicity: Ethnology in Wartime Japan and After." *Journal of Japanese Studies* 27 (1): 1–39.

Doi Takeo. 1981. *The Anatomy of Dependence*. Translated by John Bester. Tokyo: Kodansha.

Douglas, Mary. 1978. *Purity and Danger: An Analysis of Concepts of Pollution and Taboo*. London: Routledge and Kegan Paul.

Dreisinger, Baz. 2002. "Tokyo after Dark." *Vibe*. August, 130–38.

Ekman, Ivar. 2002. "Along the Other Broadway, a Japanese Accent Joins the Mix." *New York Times*. April 14.

Endo Shusaku. 1973. *Kuronbō* (Nigger). Tokyo: Kadokawa.

Enomoto Hiroaki. 1998. *"Jiko" no Shinrigaku: Jibun Sagashi e no Sasoi* ("One's Own" Psychology: An Invitation to the Search for Self). Tokyo: Saiensusha.

Eskildsen, Robert. 2002. "Of Civilization and Savages: The Mimetic Imperialism of Japan's 1874 Expedition to Taiwan." *The American Historical Review* 107 (2): 388–418.

Essed, Philomena. 1990. *Everyday Racism: Reports from Women of Two Cultures*. Claremont, Calif.: Hunter House.

Ezaki Reona. 1987. *Amerika to Nihon: Nyūyōku de Kangaeru* (Thinking about America and Japan from New York). Tokyo: Mikasa Shobō.

Fanon, Frantz. 1967. *Black Skin, White Masks*. Translated by Charles Lam Markmann. New York: Grove.

Featherstone, Mike. 1995. *Undoing Culture: Globalization, Postmoderism and Identity*. London: Sage.

Featherstone, Mike, Scott Lash, and Roland Robertson, eds. 1995. *Global Modernities*. Theory, Culture & Society. London: Sage.

Ferguson, Jane. 2006. "From Trenchtown to the Thai-Burma Border: Global Reggae, Rastafarian Aesthetics, and Politicized Music in Mainland Southeast Asia." Lecture, Chiang Mai University, Chiang Mai, Thailand, January 6.

"Fifty Yen? Japanese Hip-Hop Downtown." 2003. *New York Times*, May 25.

Figal, Gerald. 1996. "How to *Jinbunshi*: Making and Marketing Self-Histories of Showa among the Masses in Postwar Japan." *The Journal of Asian Studies* 55 (4): 902–33.

Foucault, Michel. 1988. *Madness and Civilization: A History of Insanity in the Age of Reason*. Translated by Richard Howard. New York: Vintage.

———. 1995. *Discipline and Punish: The Birth of the Prison*. 2nd Vintage ed. Translated by Alan Sheridan. New York: Vintage.

Frankenberg, Ruth. 1994. "Whiteness and Americanness: Examining Constructions of Race, Culture, and Nation in White Women's Life Narratives." In *Race*, edited by S. Gregory and R. Sanjek. New Brunswick, N.J.: Rutgers University Press.

Fujie Toshihiko. 1995. *Saraiiman no Jibun Sagashi: Ikikata no Sentaku* (The salary man's search for self: choosing a way of life). Tokyo: Sannō Daigaku Shuppan-bu.

Gage, Sue Je. 2006. "Pure Mixed Blood: The Multiple Identities of Amerasians in South Korea." Ph.D. diss., Indiana University, Bloomington.

Gallicchio, Marc S. 2000. *The African-American Encounter with Japan and China: Black Internationalism in Asia, 1895–1945*. Chapel Hill: University of North Carolina Press.

Gilroy, Paul. 1991. *"There Ain't No Black in the Union Jack": The Cultural Politics of Race and Nation, Black Literature and Culture*. Chicago: University of Chicago Press.

——. 1993. *The Black Atlantic: Modernity and Double Consciousness*. Cambridge: Harvard University Press.

Glave, Thomas. 2000. "Toward a Nobility of the Imagination: Jamaica's Shame." *Small Axe* 7: 122–26.

Gluck, Carol. 1985. *Japan's Modern Myths: Ideology in the Late Meiji Period*. Princeton, N.J.: Princeton University Press.

Goffman, Erving. 1959. *The Presentation of Self in Everyday Life*. Garden City, N.Y.: Doubleday.

Goings, Kenneth W. 1994. *Mammy and Uncle Mose: Black Collectibles and American Stereotyping*. Blacks in the Diaspora. Bloomington: Indiana University Press.

Goldson, Yvonne. 1998. *Jamaika-go o hanasō! Patowa-go handobukku* (Let's Speak Jamaican! Patois Handbook). Tokyo: Uplink.

Goodman, David G., and Masanori Miyazawa. 1995. *Jews in the Japanese Mind: The History and Uses of a Cultural Stereotype*. New York: Free Press.

Goodman, Roger, et al., eds. 2003. *Global Japan: The Experience of Japan's New Immigrant and Overseas Communities*. London: RoutledgeCurzon.

Gordon, Andrew, ed. 1993. *Postwar Japan as History*. Berkeley: University of California Press.

Gotō Wataru. 1997. *Jamaika & Regee A to Z* (Jamaica and Reggae A to Z). Tokyo: Tokyo FM.

Gramsci, Antonio. 1971. *Selections from the Prison Notebooks*. Translated and edited by Quintin Hoare and Geoffrey Nowell. New York: International Publishers.

Green, L. Shane, 2007. "Introduction: On Race, Roots/Routes, and Sovereignty in Latin America's Afro-Indigenous Multiculturalisms." *Journal of Latin American and Caribbean Anthropology* 12 (2): 329–55.

Hall, Stuart. 1996. *Stuart Hall: Critical Dialogues in Cultural Studies*. Edited by David Morley and Kuan-Hsing Chen. Comedia. London: Routledge.

——.1997a. "The Local and the Global: Globalization and Ethnicity." In *Culture, Globalization, and the World-System: Contemporary Conditions for the Representation of Identity*, edited by A. King. Minneapolis: University of Minnesota Press.

——. 1997b. "Old and New Identities, Old and New Ethnicities." In *Culture, Globalization, and the World-System: Contemporary Conditions for the Representation of Identity*, edited by A. King. Minneapolis: University of Minnesota Press.

Hanaki, Toru, et al. 2007. "Hanryu Sweeps East Asia: How 'Winter Sonata' Is Gripping Japan." *International Communication Gazette* 69 (3): 281–94.

Harris, Joseph E., ed. 1993. *Global Dimensions of the African Diaspora*. 2nd ed. Washington: Howard University Press.

Hebdige, Dick. 1979. *Subculture: The Meaning of Style*. London: Methuen.

Helg, Aline. 1990. "Race in Argentina and Cuba, 1880–1930: Theory, Policies and Popular Reaction." In *The Idea of Race in Latin America*, edited by R. Graham. Austin: University of Texas Press.

Hendry, Joy. 2000. "Foreign Country Theme Parks: A New Theme or an Old Japanese Pattern?" *Social Science Japan Journal* 3: 207–20.

Hendry, Joy, and Heung Wah Wong. 2006. *Dismantling the East-West Dichotomy: Essays in Honour of Jan van Bremen*. Japan Anthropology Workshop Series. Abingdon, England: Routledge.

Hepner, Randal. 1998. "Chanting down Babylon in the Belly of the Beast: The Rastafarian Movement in the Metropolitan United States." In *Chanting down Babylon: The Rastafari Reader*, edited by N. Samuel Murrell, W. D. Spencer, and A. A. McFarlane. Philadelphia: Temple University Press.

Hirō, Jah. 1991. *Rastaman Bibureeshon* (Rastaman Vibration). Tokyo: Japan Press.

Hobsbawm, E. J., and T. O. Ranger. 1983. *The Invention of Tradition*. Cambridge: Cambridge University Press.

Hoffman-French, Jan. 2004. "Mestizaje and Law Making in Indigenous Identity Formation in Northeastern Brazil: 'After the Conflict Came the History.' " *American Anthropologist* 10 (4): 663–74.

———. 2006. "Buried Alive: Imagining Africa in the Brazilian Northeast." *American Ethnologist* 33 (3): 340–60.

hooks, bell. 1992. *Black Looks: Race and Representation*. Boston: South End.

Hope, Donna P. 2006. *Inna di Dancehall: Popular Culture and the Politics of Identity in Jamaica*. Kingston, Jamaica: University of the West Indies Press.

Hosokawa, Shuhei. 1997. " 'Salsa no Tiene Frontera': Orquesta de la Luz or the Globalization and Japanization of Afro-Caribbean Music." *Revista Transcultural de Música* 3: 1–21.

Ikeshiro Minako. 2006. *Di Regee Bukku* (The Reggae Book). Tokyo: Shinkō.

Inoue, Masamichi. 2007. *Okinawa and the U.S. Military: Identity Making in the Age of Globalization*. New York: Columbia University Press.

Itsuki Hiroyuki. 1966. *Umi o Mitte Ita Jonii* (Johnny Who Saw the Sea). Tokyo: Kōdansha.

Ivy, Marilyn. 1995. *Discourses of the Vanishing: Modernity, Phantasm, Japan*. Chicago: University of Chicago Press.

Iwabuchi, Koichi. 2002. "Nostalgia for a (Different) Asian Modernity: Media Consumption of 'Asia' in Japan." *positions* 10 (3): 547–73.

Jameson, Fredric. 1991. *Postmodernism, or, the Cultural Logic of Late Capitalism*. Post-Contemporary Interventions. Durham, N.C.: Duke University Press.

Jenkins, Keith, ed. 1997. *The Postmodern History Reader*. London: Routledge.

Jhally, Sut. 1997. *Stuart Hall: Race, the Floating Signifier*. Northampton, Mass.:
   Media Education Foundation. Videorecording.
Johnson, E. Patrick. 2003. *Appropriating Blackness: Performance and the Politics of
   Authenticity*. Durham, N.C.: Duke University Press.
Jones, Andrew F. 2001. *Yellow Music: Media Culture and Colonial Modernity in the
   Chinese Jazz Age*. Durham, N.C.: Duke University Press.
Jones, Andrew F., and Nikhil Pal Singh, eds. 2003. "The Afro-Asian Century." Spe-
   cial issue. *Positions* 11 (1).
Kawamura, Nozomu. 1980. "The Historical Background of Arguments Emphasiz-
   ing the Uniqueness of Japanese Society." *Social Analysis* 5–6: 44–62.
Kawazoe Hitoshi. 1995. *Jibun Sagashi: Kawazoe Hitoshi Shōsetsu-shū* (The Search for
   Self: The Collected Fiction of Kawazoe Hitoshi). Takaoka, Japan: Honda Kikaku.
Keita. 1993. *Shinkuro Baibusu* (Synchro Vibes). Tokyo: JICC.
Kelsky, Karen. 1994. "Intimate Ideologies: Transnational Theory and Japan's
   Yellow Cabs." *Public Culture* 6: 465–78.
———. 2001. *Women on the Verge: Japanese Women, Western Dreams, Asia-Pacific*.
   Durham, N.C.: Duke University Press.
Kelts, Roland. 2006. *Japanamerica: How Japanese Pop Culture Has Invaded the U.S.*
   New York: Palgrave Macmillan.
Kimoto Yuko. 1994. *Honjama Jamaika*. Tokyo: Kadokawa Shoten.
Kinsella, Sharon. 1995. "Cuties in Japan." In *Women, Media and Consumption in Ja-
   pan*, edited by Lise Skov and Brian Moeran. Honolulu: University of Hawaii Press.
Koike Noriko. 2002. *Jibun Sagashi Serapii: Chiisana Shiawase o Mitsukeru Koto kara
   Hajimeyō* (Search-for-Self Therapy: Let's Start from the Discovery of Small Joy).
   Tokyo: Besutoseraazu.
Kokoro no Waakubukku Seisaki Gurūpu. 2006. *Kokoro no Waakubukku = Workbook
   of the Mind: Dare Demo Dekiru Hitori Demo Dekiru Jibun Sagashi Commyunikeeshon
   Gaido* (Workbook of the Mind: A Search-for-Self Communication Guide that
   Anyone, Even Alone, Can Do). Okayama, Japan: Fukurō Shuppan.
Kondo, Dorinne K. 1990. *Crafting Selves: Power, Gender, and Discourses of Identity in
   a Japanese Workplace*. Chicago: University of Chicago Press.
Krauze, Enrique. 2005. "The Pride in Memín Pinguín." *Washington Post*, July 12.
Kurokawa, Yoko. 2004. "Yearning for a Distant Music: Consumption of Hawaiian
   Music and Dance in Japan." Ph.D. diss., University of Hawaii at Manoa.
Lebra, Takie Sugiyama. 1976. *Japanese Patterns of Behavior*. Honolulu: University
   Press of Hawaii.
Leland, John. 1992. "When Rap Meets Reggae: The Dynamic New Music from
   Jamaica." *Newsweek*. September 7, 59.
Leupp, Gary. 1995. "Images of Black People in Late Mediaeval and Early Modern
   Japan, 1543–1900." *Japan Forum* 7 (1): 1–13.
Lewellen, Ted C. 2002. *The Anthropology of Globalization: Cultural Anthropology
   Enters the 21st Century*. Westport, Conn.: Bergin and Garvey.
Lewis, John Lowell. 1992. *Ring of Liberation: Deceptive Discourse in Brazilian
   Capoeira*. Chicago: University of Chicago Press.

Lewis, Marvin A. 1995. *Afro-Argentine Discourse: Another Dimension of the Black Diaspora*. Columbia: University of Missouri Press.

Lewis, William F. 1994. "The Social Drama of the Rastafari." *Dialectical Anthropology* 19: 283–94.

Lie, John. 2001. *Multiethnic Japan*. Cambridge: Harvard University Press.

Lindfors, Bernth. 1999. *Africans on Stage: Studies in Ethnological Show Business*. Bloomington: Indiana University Press.

Linicome, Mark. 1993. "Nationalism, Internationalization, and the Dilemma of Educational Reform in Japan." *Comparative Education Review* 37: 123–51.

Lopez Ropero, Lourdes. 2006. "One People, One Nation? Creolization and Its Tensions in Trinidadian and Guyanese Fiction." In *AfroAsian Encounters: Culture, History, Politics*, edited by Heike Raphael-Hernandez and Shannon Steen. New York: New York University Press.

Lyotard, Jean François. 1984. *The Postmodern Condition: A Report on Knowledge*. Translated by Geoff Bennington and Brian Massumi. Minneapolis: University of Minnesota Press.

Makoto, Oda. 1961. *Nan de mo Mite Yarō* (I'll Give Anything a Look). Tokyo: Kawade Shobō.

Malkki, Liisa. 1995. *Purity and Exile: Violence, Memory, and National Cosmology among Hutu Refugees in Tanzania*. Chicago: University of Chicago Press.

Manuel, Peter, and Wayne Marshall. 2006. "The Riddim Method: Aesthetics, Practice, and Ownership in Jamaican Dancehall." *Popular Music* 25 (3): 447–70.

Mathews, Gordon. 1996. "The Stuff of Dreams, Fading: Ikigai and 'The Japanese Self.'" *Ethos* 24: 718–47.

McGill, Douglas. 1989. "Colgate to Rename a Toothpaste." *New York Times*. January 27.

McGray, Douglas. 2002. "Japan's Gross National Cool." *Foreign Policy* 130: 44–54.

McLelland, Mark J. 2000. *Male Homosexuality in Modern Japan: Cultural Myths and Social Realities*. New York: Routledge.

Miller, Laura, and Jan Bardsley, eds. 2005. *Bad Girls of Japan*. New York: Palgrave Macmillan.

Min, Pyong Gap. 2003. "Korean 'Comfort Women': The Intersection of Colonial Power, Gender, and Class." *Gender and Society* 17 (6): 938–57.

Miyake, Hitoshi. 2001. *Shugendō: Essays on the Structure of Japanese Folk Religion*. Ann Arbor: University of Michigan Press.

Miyoshi, Masao, and H. D. Harootunian, eds. 1989. *Postmodernism and Japan*. Durham, N.C.: Duke University Press.

Montague, Masani. 1994. *Dread Culture: A Rastawoman's Story*. Toronto: Sister Vision.

More, Blake. 1994. "Jamming in Jah-pan." http://snakelyone.com/jahpan.htm (accessed July 19, 2009).

Morimoto Junji, ed. 1998. *Sekai Ururun Taizaiki: "Tabibito" 20 Nin ga Tsuzuru Kandō no Jibun Sagashi* (Homestay in the world: the moving search for self as told by twenty travelers). Tokyo: Kōbunsha.

Morrison, Toni. 1992. *Playing in the Dark: Whiteness and the Literary Imagination.* Cambridge: Harvard University Press.

Mullen, Bill V. 2004. *Afro-Orientalism.* Minneapolis: University of Minnesota Press.

Murakami Ryū. 1976. *Kagirinaku Tōmei ni Chikai Burū* (Almost transparent blue). Tokyo: Kodansha.

Mussche, Steffen Patrick. 2008. "Wi Likkle but Wi Tallawah: Narratives of Nation Branding—Intellectual Property Governance and Identity Politics in Jamaica." Master's thesis, University of Oslo.

Nakamura, Akira, Tadashi Nakamura, and Kazuaki Inoue, eds. 1997. *Otoko ga Miete Kuru Jinbun Sagashi no 100 Satsu* (A Hundred Books on the Search for Self in Which Men Appear). Kyoto, Japan: Kamogawa Shuppan.

Napier, Susan. 1996. *The Fantastic in Modern Japanese Literature: The Subversion of Modernity.* Nissan Institute/Routledge Japanese Studies Series. London: Routledge.

Nassy Brown, Jacqueline. 1998. "Black Liverpool, Black America, and the Gendering of Diasporic Space." *Cultural Anthropology* 13 (3): 291–325.

Nederveen, Jan Pieterse. 1992. *White on Black: Images of Africa and Blacks in Western Popular Culture.* New Haven, Conn.: Yale University Press.

Nelson, John. 2003. "Social Memory as Ritual Practice: Commemorating Spirits of the Military Dead at Yasukuni Shinto Shrine." *The Journal of Asian Studies* 62 (2): 443–67.

Oates, Joyce Carol. 1990. *Because It Is Bitter, and Because It Is My Heart.* New York: Dutton.

Ōe Kenzaburō. 1958. *Shisha no Ogori–Shiiku* (Lavish Are the Dead and Prize Stock). Tokyo: Shinchō.

Ōga Tamanosuke. 1998. *Jamaika ga Suki da!* (I Love Jamaica!). Tokyo: K. K. Besutoseraazu.

Ogasawara, Yuko. 1998. *Office Ladies and Salaried Men: Power, Gender, and Work in Japanese Companies.* Berkeley: University of California Press.

Ogawa Akira. 1998. *Kaisha ga Iya ni Natta Toki Yomu Hon: Kyūkoku no "Jibun Sagashi" no Susume* (The Book to Read When Work Goes Bad: The Ultimate Advice on "The Search for Self"). Tokyo: PHP Kenkyūjo.

Ōgon Toshio. 1998. *Torauma: Jibun mo Shiranai Jibun Sagashi* (Trauma: The Search for a Self Unknown Even to the Searcher). Tokyo: Hakuju-sha.

Oguma, Eiji. 2002. *A Genealogy of "Japanese" Self-Images.* Translated by David Askew. Japanese Society Series. Melbourne, Australia: Trans Pacific.

Ohba, Toshiaki. 2000. "Power of Woman: Sister Kaya for Sistren." *Riddim* 204: 20–21.

Okonogi Keigo. 1981. *Moratoriamu Ningen no Jidai* (The Age of Moratorium People). Tokyo: Chūō Kōronsha.

Ōmori, Osamu. 1997. *Miyazawa Kenji to Ayumu Jibun Sagashi no Tabi: Kokoro no Kyōiku de Ikiru Chikara o* (Walking with Miyazawa Kenji, Journeying into a Search for Self: Increasing the Strength to Live by Educating the Spirit). Tokyo: Meiji Tosho Shuppan.

Ong, Aihwa. 1999. *Flexible Citizenship: The Cultural Logics of Transnationality*. Durham, N.C.: Duke University Press.

Orenstein, Peggy. 2001. "Parasites in Prêt-à-Porter are Threatening Japan's Economy." *New York Times*. July 1.

Ôsumi, Makoto. 2001. *Yongu Shinrigaku + "Bukkyō" no Kaunseringu: Kokoro o Iyashi, "Hontō no Jibun Sagashi" o Fukameru tame ni* (Jungian Psychology and "Buddhist" Counseling: To Mend the Spirit and Deepen a "True Search for Self"). Tokyo: Gakuyō.

Park, Kyeyoung. 1996. "Use and Abuse of Race and Culture: Black-Korean Tension in America." *American Anthropologist* 98 (3): 492–99.

Pollard, Velma. 1980. "Dread Talk." *Caribbean Quarterly* 26: 32–42.

Prashad, Vijay. 2001. *Everybody Was Kung Fu Fighting: Afro-Asian Connections and the Myth of Cultural Purity*. Boston: Beacon.

Prasso, Sheridan. 2006. "Escape from Japan." *New York Times*. October 15.

Rahier, Jean. 1999. *Representations of Blackness and the Performance of Identities*. Westport, Conn.: Bergin and Garvey.

Raphael-Hernandez, Heike, and Shannon Steen, eds. 2006. *AfroAsian Encounters: Culture, History, Politics*. New York: New York University Press.

Reader, Ian, and George Joji Tanabe. 1998. *Practically Religious: Worldly Benefits and the Common Religion of Japan*. Honolulu: University of Hawaii Press.

"Reggae Music: Trench Town East." 1994. *The Economist*. January 22.

Roach, Joseph R. 1996. *Cities of the Dead: Circum-Atlantic Performance*. New York: Columbia University Press.

Roberson, James E., and Nobue Suzuki. 2003. *Men and Masculinities in Contemporary Japan: Dislocating the Salaryman Doxa*. London: Routledge.

Robertson, Jennifer Ellen. 1998. *Takarazuka: Sexual Politics and Popular Culture in Modern Japan*. Berkeley: University of California Press.

Rose, Tricia. 1994. *Black Noise: Rap Music and Black Culture in Contemporary America*. Middletown, Conn.: Wesleyan University Press.

Rubin, Arnold. 1974. *Black Nanban: Africans in Japan during the Sixteenth Century*. Bloomington: African Studies Program, Indiana University.

Russell, John G. 1991a. "Race and Reflexivity: The Black Other in Contemporary Japanese Mass Culture." *Cultural Anthropology* 6: 3–23.

——. 1991b. "Narratives of Denial: Racial Chauvinism and the Black Other in Japan." *Japan Quarterly* 38: 416–28.

——. 1991c. *Nihonjin no Kokujinkan: Mondai wa "Chibikuro Sambo" Dake De Wa Nai* (Japanese Views of Black People: The Problem Is Not Only "Little Black Sambo"). Tokyo: Shinhyōron.

——. 1998. "Consuming Passions: Spectacle, Self-Transformation, and the Commodification of Blackness in Japan." *positions* 6: 113–77.

Said, Edward W. 1979. *Orientalism*. New York: Vintage.

Sato, Ikuya. 1991. *Kamikaze Biker: Parody and Anomy in Affluent Japan*. Chicago: University of Chicago Press.

Sautman, Barry. 1994. "Anti-Black Racism in Post-Mao China." *The China Quarterly* 138: 413–37.

Savigliano, Marta. 1995. "Tango in Japan and the World Economy of Passion." In *Remade in Japan: Everyday Life and Consumer Taste in a Changing Society*. Edited by Joseph Tobin. New Haven, Conn.: Yale University Press.

Savishinsky, Neil J. 1994. "Rastafari in the Promised Land: The Spread of a Jamaican Socioreligious Movement among the Youth of Africa." *African Studies Review* 37 (3): 19–50.

Sawaki Kōtaro. 1986. *Shinya Tokkyū: Honkon, Makao* (Midnight Express: Hong Kong, Macao). Tokyo: Shinchōsha.

Scott, James C. 1985. *Weapons of the Weak: Everyday Forms of Peasant Resistance*. New Haven, Conn.: Yale University Press.

Silverberg, Miriam. 1991. "The Modern Girl as Militant." In *Recreating Japanese Women, 1600–1945*, edited by G. L. Bernstein. Berkeley: University of California Press.

Skov, Lise, and Brian Moeran, eds. 1995. *Women, Media and Consumption in Japan*. Honolulu: University of Hawaii Press.

Smith, M. G., Roy Augier, and Rex M. Nettleford. 1960. *The Ras Tafari Movement in Kingston, Jamaica*. Mona, Jamaica: University College of the West Indies, Institute of Social and Economic Research.

Smith, Robert John. 1983. *Japanese Society: Tradition, Self and the Social Order*. Cambridge: Cambridge University Press.

Soma, Emi. 2001. "Powder Room Talk." *Strive* 1: 36.

Stanley-Niaah, Sonjah. 2004. "Kingston's Dancehall: A Story of Space and Celebration." *Space & Culture* 7 (1): 102–18.

Stetz, Margaret D., and Bonnie B. C. Oh, eds. 2001. *Legacies of the Comfort Women of World War II*. Armonk, N.Y.: M. E. Sharpe.

Stoler, Ann Laura. 1995. *Race and the Education of Desire: Foucault's History of Sexuality and the Colonial Order of Things*. Durham, N.C.: Duke University Press.

——. 2002. *Carnal Knowledge and Imperial Power: Race and the Intimate in Colonial Rule*. Berkeley: University of California Press.

Stolzoff, Norman C. 2000. *Wake the Town and Tell the People: Dancehall Culture in Jamaica*. Durham, N.C.: Duke University Press.

Sugimoto, Yoshio, and Ross Mouer. 1986. "Reappraising Images of Japanese Society." *Social Analysis* 5–6: 5–19.

Suttmeier, Bruce. 2009. "Ethnography as Consumption: Travel and National Identity in Oda Makoto's *Nan de mo mite yarō*." *Journal of Japanese Studies*, 35(1): 61–86.

Suzuki Shinichirō. 2000. *Reggae Train: Diaspora no Hibiki* (Reggae Train: Sounds of Diaspora). Tokyo: Seido-sha.

Tagawa, Tadasu. 1985. *Reggae: Jamaika no Kaze to Hikari* (Reggae: Jamaica's Wind and Light). Tokyo: Ongaku No Tomosha.

Takeda Mayumi. 1999. *Faito!* (Fight!). Tokyo: Gentōsha.

Takezawa, Yasuko. 2005. *Jinshu Gainen no Fuhensei o Tō–Seiyōteki Paradiamu o Koete* (Questioning the Universality of the Concept of Race: Transcending the Western Paradigm). Tokyo: Jinbunshoin.

Tamanoi, Mariko. 1998. *Under the Shadow of Nationalism: Politics and Poetics of Rural Japanese Women*. Honolulu: University of Hawaii Press.

———. 2000. "Knowledge, Power, and Racial Classification: The 'Japanese' in 'Manchuria.'" *Journal of Asian Studies* 59 (2): 248–76.

Thomas, Deborah A. 2004. *Modern Blackness: Nationalism, Globalization, and the Politics of Culture in Jamaica*. Durham, N.C.: Duke University Press.

Thornton, Michael Charles. 1983. "A Social History of a Multiethnic Identity: The Case of Black Japanese Americans." Ph.D. diss., University of Michigan at Ann Arbor.

Tierney, R. Kenji. 2002. "Wrestling with Tradition: Sumo, Popular Culture and Trans/Nationalism." Ph.D. diss., University of California, Berkeley.

Tobin, Joseph, ed. 1992a. *Re-Made in Japan: Everyday Life and Consumer Taste in a Changing Society*. New Haven, Conn.: Yale University Press.

———. 1992b. "Introduction: Domesticating the West." In *Re-Made in Japan: Everyday Life and Consumer Taste in a Changing Society*, edited by Joseph Tobin. New Haven, Conn.: Yale University Press.

———. 2006. *Pikachu's Global Adventure: The Rise and Fall of Pokémon*. Durham, N.C.: Duke University Press.

Turner, Terisa E. 1991. "Women, Rastafari and the New Society: Caribbean and East African Roots of a Popular Movement against Structural Adjustment." *Labour, Capital and Society* 21: 66–89.

Turner, Victor Witter. 1982. *From Ritual to Theatre: The Human Seriousness of Play*. New York: PAJ Publications.

———. 1987. *The Anthropology of Performance*. New York: PAJ Publications.

Turner, Victor Witter, and Edward M. Bruner. 1986. *The Anthropology of Experience*. Urbana: University of Illinois Press.

Ullestad, Neal. 1999. "American Indian Rap and Reggae: Dancing 'to the Beat of a Different Drummer.'" *Popular Music and Society* 23 (2): 62–90.

Uno, Masami. 1985. *Yudaya ga Wakaru to Sekai ga Miete Kuru* (If You Understand the Jews, You Will Come to Understand the World). Tokyo: Tokuma Shoten.

———. 1995. *Kodai Yudaya wa Nihon de Fukkatsu Suru* (The Ancient Jews Will Rise Again in Japan). Tokyo: Nihon Bunkgeisha.

van Dijk, Frank. 1998. "Chanting down Babylon Outernational: The Rise of Rastafari in Europe, the Caribbean, and the Pacific." In *Chanting down Babylon: The Rastafari Reader*, edited by N. Samuel Murrell, W. D. Spencer, and A. A. McFarlane. Philadelphia: Temple University Press.

van Wolferen, Karel. 1990. *The Enigma of Japanese Power: People and Politics in a Stateless Nation*. New York: Vintage.

Wade, Peter. 1995. "The Cultural Politics of Blackness in Colombia." *American Ethnologist* 22 (2): 341–57.

Wagatsuma, Hiroshi. 1967. "The Social Perception of Skin Color in Japan." *Daedalus* (spring): 407–43.

Wallerstein, Immanuel Maurice. 1974. *The Modern World-System*. New York: Academic.

Wang, Oliver. 2006. "These Are the Breaks: Hip-Hop and AfroAsian Cultural (Dis)Connections." In *AfroAsian Encounters: Culture, History, Politics*, edited by Heike Raphael-Hernandez and Shannon Steen. New York: New York University Press.

Watanabe Kasuko. 1993. *Feminizumu Shōsetsuron: Josei Sakka no Jibun Sagashi* (Theorizing the Feminist Novel: Female Authors' Search for Self). Tokyo: Tsugeshin Shobō.

Watson, James, ed. 1997. *Golden Arches East: McDonald's in East Asia*. Stanford, Calif.: Stanford University Press.

Watts, Jonathan. 2001. "The Emperor's New Roots." *Guardian*, December 28.

Weiner, Michael. 1995. *Race and Migration in Imperial Japan*. Sheffield Centre for Japanese Studies/Routledge Series. London: Routledge.

——, ed. 2004. *Race, Ethnicity and Migration in Modern Japan*. London: Routledge.

Wekker, Gloria. 2006. *The Politics of Passion: Women's Sexual Culture in the Afro-Surinamese Diaspora*. New York: Columbia University Press.

White, Merry I. 1988. *The Material Child: Coming of Age in Japan and America*. New York: Free Press.

——. 1993. *The Japanese Overseas: Can They Go Home Again?* New York: Free Press.

Whitten, Norman E., and Arlene Torres. 1998. *Blackness in Latin America and the Caribbean: Social Dynamics and Cultural Transformations*. Blacks in the Diaspora. Bloomington: Indiana University Press.

Williams, Lawson. 2000. "Homophobia and Gay Rights Activism in Jamaica." *Small Axe* 7: 106–11.

Wood, Joe. 1997. "The Yellow Negro." *Transition* 73:40–66.

Woronoff, Jon. 1983. *Japan's Wasted Workers*. Totowa, N.J.: Allanheld, Osmun.

Wright, Keril. 2007. "Anger over Winner Spoils Dancehall Queen Competition." *Jamaica Observer*. July 31.

Wright, Michelle M. 2003. "Others-from-within from without: Afro-German Subject Formation and the Challenge of a Counter-Discourse." *Callaloo* 26 (2): 296–305.

Yamada Eimi. 1987. *Beddotaimu Aizu* (Bedtime Eyes). Tokyo: Kawade.

Yamakawa Kenichi. 1985. *Hoshi to Regee no Shima* (Island of Stars and Reggae). Tokyo: Kakukawa.

——. 1993. *Wan Rabu Jamaika* (One Love Jamaica). Tokyo: Tokyo FM.

Yang, Hyunah. 2008. "Finding the 'Map of Memory': Testimony of the Japanese Military Sexual Slavery Survivors." *positions* 16 (1): 79–107.

Yawney, Carole. 1994. "Rasta Mek a Trod: Symbolic Ambiguity in a Globalizing Region." In *Arise Ye Mighty People! Gender, Class and Race in Popular Struggles*, edited by Terisa E. Turner. Trenton, N.J.: Africa World Press.

Yellin, Victor. 1996. "Mrs. Belmont, Matthew Perry, and the 'Japanese Minstrels.'" *American Music* 14 (3): 257–75.

Yoda, Tomiko, and Harry D. Harootunian, eds. 2006. *Japan after Japan: Social and Cultural Life from the Recessionary 1990s to the Present*. Durham, N.C.: Duke University Press.

Yoshiaki, Yoshimi. 2000. *Comfort Women*. New York: Columbia University Press.

Yoshida Ruriko. 1979. *Harlem no Atsui Hibi* (Hot Harlem Days). Tokyo: Kodansha.

Yoshikawa Hideki. 1999. *Bankoku Jibun Sagashi no Ringu: Muetai o Eranda Gonin no Wakamono* (The Ring of Bangkok Search for Self: Five Young People Who Chose Muay Thai). Tokyo: Mekon.

Yúdice, George. 2001. "Afro Reggae." *Social Text* 19 (4): 53–65.

Zielenziger, Michael. 2006. *Shutting out the Sun: How Japan Created Its Own Lost Generation*. New York: Nan A. Talese.

Page numbers in italics refer to photographs and illustrations.

"Boom Bye-Bye," 105–6, 108–9
Born in JAHpan (documentary), 133
Bourdieu, Pierre, 62, 99
Buell, Frederick, 144
burakumin (hamlet people), 43, 162–64, 231–32, 234, 254, 259n13, 263n1
Butler, Judith, 258n11, 261n1

Campbell, Horace, 149
Cashmore, Ernest, 36, 149
Cham, Baby, 93–94, 97
Cherish, 134–35, 139
China and Chinese culture: Chinese-Japanese ethnicity and, 43, 50–51, 167, 233–36, 235; Greater East Asia Co-Prosperity Sphere and, 76–77; internationalization and, 72–74; misidentification of Japanese as Chinese in Jamaica and, 79, 81–82, 130, 216–17, 240, 255
Chinatsu, 120, 137
civil and human rights, 20, 45, 164, 259n15
class difference: for Afro-Jamaican women, 104, 126, 141; in corporate workplace, 50; in dancehall culture, 22, 107, 231; dancehall culture in Japan and, 22, 231; DJs and, 107; dub musicians and, 161, 162, 231; ethnonational view of, 231–32; MCs and, 107; for men in Jamaica, 6, 141, 230–31, 237; for men in Japan, 6, 141, 230–31, 237; social identity dynamics and, 4, 230–31; for women in Japan, 50, 103, 104, 126, 141, 142
Cliff, Jimmy, 9, 71
Club Citta, 2, 61, 93
Cojie, 80, 84, 87, 235, 261n7
Collinwood, Dean W., 154
colonialism: Japan and, 6, 23, 74, 76–77, 166, 217; Rasta culture in Jamaica, and critique of, 145–48
colonial-modern discourse, and global blackness, 246–47, 252–53

Condry, Ian, 58–59, 120
"Cool Runnings," 11, 12
Cooper, Carolyn, x, 64, 140, 147
Cornyetz, Nina, 55–57, 110–11, 260n6, 262n3
corporate workplace: class difference in, 50; marginalization of women and, 103, 112, 123; office ladies and, 21, 110, 193, 257–58n9; racism in, 26; rejection of, 194, 198, 231; *sararii-man*, 21, 193, 257–58n9
"cos play," 226, 265n1
cultural consumption, global politics of, 20, 28–29, 42, 224–25, 249
cultural theft and exploitation accusations, 240–41, 244

Dakko-chan (golliwog-like dolls), 25, 55, 246
Dale, Peter N., 20, 48
dancehall culture in Jamaica: Afro-centric culture of, 141; Afro-Jamaican women in, 56–57, 104, 110, 126, 132, 140, 141, 262n3; dance and fashion scene for men in, 106; dub musicians, and travels to experience, 29, 157; ethnoracial energies associated with, 63; gender and sexuality issues in, 69, 90–91, 104, 105; homophobia in, 69, 77–78, 105–9, 120, 261–62n2; postcolonial blackness, and "browning" for men in, 240; rhetorical violence and aggressiveness in, 105; slackness in, 68–70, 105, 140; social tension, and local performative field of, 64–65; songs, and sexualization of women in, 238; sound clash event in, 90–91; violence and aggressiveness, and rhetoric in, 105; vulgarity complaints about, 105, 239. *See also* international dancehall competitions; performative field of international dancehall culture; sound clash events

dancehall culture in Japan: Afrocentric culture of Rasta in, 46, 157; authenticity and authority of Japaneseness in, 71–78, 98–99, 118–19, 261n12; as business enterprise, 17, 79, 85, 261n7; career opportunities in, 82–83, 88, 231; class difference, and culture of, 22, 231; Club Citta and, 2, 61, 93; continuum of Rasta in Japan and, 1–4, 151–54; dance and fashion scene for men and, 106–7; DJs and, 68–71, 90; domestication of foreign culture in, 77–78; dub reggae and, 19, 63–67, 152–53, 260n1; economic recession in Japan and, 119; emotional investment in, 46–47, 50–51; engineer role in, 63, 84–89, 91; fans and, 17–18, 63, 66, 86; gender and sexuality issues in, 22, 57, 104–5, 109–11, 225–26; homosexuality and, 94, 106–9, 120, 261n8, 261–62n2; imagined sexually available discourse on, 109–10; Jamaican perspectives on, 30, 236–38; Jamaican presence and, 77–78, 89; juggling and, 64, 88, 90, 261n7; local performative practice and, 64, 97; marginalization of individuals in, 83, 99, 111, 117; masculinity performance in, 78–79, 104; media and, 9, 17, 85, 113–19, 125, 243–45, 266n5; men's rivals in, 104–5; music videos, 118–19; national pride, and songs in, 70–78, 89; New York, and views of musicians in, 264–65n4; overview, 7–8, 12–13, 15–19, 61–63, 65, 66, 97, 223, 255; Papa Bon and, 78–84, 97, 98, 118, 122; patron experience in, 97–98, 103, 134; power, and misrecognition in, 99; ragga/raggamuffin and, 6, 7–8, 106–7; romantic love in songs, 70–71, 120–21; roots reggae in, 90; rub-a-dub events in, 58, 64, 90–91, 124; search for self and, 46, 50–51, 79, 83–84; selectors role, 61, 84, 90, 91; singers and, 68, 71–76, 121; slackness in, 70–71; socialization, and performative in, 62, 97–99; sound clash event in, 90–91, 93–97, 261n11; sounds and, 11, 62, 65, 236; symbolic capital acquisition in, 61, 62, 66–67, 85, 91–96, 224; Tokyo and, 79, 80–82; travels overseas by artists and fans in, 66–67, 79, 80–82, 85, 87–88; as vulgar, 99; websites and, 17–18; women and, 104, 109–11. *See also* dancehall (reggae) subculture in Japan; MCs (emcees); international dancehall competitions; performative field of international dancehall culture; sound clash events

dancehall (reggae) music in Japan: Afrocentric culture of Rasta, 46, 254; authority of Jamaican referenced by, 261n12; Babylon and, 159–60; corporate foundations for, 10–11; in dancehall culture in Japan, 90; dub musicians and exposure to, 158; the *esunikku*, 13; female singers in, 115, 121; gender and sexuality issues, and power expressed in, 57–58; *iemoto* system of apprenticeship and, 262–63n5; "J-reggae," 17, 47; local performative practice and, 59; media and, 115; natural world valuation in, 13, 18; opportunism for Jamaican-Japanese cultural exchange and, 241–42; overview, 9–15, 223, 257nn3–4; print media, and role in, 10, 12, 13, 17; rural band, 175–76, 179, 263n7; social identity dynamics and, 46, 225; spectrum of, 151–54; websites and, 113–14. *See also* dancehall culture in Japan; Rasta culture in Japan; reggae dance performance by women in Japan; Yoshino Rasta yard

Dancehall Queen (film), 137, 250

dancehall (reggae) subculture in Japan:

Babylon east and, 5–6, 142; dancehall, and links and tension with, 119, 121, 157; dancehall culture in Japan, and continuum of, 1–4, 151–54; as deviant from norm, 154; domestication of foreign culture in, 21, 47, 62, 77–78, 212, 224, 239; ethnicity in, 22, 43; ethnoracial encounters in, 59; global politics of cultural consumption and reproduction in, 20, 28–29, 42, 224–25, 254; individualist Rasta lifestyle and, 155, 228, 230; "J-reggae," 123; natural world valuation in, 122, 228; social identity dynamics, and emotional investment in, 50–51; spectrum of, 1–4; thirdness and, 52–53; traditional festival fashion and costumes in, 1–2; websites, 113–14. *See also* Rasta culture in Japan; reggae dance performance by women in Japan

Dear Chicks, 124–26, 134, 138

de Certeau, Michel, 103

De Vos, George, 109

diaspora community: in Africa, 36, 149–50; beyond the, 5, 6, 150–51; in Great Britain, 9, 36, 38, 66, 149, 255; in Latin America, 36–37, 260n1; in New York, 9, 149, 255; roots reggae music in, 36–37, 42; social identity dynamics and, 36, 255

digital musical tracks (*riddim*), DJs, and performances over, 8, 90; dub plates and, 67; history of, 12, 14, 64; rub-a-dub events and, 90; singers' performances over, 90

Dikötter, Frank, 23, 24–25

Di Reggae Book (Ikeshiro), 115

divas. *See* reggae dance performance by women in Japan

DJs (deejays), 68–71, 70, 90, 96, 107–9, 120–21, 137

domestication of foreign culture, in Rasta culture in Japan, 21, 47, 62, 77–78, 212, 224, 239

Donnette, 8, 136

donnettes. *See* reggae dance performance by women in Japan

D[omacron]zan, Miki, 73–74, 76, 77

dreadlocks: Rasta tam, and fake, 21, 147, 148, 171–72; as symbol of Rasta, 28, 55, 146–48, 150, 151, 155; for women, 21, 227

dread talk, 92, 147, 159–60

Dreisinger, Baz, 243–45

dub musicians in Japan: Afrocentric culture and, 157; Babylon east and, 157, 160, 162–63; *burakumin* discrimination and, 162–64; character of, 158–59, 161–62; class difference, and experience of, 161, 162, 231; ethnicity and, 163; marijuana consumption by, 157, 160–61; overview, 157; patois, 158–59; patriarchal Rasta attitude toward Afro-Jamaican women by, 161; roots reggae and, 158; Taffy (pseud.) and, 161–64, 186, 231–32, 234, 254; travels by, 29, 157, 159, 264–65n4; urban perspectives and, 164–66

dub plates, 67, 85, 92, 94–95, 224

dub reggae (dub version; version), 19, 63–67, 152–53, 260n1

economic recession in Japan, 4–5, 112, 119, 193–95, 197, 202–3

electronica, 64, 152

Elephant Man, 16–17, 122, 238, 240

En no Gy[omacron]ja, 181–82

the *esunikku* (the ethnic), 13, 21, 111, 166–69, 220

eta outcastes, 43; otherwise known as *burakumin* (hamlet people), 43, 162–64, 231–32, 234, 254, 259n13, 263n1

ethnicity (*minzoku*): *burakumin* and, 43, 162–64, 231–32, 234, 254, 259n13, 263n1; Chinese-Japanese ethnicity and, 43, 50–51, 167, 233–36, 235,

Greater East Asia Co-Prosperity Sphere, 76

Hall, Stuart, 145, 249
hamlet people (*burakumin*), 43, 162–64, 231–32, 234, 254, 259n13, 263n1
headtop (dance move), 102, 128, 135, 136, 137
Helg, Aline, 260n1
Hepner, Randall, 149
Hideaki, Takagi (Papa Bon), 78–84, *81*, 97, 98, 118, 122
hip-hop, 56–59, 105, 119, 120, 241, 244
Hir[omacron], Jah, 221. *See also Rastaman Vibration* (book by Jah Hir[omacron])
H-Man, 68, 70–71, 122
homogeneous concept, 20, 50–51, 59, 121, 200, 213, 231, 259n13
homophobia, in dancehall culture, 69, 77–78, 105–9, 120, 261–62n2
homosexuality, and sound system, 94, 106–9, 120, 261n8, 261–62n2
Honey Butts, 136
Honjama Jamaika (Kimoto), 205
Hoshi to regee no shima (Island of Stars and Reggae; Yamakawa), 206–9, 265nn6–7

iemoto system, 262–63n5
Ikeshiro, Minako, 115, 261n3
I'll Give Anything a Look (Nan de mo mite yar[omacron]; Makoto), 197
images in print media, 16, 25, 78, 108, 131, 203, 209. *See also* literature of Rasta
imagination of blackness. *See* blackness, imagination of
industrial modernization era, 19–20, 48, 144
Inochi no Matsuri (Festival of Life), 167–68, 199
Inoue, Masamichi, 20

instrumental music, Jamaican, 152
international dancehall competitions: International Dancehall Queen Contest, 22, 101–3, 126, 133, 226, 240, 261n1; national and racial pride in victories in, 49–50
internationalization (*kokusaika*), 4, 49, 72–74, 126, 196, 237, 250–51
Island of Stars and Reggae (Hoshi to regee no shima), 206–9, 265nn6–7
Israel and lost tribes heritage of Rastas, 49, 151, 173, 191, 198–203, 223, 229, 264n2
"I-tal" (natural) concept, 2, 147, 181
Ivy, Marilyn, 144
Iwabuchi, Koichi, 76

Jamaican culture and society: Afrocentric culture of, 69, 126–32, 145, 198, 253, 254; class difference in, 126, 141, 145–48, 165, 230–31, 237; colonial past critique, and ideological features of, 145–48; culture and history of, 203–4; gender and sexuality issues, and power in, 57–58; history of, 64–65; instrumental music in, 152; Jamaican-Japanese cultural exchange opportunities and, 241–43, 244–45; Jamaican presence and, 77–78, 89; Japanese dancehall culture, and Jamaican perspectives in, 30, 236–38; "the male deal," and power relationships in, 140–41; misidentification of Japanese in, 81–82, 128, 130, 216–17, 240, 255, 261n6, 265n4; negative pride in, 239–40; postcolonial discourse of global blackness in, 240, 247–48, 253; postmodernism, and apolitical effacement of meaning in, 248; power and location in ethnoracial terms and transnational sites of, 58–59; Rasta culture in Japan, and Jamaican perspectives in, 239–43; reggae dance

style of, 128; family's opinion of reggae dance success by, 132; and Japanese Dancehall Queen competition in
2000 in Tokyo, 128; language and,
126; as National Dancehall Queen
competition winner in Jamaica in
2002, 8, 9, 15, 101, 102, 126, 129–
31, 247; photograph of, 129; popularity of, 131; race in politics of Rasta
in Jamaica and, 126–32, 240, 241,
247; socioeconomically marginalization of women and, 141; travels to
Jamaica by, 127–28
Kurokawa, Yoko, 262–63n5
Kurosawa, Minako, 133
Kusatsu, Osamu, 154
Kyoto, 169–70

Latin America, 36–37, 260n1
Let's Speak Jamaican! . . . (Jamaika-go o
hanas[omacron]! . . . ; Goldson), 203
Lewellen, Ted C., 249
Lewis, W., 147, 150
Lie, John, 234
Lindfors, Bernth, 246
lion-shaped (*shiisaa*) sculptures, 172,
173
literature of Rasta: autobiography,
196–98; black otherness, 24–25,
218–20, 265nn6–7; culture and history of Jamaica and, 203–4; images
in, 203, 209; Japaneseness and, 196,
198, 210, 213–15, 224; lost tribes of
Israel heritage of Rasta and, 198–
203, 264n2; nonfiction about travels
to Jamaica, 203–6; overview, 22,
29, 191–92; spiritual beliefs in, 205–
6, 228; violence and badness in Jamaica and, 204–5, 206. *See also* fictional accounts of travels to Jamaica;
search for self (*jibun sagashi*) discourse in literature
local performative practice: dancehall
culture in Japan and, 64, 97; roots

reggae music in Japan and, 59; rural
Rasta culture in Japan, and mythologized, 59, 144, 166–69, 174,
176–79, 183, 187–89; social tension
between Rasta culture in Jamaica
and Japanese, 64–65; urban Rasta
culture in Japan and, 59, 158–59,
165, 186, 231
lonely (*sabishii*) or aloneness, 139, 210,
213
Love Milk, 115, 119, 136–37
Lyotard, Jean François, 249

Makoto, Oda, 197
manga (comic books), 16, 25, 78, 108,
131
Maori people, 150–51
marijuana consumption, 32–33, 146,
147, 157, 160–61, 170
Marley, Bob: history of Jamaican popular subculture in Japan and, 10, 78,
89, 163, 165; images of, 137, 164,
167, 177, 221; as male role model,
263–64n8; as mixed race, 241; songs
by, 2, 165
masculinity performance, in dancehall
culture, 68–70, 78–79, 104, 105,
107–9, 140
Mathews, Gordon, 50, 195
McLelland, Mark J., 108
MCs (emcees): character of, 69, 85–86;
class difference and, 107; dancehall
terms used by, 91–92; female, 120;
homophobia in, 108–9, 120; imagination of blackness and, 246–47;
masculinity performance of, 107–9;
men as, 84–86; patois and, 91–92;
reggae dance performance by women
and, 131–38; in sound clash events,
90–91, 93–94, 95–96; vulgar speech
of, 70, 107, 108; women as, 84, 120
media: dancehall culture in Japan and,
9, 17, 85, 113–19, 125, 243–45,
266n5; global postmodern, and cap-

media (*cont.*)

italist dissociation in, 249–50; imagination of blackness, and racism in,
39–42, 55; Japanese women's relationships with Western men, and
sensationalism in, 48, 56–57, 110,
195–96, 262n3; power and location,
and transnational sites of Rasta, 59;
race and, 25; subcultural identifications, and global postmodern, 250

Memín Pinguín, 40

men in Jamaica: class difference for, 6,
141, 230–31, 237; neoliberalism, and
effects on, 141, 242; patriarchy, 103,
147–48, 161

men in Japan: class difference for, 6,
50, 141, 161, 186, 230–31, 237;
dance and fashion scene for, 106–7;
dreadlocks worn by, 1, 147, 148,
171–72; as fans of reggae dance performance, 134–35, 136, 138, 139;
gangsta man, and aggressive music
of, 68–69, 94, 158–59; hip-hop, and
gender and sexuality issues for, 56–
57; marginalization of, 83, 111; as
MCs, 84–86; patriarchy, 103, 147–
48, 161; reggae dance performance
by women in Japan, and power of,
138; rural Rasta culture and, 175,
176, 179, 182, 183–89, 212; *sarariiman* and, 21, 193, 257–58n9; sexual
independence for women, and fears
of, 104; sound system, and rivals
among, 104–5; Western Orientalist
discourse, and participation by, 56,
260n6

Midnight Express (Shinya Tokky[umacron]; book by Sawaki), 198

Mighty Crown: Chinese-Japanese ethnicity and, 233–36, 235; Cojie as selector for, 80, 84, 87, 235, 261n7;
cultural theft accusations and, 241;
Judgment Sound Station sound clash
with, 90–91, 93–97; Papa Bon and,
78–83, 97, 98, 118; performance
style, 69; Sammy T as selector for,
84, 87, 93–94, 96, 233–35, 235,
261n7; Simon as MC for, 15, 65, 84,
87, 234–37, 235; in World Clash competitions, 8–9, 15, 62, 224, 237;
Yokohama Reggae Sai (Festival) and,
232, 232; in Yokohama's Chinatown,
235

Mighty Crown Entertainment, 17, 79,
85, 261n7

Miller, Laura, 226

minzoku (ethnicity). *See* ethnicity

Mixi (social networking site), 122, 244

Miyake, Hitoshi, 175

Miyazawa, Masanori, 199–202

modern girl (*moga*), 109–10, 112, 195,
226

Moeran, Brian, 110, 112

moga (modern girl), 109–10, 112, 195,
226

Morioka, Naoko, 153, 180

Morrison, Toni, 54

Munehiro, 17, 68, 71–73, 75–77, 118–
19, 121, 234

music videos, 71–73, 75, 118–19

Nagano, 12, 166, 168

Nahki, 11, 12, 14, 53, 68, 122

Nan de mo mite yar[omacron] (I'll Give
Anything a Look; book by Makoto),
197

Nanjaman, 74–78, 87

Napier, Susan, 259n14

Nara prefecture, 174–75, 263n6

National Dancehall Queen competition:
in Jamaica, 8, 9, 15, 101, 102, 126,
129–31, 247; in Tokyo, 128

national pride: industrial modernization era, 19–20; *nihonjinron* and, 20,
48–50, 73, 201, 213; roots reggae
music in Japan and, 119; social identity dynamics and, 4, 232–36; songs
in dancehall culture and, 70–78, 89

Native Americans, 75, 76, 150, 156, 167, 168

natural world: Africa, and valuation of, 188; imagination of blackness, and reclaimed, 170–71, 189, 264n10; Rasta culture, and valuation of, 2, 13, 18, 122, 146–47, 181, 188, 228

Nederveen, Jan Pieterse, 246

neoliberalism: Babylon and, 5–6, 142, 145, 146, 148, 159, 162, 257n2; cultural consumption and, 29; individuals in Jamaica and, 141, 242; in Japan, 194; lost tribes of Israel heritage of Rasta and, 202–3; roots reggae music in Jamaica, 111; U.S. and, 47, 75, 261n5. *See also* Babylon east

New York: as Babylon, 212, 264–65n4; dancehall in, 264–65n4; dub musicians, and travels to, 29, 157, 264–65n4; hip-hop in, 264–65n4; in Japanese imagination of the global, 264–65n4; misidentification of Japanese in, 81; as racialized with black presence, 264–65n4; Rasta diaspora community in, 9, 149, 255; settlement by Rasta from Japan in, 251; travels to, 66–67, 79, 80–82, 88

New Zealand, 150–51

nihonjinron (theories of the Japanese), 20, 48–50, 73, 201, 213

Nihon no haji da na (shame, Japan's), 133, 226

nonfiction about travels to Jamaica, 203–6

office ladies, 21, 110, 112, 198, 230, 257–58n9

[Omaron]ga Tamanosuke, *Jamaika ga Suki da!* (I Love Jamaica!), 204

Ogawa Akira, 193

Ohba, Toshiaki, 115

Okinawa, 20, 45, 47, 172–73, 259n13

Okonogi Keigo, 195

[Omacron]mori, Osamu, 193

One and G website and registry, 115, 120, 124

One Love Jamaica (Yamakawa), 205–6

One Love Jamaica Festival, 18, 139

Ong, Aihwa, 250

orientalism, 19, 76, 77

otherness, black, 23–28, 38, 48, 50, 54, 218–20, 258–59n12, 265nn6–7

outcastes, 43, 162–64, 231–32, 234, 254, 259n13, 263n1

Pablo, Augustus, 172, 263n5

Pacific roots reggae, 150–51

patois: dub musicians in Japan, 158–59; as lingua franca in Jamaica, 159; MCs, 91–92; as symbolic capital, 61, 62, 67, 85, 91–93, 224; as vulgar, 147

patriarchy, 103, 147–48, 161

patron experience, in dancehall culture, 97–98, 103, 134

performative field of international dancehall culture: bus taking female dance contestants to competition in Jamaica and, 22, 129–30, 132; homophobia in, 69, 105–9, 261–62n2; Jamaican powder room, and international dancehall sisterhood experience for Japanese performers in, 22, 29, 125–26, 132, 238; overview, 22, 62, 223–24; patois and, 61, 62, 97; politics of, 126; "Powder Room Talk" (column in *Strive*) and, 125–26, 129, 132, 138, 238; power and, 99, 138. *See also* social performance

performative thirdness, 51–54, 53, 56, 110, 122, 231, 234

Planno, Mortimo, 173, 262n5

politics of divas' performances. *See* reggae dance performance by women in Japan

postcolonial discourse, and global blackness, 240, 247–48, 252, 253, 255

"Powder Room Talk" (column in *Strive*), 125–26, 129, 132, 138, 238

power: Afro-Jamaican women, and perceptions of, 124–25, 131; dancehall culture and, 99, 138; gender and sexuality issues in Rasta culture, 57–58; hip-hop location and, 58–59; imagination of blackness and, 56–58; Japan as global cultural, 4, 6, 15–16, 242; "the male deal," and relationships of, 140–41; reggae dance performance by women, and perceptions about, 124–25, 131, 138, 139, 140; transnational sites of, 58–59; "word sound power," 149, 228

race (*jinshu*): ethnonational view of, 5; homosexuality, in context of, 261–62n2; imagination of blackness and, 23–24, 58, 104, 218–20, 246–47, 255, 265nn6–7; in Japan, 23–26, 260n3; performative thirdness and, 22, 51–54, 53, 56, 110, 122, 231, 234; social identity dynamics and, 23–26, 37; social performance, 22, 23–24, 258–59n12. *See also* blackness, imagination of; class difference; gender and sexuality issues; global blackness

racism: in corporate workplace, 26; in mass media, 39–42, 54–55; social performance and, 23–25, 26–27, 259nn13–15; structural, 23–26

ragga/raggamuffin, 6, 7–8, 106–7

Rankin' Taxi, 11, 14, 70, 82, 95–97, 134

Ras, defined, 263n4

Rastafarian (Rasta). *See* Rasta culture in Jamaica; Rasta culture in Japan; rural Rasta culture in Japan; urban Rasta culture in Japan

Rasta culture in Jamaica: Afro-Jamaican women's status, and mar-

ginalization in, 104, 132, 140, 141, 147–48, 160, 161; Babylon and, 5–6, 142, 145, 146, 148, 159, 162, 257n2; blackness as a sexual political statement and, 58; colors as symbolic of, 2, 17, 55, 72, 148, 178, 232; consumerism critique, and ideological features of, 145–48; described, 42; diet and, 2, 181; history and description of, 145; imagination and fear of, 54; imaginations of history and, 187; as international symbol, 54; Japanese presence in, 251–52; language and, 147; lion as symbolic in, 146, 148, 172; lost tribes of Israel heritage in, 49, 191, 201; natural world valuation in, 2, 146–47, 181, 188; objectification and commodification of women's bodies in, 141, 240; patriarchy in, 147–48; performative practices in, 149, 170; personally achieved wisdom feature of, 146; religion, and social identity in, 230; Selassie as symbolic in, 148–49, 164, 177, 178; travels by artists and fans in dancehall culture in Japan to connect with, 66–67, 85, 87–88; travels from rural Rasta in Japan to connect with, 29, 171, 173. *See also* Jamaican culture and society

Rasta culture in Japan: authority of Jamaican referenced by, 33, 98–99; Jamaican perspectives on, 239–43; marginalization of Jamaica in, 225; mutual recognition of marginalization and connections made between Jamaican and Japanese situations in, 6, 29; opportunism for Jamaican-Japanese cultural exchange and, 241–43, 244–45; spiritual beliefs and, 205–6, 228. *See also* dancehall (reggae) music in Japan; dancehall (reggae) subculture in Japan

Rasta-identifying Japanese: Babylon

and, 156, 157; class difference for
men and, 230–31; defined, 155–56;
economic recession in Japan, and effects on, 202–3; Israelite lost tribes
heritage, and social identity of, 49,
173, 191, 198–202, 223, 229, 264n2;
"Japanese Rastafari" defined, 228–
29; romanticism about Rasta in Jamaica and, 216–17; social and global
individual in Japan, and context for,
203; social identity through encounters with Jamaican, 207–9; women's
identification with Rasta and, 180,
226–27, 263–64n8. *See also* rural
Rasta culture in Japan; urban Rasta
culture in Japan
Rastaman Vibration (book by Jah
Hir[omacron]): Babylon, and political
social identity for Gor[omacron] in,
211–14; dissatisfaction with religious traditions in Japan and spiritual beliefs of Rasta in, 215–16;
Jamaican views of Japanese, and political social identity for
Gor[omacron] in, 215–17, 265n5;
Japaneseness and, 210, 213–15, 224;
Japanese views of Jamaicans, and political social identity for
Gor[omacron] in, 218–20; plot sum-
mary, x, 210–11; rural refuge from
urban modernity, 211–12, 213; social identity dynamics in, 209–10;
third world, and search for self in,
210, 213, 215; travel and safe return
metaphor in, 212
Rasta yard, 174
reggae. *See* dancehall (reggae) music in
Japan; roots reggae music in Jamaica
Reggae (Tagawa), 204
Reggae Academy Awards, 242–43
reggae dance performance by women in
Jamaica: blackness and black womanhood in, 104; bus taking contestants
to competition by Afro-Jamaican

women in, 22, 129–30, 132; class difference for Afro-Jamaican women in,
104, 141; gender, and international
dancehall sisterhood in Jamaican
powder room for Japanese performers in, 104, 125–26, 132, 238;
iemoto system of apprenticeship and,
262–63n5; Japaneseness and, 130–
31; National Dancehall Queen competition winner in Jamaica in 2002
and, 8, 9, 15, 101, 102, 126, 129–31,
247; phenotypic and racial sensitivities for Japanese during performance in, 104, 130–31; "Powder
Room Talk" and, 125–26, 129, 132,
138, 238; race differences, and cross-
culturally relative notions of, 57,
104, 126, 130–31. *See also* Afro-
Jamaican women; Rasta culture in
Jamaica; roots reggae music in Jamaica
reggae dance performance by women in
Japan: Afrocentric culture in, 46;
agency of women's performances
and, 103–4, 134–38; autonomy, and
solo, 139; biographical information
about women in Dear Chicks duo
and, 124–25; choreography of dance
moves and, 102, 128, 135; class difference and, 103, 104, 126, 142;
DVDs of, 101, 115–18; fandom concept and, 121–23; fans of, 134–35,
136, 138, 139; fashion and costumes
of women in, 2, 8, 102, 125, 127, 134–
37, 139, 226, 265n1; female power
in, 139, 140; gender and sexuality issues for women, and imagined sexually available discourse on, 56, 117–
18, 226–27; gendered economy, marginalization of women and, 103, 104;
gender in politics of, 126; imagined
sexually available discourse on, 103,
110, 112, 123, 142; Jamaican perspectives on popularity of Jamaican

reggae dance performance by (*cont.*)
culture in Japan and, 237; Japanese
Dancehall Queen competition in
1999 in Tokyo, 104, 133–38; male
power in, 138; marginalization of
women and, 111; MCs and, 131–38;
misidentification of Japanese in Jamaica and, 81–82, 128, 130, 255,
261n6; National Dancehall Queen
competition donnette winner Kudo
and, 8, 9, 15, 101, 102; objectification and commodification of wom-
en's bodies in, 103, 119–20, 134–38,
141, 240, 248; overview, 2, 8, 101–4,
224, 227; perception of power of
Afro-Jamaican women, and social
identity of women in, 124–25, 131;
physical toll for, 134, 136; "Powder
Room Talk" and, 125–26, 129, 132,
138, 238; race in politics of, 126; race
in politics of Rasta in Jamaica and,
126–32, 240, 241, 247; social identity dynamics and, 116–17, 124–25,
131, 133; songs selected by women
and played during, 135, 136, 138;
travels to Jamaica by women in, 22,
123–24, 125, 127–30, 132, 263–
64n8; vulgar status of, 8, 39, 99, 103,
105; women's experience in, 21,
115–16, 120–21, 125–26, 129, 132,
138, 238
Reggae JapanSplash, 11–13, 18, 152
Reggae Sunsplash, 11, 68
religions: Japanese Buddhism, 170–73,
184, 199, 215–16, 227, 230, 233;
"Japanese Rastafari," 227–30. *See
also* Shugend[omacron]
research method: gender of researcher
and, 32; marijuana consumption and,
32–33; multi-sited, 5, 29–31, 224;
patois and, 30–31; positionality and,
32–34
rhythm and blues, 4, 7, 16, 115, 151,
152

riddim (digital musical tracks): DJs, and
performances over, 8, 90; dub plates
and, 67; history of, 12, 14, 64; rub-
a-dub events and, 90; singers' performances over, 90
rikishi (sumo wrestler), 51, 52, 233–34
rocksteady, 7, 18, 63, 152
romanticism, 58, 70–71, 120–21, 216–
17
roots reggae music in Jamaica: gender
and sexuality issues, and power expressed in, 58; history of, 7, 9–10,
11–15, 18; as international symbol,
54; overview, 7, 8, 18, 119, 255; romanticism in, 58; spiritual beliefs of
Rasta and, 65. *See also* Rasta culture
in Jamaica; reggae dance performance by women in Jamaica
roots reggae music in Japan. *See* dancehall (reggae) music in Japan
roots reggae music in Pacific, 150–51,
168, 172
rub-a-dub events, 58, 64, 90–91, 124,
128
Rubin, Arnold, 43
rural Rasta culture in Japan: Afrocentric culture and, 169, 171; biographical information about
individuals in, 171, 182–83; counterculture movement and, 154, 166–69;
daily life, and embodiment of Rasta
in, 179–81, 189; dancehall (reggae)
music band and, 175–76, 179,
263n7; described, 171, 175–76; diet,
and embodiment of Rasta in, 180–
81; dreadlocks, and embodiment of
Rasta in, 171, 172, 180, 181–82,
189; frog jump festival and, 212;
frog jump festival, and participation
by members of, 176, 179, 183–89;
gender differences and, 179–81;
global cultural experiences and, 174,
178, 181–82; imagination of blackness, and natural world reclaimed in,

170–71, 189; imaginations of history and, 187–89; individual's route to identification with Rasta in, 169–74, 228; *Inochi no Matsuri* and, 167–68, 199; local performative practice, and mythologized local in, 59, 144, 166–69, 174, 176–79, 183, 187–89; lost tribes of Israel heritage, and social identity of, 173, 264n2; marijuana consumption in, 154, 168; medicinal practice, and embodiment of Rasta in, 182–83; medicinal practice in, 173; men in, 175, 176, 179, 182, 183–89, 212; overview, 186; patois, 171; Rasta yard and, 174, 176–79; as refuge from urban modernity, 211–12, 213; religion in Japan and, 4, 170–72, 176, 179, 181–89; religious traditions, and dissatisfaction in, 171–72, 215–16; spiritual beliefs of Rasta and, 169–74, 189, 215–16, 224, 228; travels overseas by individuals in, 29, 171–73, 188; uncanny Japanese self and, 144, 171, 174, 201–2; urban Rasta, and relation to imagination of rural for, 122, 143–44, 187, 213; valorization of premodern rural through global in, 176, 178–79, 183, 186, 189, 254; women in, 179, 180, 227, 263–64n8. *See also* Yoshino Rasta yard

Russell, John, 44, 47–48, 54–55, 209

Ry[omacron]anji Temple, 170–71

Ryo the Skywalker, 68, 74–77

Ry[umacron]ha-R (television program), 119

sabishii (lonely) or aloneness, 139, 210, 213

Said, Edward, 19, 41, 159

salaryman (*sarariiman*), 21, 198, 230, 257–58n9

Sammy T, 84, 87, 93–94, 96, 233–35, 235, 261n7

samurai, 19, 73, 75–77

sarariiman (salaryman), 21, 198, 230, 257–58n9

Savigliano, Marta, 239

Savishinsky, Neil, 36, 150

Sawaki K[omacron]taro, *Shinya Tokky[umacron]* (Midnight Express), 198

Scott, James C., 247

search for self (*jibun sagashi*) discourse in literature: audience and readers of, 22, 191, 220–21; dancehall culture in Japan and, 46, 50–51, 79, 83–84; economic recession in Japan and, 4, 112, 194, 195, 197, 202–3; individual in Japan, and social and global context for, 194–96, 203; Israelite lost tribes heritage of Rasta-identifying Japanese and, 198–203, 264n2; *nihonjinron* and, 73; overview, 192–93; performative literary representations of ideas in, 196, 220–21; social and historical context for, 193–98; third world and, 197, 210, 213, 220–22; travel and safe return metaphor in, 196–98, 212, 251; youth, and "lost generation" context for, 4, 193–95. *See also* literature of Rasta; social identity dynamics

Seek, Ras (pseud.), 171, 173, 187, 199

Selassie, Haile, I: ambiguous attitude in Japan towards, 229; as divine, 146, 151, 155, 170, 228, 254; as messiah, 4, 145; Rasta imagination of history and, 187, 224, 229; as representation of spiritual self, 170–71, 228, 254; search for self, and words of, 198; speech on war by, 165; as symbol of Rasta, 148–49, 164, 177, 178

selector/selectors: Cojie as dancehall, 80, 84, 87, 235, 261n7; role of, 61, 84, 90, 91; Sammy T as dancehall, 84, 87, 93–94, 96, 233–35, 235, 261n7; in sound clash events, 93–94; Spicy selector/selectors (*cont.*)

    Chocolate as dance contest, 133–34, 138; Sticko as dancehall, 89

self, search for. *See* search for self (*jibun sagashi*) discourse in literature

shame, Japan's (*Nihon no haji da na*), 133, 226

shiisaa (lion-shaped) sculptures, 172, 173

Shint[omacron], 170, 172, 215, 227, 233, 263n1

Shinya Tokky[umacron] (Midnight Express; book by Sawaki), 198

Shugend[omacron]: described, 175; frog jump festival and, 175, 176, 183–85, 212; Rasta roots in, 181–82, 188, 189, 201, 229, 254

Silverberg, Miriam, 109–10

Simon, Masta, 15, 65, 84, 87, 93, 234–37, *235*

singers, 68, 71–76, 90, 121

ska, 7, 11, 18, 63, 152

Skov, Lise, 110, 112

slackness, 68–71, 105, 140

social identity dynamics: Afro-Asian perspective in, 5, 29–30, 40, 62, 254–55; Afrocentric culture of Rasta and Japanese, 50, 58–59; Ainu indigenous people and, 43, 44–45, 50, 173, 259n13; black otherness in, 23, 47–48, 218–20, 265nn6–7; Chinese-Japanese ethnicity and, 43, 50–51, 167, 233–36, *235*; class difference across subcultures, 4, 230–31; diaspora community and, 36, 255; emotional investment in Rasta culture in Japan and, 50–51; ethnicity in, 4, 48, 163, 220, 225, 231–36, 247–48, 259n13; ethnic outness continuum and, 234–35; ethnic transvestism and, 51, 233; gender and sexuality issues across subcultures and, 225–27; imagination of blackness and, 23–24, 250–51, 255; internationaliza-

tion and, 4, 250–51; Jamaican perspectives on Japanese dancehall culture and, 30, 236–38; Jamaican perspectives on Rasta culture in Japan and, 239–43; "Japanese Rastafari" and, 227–30; Korean culture and, 74, 76, 259n13; in literature, 209–10; lost tribes of Israel heritage and, 49, 173, 191, 198–202, 223, 229, 264n2; national pride and, 4, 232–36; *nihonjinron* and, 20, 48–50, 73, 201, 213; overview, 4–5, 30, 224–25; race and, 23–26, 37; Rasta religion in culture in Jamaica and, 230; reggae dance performance by women in Japan and, 116–17, 124–25, 131, 133; women's relationships with African Americans and, 48, 56–57, 110, 195–96, 262n3. *See also* class difference; Japaneseness; Rasta culture in Japan; *Rastaman Vibration* (book by Jah Hir[omacron]); search for self (*jibun sagashi*) discourse in literature; social performance

social performance: blackness defined/use of term and, 23–25, 258–59n12; black otherness and, 27–28; defined, 21, 258n10; ethnoracism and, 26–27, 259n13; gender and sexuality issues and, 22, 23, 258n11; performance defined, 258n11; performative field defined, 22; in proximal settings, 21; race and, 22, 23–24, 258–59n12; racism and, 23–25, 259nn14–15; in remote settings, 21; structural racism, 23–26. *See also* performative field of international dancehall culture; social identity dynamics

Soma, Emi, 125, 129, 132, 139, 238

songs, dancehall: economic recession in Japan and search for self in, 75–77; national pride in, 70–78, 89; romantic love in, 70–71, 120–21; sexualiz-

UWI's 2008 Global Reggae Conference, 242–43

Van Dijk, Frank, 150–51
version (dub reggae; dub version), 19, 63–67, 152–53, 260n1
violence, and aggressiveness in Jamaican culture and society, 105, 204–5, 206
vulgarity: in patois, 147; reggae dance performance by women in Japan and, 8, 39, 99, 103, 105; sound system, and complaints about, 70, 99, 105, 107, 108, 239

Wagatsuma, Hiroshi, 44
Wallerstein, Immanuel Maurice, 37–38
Watson, James, 20
websites, 17–18, 113–14, 115, 120, 124
Weiner, Michael, 43–44
whiteness idea, 25, 36, 44, 54
women in Jamaica. See Afro-Jamaican women
women in Japan: agency and, 56; autobiography and, 196, 264n1; class difference and, 50, 103, 104, 126, 141, 142; dancehall culture and, 84, 104, 109–11, 120, 137; dreadlocks worn by, 3, 21, 227; as fans of reggae dance performance, 139; gender-specific language for, 107; homophobia and, 120; imagination of blackness, and Western men's relationships with, 48, 56–57, 110, 195–96, 238, 262n3; imagined sexually available discourse on, 56, 117–18, 226–27; immigration to New York and, 264–65n4; marginalization of, 104, 111, 117, 141; as office ladies in corporate workplace, 21, 110, 112, 257–58n9; patriarchal limitations on opportunities for, 103; reggae dance performance, and power of, 139, 140;

rural Rasta-identifying, 179–80, 226–27, 263–64n8; as singers, 121; social identity reflected in relationships between African Americans and, 48, 56–57, 110, 195–96, 262n3; songs in dancehall culture, and sexualization of, 238; Takarazuka Revue, and valorization of, 51, 121, 122. See also reggae dance performance by women in Japan
"word sound power," 149, 228
World Clash competitions, 8–9, 15, 62, 65, 224, 237
Woronoff, Jon (author of Japan's Wasted Workers), 194
Wright, Keril, 261n1

X-Rated Japanese Reggae Dancers (DVD), 115–16

Yamakawa Kenichi, 205–6, 206–9, 221–22, 265nn6–7
yamato damashii (Japanese spirit), 75–76, 216–17
Yamato (regular) Japanese, 213–15, 234
Yawney, Carole, 150
"yellow cabs," 56
Yokohama, 2–3, 11, 17, 62, 85–87, 235, 235
Yokohama Reggae Sai Festival, 232, 232
Yoshikawa Hideki, 198
Yoshino community, 174–76, 183–85
Yoshino Rasta yard: biographical information about individuals in, 182–83; daily life, and embodiment of Rasta in, 179–81, 189; dancehall (reggae) music band and, 175–76; diet, and embodiment of Rasta in, 180–81; dreadlocks, and embodiment of Rasta in, 180, 181–82; frog jump festival, and participation by members of, 176, 179, 183–89; gender differences and, 179–81; global cultural

experiences and, 174, 178, 181–82; imaginations of history and, 187–89; local performative practice, and mythologized rural in, 174, 176–79, 183, 187; medicinal practice, and embodiment of Rasta in, 182–83; men in, 175, 176, 179, 182, 183–89, 212; Rasta yard and, 174, 176–79; roots reggae music band and, 179, 263n7; valorization of premodern rural through global in, 176, 178–79, 183, 186, 189, 254; women in, 179, 180

Zielenziger, Michael, 194

MARVIN D. STERLING is an assistant professor of anthropology at
Indiana University, Bloomington.

Library of Congress Cataloging-in-Publication Data

Sterling, Marvin D.
Babylon East : performing dancehall, roots reggae,
and Rastafari in Japan / Marvin D. Sterling.
p. cm.
Includes bibliographical references and index.
ISBN 978-0-8223-4705-7 (cloth : alk. paper)
ISBN 978-0-8223-4722-4 (pbk. : alk. paper)
1. Rastafari movement—Japan. 2. Popular culture—Japan.
3. Subculture—Japan. 4. Japan—Social life and customs.
I. Title.
BL2532.R7S74 2010
306.4'842460952—dc22   2010000608